SHERIDAN AND
HIS GENERALS./USAMHI
(U.S. Army Military History Institute,
Carlisle Barracks, PA.)

SHERIDAN'S CIVIL WAR MEMOIRS

Abraham Lincoln, upon first meeting General Philip H. Sheridan, was decidedly unimpressed. Sheridan, according to the president, was a "brown, chunky little chap, with a long body, short legs, not enough neck to hang him, and such long arms that if his ankles itch he can scratch them without stooping."

By war's end President Lincoln had had a change of opinion. "General Sheridan," the president remarked to the Union hero, "when this particular war began, I thought a cavalryman would be at least six feet four inches high, but I have changed my mind. Five feet four will do in a pinch."

—from the Introduction by
Paul Andrew Hutton

CIVIL WAR MEMOIRS

Philip Sheridan

★ ★ ★

Introduction by Paul Andrew Hutton
General Series Editor, Paul Andrew Hutton

BANTAM BOOKS
New York • Toronto • London • Sydney • Auckland

CIVIL WAR MEMOIRS

A Bantam Domain Book / November 1991

PRINTING HISTORY

Originally published as *Personal Memoirs of P. H. Sheridan*
Charles L. Webster & Company edition published 1888

ISBN 0-553-29379-6

Published simultaneously in the United States and Canada

PRINTED IN THE UNITED STATES OF AMERICA

OPM   0   9   8   7   6   5   4   3   2   1

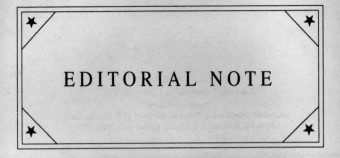

EDITORIAL NOTE

THIS EDITION OF **PERSONAL MEMOIRS OF P. H. SHER-IDAN, GENERAL UNITED STATES ARMY** (2 vols., New York: Charles L. Webster & Co., 1888) contains the complete text of the original as it concerns the Civil War except for explanatory chapter headings, some reprinted correspondence, and organizational listings for military units. Chapters concerning Sheridan's years before and after the Civil War have been omitted. Readers interested in those years, chiefly concerned with frontier issues, might wish to consult Paul Andrew Hutton, PHIL SHERIDAN AND HIS ARMY (Lincoln: University of Nebraska Press, 1985).

INTRODUCTION

by Paul Andrew Hutton

ABRAHAM LINCOLN, upon first meeting General Philip H. Sheridan, was decidedly unimpressed. Sheridan, according to the president, was a "brown, chunky little chap, with a long body, short legs, not enough neck to hang him, and such long arms that if his ankles itch he can scratch them without stooping." To make matters worse, the five-foot-five general was blessed with a bullet-shaped head with two large bumps in back that made it nearly impossible for him to keep a hat on. This oversized head was crowned by coarse, short-cropped hair that one wag described as resembling a "coat of black paint."

Sheridan's eyes, however, were the mark of the man. His friend and aide John Schuyler Crosby insisted that "one could tell from his eyes in a moment whether he was serious, sad, or humorous, without noticing another feature of his face." Another friend admitted that while Sheridan might well be a "stumpy, quadrangular little man" with a "forehead of no promise," it was "his eye and his mouth" that marked him a fierce warrior. These facial features betrayed Sheridan's Irish origins, although his voice carried no trace of a brogue. It was those dark eyes, long and narrow beneath arched eyebrows, that sparkled with the fire that had held the line at Stones River, had sent a bruised army roaring up Missionary Ridge, had turned defeat into victory at Cedar Creek, and had crushed Lee's last hope at Five Forks.

"Bold in conception, self-reliant, demonstrating by his acts that 'much danger makes great hearts most resolute,' fertile in resources, combining the restlessness of a Hotspur with the patience of a Fabius, it is no wonder that he should have been looked upon as the wizard of the battlefield," gushed General Horace Porter. "Wherever blows fell thickest," Porter recalled, "there was his crest."

By war's end President Lincoln had had a change of opinion. "General Sheridan," the president remarked to the Union hero, "when this particular war began, I thought a cavalryman should be at least six feet four inches high, but I have changed my mind. Five feet four will do in a pinch."

Sheridan was a latecomer to the war, for by the time he assumed command of a desk at General Henry Halleck's Missouri headquarters, Ulysses S. Grant had already won victories at Forts Henry and Donelson, and William Tecumseh Sherman commanded a division. Yet within four years he would rise from captain to major general in the regular army (at age thirty-three) and stand with Grant and Sherman as one of the Union's trinity of great captains.

Sheridan's origins gave little hint of the military glory that awaited him. The exact place of his birth is unknown, and he confused the issue considerably by claiming Albany, New York, and Somerset, Ohio, on various official documents. Almost certainly neither was true, although the March 6, 1831, birth date he claimed can probably be trusted. He most likely was born in County Cavan, Ireland, where his parents were tenant farmers, or on the boat en route to the United States. He was an infant when John and Mary Sheridan settled in Somerset, Ohio. Considering the fierce anti-Irish prejudice of the time, the subterfuge is quite natural.

Sheridan was educated in Somerset's one-room school-house and came away deeply influenced by the experience. "The little white schoolhouse made us superior to the South," he later remarked. "Education is invincible." At fourteen, his schooling over, he secured a clerk's position in a local general store. He quickly rose to be the book-keeper of Somerset's largest dry-goods shop. His attention, however, was often distracted by news of battles in distant Mexico. The war, and dreams of martial glory, captivated the youngster, so that when he heard that the 1848 ap-pointee from his district to West Point had failed the en-trance exam, he appealed to his congressman to be allowed to fill the vacancy. Congressman Thomas Ritchie promptly returned a warrant for the class of 1848.

This horrified Sheridan's parents. They shared the com-mon western view that West Point was a bastion of aris-tocracy, special privilege, and militarism hardly in keeping with the republic's ideals. John Sheridan also feared the impact of West Point on his son's religious values. He consulted the local Dominican priest, who advised: "Rather than send him to West Point take him out into the back yard, behind the chicken coop, and cut his throat."

Ignoring this sober advice, John Sheridan relented and allowed his son to head east to West Point. His experience there was not a happy one. The traditional hazing frayed his volatile temper, the refined manners and aristocratic pretensions of the academy's southern clique irritated him, and his studies failed to prosper. These frustrations finally broke forth on the drill field one September afternoon in 1851 when he assaulted his southern drill instructor. Sus-pended for one year, he returned unrepentant after spend-ing nine humiliating months back at his Somerset bookkeeping job. He now compounded his poor grades with a miserable attitude that left him but eleven demerits from expulsion when he graduated thirty-fourth in a class of fifty-two in July 1853.

Brevet Second Lieutenant Sheridan was assigned to the First Infantry and ordered to Fort Duncan, Texas, perhaps the most isolated post on the frontier. Sheridan still found the fort a decided improvement over West Point, but he was not there long. He was assigned to the Fourth Infantry and transferred to Fort Reading, California, where pressure from gold miners and squatters was driving the local Indians to war. Sheridan's best friend from West Point, George Crook, was also there, and he characterized the situation as "the fable of the wolf and the lamb." It was cruel, Crook lamented, that the soldiers "had to fight when our sympathies were with the Indians."

Sheridan did not share his friend's liberal sensibilities and was delighted to march north against Yakima and Rogue River Indians in October 1855. The young officer distinguished himself in a series of sharp campaigns, being commended in general orders by General Winfield Scott for his heroism in a fight at the Cascades of the Columbia River in March 1856.

Sheridan's last years in the Pacific Northwest were spent guarding the Grande Ronde Indian Reservation in western Oregon. He was ill fitted by temperament for such quiet duty and so was naturally delighted when orders finally arrived in September 1861 promoting him to captain in the Thirteenth Infantry.

Sheridan hurried eastward, fearful the war might end before he could join his new regiment. If conflict lasted long enough, he confided to a friend, he hoped to "have a chance to earn a major's commission." He took pride in the fact that he was "untainted by politics," and that his thoughts had never "been disturbed by any discussion of the questions out of which the war grew." That was to change dramatically.

After impressive service on the staffs of Generals Samuel R. Curtis and Henry W. Halleck, Captain Sheridan was appointed colonel of the Second Michigan Cavalry on May 26, 1862. The new colonel fought a masterful battle at Booneville, Missouri, against a force over four times the size of his own, prompting General William Rosecrans and four of his brigadiers to wire Halleck: "Brigadiers scarce;

good ones scarcer... The undersigned respectfully beg that you will obtain the promotion of Sheridan. He is worth his weight in gold."

Promoted to brigadier general of volunteers dating from July 1, 1862, the date of the Battle of Booneville, and given command of the newly organized Eleventh Division of Don Carlos Buell's Army of the Ohio, Sheridan proved his mettle by holding the Union line against five Rebel assaults at Perryville, Kentucky, on October 8, 1862. The northern press dubbed the bantam brigadier the "paladin of Perryville."

Rosecrans replaced Buell as commander of the redesignated Army of the Cumberland, and Sheridan was assigned to command of the Third Division of General Alexander McCook's right wing of that army. At Stones River, Tennessee, from December 31, 1862, to January 3, 1863, Sheridan tenaciously held on amid incredible slaughter to form the anchor that allowed General George Thomas's line to hold, bringing the Union an important but grisly victory. In this work his division suffered 1,633 casualties out of 4,164 men.

Stones River confirmed Sheridan's growing reputation for courage and tenacity. "I knew it was infernal in there before I got in," declared General Lovell Rousseau in describing the battle, "but I was convinced of it when I saw Phil Sheridan, with hat in one hand and sword in the other, fighting as if he was the devil incarnate, and swearing as if he had a fresh indulgence from Father Tracy every five minutes."

General Rosecrans dissaproved of Sheridan's vivid language, which eventually became legendary in the army, and admonished him during the fighting at Stones River. "Watch your language," he lectured his young brigadier. "Remember, the first bullet may send you to eternity." But eternity did not much concern Sheridan during battle; his mind was consumed instead with how to destroy his enemy. "I have never in my life taken a command into battle," Sheridan told Horace Porter, "and had the slightest desire to come out alive unless I won."

Stones River won another star in the volunteer army for Sheridan, but it was his actions at Chattanooga in November that earned him Grant's esteem and secured his future. Sheridan shared in the humiliation of the Army of the Cumberland, first defeated at Chickamauga on September 20, and then besieged in Chattanooga. He and his men were anxious to redeem themselves in front of the reinforcements from the Army of the Potomac under Joe Hooker and the Army of the Tennessee under Sherman. Grant, now in overall command west of the Alleghenies, instead held the Cumberlanders in reserve while the troops under Hooker and Sherman assaulted the Confederate positions looming over the city on Lookout Mountain and Missionary Ridge.

Sheridan finally got his chance on November 25, 1863. Sherman's forces had been repulsed four times from the north slope of Missionary Ridge when Grant ordered the Cumberlanders forward to assault rifle pits at the base of the central ridge, hoping to take the pressure off Sherman. Sheridan's Second Division, one of four in the assault, overran the rifle pits with ease but then faced a murderous fire from the crest of the ridge. Sheridan sent an aide off to his commander, Gordon Granger, begging permission to assault the crest. When an officer returned with Granger's assent, Sheridan beamed.

Taking a pewter flask from the aide, Sheridan toasted the Rebel headquarters directly above him. As he gulped down the brandy the Confederate batteries answered his impertinence with a volley that sent dirt and rocks flying all around him. Cursing Rebel rudeness, Sheridan tossed the flask up the ridge, mounted his black charger, Rienzi, and led his division roaring up the ridge.

Newspapers later called it the miracle of Missionary Ridge. The Cumberlanders swept up the face of the ridge as one, each regiment struggling to plant its colors on the crest first. Sheridan, unlike the other Union commanders, did not halt on the summit, but pushed on after the fleeing Rebels to Chickamauga Station.

"Sheridan showed his genius in that battle," declared a delighted Grant, "and to him I owe the capture of most of the prisoners that were taken. Although commanding a division only, he saw in the crisis of that engagement that it was necessary to advance beyond the point indicated by his orders . . . and with the instinct of military genius pushed ahead." Sheridan never quit, and Grant, who was much the same, prized him for that quality. When Grant went east in March 1864 as general in chief, he offered Sheridan command of the cavalry of the Army of the Potomac. When Grant visited the War Department with his new cavalry chief, one officer remarked: "The officer you brought on from the West is rather a little fellow to handle your cavalry." To which Grant responded, "You will find him big enough for the purpose before we get through with him."

Sheridan and General George Gordon Meade developed an immediate dislike for each other. Meade believed the only role of cavalry was to provide escorts for provision trains and infantry columns and do picket and scouting duty. Sheridan wanted to concentrate his ten thousand troopers and engage J.E.B. Stuart's supposedly invincible horsemen. After one particularly heated argument Meade went to Grant to complain about Sheridan, and for his troubles was ordered by the general in chief to allow Sheridan to go out and whip Stuart. Sheridan's troopers proceeded to avenge three years of humiliation by brushing aside the Rebel cavalry at Yellow Tavern, mortally wounding Stuart in the process, and then raiding to the gates of Richmond before rejoining the Union army.

When Lee sent Jubal Early up the Shenandoah Valley to threaten Washington and relieve the pressure on Richmond, Grant countered by placing Sheridan in command of the Army of the Shenandoah. Lincoln objected because of Sheridan's youth, but Grant felt youthful audacity was needed to seal off the Shenandoah from the Rebels once and for all. The reputations of Frémont, Banks, Sigel, and Hunter had been shattered in the Shenandoah, but Sheridan was to fare much better. In September 1864 he defeated Early at Winchester and Fisher's Hill. Lincoln rewarded him with a brigadier's star in the regulars.

At Cedar Creek, however, Early caught the federals napping while Sheridan was away and routed a portion of the army. Sheridan, returning from a conference in Washington, was fourteen miles away in Winchester and now raced to the sound of the guns. His sudden return electrified the stricken army, so that they rallied and crushed their foe before nightfall. Coming on the very eve of the presidential election, the victory at Cedar Creek proved a tonic for Lincoln and the Republicans. "Sheridan's Ride" became one of the most storied events of the war, quickly immortalized in a popular poem by T. Buchanan Read that was memorized by generations of schoolchildren. That poem made Sheridan's black charger Rienzi one of the most famous horses in history (and he can still be seen today on exhibit in the American history museum of the Smithsonian Institution in Washington, D.C.). Congress tendered its thanks to the victor of Cedar Creek, who also received a promotion to major general in the regular army. Sheridan now stood firmly with Grant and Sherman in the front rank of Union generals.

Sheridan had eliminated the Confederate army at Cedar Creek, but Grant also wanted him to destroy Rebel resources in the valley as well. Sheridan's Robbers, as his army was thereafter known by their enemies, so effectively ravaged Virginia's most bountiful valley that Sheridan could boast, with but little exaggeration, that "a crow would be compelled to carry his own rations" when crossing the Shenandoah.

Sheridan, sensing the war would soon end and anxious to "be in at the death," gave up his independent command and hurriedly rejoined Grant. He then scored a smashing victory at Five Forks, captured Ewell and the right wing of the Rebel army at Sayler's Creek, and blocked Lee's retreat at Appomattox. As he walked with Grant to the McLean house at Appomattox the thirty-four-year-old Sheridan triumphantly capped off one of the most remarkable ascensions in modern military history.

War had been a tonic to Sheridan. "He was a wonderful man on the battlefield," one of his officers recalled, "and never in as good humor as when under fire." As for many of his generation, it was the days in camp and field that gave Sheridan his fondest memories. Yet his view of war was far from romantic, for Sheridan was a modern soldier.

Sheridan shared his friend Sherman's vision of war as "power unrestrained by constitution or compact." This power was to be used to cripple the enemy people as well as the enemy army. "I do not hold war to mean simply that lines of men shall engage each other in battle," Sheridan later wrote. "This is but a duel, in which one combatant seeks the other's life; war means much more, and is far worse than this." The key to success in war was the destruction of the enemy homeland and the eradication of the people's will to resist. Sheridan understood that "the loss of property weighs heavy with the most of mankind; heavier often, than the sacrifices made on the field of battle." For Phil Sheridan the torch proved as mighty a weapon as the sword. "Reduction to poverty brings prayers for peace more surely and more quickly than does the destruction of human life," he declared.

In October 1870, while serving as an observer with the Prussian army during the Franco-Prussian War, Sheridan advised Count Otto von Bismarck that his troops were too mild in their handling of French guerrillas. "The proper strategy," he told the Prussian, "consists in the first place in inflicting as telling blows as possible upon the enemy's army, and then causing the inhabitants so much suffering that they must long for peace, and force their government to demand it. The people must be left nothing but their eyes to weep with over the war."

Sheridan's heartlessness toward an enemy contrasted sharply with the compassion he displayed toward his own soldiers. He not only selected their campsites, but also went to great pains to be certain they were well fed and clothed. He viewed the relationship between officers and men as a social contract with obligations on each side. An officer who failed in his obligations was worthless, for according to Sheridan, "a General lacking the confidence of his men is not less helpless than a general without an Army."

Although often described as the embodiment of the reckless cavalryman, Sheridan actually rarely if ever exposed his men to needless danger. He respected the intelligence of the common soldier and understood that "none realized more quickly than they the blundering that often takes place on the field of battle." If soldiers were to be called on to die, they must have "some tangible indemnity for the loss of life." He thus never sought glory at the expense of his soldiers. Sheridan's men responded to this concern with unqualified devotion. War provides few examples of a commander's influence over his men as was provided by Sheridan at Cedar Creek when his mere presence on the field rallied a stricken army.

If, however, an officer or soldier failed to perform his duty, or even failed to display Sheridan's intense zeal for combat, the general's wrath was unmerciful. In February 1865, at the close of the Shenandoah campaign, Sheridan replaced General Alfred Torbert, long his cavalry chief, with Wesley Merritt. Torbert's undoing was not the result of failure—on the contrary his cavalry had performed spectacularly—but rather was the result of his not proving aggressive enough on two occasions at Luray Valley and Gordonsville. When the army was reorganized after the war, most of Sheridan's division commanders received regiments, but Torbert reverted to his prewar rank of captain. General William W. Averell, commander of a cavalry division in the Shenandoah, was replaced after Fisher's Hill for failing to aggressively press the retreating Rebels. Averell resigned his regular-army commission.

Even more notorious was Sheridan's treatment of General Gouverneur K. Warren, the hero of Gettysburg who commanded the Fifth Corps at Five Forks. On the very eve of victory and right after the triumph at Five Forks, Sheridan removed Warren from command. Warren's sins were in moving his troops into position too slowly and displaying a quiet calm in the face of the enemy that the excitable Sheridan regarded as apathy. Warren remained in the army, reverting to his regular rank of major in the engineers, and diligently worked to clear his name. President Rutherford B. Hayes, who had served under Sheridan but was not a great admirer, finally granted Warren a court of inquiry in 1879. The 1882-published findings of the court exonerated Warren on three of the four reasons upon which Sheridan had based the removal. The verdict was a hard blow to Sheridan's pride. He loudly complained that the findings were "more in the nature of apologies than annunciation of the facts shown in the evidence." It did not matter to Warren, for that anguished officer had died a few months before the court vindicated him.

Sheridan was a good hater. His contempt for Meade was notorious, but his persecution of General William B. Hazen displayed even more glaringly a cruel, vindictive pettiness. After Missionary Ridge, Sheridan and Hazen had argued over whose troops reached the crest first and captured eleven Rebel cannons. Although Grant sided with Sheridan, the argument continued and Sheridan never forgave Hazen. Both men devoted a disproportionate share of their memoirs to the controversy. Sheridan again clashed with Hazen on the Indian frontier in 1868, and their inability to cooperate damaged the effectiveness of Sheridan's campaign. Hazen's friendship with General Sherman made it difficult for Sheridan to persecute him, but he did manage to transfer his rival and his regiment to Fort Buford, North Dakota, in 1872. Hazen regarded his "banishment" to the army's most desolate and remote post to be the direct result of Sheridan's enmity. The final victory, however, went to Hazen when his close friend James A. Garfield was elected president. Hazen was promptly promoted to brigadier general and appointed chief signal officer, finally escaping Sheridan's persecution.

Sheridan emerged from the Civil War as the Union's premier combat officer. Rarely innovative, he nevertheless developed the cavalry into a more powerful force by dismounting them in battle and supplying them with artillery support. He utilized intelligence gathering, scouting, and spying at a level far above other generals and always had a reputation for being remarkably well informed. Although cautious and painstaking in preparation for battle, once on the field he was quick thinking, bold, and decisive. "A persevering terrier dog," was how his friend Sherman characterized him, "honest, modest, plucky and smart enough."

Adam Badeau, Grant's military secretary, described the relationship between his commander and Sheridan as "the love of strong men who had stood side by side in war, and watched each other's deeds. . . . The affection was founded on admiration; the intimacy grew out of achievement. It was the strange, rich fruit of battle, watered by blood and ripened by patriotism into a close and tender regard." Grant's affections were notoriously expressed through poor judgment, and his assessments of Sheridan were often given over to hyperbole. Yet this estimate, given to Senator George Hoar, has the ring of truth: "I believe General Sheridan has no superior as a general, either living or dead, and perhaps not an equal. . . . He has judgment, prudence, foresight and power to deal with dispositions needed in a great war. I entertained this opinion of him before he became generally known in the late war."

With the war over, Grant immediately sent Sheridan to the Texas border with orders to provide material and moral support to the forces of Benito Juárez in their struggle with Maximilian, the puppet emperor of Mexico installed by Louis Napoleon of France. Sheridan relished the opportunity to confront French troops in battle, but he was restrained by the Department of State. Still, Sheridan provided arms and ammunition to the forces of Juárez while his forces on the Rio Grande bluffed French troops out of northern Mexico. The French soon abandoned Maximilian to his fate.

Although preoccupied with border affairs, Sheridan still kept a wary eye on civil affairs in Texas and Louisiana. He distributed troops at critical points to suppress night-riding white terrorists who attacked the freed blacks and white Unionists. The war had radicalized the general, so that by the time of Appomattox he was one of the most stridently Republican and bitterly antisouthern officers in the army. He was particularly enraged by the various vagrancy and apprentice laws—called Black Codes—enacted by the Texans. Sheridan angrily declared that they resulted in "a policy of gross injustice toward the colored people on the part of the courts, and a reign of lawlessness and disorder ensued."

Sheridan was hardly a crusader, clearly subscribing to the racial prejudices of his time, but he was determined to protect the emancipated blacks. He felt that black Americans had earned their freedom during the war, and "it was the plain duty of those in authority to make it secure" and "see that they had a fair chance in the battle of life."

Keeping his troops close to the Texas urban centers to protect the blacks. Sheridan was heavily criticized for not protecting frontier Texans from the Comanches. The general refused to move his men, noting that "if a white man is killed by the Indians on an extensive Indian frontier, the greatest excitement will take place, but over the killing of many freedmen in the settlements, nothing is done." Sheridan further angered the Texans when, on being asked by a reporter what he thought of the Lone Star State, he replied: "If I owned hell and Texas, I would rent Texas out and live in hell."

Sheridan's determined defense of the blacks, his bitter disputes with local politicians, his forceful suppression of white terrorism, and his zealous application of the reconstruction laws of the congressional radical Republicans led President Andrew Johnson to dismiss him as commander of the Fifth Military District on July 31, 1867. Reassigned to command the Department of the Missouri, which included present-day Kansas, Oklahoma, New Mexico, and Colorado, Sheridan soon found the task of frontier defense equally difficult but far more congenial to his temperament.

Throughout late 1868 and early 1869 Sheridan conducted a masterful winter campaign against the Cheyennes and allied tribes. In sharp encounters at the Washita in November 1868, at Soldier Springs in December, and at Summit Springs in July 1869, Sheridan's troopers broke the power of the Cheyennes and forced them onto reservations in Indian Territory (Oklahoma). The campaign won Sheridan a new reputation as the nation's top Indian fighter.

After Grant took office as president in March 1869, he appointed Sheridan lieutenant general and gave him command of the Division of the Missouri. This vast command extended from Sheridan's Chicago headquarters on the east to the western borders of Montana, Wyoming, Utah, and New Mexico on the west, and from the Canadian line on the north to the Mexican border on the south. Most of the Indian population of the United States was scattered about the million square miles of Sheridan's command: Sioux, Northern and Southern Cheyennes, Kiowas, Arapahos, Comanches, Utes, Piegans, Kickapoos, and Apaches all battled Sheridan's troopers. He gave overall direction to the final, and greatest, Indian campaigns waged on this continent. Between 1867 and 1884, his troops fought 619 engagements with the western tribes, finally completing the subjugation of America's native peoples that had been set in motion almost four hundred years before.

In these campaigns Sheridan usually employed the same strategy that had worked so well in 1868 and 1869. In the Red River War of 1874 to 1875 on the southern plains and the Great Sioux War of 1876 to 1877 on the northern plains he again attempted to employ winter as an ally (although both campaigns saw summer fighting) and to have converging columns trap the Indians. Recognizing the difficulties of distance and terrain, he never expected these columns to meet or to work in concert, but rather to keep the natives insecure, off balance, and constantly on the move. In neither of these great campaigns did the Indians suffer much loss of life in battle (in fact, far more soldiers were killed on the battlefield than Indians), but they were finally defeated by starvation, exposure, stock and property losses, and unrelenting insecurity. Such campaigns reaffirmed the effectiveness of Sheridan's total-war philosophy, for it was concern over the suffering of their families that forced the warriors onto the reservation to surrender. If Indian women and children had been allowed to find sanctuary on the reservation, which they were not, or if the soldiers had been prohibited from attacking the Indian villages, then Sheridan's strategy would have failed. Only by making war on the entire tribe—men, women, and children—could Sheridan hope for quick and decisive results. This brutally simple strategy proved eminently successful.

Sheridan's innate conservatism led him to cling to his converging-column, winter campaign strategy when alternatives might have proven more effective. Sheridan, and many other officers, also tended to underestimate the tenacity, courage, and ability of the Indians. This could have disastrous consequences, as it did on the northern plains during the Great Sioux War when the Sioux outgeneraled George Crook and George Custer at the Rosebud and Little Big Horn. Only after Sheridan turned to occupying the Sioux hunting grounds, to constant harassing tactics, and to military control over the reservations did the Indians capitulate.

After the Great Sioux War the nature of Indian campaigning changed, for no longer did Sheridan's troopers march into strange country against a foe of unknown numbers. Instead the soldiers ringed the various reservations with their forts, guarding against any outbreak. Any Indian off the reservation was branded as a "hostile." The char-

acteristic type of campaign after 1877 was the pursuit of
Indian fugitives over a great expanse of territory. Such was
the case with Chief Joseph's Nez Percé band, with the
Northern Cheyennes of Dull Knife and Little Wolf, and
with Geronimo's Apaches.

Keeping the peace on the Indian frontier remained
Sheridan's primary duty throughout his years as commander of the Division of the Missouri, but even during
times of Indian unrest his troops were quickly pulled from
the frontier to meet various threats to national order.
Sheridan and his troopers were called east to duty, for
example, during the 1871 Chicago fire crisis, during 1875
when the general was again placed in command in Louisiana, during the tense election crisis of 1876, and during
the great railroad strike of 1877. Indian wars were already
anachronistic to Gilded Age Americans, and the needs of
the western frontier were usually subordinated to more
pressing political, economic, or social needs in the East.

Sheridan's pragmatism and elastic ethics made him the
perfect soldier for an expansionistic republic. He ruthlessly
carried out the dictates of his government, never faltering
in his conviction that what he did was right. Hardly ce-
rebral, he nevertheless possessed a truly continental vision
of the nation. He was determined to open the West and
unite it with the rest of the country. That he could be
cruel and vindictive in this enterprise found expression in
a frontier military policy that was but an extension of his
Civil War strategies. Knowing but the soldier's life, Sheridan tended to view every situation in light of how military
power could establish order. Deeply affected by the chaos
of the Civil War, he was quick to apply force against all
those who opposed his government's wishes—be they un-
reconstructed Southerners, striking Northern laborers, or
Western Indians.

On November 1, 1883, General Sherman retired from
the army and Sheridan moved to Washington to assume
the position of commanding general. By law, however,
Sherman's four stars retired with him. Sheridan found his

new position frustrating, for the office was devoid of any real power in peacetime. The bureau chiefs actually administered the army and they reported directly to the secretary of war. There was considerable talk in the eighties of running Sheridan for president, although his identification as a Roman Catholic made his nomination unlikely. Sheridan had no desire to run for political office anyway, and the blandishments of the professional politicians did not sway him. He had seen what politics had done to "the old man," as he called Grant, and he had no wish to chance such a fate. "I have led forlorn hopes enough in the Army," he declared in March 1888. "This being pulled and hauled by politicians does not suit a soldier."

Another reason to decline politics was the precarious state of his health, for despite his relative youth, Sheridan suffered from severe heart disease. By 1883 his oddly shaped figure had grown increasingly portly, his face flushed and fleshy, and his hair snow white. He now withdrew from the public limelight to spend more time with his wife, Irene Rucker Sheridan (they were married in 1875), and their four young children.

He spent much of his time working on his memoirs in the study of his roomy home at Rhode Island Avenue and Seventeenth Street in Washington. He had been working on them for a year when, in November 1887, his physician diagnosed the heart disease that would soon kill him. This medical news caused him to redouble his writing efforts, and although he despised the hard labor of writing, he now passionately stuck to a daily routine. He had hoped to take the memoirs up to his appointment as commanding general, but his declining health forced him to end the manuscript with the 1871 Franco-Prussian War. On March 23, 1888, he sent the manuscript to his publisher, Charles L. Webster and Company of New York. They issued it in a beautiful two-volume edition with bindings to match the memoirs of Grant and Sherman. While Sheridan's book lacks the literary grace of Grant's memoirs and the bluntness and frank insight of Sherman's, it nevertheless remains a compelling, informative memoir of grand literary and historical merit. The memoirs deserve to rank with the works of his two military friends. In 1902, D. Appleton and Company issued an expanded edition of the memoirs with additional material by Michael V. Sheridan, the general's brother and longtime military aide, that dealt with the final seventeen years of the general's life.

Completion of the manuscript came none too soon, for on May 22, 1888, just after returning from Chicago, where he had inspected the site for Fort Sheridan, the fifty-seven-year-old general collapsed with a severe heart attack. This news prompted Congress to revive the grade of general of the army, and President Grover Cleveland promptly signed the commission so that Sheridan joined Washington, Grant, and Sherman in holding the four-star grade. His spirits were lifted by the promotion, even though his increasingly frail body had been racked by more heart attacks, and he requested that he be taken to his seaside cottage at Nonquitt, Massachusetts. There he died on Sunday, August 5, 1888.

They buried him at Arlington National Cemetery as he had requested. His impressive gravestone was placed on a high, green knoll directly in front of the Custiss-Lee Mansion, the home of his old foe, looking eastward toward the city of Washington. There it stands today, still guarding the sacred Union Phil Sheridan had done so much to save.

"SHERIDAN'S RIDE"
by T. Buchanan Read

Up from the South at break of day,
Bringing to Winchester fresh dismay,
The affrighted air with a shudder bore,
Like a herald in haste, to the chieftain's door,
The terrible grumble, and rumble, and roar,
Telling the battle was on once more,
And Sheridan twenty miles away.

And wider still those billows of war
Thundered along the horizon's bar;
And louder yet into Winchester rolled
The roar of that red sea uncontrolled,
Making the blood of the listener cold,
As he thought of the stake in that fiery fray,
And Sheridan twenty miles away.

But there is a road from Winchester town,
A good broad highway leading down;
And there, through the flush of the morning light,
A steed as black as the steeds of night
Was seen to pass, as with eagle flight,
As if he knew the terrible need;
He stretched away with his utmost speed
Hills rose and fell; but his heart was gay,
With Sheridan fifteen miles away.

Still sprung from those swift hoofs, thundering South,
The dust, like smoke from the cannon's mouth;
Or the trail of a comet, sweeping faster and faster,
Foreboding to traitors the doom of disaster.
The heart of the steed, and the heart of the master,
Were beating like prisoners assaulting their walls,
Impatient to be where the battle-field calls;
Every nerve of the charger was strained to full play,
With Sheridan only ten miles away.

Under his spurning feet the road
Like an arrowy Alpine river flowed,
And the landscape sped away behind
Like an ocean flying before the wind,
And the steed, like a barque fed with furnace ire,
Swept on, with his wild eye full of fire.
But lo! he is nearing his heart's desire;
He is snuffing the smoke of the roaring fray,
With Sheridan only five miles away.

The first that the general saw were the groups
Of stragglers, and then the retreating troops.
What was done? what to do? a glance told him both;
Then, striking his spurs, with a terrible oath,
He dashed down the line, 'mid a storm of huzzas,
And the wave of retreat checked its course there, because
The sight of the master compelled it to pause.
With foam and with dust, the black charger was gray;
By the flash of his eye, and the red nostril's play,
He seemed to the whole great army to say,
"I have brought you Sheridan all the way
From Winchester, down to save the day!"

Hurrah! hurrah for Sheridan!
Hurrah! hurrah for horse and man!
And when their statues are placed on high,
Under the dome of the Union sky,
The American soldiers' Temple of Fame,
There, with the glorious general's name,

Be it said, in letters both bold and bright,
"Here is the steed that saved the day,
By carrying Sheridan into the fight,
From Winchester, twenty miles away!"

CIVIL WAR MEMOIRS

CHAPTER I

THE NEWS OF THE FIRING ON FORT SUMTER brought us an excitement which overshadowed all else, and though we had no officers at the post who sympathized with the rebellion, there were several in our regiment—the Fourth Infantry—who did, and we were considerably exercised as to the course they might pursue, but naturally far more so concerning the disposition that would be made of the regiment during the conflict.

In due time orders came for the regiment to go East, and my company went off, leaving me, however—a second lieutenant—in command of the post [Fort Yamhill, Oregon] until I should be relieved by Captain James J. Archer, of the Ninth Infantry, whose company was to take the place of the old garrison. Captain Archer, with his company of the Ninth, arrived shortly after, but I had been notified that he intended to go South, and his conduct was such after reaching the post that I would not turn over the command to him for fear he might commit some rebellious act. Thus a more prolonged detention occurred that than I had at first anticipated. Finally the news came that he had tendered his resignation and been granted a leave of absence for sixty days. On July 17 he took his departure, but I continued in command till September 1, when Captain Philip A. Owen, of the Ninth Infantry, arrived and, taking charge, gave me my release.

From the day we received the news of the firing on Sumter until I started East, about the first of September, 1861, I was deeply solicitous as to the course of events, and though I felt confident that in the end the just cause of the Government must triumph, yet the thoroughly crystallized organization which the Southern Confederacy quickly exhibited disquieted me very much, for it alone was evidence that the Southern leaders had long anticipated the struggle and prepared for it. It was very difficult to obtain direct intelligence of the progress of the war. Most of the time we were in the depths of ignorance as to the true condition of affairs, and this tended to increase our anxiety. Then, too, the accounts of the conflicts that had taken place were greatly exaggerated by the Eastern papers, and lost nothing in transition. The news came by the pony express across the Plains to San Francisco, where it was still further magnified in republishing, and gained somewhat in Southern bias. I remember well that when the first reports reached us of the battle of Bull Run— that sanguinary engagement—it was stated that each side had lost *forty* thousand men in killed and wounded, and none were reported missing nor as having run away. Week by week these losses grew less, until they finally shrunk into the hundreds, but the vivid descriptions of the gory conflict were not toned down during the whole summer.

We received our mail at Yamhill only once a week, and then had to bring it from Portland, Oregon, by express. On the day of the week that our courier, or messenger, was expected back from Portland, I would go out early in the morning to a commanding point above the post, from which I could see a long distance down the road as it ran through the valley of the Yamhill, and there I would watch with anxiety for his coming, longing for good news; for, isolated as I had been through years spent in the wilderness, my patriotism was untainted by politics, nor had it been disturbed by any discussion of the questions out of which the war grew, and I hoped for the success of the Government above all other considerations. I believe I was also uninfluenced by any thoughts of the promotion that might result to me from the conflict, but, out of a sincere desire to contribute as much as I could to the preservation of the Union, I earnestly wished to be at the seat of war, and feared it might end before I could get East. In no sense did I anticipate what was to happen to me afterward, nor that I was to gain any distinction from it. I was ready to do my duty to the best of my ability wherever I might be called, and I was young, healthy, insensible to fatigue, and desired opportunity, but high rank was so distant in our service that not a dream of its attainment had flitted through my brain.

During the period running from January to September, 1861, in consequence of resignations and the addition of some new regiments to the regular army, I had passed through the grade of first lieutenant and reached that of captain in the Thirteenth United States Infantry, of which General W. T. Sherman had recently been made the colonel. When relieved from further duty at Yamhill by Captain Owen, I left for the Atlantic coast to join my new regiment. A two days' ride brought me down to Portland, whence I sailed to San Franciso, and at that city took passage by steamer for New York via the Isthmus of Panama, in company with a number of officers who were coming East under circumstances like my own.

At this time California was much agitated on the question of secession, and the secession element was so strong that considerable apprehension was felt by the Union people lest the State might be carried into the Confederacy. As a consequence great distrust existed in all quarters, and the loyal passengers on the steamer, not knowing what might occur during our voyage, prepared to meet emergencies by thoroughly organizing to frustrate any attempt that might possibly be made to carry us into some South-

CHAPTER II

SOME DAYS AFTER I had reached the headquarters of my regiment near St. Louis, General Halleck sent for me, and when I reported he informed me that there existed a great deal of confusion regarding the accounts of some of the disbursing officers in his department, whose management of its fiscal affairs under his predecessor, General John C. Fremont, had been very loose; and as the chaotic condition of things could be relieved only by auditing these accounts, he therefore had determined to create a board of officers for the purpose, and intended to make me president of it. The various transactions in question covered a wide field, for the department embraced the States of Missouri, Iowa, Minnesota, Illinois, Arkansas, and all of Kentucky west of the Cumberland River.

The duty was not distasteful, and I felt that I was qualified to undertake it, for the accounts to be audited belonged exclusively to the Quartermaster and Subsistence departments, and by recent experience I had become familiar with the class of papers that pertained to those branches of the army. Indeed, it was my familiarity with such transactions, returns, &c., that probably caused my selection as president of the board.

I entered upon the work forthwith, and continued at it until the 26th of December, 1861. At that date I was relieved from the auditing board and assigned to duty as Chief Commissary of the Army of Southwest Missouri, commanded by General Samuel R. Curtis. This army was then organizing at Rolla, Missouri, for the Pea Ridge campaign, its strength throughout the campaign being in the aggregate about fifteen thousand men.

As soon as I received information of my selection for this position, I went to General Halleck and requested him to assign me as Chief Quartermaster also. He was reluctant to do so, saying that I could not perform both duties, but I soon convinced him that I could do both better than the one, for I reminded him that as Chief Quartermaster I should control the transportation, and thus obviate all possible chances of discord between the two staff departments; a condition which I deemed essential to success, especially as it was intended that Curtis's army should mainly subsist on the country. This argument impressed Halleck, and becoming convinced, he promptly issued the order making me Chief Quartermaster and Chief Commissary of Subsistence of the Army of Southwest Missouri, and I started for Rolla to enter upon the work assigned me.

Having reported to General Curtis, I quickly learned that his system of supply was very defective, and the transportation without proper organization, some of the regiments having forty to fifty wagon each, and others only three or four. I labored day and night to remedy these and other defects, and with the help of Captain Michael P. Small, of the Subsistence Department, who was an invaluable assistant, soon brought things into shape, putting the transportation in good working order, giving each regiment its proper quota of wagons, and turning the surplus into the general supply trains of the army. In accomplishing this I was several times on the verge of personal conflict with irate regimental commanders, but Colonel G. M. Dodge so greatly sustained me with General Curtis by strong moral support, and by such efficient details from his regiment—the Fourth Iowa Volunteer Infantry—that I still bear him and it great affection and lasting gratitude.

On January 26, 1862, General Curtis's army began its march from Rolla to Springfield, Missouri, by way of Lebanon. The roads were deep with mud, and so badly cut up that the supply trains in moving labored under the most serious difficulties, and were greatly embarrassed by swollen streams. Under these circumstances many delays occurred, and when we arrived at Lebanon nearly all the supplies with which we had started had been consumed, and the work of feeding the troops off the country had to begin at that point. To get flour, wheat had to be taken from the stacks, threshed, and sent to the mills to be ground. Wheat being scarce in this region, corn as a substitute had to be converted into meal by the same laborious process. In addition, beef cattle had to be secured for the meat ration.

By hard work we soon accumulated a sufficient quantity of flour and corn meal to justify the resumption of our march on Springfield, at or near which point the enemy was believed to be awaiting us, and the order was given to move forward, the commanding general cautioning me, in the event of disaster, to let no salt fall into General Price's hands. General Curtis made a hobby of this matter of salt, believing the enemy was sadly in need of that article, and he impressed me deeply with his conviction that our cause would be seriously injured by a loss which would inure so greatly and peculiarly to the enemy's benefit; but we afterward discovered, when Price abandoned his position, that about all he left behind was salt.

When we were within about eight miles of Springfield, General Curtis decided to put his troops in line of battle for the advance on the town, and directed me to stretch out my supply trains in a long line of battle, so that in falling back, in case the troops were repulsed, he could rally the men on the wagons. I did not like the tactics, but of course obeyed the order. The line moved on Springfield, and took the town without resistance, the enemy having fled southward, in the direction of Pea Ridge, the preceding day. Of course our success relieved my anxiety about the wagons; but fancy has often pictured since, the stampede of six mule teams that, had we met with any reverse, would have taken place over the prairies of southwest Missouri.

The army set out in pursuit of Price, but I was left at Springfield to gather supplies from the surrounding country, by the same means that had been used at Lebanon, and send them forward. To succeed in this useful and necessary duty required much hard work. To procure the grain and to run the mills in the country, replacing the machinery where parts had been carried away, or changing the principle and running the mills on some different plan when necessary, and finally forward the product to the army, made a task that taxed the energy of all engaged in it. Yet, having at command a very skillful corps of mill-wrights, machinists, and millers, detailed principally from the Fourth Iowa and Thirty-sixth Illinois volunteer regiments, we soon got matters in shape, and were able to send such large quantities of flour and meal to the front, that only the bacon and small parts of the ration had to be brought forward from our dépôt at Rolla. When things were well systematized, I went forward myself to expedite the delivery of supplies, and joined the army at Cross Hollows, just south of Pea Ridge.

Finding everything working well at Cross Hollows, I returned to Springfield in a few days to continue the labor of collecting supplies. On my way back I put the mills at Cassville in good order to grind the grain in that vicinity, and perfected there a plan for the general supply from the neighboring district of both the men and animals of the army, so that there should be no chance of a failure of the campaign from bad roads or disaster to my trains. Springfield thus became the center of the entire supply section.

Just after my return to Springfield the battle of Pea Ridge was fought. The success of the Union troops in this battle was considerable, and while not of sufficient magnitude to affect the general cause materially, it was decisive as to that particular campaign, and resulted in driving all organized Confederate forces out of the State of Missouri. After Pea Ridge was won, certain efforts were made to deprive Curtis of the credit due him for the victory; but, no matter what merit belonged to individual commanders, I was always convinced that Curtis was deserving of the highest commendation, not only for the skill displayed on the field, but for a zeal and daring in campaign which was not often exhibited at that early period of the war. Especially should this credit be awarded him, when we consider the difficulties under which he labored, how he was hampered in having to depend on a sparsely settled country for the subsistence of his troops. In the reports of the battle that came to Springfield, much glory was claimed for some other general officers, but as I had control of the telegraph line from Springfield east, I detained all despatches until General Curtis had sent in his official report. He thus had the opportunity of communicating with his superior in advance of some of his vain subordinates, who would have laid claim to the credit of the battle had I not thwarted them by this summary means.

Not long afterward came the culmination of a little difference that had arisen between General Curtis and me, brought about, I have since sometimes thought, by an assistant quartermaster from Iowa, whom I had on duty with me at Springfield. He coveted my place, and finally succeeded in getting it. He had been an unsuccessful banker in Iowa, and early in the war obtained an appointment as assistant quartermaster of volunteers with the rank of captain. As chief quartermaster of the army in Missouri, there would be opportunities for the recuperation of his fortunes which would not offer to one in a subordinate place; so to gain this position he doubtless intrigued for it while under my eye, and Curtis was induced

to give it to him as soon as I was relieved. His career as
my successor, as well as in other capacities in which he
was permitted to act during the war, was to say the least
not savory. The war over he turned up in Chicago as president of a bank, which he wrecked; and he finally landed
in the penitentiary for stealing a large sum of money from
the United States Treasury at Washington while employed
there as a clerk. The chances that this man's rascality
would be discovered were much less when chief of the
departments of transportation and supply of an army than
they afterward proved to be in the Treasury. I had in my
possession at all times large sums of money for the needs
of the army, and among other purposes for which these
funds were to be disbursed was the purchase of horses and
mules. Certain officers and men more devoted to gain than
to the performance of duty (a few such are always to be
found in armies) quickly learned this, and determined to
profit by it. Consequently they began a regular system of
stealing horses from the people of the country and prof-
fering them to me for purchase. It took but a little time
to discover this roguery, and when I became satisfied of
their knavery I brought it to a sudden close by seizing the
horses as captured property, branding them U. S., and
refusing to pay for them. General Curtis, misled by the
misrepresentations that had been made, and without fully
knowing the circumstances, or realizing to what a base
and demoralizing state of things this course was inevitably
tending, practically ordered me to make the payments, and
I refused. The immediate result of this disobedience was
a court-martial to try me; and knowing that my usefulness
in that army was gone, no matter what the outcome of
the trial might be, I asked General Halleck to relieve me
from duty with General Curtis and order me to St. Louis.
This was promptly done, and as my connection with the
Army of Southwest Missouri was thus severed before the
court could be convened, my case never came to trial.
The man referred to as being the cause of this condition
of affairs was appointed by General Curtis to succeed me.

I turned over to the former all the funds and property for which I was responsible, also the branded horses and mules stolen from the people of the country, requiring receipts for everything. I heard afterward that some of the blooded stock of southwest Missouri made its way to Iowa in an unaccountable manner, but whether the administration of my successor was responsible for it or not I am unable to say.

On my arrival at St. Louis I felt somewhat forlorn and disheartened at the turn affairs had taken. I did not know where I should be assigned, nor what I should be required to do, but these uncertainties were dispelled in a few days by General Halleck, who, being much pressed by the Governors of some of the Western States to disburse money in their sections, sent me out into the Northwest with a sort of roving commission to purchase horses for the use of the army. I went to Madison and Racine, Wis., at which places I bought two hundred horses, which were shipped to St. Louis. At Chicago I bought two hundred more, and as the prices paid at the latter point showed that Illinois was the cheapest market—it at that time producing a surplus over home demands—I determined to make Chicago the centre of my operations.

While occupied in this way at Chicago the battle of Shiloh took place, and the desire for active service with troops became uppermost in my thoughts, so I returned to St. Louis to see if I could not get into the field. General Halleck having gone down to the Shiloh battle-field, I reported to his Assistant Adjutant-General, Colonel John C. Kelton, and told him of my anxiety to take a hand in active field-service, adding that I did not wish to join my regiment, which was still organizing and recruiting at Jefferson Barracks, for I felt confident I could be more useful elsewhere. Kelton knew that the purchasing duty was but temporary, and that on its completion, probably at no distant date, I should have to join my company at the barracks; so, realizing the inactivity to which that situation of affairs would subject me, he decided to assume

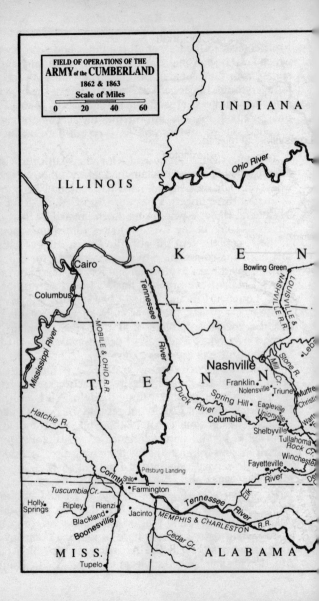

FIELD OF OPERATIONS OF THE
ARMY of the **CUMBERLAND**
1862 & 1863
Scale of Miles
0   20   40   60

INDIANA

ILLINOIS

Ohio River

K   E   N

Cairo

Bowling Green

Columbus

Tennessee River

LOUISVILLE & NASHVILLE R.R.

MOBILE & OHIO R.R.

Mississippi River

Nashville

Mill Cr.

Stone R.

Leb

T   E

Franklin

N

Duck River

Nolensville   Triune

Murfre

Christi

Spring Hill   Eagleville

Columbia   Unionville

War

Hatchie R.

Shelbyville

Tullahoma
Rock Cr.

Winchester

Fayetteville

Corinth

Pittsburg Landing

Shilo

River

De

Tuscumbia Cr.   Farmington

Holly
Springs   Ripley   Rienzi

Blackland

Tennessee River

Elk

Jacinto

MEMPHIS & CHARLESTON R.R.

Boonesville

Cedar Cr.

MISS.   ALABAMA

Tupelo

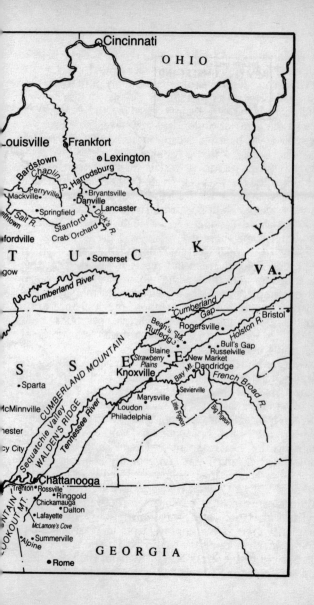

the responsibility of sending me to report to General Halleck at Shiloh, and gave me an order to that effect.

This I consider the turning-point in my military career, and shall always feel grateful to Colonel Kelton for his kindly act which so greatly influenced my future. My desire to join the army at Shiloh had now taken possession of me, and I was bent on getting there by the first means available. Learning that a hospital-boat under charge of Dr. Hough was preparing to start for Pittsburg Landing, I obtained the Doctor's consent to take passage on it, and on the evening of April 15 I left St. Louis for the scene of military operations in northeastern Mississippi.

At Pittsburg Landing I reported to General Halleck, who, after some slight delay, assigned me to duty as an assistant to Colonel George Thom, of the topographical engineers. Colonel Thom put me at the work of getting the trains up from the landing, which involved the repair of roads for that purpose by corduroying the marshy places. This was rough, hard work, without much chance of reward, but it was near the field of active operations, and I determined to do the best I could at it till opportunity for something better might arise.

General Halleck did not know much about taking care of himself in the field. His camp arrangements were wholly inadequate, and in consequence he and all the officers about him were subjected to much unnecessary discomfort and annoyance. Some one suggested to him to appoint me quartermaster for his headquarters, with a view of systematizing the establishment and remedying the defects complained of, and I was consequently assigned to this duty. Shortly after this assignment I had the satisfaction of knowing that General Halleck was delighted with the improvements made at headquarters, both in camp outfit and transportation, and in administration generally. My popularity grew as the improvements increased, but one trifling incident came near marring it. There was some hitch about getting fresh beef for General Halleck's mess, and as by this time everybody had come to look to me for anything and everything in the way of comfort, Colonel Joe McKibben brought an order from the General for me to get fresh beef for the headquarters mess. I was not caterer for this mess, nor did I belong to it even, so I refused point-blank. McKibben, disliking to report my disobedience, undertook persuasion, and brought Colonel Thom to see me to aid in his negotiations, but I would not give in, so McKibben in the kindness of his heart rode several miles in order to procure the beef himself, and thus save me from the dire results which he thought would follow should Halleck get wind of such downright insubordination. The next day I was made Commissary of Subsistence for the headquarters in addition to my other duties, and as this brought me into the line of fresh beef, General Halleck had no cause thereafter to complain of a scarcity of that article in his mess.

My stay at General Halleck's headquarters was exceedingly agreeable, and my personal intercourse with officers on duty there was not only pleasant and instructive, but offered opportunities for improvement and advancement for which hardly any other post could have afforded like chances. My special duties did not occupy all my time, and whenever possible I used to go over to General Sherman's division, which held the extreme right of our line in the advance on Corinth, to witness the little engagements occurring there continuously during the slow progress which the army was then making, the enemy being forced back but a short distance each day. I knew General Sherman very well. We came from near the same section of country in Ohio, and his wife and her family had known me from childhood. I was always kindly received by the General, and one day he asked me if I would be willing to accept the colonelcy of a certain Ohio regiment if he secured the appointment. I gladly told him yes, if General Halleck would let me go; but I was doomed to disappointment, for in about a week or so afterward General Sherman informed me that the Governor of Ohio would not consent, having already decided to appoint some one else.

A little later Governor Blair, of Michigan, who was with the army temporarily in the interest of the troops from his State, and who just at this time was looking around for a colonel for the Second Michigan Cavalry, and very anxious to get a regular officer, fixed upon me as the man. The regiment was then somewhat run down by losses from sickness, and considerably split into factions growing out of jealousies engendered by local differences previous to organization, and the Governor desired to bridge over all these troubles by giving the regiment a commander who knew nothing about them. I presume that some one said to the Governor about this time, "Why don't you get Sheridan?" This, however, is only conjecture. I really do not know how my name was proposed to him, but I have often been told since that General Gordon Granger, whom I knew slightly then, and who had been the former colonel of the regiment, first suggested the appointment. At all events, on the morning of May 27, 1862, Captain Russell A. Alger—recently Governor of Michigan—accompanied by the quartermaster of the regiment, Lieutenant Frank Walbridge, arrived at General Halleck's headquarters and delivered to me this telegram:

[By Telegraph.]   "MILITARY DEP'T OF MICHIGAN,
                         "ADJUTANT-GENERAL'S OFFICE,
                         "DETROIT, May 25, 1862.

"GENERAL ORDERS No. 148.
    "Captain Philip H. Sheridan, U. S. Army, is hereby appointed Colonel of the Second Regiment Michigan Cavalry, to rank from this date.
    "Captain Sheridan will immediately assume command of the regiment.
    "By order of the Commander-in-Chief,
                              "JNO. ROBERTSON,
                                   "*Adjutant-General.*"

I took the order to General Halleck, and said that I would like to accept, but he was not willing I should do so until the consent of the War Department could be obtained. I returned to my tent much disappointed, for in those days, for some unaccountable reason, the War Department did not favor the appointment of regular officers to volunteer regiments, and I feared a disapproval at Washington. After a further consultation with Captain Alger and Lieutenant Walbridge, I determined to go to the General again and further present the case. Enlarging on my desire for active service with troops, and urging the utter lack of such opportunity where I was, I pleaded my cause until General Halleck finally resolved to take the responsibility of letting me go without consulting the War Department. When I had thanked him for the kindness, he said that inasmuch as I was to leave him, he would inform me that the regiment to which I had just been appointed was ordered out as part of a column directed to make a raid to the south of the enemy, then occupying Corinth, and that if I could turn over my property, it would probably be well for me to join my command immediately, so that I could go with the expedition. I returned to my tent, where Alger and Walbridge were still waiting, and told them of the success of my interview, at the same time notifying them that I would join the regiment in season to accompany the expedition of which Halleck had spoken.

In the course of the afternoon I turned over all my property to my successor, and about 8 o'clock that evening made my appearance at the camp of the Second Michigan Cavalry, near Farmington, Mississippi. The regiment was in a hubbub of excitement making preparations for the raid, and I had barely time to meet the officers of my command, and no opportunity at all to see the men, when the trumpet sounded to horse. Dressed in a coat and trousers of a captain of infantry, but recast as a colonel of cavalry by a pair of well-worn eagles that General Granger had kindly given me, I hurriedly placed on my saddle a haversack, containing some coffee, sugar, bacon, and hard bread, which had been prepared, and mounting my horse, I reported my regiment to the brigade commander as ready for duty.

CHAPTER III

THE EXPEDITION REFERRED TO by General Halleck in his parting conversation was composed of the Second Michigan and Second Iowa regiments of cavalry, formed into a brigade under command of Colonel Washington L. Elliott, of the Second Iowa. It was to start on the night of the 27th of May at 12 o'clock, and proceed by a circuitous route through Iuka, Miss., to Booneville, a station on the Mobile and Ohio Railroad, about twenty-two miles below Corinth, and accomplish all it could in the way of destroying the enemy's supplies and cutting his railroad communications.

The weather in that climate was already warm, guides unobtainable, and both men and horses suffered much discomfort from the heat, and fatigue from the many delays growing out of the fact that we were in almost total ignorance of the roads leading to the point that we desired to reach. In order that we might go light we carried only sugar, coffee, and salt, depending on the country for meat and bread. Both these articles were scarce, but I think we got all there was, for our advent was so unexpected by the people of the region through which we passed that, supposing us to be Confederate cavalry, they often gave us all they had, the women and servants contributing most freely from their reserve stores.

Before reaching Booneville I had the advance, but just as we arrived on the outskirts of the town the brigade was formed with the Second Iowa on my right, and the whole force moved forward, right in front, preceded by skirmishers. Here we encountered the enemy, but forced him back with little resistance. When we had gained possession of the station, Colonel Elliott directed me to take the left wing of my regiment, pass to the south, and destroy a bridge or culvert supposed to be at a little distance below the town on the Mobile and Ohio Railroad. The right wing, or other half of the regiment, was to be held in reserve for my support if necessary. I moved rapidly in the designated direction till I reached the railroad, and then rode down it for a mile and a half, but found neither bridge nor culvert. I then learned that there was no bridge of any importance except the one at Baldwin, nine miles farther down, but as I was aware, from information recently received, that it was defended by three regiments and a battery, I concluded that I could best accomplish the purpose for which I had been detached—crippling the road—by tearing up the track, bending the rails, and burning the cross-ties. This was begun with alacrity at four different points, officers and men vieing with one another in the laborious work of destruction. We had but few tools, and as the difficulties to overcome were serious, our progress was slow, until some genius conceived the idea that the track, rails and ties, might be lifted from its bed bodily, turned over, and subjected to a high heat; a convenient supply of dry fence-rails would furnish ample fuel to render the rails useless. In this way a good deal of the track was effectively broken up, and communication by rail from Corinth to the south entirely cut off. While we were still busy in wrecking the road, a dash was made at my right and rear by a squadron of Confederate cavalry. This was handsomely met by the reserve under Captain Archibald

P. Campbell, of the Second Michigan, who, dismounting a portion of his command, received the enemy with such a volley from his Colt's repeating rifles that the squadron broke and fled in all directions. We were not molested further, and resumed our work, intending to extend the break toward Baldwin, but receiving orders from Elliott to return to Booneville immediately, the men were recalled, and we started to rejoin the main command.

In returning to Booneville, I found the railroad track above where I had struck it blocked by trains that we had thus cut off, and the woods and fields around the town covered with several thousand Confederate soldiers. These were mostly convalescents and disheartened stragglers belonging to General Beauregard's army, and from them we learned that Corinth was being evacuated. I spent some little time in an endeavor to get these demoralized men into an open field, with a view to some future disposition of them; but in the midst of the undertaking I received another order from Colonel Elliott to join him at once. The news of the evacuation had also reached Elliott, and had disclosed a phase of the situation so different from that under which he had viewed it when we arrived at Booneville, that he had grown anxious to withdraw, lest we should be suddenly pounced upon by an overwhelming force from some one of the columns in retreat. Under such circumstances my prisoners would prove a decided embarrassment, so I abandoned further attempts to get them together—not even paroling them, which I thought might have been done with but little risk.

In the meantime the captured cars had been fired, and as their complete destruction was assured by explosions from those containing ammunition, they needed no further attention, so I withdrew my men and hastened to join Elliott, taking along some Confederate officers whom I had retained from among four or five hundred prisoners captured when making the original dash below the town.

The losses in my regiment, and, in fact, those of the entire command, were insignificant. The results of the expedition were important; the railroad being broken so thoroughly as to cut off all rolling stock north of Booneville, and to place at the service of General Halleck's army the cars and locomotives of which the retreating Confederates were now so much in need. In addition, we burned twenty-six cars containing ten thousand stand of small arms, three pieces of artillery, a great quantity of clothing, a heavy supply of ammunition, and the personal baggage of General Leonidas Polk. A large number of prisoners, mostly sick and convalescent, also fell into our hands; but as we could not carry them with us—such a hurried departure was an immediate necessity, by reason of our critical situation—the process of paroling them was not completed, and they doubtless passed back to active service in the Confederacy, properly enough unrecognized as prisoners of war by their superiors.

In returning, the column marched back by another indirect route to its old camp near Farmington, where we learned that the whole army had moved into and beyond Corinth, in pursuit of Beauregard, on the 13th of May, the very day we had captured Booneville. Although we had marched about one hundred and eighty miles in four days, we were required to take part, of course, in the pursuit of the Confederate army. So, resting but one night in our old camp, we were early in the saddle again on the morning of the 2d of June. Marching south through Corinth, we passed on the 4th of June the scene of our late raid, viewing with much satisfaction, as we took the road toward Blackland, the still smoldering embers of the burned trains.

On the 4th of June I was ordered to proceed with my regiment along the Blackland road to determine the strength of the enemy in that direction, as it was thought possible we might capture, by a concerted movement which General John Pope had suggested to General Halleck, a portion of Beauregard's rear guard. Pushing the Confederate scouts rapidly in with a running fire for a mile or more, while we were approaching a little stream, I hoped to gobble the main body of the enemy's pickets. I therefore directed the sabre battalion of the regiment, followed by that portion of it armed with revolving rifles, to dash forward in column, cut off these videttes before they could cross the stream, and then gather them in. The pickets fled hastily, however, and a pell-mell pursuit carried us over the stream at their heels by a little bridge, with no thought of halting till we gained a hill on the other side, and suddenly found ourselves almost in the camp of a strong body of artillery and infantry. Captain Campbell being in advance, hurriedly dismounted his battalion for a further forward movement on foot, but it was readily seen that the enemy was present in such heavy force as almost to ensure our destruction, and I gave orders for a hasty withdrawal. We withdrew without loss under cover of thick woods, aided much, however, by the consternation of the Confederates, who had hardly recovered from their surprise at our sudden appearance in their camp before we had again placed the stream between them and us by recrossing the bridge. The reconnoissance was a success in one way—that is, in finding out that the enemy was at the point supposed by General Pope; but it also had a tendency to accelerate Beauregard's retreat, for in a day or two his whole line fell back as far south as Guntown, thus rendering abortive the plans for bagging a large portion of his army.

General Beauregard's evacuation of Corinth and retreat southward were accomplished in the face of a largely superior force of Union troops, and he reached the point where he intended to halt for reorganization without other loss than that sustained in the destruction of the cars and supplies at Booneville, and the capture of some stragglers and deserters that fell into our hands while we were pressing his rear from General Pope's flank. The number of these was quite large, and indicated that the enemy was considerably demoralized. Under such circumstances, an energetic and skillfully directed pursuit might not have made certain the enemy's destruction, but it would largely have aided in disintegrating his forces, and I never could quite understand why it was not ordered. The desultory affairs between rear and advance guards seemed as a general thing to have no particular purpose in view beyond finding out where the enemy was, and when he was found, since no supporting columns were at hand and no one in supreme control was present to give directions, our skirmishing was of little avail and brought but small reward.

A short time subsequent to these occurrences, Colonel Elliott was made a brigadier-general, and as General Pope appointed him his Chief-of-Staff, I, on the 11th of June, 1862, fell in command of the brigade by seniority. For the rest of the month but little of moment occurred, and we settled down into camp at Booneville on the 26th of June, in a position which my brigade had been ordered to take up some twenty miles in advance of the main army for the purpose of covering its front. Although but a few days had elapsed from the date of my appointment as colonel of the Second Michigan to that of my succeeding to the command of the brigade, I believe I can say with propriety that I had firmly established myself in the confidence of the officers and men of the regiment, and won their regard by thoughtful care. I had striven unceasingly to have them well fed and well clothed, had personally looked after the selection of their camps, and had maintained such a discipline as to allay former irritation.

Men who march, scout, and fight, and suffer all the hardships that fall to the lot of soldiers in the field, in order to do vigorous work must have the best bodily sustenance, and every comfort that can be provided. I knew from practical experience on the frontier that my efforts in this direction would not only be appreciated, but requited by personal affection and gratitude; and, further, that such exertions would bring the best results to me. Whenever my authority would permit I saved my command from needless sacrifices and unnecessary toil; therefore, when hard or daring work was to be done I expected the heartiest response, and always got it. Soldiers are averse to seeing their comrades killed without compensating results, and none realize more quickly than they the blundering that often takes place on the field of battle. They want some tangible indemnity for the loss of life, and as victory is an offset the value of which is manifest, it not only makes them content to shed their blood, but also furnishes evidence of capacity in those who commanded them. My regiment had lost very few men since coming under my command, but it seemed, in the eyes of all who belonged to it, that casualties to the enemy and some slight successes for us had repaid every sacrifice, and in consequence I had gained not only their confidence as soldiers, but also their esteem and love as men, and to a degree far beyond what I then realized.

As soon as the camp of my brigade was pitched at Booneville, I began to scout in every direction, to obtain a knowledge of the enemy's whereabouts and learn the ground about me. My standing in drawing at the Military Academy had never been so high as to warrant the belief that I could ever prove myself an expert, but a few practical lessons in that line were impressed on me there, and I had retained enough to enable me to make rough maps that could be readily understood, and which would be suitable to replace the erroneous skeleton outlines of northern Mississippi, with which at this time we were scantily furnished; so as soon as possible I compiled for the use of myself and my regimental commanders an information map of the surrounding country. This map exhibited such details as country roads, streams, farmhouses, fields, woods, and swamps, and such other topographical features as would be useful. I must confess that my crude sketch did not evidence much artistic merit, but it was an improvement on what we already possessed in the way of details to guide the command, and this was what I most needed; for it was of the first importance that in our exposed condition we should be equipped with a thorough knowledge of the section in which we were operating, so as to be prepared to encounter an enemy already indicating recovery from the disorganizing effects of his recent retreat.

In the immediate vicinity of Booneville the country was covered with heavy forests, with here and there clearings or intervening fields that had been devoted to the cultivation of cotton and corn. The ground was of a low character, typical of northeastern Mississippi, and abounded in small creeks that went almost totally dry even in short periods of drought, but became flooded with muddy water under the outpouring of rain peculiar to a semi-tropical climate. In such a region there were many chances of our being surprised, especially by an enemy who knew the country well, and whose ranks were filled with local guides; and great precautions as well as the fullest information were necessary to prevent disaster. I therefore endeavored to familiarize all with our surroundings, but scarcely had matters begun to shape themselves as I desired when our annihilation was attempted by a large force of Confederate cavalry.

On the morning of July 1, 1862, a cavalry command of between five and six thousand men, under the Confederate General James R. Chalmers, advanced on two roads converging near Booneville. The head of the enemy's column on the Blackland and Booneville road came in contact with my pickets three miles and a half west of Booneville. These pickets, under Lieutenant Leonidas S. Scranton, of the Second Michigan Cavalry, fell back slowly, taking advantage of every tree or other cover to fire from till they arrived at the point where the converging roads joined. At this junction there was a strong position in the protecting timber, and here Scranton made a firm stand, being reinforced presently by the few men he had out as pickets on the road to his left, a second company I had sent him from camp, and subsequently by three companies more, all now commanded by Captain Campbell. This force was dismounted and formed in line, and soon developed that the enemy was present in large numbers. Up to this time Chalmers had shown only the heads of his columns, and we had doubts as to his purpose, but now that our resistance forced him to deploy two regiments on the right and left of the road, it became apparent that he meant business, and that there was no time to lose in preparing to repel his attack.

Full information of the situation was immediately sent me, and I directed Campbell to hold fast, if possible, till I could support him, but if compelled to retire he was authorized to do so slowly, taking advantage of every means that fell in his way to prolong the fighting. Before this I had stationed one battalion of the Second Iowa in Booneville, but Colonel Edward Hatch, commanding that regiment, was now directed to leave one company for the protection of our camp a little to the north of the station, and take the balance of the Second Iowa, with the battalion in Booneville except two sabre companies, and form the whole in rear of Captain Campbell, to protect his flanks and support him by a charge should the enemy break his dismounted line.

While these preparations were being made, the Confederates attempted to drive Campbell from his position by a direct attack through an open field. In this they failed, however, for our men, reserving their fire until the enemy came within about thirty yards, then opened on him with such a shower of bullets from our Colt's rifles that it soon became too hot for him, and he was repulsed with considerable loss. Foiled in this move, Chalmers hesitated to attack again in front, but began overlapping both flanks of Campbell's line by force of numbers, compelling Campbell to retire toward a strong position I had selected in his rear for a line on which to make our main resistance. As soon as the enemy saw this withdrawing he again charged in front, but was again as gallantly repelled as in the first assault, although the encounter was for a short time so desperate as to have the character of a hand-to-hand conflict, several groups of friend and foe using on each other the butts of their guns. At this juncture the timely arrival of Colonel Hatch with the Second Iowa gave a breathing-spell to Campbell, and made the Confederates so chary of further direct attacks that he was enabled to retire; and at the same time I found opportunity to make disposition of the reinforcement to the best advantage possible, placing the Second Iowa on the left of the new line and strengthening Campbell on its right with all the men available.

In view of his numbers, the enemy soon regained confidence in his ability to overcome us, and in a little while again began his flanking movements, his right passing around my left flank some distance, and approaching our camp and transportation, which I had forbidden to be moved out to the rear. Fearing that he would envelop us and capture the camp and transportation, I determined to take the offensive. Remembering a circuitous wood road that I had become familiar with while making the map heretofore mentioned, I concluded that the most effective plan would be to pass a small column around the enemy's left, by way of this road, and strike his rear by a mounted charge simultaneously with an advance of our main line on his front. I knew that the attack in rear would be a most hazardous undertaking, but in the face of such odds as the enemy had the condition of affairs was most critical, and could be relieved only by a bold and radical change in our tactics; so I at once selected four sabre companies, two from the Second Michigan and two from the Second Iowa, and placing Captain Alger, of the former regiment, in command of them, I informed him that I expected of them the quick and desperate work that is usually imposed on a forlorn hope.

To carry out the purpose now in view, I instructed Captain Alger to follow the wood road as it led around the left of the enemy's advancing forces, to a point where it joined the Blackland road, about three miles from Booneville, and directed him, upon reaching the Blackland road, to turn up it immediately, and charge the rear of the enemy's line. Under no circumstances was he to deploy the battalion, but charge *in column* right through whatever he came upon, and report to me in front of Booneville, if at all possible for him to get there. If he failed to break through the enemy's line, he was to go ahead as far as he

could, and then if any of his men were left, and he was
able to retreat, he was to do so by the same route he had
taken on his way out. To conduct him on this perilous
service I sent along a thin, sallow, tawny-haired Missis-
sippian named Beene, whom I had employed as a guide
and scout a few days before, on account of his intimate
knowledge of the roads, from the public thoroughfares
down to the insignificant by-paths of the neighboring
swamps. With such guidance I felt sure that the column
would get to the desired point without delay, for there was
no danger of its being lost or misled by taking any of the
many by-roads which traversed the dense forests through
which it would be obliged to pass. I also informed Alger
that I should take the reserve and join the main line in
front of Booneville for the purpose of making an advance
of my whole force, and that as a signal he must have his
men cheer loudly when he struck the enemy's rear, in
order that my attack might be simultaneous with his.

I gave him one hour to go around and come back
through the enemy, and when he started I moved to the
front with the balance of the reserve, to put everything I
had into the fight. This meant an inestimable advantage
to the enemy in case of our defeat, but our own safety
demanded the hazard. All along our attenuated line the
fighting was now sharp, and the enemy's firing indicated
such numerical strength that fear of disaster to Alger increased my anxiety terribly as the time set for his cheering
arrived and no sound of it was heard.

Relying, however, on the fact that Beene's knowledge
of the roads would prevent his being led astray, and confident of Alger's determination to accomplish the purpose
for which he set out, as soon as the hour was up I ordered
my whole line forward. Fortunately, just as this moment
a locomotive and two cars loaded with grain for my horses
ran into Booneville from Corinth. I say fortunately, because it was well known throughout the command that in
the morning, when I first discovered the large numbers
of the enemy, I had called for assistance; and my troops,
now thinking that reinforcements had arrived by rail from

Rienzi, where a division of infantry was encamped, and inspirated by this belief, advanced with renewed confidence and wild cheering. Meantime I had the engineer of the locomotive blow his whistle loudly, so that the enemy might also learn that a train had come; and from the fact that in a few moments he began to give way before our small force, I thought that this strategem had some effect. Soon his men broke, and ran in the utmost disorder over the country in every direction. I found later, however, that his precipitous retreat was due to the pressure on his left from the Second Iowa, in concert with the front attack of the Second Michigan, and the demoralization wrought in his rear by Alger, who had almost entirely accomplished the purpose of his expedition, though he had failed to come through, or so near that I could hear the signal agreed upon before leaving Booneville.

After Alger had reached and turned up the Blackland road, the first thing he came across was the Confederate headquarters; the officers and orderlies about which he captured and sent back some distance to a farm-house. Continuing on a gallop, he soon struck the rear of the enemy's line, but was unable to get through; nor did he get near enough for me to hear his cheering; but as he had made the distance he was to travel in the time allotted, his attack and mine were almost coincident, and the enemy, stampeded by the charges in front and rear, fled toward Blackland, with little or no attempt to capture Alger's command, which might readily have been done. Alger's troopers soon rejoined me at Booneville, minus many hats, having returned by their original route. They had sustained little loss except a few men wounded and a few temporarily missing. Among these was Alger himself, who was dragged from his saddle by the limb of a tree that, in the excitement of the charge, he was unable to flank. The missing had been dismounted in one way or another, and run over by the enemy in his flight; but they all turned up later, none the worse except for a few scratches and bruises.

My effective strength in this fight was 827 all told, and Alger's command comprised ninety officers and men. Chalmers's force was composed of six regiments and two battalions, and though I have been unable to find any returns from which to verify his actual numbers, yet, from the statements of prisoners and from information obtained from citizens along his line of march, it is safe to say that he had in the action not less than five thousand men. Our casualties were not many—forty-one in all. His loss in killed and wounded was considerable, his most severely wounded—forty men—falling into our hands, having been left at farm-houses in the vicinity of the battlefield.

The victory in the face of such odds was most gratifying, and as it justified my disinclination—in fact, refusal—to retire from Booneville without fighting (for the purpose of saving my transportation, as directed by superior authority when I applied in the morning for reinforcements), it was to me particularly grateful. It was also very valuable in view of the fact that it increased the confidence between the officers and men of my brigade and me, and gave us for the balance of the month not only comparative rest, but entire immunity from the dangers of a renewed effort to gobble my isolated outpost. In addition to all this, commendation from my immediate superiors was promptly tendered through oral and written congratulations; and their satisfaction at the result of the battle took definite form a few days later, in the following application for my promotion, when, by an expedition to Ripley, Miss., most valuable information as to the enemy's location and plans was captured:

"HEADQUARTERS ARMY OF THE MISSISSIPPI,
"J . . . 30, 1862.—3.05 P.M.

"MAJOR-GENERAL HALLECK,
        "Washington, D. C.

"Brigadiers scarce; good ones scarce. Asboth goes on the month's leave you gave him ten months since; Granger has temporary command. The undersigned respectfully beg that you will obtain the promotion of Sheridan. He is worth his weight in gold. His Ripley expedition has brought us captured letters of immense value, as well as prisoners, showing the rebel plans and dispositions, as you will learn from District Commander.

"W. S. ROSECRANS,　Brigadier -General.
"C. C. SULLIVAN,　　　"　　"
"G. GRANGER,　　　　 "　　"
"W. L. ELLIOTT,　　　　"　　"
"A. ASBOTH,　　　　　 "　　" "

CHAPTER IV

After the battle of Booneville, it was decided by General Rosecrans, on the advice of General Granger, that my position at Booneville was too much exposed, despite the fact that late on the evening of the fight my force had been increased by the addition of a battery of four guns and two companies of infantry, and by the Third Michigan Cavalry, commanded by Colonel John K. Mizner; so I was directed to withdraw from my post and go into camp near Rienzi, Mississippi, where I could equally well cover the roads in front of the army, and also be near General Asboth's division of infantry, which occupied a line in rear of the town. This section of country, being higher and more rolling than that in the neighborhood of Booneville, had many advantages in the way of better camping-grounds, better grazing and the like, but I moved with reluctance, because I feared that my proximity to Asboth would diminish to a certain extent my independence of command.

General Asboth was a tall, spare, handsome man, with gray mustache and a fierce look. He was an educated soldier, of unquestioned courage, but the responsibilities of outpost duty bore rather heavily on him, and he kept all hands in a state of constant worry in anticipation of imaginary attacks. His ideas of discipline were not very rigid either, and as by this time there had been introduced into my brigade some better methods than those obtaining when it first fell to my command, I feared the effect should he have any control over it, or meddle with its internal affairs. However, there was nothing to do but to move to the place designated, but General Granger, who still commanded the cavalry division to which the brigade belonged, so arranged matters with General Rosecrans, who had succeeded to the command of the Army of the Mississippi, that my independence was to be undisturbed, except in case of a general attack by the enemy.

We went into camp near Rienzi, July 22, sending back to the general field-hospital at Tuscumbia Springs all our sick—a considerable number—stricken down by the malarial influences around Booneville. In a few days the fine grazing and abundance of grain for our exhausted horses brought about their recuperation; and the many large open fields in the vicinity gave opportunity for drills and parades, which were much needed. I turned my attention to those disciplinary measures which, on account of active work in the field, had been necessarily neglected since the brigade had arrived at Pittsburg Landing, in April; and besides, we had been busy in collecting information by scouting parties and otherwise, in prosecution of the purpose for which we were covering the main army.

I kept up an almost daily correspondence with General Granger, concerning the information obtained by scouts and reconnoitring parties, and he came often to Rienzi to see me in relation to this and other matters. Previously I had not had much personal association with Granger. While I was at Halleck's headquarters we met on one or two occasions, and the day I joined the Second Michigan at Farmington I saw him for a few moments, but, with such slight exception, our intercourse had been almost exclusively official. He had suggested my name, I was told, to Governor Blair, when the Governor was in search of an officer of the regular army to appoint to the colonelcy of the Second Michigan Cavalry, but his recommendation must have been mainly based on the favorable opinions he had heard expressed by General Halleck and by some of the officers of his staff, rather than from any personal knowledge of my capacity. Of course I was very grateful for this, but some of his characteristics did not impress me favorably, and I sometimes wished the distance between our camps greater. His most serious failing was an uncontrollable propensity to interfere with and direct the minor matters relating to the command, the details for which those under him were alone responsible. Ill-judged meddling in this respect often led to differences between us, only temporary it is true, but most harassing to the subordinate, since I was compelled by the circumstances of the situation not only invariably to yield my own judgment, but many a time had to play peacemaker—smoothing down ruffled feelings, that I knew had been excited by Granger's freaky and spasmodic efforts to correct personally some trifling fault that ought to have been left to a regimental or company commander to remedy. Yet with all these small blemishes Granger had many good qualities, and his big heart was so full of generous impulses and good motives as to far outbalance his short-comings; and notwithstanding the friction and occasional acerbity of our official intercourse, we maintained friendly relations till his death.

In pursuance of the fatal mistake made by dispersing Halleck's forces after the fall of Corinth, General Don Carlos Buell's Army of the Ohio had been started some time before on its march eastward toward Chattanooga; and as this movement would be followed of course by a manoeuvre on the part of the enemy, now at Tupelo under General Braxton Bragg, either to meet Buell or frustrate his designs by some counter-operation, I was expected to furnish, by scouting and all other means available, information as to what was going on within the Confederate lines. To do the work required, necessitated an increase of my command, and the Seventh Kansas Cavalry was therefore added to it, and my picket-line extended so as to cover from Jacinto southwesterly to a point midway between Rienzi and Booneville, and then northwesterly to the Hatchie River. Skirmishes between outposts on this line were of frequent occurrence, with small results to either side, but they were somewhat annoying, particularly in the direction of Ripley, where the enemy maintained a considerable outpost. Deciding to cripple if not capture this outpost, on the evening of July 27 I sent out an expedition under Colonel Hatch, which drove the enemy from the town of Ripley and took a few prisoners, but the most valuable prize was in the shape of a package of thirty-two private letters, the partial reading of which disclosed to me the positive transfer from Mississippi of most of Bragg's army, for the purpose of counteracting Buell's operations in northern Alabama and East Tennessee. This decisive evidence was of the utmost importance, and without taking time to read all the letters, I forwarded them to General Granger July 28, in a despatch which stated: "I deem it necessary to send them at once; the enemy is moving in large force on Chattanooga." Other than this the results of the expedition were few; and the enemy, having fled from Ripley with but slight resistance, accompanied by almost all the inhabitants, re-occupied the place next day after our people had quitted it, and resumed in due time his annoying attacks on our outposts, both sides trying to achieve something whenever occasion offered.

The prevalence of a severe drought had resulted in drying up many of the streams within the enemy's lines, and, in consequence, he was obliged to shift his camps often, and send his beef-cattle and mules near his outposts for water. My scouts kept me well posted in regard to the movements of both camps and herds; and a favorable opportunity presenting itself, I sent an expedition on August 14 to gather in some animals located on Twenty-Mile Creek, a stream always supplied with water from a source of never-failing springs. Our side met with complete success in this instance, and when the expedition returned, we were all made happy by an abundance of fresh beef, and by some two hundred captured mules, that we thus added to our trains at a time when draft animals were much needed.

Rations for the men were now supplied in fair quantities, and the only thing required to make us wholly contented was plenty of grain for our animals. Because of the large number of troops then in West Tennessee and about Corinth, the indifferent railroad leading down from Columbus, Ky., was taxed to its utmost capacity to transport supplies. The quantity of grain received at Corinth from the north was therefore limited, and before reaching the different outposts, by passing through intermediate dépôts of supply, it had dwindled to insignificance. I had hopes, however, that this condition of things might be ameliorated before long by gathering a good supply of corn that was ripening in the neighborhood, and would soon, I thought, be sufficiently hard to feed to my animals. Not far from my headquarters there was a particularly fine field, which, with this end in view, I had carefully protected through the milky stage, to the evident disappointment of both Asbcth's men and mine. They bore the prohibition well while it affected only themselves, but the trial was too great when it came to denying their horses; and men whose discipline kept faith with my guards during the roasting-ear period now fell from grace. Their horses were growing thin, and few could withstand the mute appeals of their suffering pets; so at night the corn, because of individual foraging, kept stealthily and steadily vanishing, until the field was soon fringed with only earless stalks. The disappearance was noticed, and the guard increased, but still the quantity of corn continued to grow less, the more honest troopers bemoaning the loss, and questioning the honor of those to whose safe-keeping it had been entrusted. Finally, doubtless under the apprehension that through their irregularities the corn would all disappear and find its way to the horses in accordance with the stealthy enterprise of their owners, a general raid was made on the field in broad daylight, and though the guard drove off the marauders, I must admit that its efforts to keep them back were so unsuccessful that my hopes for an equal distribution of the crop were quickly blasted. One look at the field told that it had been swept clean of its grain. Of course a great row occurred as to who was to blame, and many arrests and trials took place, but there had been such an interchanging of cap numbers and other insignia that it was next to impossible to identify the guilty, and so much crimination and acrimony grew out of the affair that it was deemed best to drop the whole matter.

On August 27 about half of the command was absent reconnoitring, I having sent it south toward Tupelo, in the hope of obtaining some definite information regarding a movement to Holly Springs of the remainder of the Confederate army, under General Price, when about mid-day I was suddenly aroused by excited cries and sounds of firing, and I saw in a moment that the enemy was in my camp. He had come in on my right flank from the direction of the Hatchie River, pell-mell with our picket-post stationed about three miles out on the Ripley road. The whole force of the enemy comprised about eight hundred, but only his advance entered with my pickets, whom he had charged and badly stampeded, without, on their part, the pretense of a fight in behalf of those whom it was their duty to protect until proper dispositions for defense could be made. The day was excessively hot, one of those sultry debilitating days that had caused the suspending of all military exercises; and as most of the men were lounging or sleeping in their tents, we were literally caught napping. The alarm spread instantly through the camp, and in a moment the command turned out for action, somewhat in deshabille it is true, but none the less effective, for every man had grabbed his rifle and cartridge-box at the first alarm. Aided by a few shots from Captain Henry Hescock's battery, we soon drove the intruders from our camp in about the same disorder in which they had broken in on us. By this time Colonel Hatch and Colonel Albert L. Lee had mounted two battalions each, and I moved them out at a lively pace in pursuit, followed by a section of the battery. No halt was called till we came upon the enemy's main body, under Colonel Faulkner, drawn up in line of battle near Newland's store. Opening on him with the two pieces of artillery, I hurriedly formed line confronting him, and quickly and with but little resistance drove him in confusion from the field. The sudden turning of the tables dismayed Faulkner's men, and panic seizing them, they threw away every loose article of arms or clothing of which they could dismember themselves, and ran in the wildest disorder in a mad effort to escape. As the chase went on the panic increased, the clouds of dust from the road causing an intermingling of friend and foe. In a little while the affair grew most ludicrous, Faulkner's hatless and coatless men taking to the woods in such dispersed order and so demoralized that a good many prisoners were secured, and those of the enemy who escaped were hunted until dark. When the recall was sounded, our men came in loaded down with plunder in the shape of hats, haversacks, blankets, pistols, and shotguns, in a quantity which amply repaid for the surprise of the morning, but did not excuse the delinquent commander of our picket-guard, who a few days later was brought to a realizing sense of his duty by a court-martial.

Shortly after this affair Captain Archibald P. Campbell, of the Second Michigan Cavalry, presented me with the black horse called Rienzi, since made historical from having been ridden by me in many battles, conspicuously in the ride from Winchester to Cedar Creek, which has been celebrated in the poem by T. Buchanan Read. This horse was of Morgan stock, and then about three years old. He was jet black, excepting three white feet, sixteen hands high, and strongly built, with great powers of endurance. He was so active that he could cover with ease five miles an hour at his natural walking gait. The gelding had been ridden very seldom; in fact, Campbell had been unaccustomed to riding till the war broke out, and, I think, felt some disinclination to mount the fiery colt. Campbell had an affection for him, however, that never waned, and would often come to my headquarters to see his favorite, the colt being cared for there by the regimental farrier, an old man named John Ashley, who had taken him in charge when leaving Michigan, and had been his groom ever since. Seeing that I liked the horse—I had ridden him on several occasions—Campbell presented him to me on one of these visits, and from that time till the close of the war I rode him almost continuously, in every campaign and battle in which I took part, without once finding him overcome by fatigue, though on many occasions his strength was severely tested by long marches and short rations. I never observed in him any vicious habit; a nervousness and restlessness and switch of the tail, when everything about him was in repose, being the only indication that he might be untrustworthy. No one but a novice could be deceived by this, however, for the intelligence evinced in every feature, and his thoroughbred appearance, were so striking that any person accustomed to horses could not misunderstand such a noble animal. But Campbell thought otherwise, at least when the horse was to a certain degree yet untrained, and could not be persuaded to ride him; indeed, for more than a year after he was given to me, Campbell still retained suspicions of his viciousness, though, along with this mistrust, an undiminished affection. Although he was several times wounded, this horse escaped death in action; and living to a ripe old age, died in 1878, attended to the last with all the care and surrounded with every comfort due the faithful service he had rendered.

In moving from Corinth east toward Chattanooga, General Buell's army was much delayed by the requirement that he should repair the Memphis and Charleston railroad as he progressed. The work of repair obliged him to march very slowly, and was of but little use when done, for guerrillas and other bands of Confederates destroyed the road again as soon as he had passed on. But worst of all, the time thus consumed gave General Bragg the opportunity to reorganize and increase his army to such an extent that he was able to contest the possession of Middle Tennessee and Kentucky. Consequently, the movement of this army through Tennessee and Kentucky toward the Ohio River— its objective points being Louisville and Cincinnati—was now well defined, and had already rendered abortive General Buell's designs on Chattanooga and East Tennessee. Therefore extraordinary efforts on the part of the Government became necessary, and the concentration of National troops at Louisville and Cincinnati to meet the contingency of Bragg's reaching those points was an obvious requirement. These troops were drawn from all sections in the West where it was thought they could be spared, and among others I was ordered to conduct thither—to Louisville or Cincinnati, as subsequent developments might demand—my regiment, Hescock's battery, the Second and Fifteenth Missouri, and the Thirty-sixth and Forty-fourth Illinois regiments of infantry, known as the "Pea Ridge Brigade." With this column I marched back to Corinth on the 6th of September, 1862, for the purpose of getting railroad transportation to Columbus, Kentucky.

At Corinth I met General Grant, who by this time had been re-established in favor and command somewhat, General Halleck having departed for Washington to assume command of the army as General-in-Chief. Before and during the activity which followed his reinstatement, General Grant had become familiar with my services through the transmission to Washington of information I had furnished concerning the enemy's movements, and by reading reports of my fights and skirmishes in front, and he was loth to let me go. Indeed, he expressed surprise at seeing me in Corinth, and said he had not expected me to go; he also plainly showed that he was much hurt at the inconsiderate way in which his command was being depleted. Since I was of the opinion that the chief field of usefulness and opportunity was opening up in Kentucky, I did not wish him to retain me, which he might have done, and I impressed him with my conviction, somewhat emphatically, I fear. Our conversation ended with my wish gratified. I afterward learned that General Granger, whom General Grant did not fancy, had suggested that I should take to Cincinnati the main portion of Granger's command—the Pea Ridge Brigade—as well as the Second Michigan Cavalry, of which I was still colonel.

We started that night, going by rail over the Mobile and Ohio road to Columbus, Ky., where we embarked on steamboats awaiting us. These boats were five in number, and making one of them my flag-ship, expecting that we might come upon certain batteries reported to be located upon the Kentucky shore of the Ohio, I directed the rest to follow my lead. Just before reaching Caseyville, the captain of a tin-clad gunboat that was patrolling the river brought me the information that the enemy was in strong force at Caseyville, and expressed a fear that my fleet could not pass his batteries. Accepting the information as correct, I concluded to capture the place before trying to pass up the river. Pushing in to the bank as we neared the town, I got the troops ashore and moved on Caseyville, in the expectation of a bloody fight, but was agreeably surprised upon reaching the outskirts of the village by an outpouring of its inhabitants—men, women, and children—carrying the Stars and Stripes, and making the most loyal professions. Similar demonstrations of loyalty had been made to the panic-stricken captain of the gunboat when he passed down the river, but he did not stay to ascertain their character, neither by landing nor by inquiry, for he assumed that on the Kentucky bank of the river there could be no loyalty. The result mortified the captain intensely; and deeming his convoy of little further use, he steamed toward Cairo in quest of other imaginary batteries, while I re-embarked at Caseyville, and continued up the Ohio undisturbed. About three miles below Cincinnati I received instructions to halt, and next day I was ordered by Major-General H. G. Wright to take my troops back to Louisville,

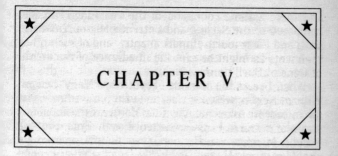

CHAPTER V

I REPORTED TO MAJOR-GENERAL NELSON at the Galt House in Louisville, September 14, 1862, who greeted me in the bluff and hearty fashion of a sailor—for he had been in the navy till the breaking out of the war. The new responsibilities that were now to fall upon me by virtue of increased rank caused in my mind an uneasiness which, I think, Nelson observed at the interview, and he allayed it by giving me much good advice, and most valuable information in regard to affairs in Kentucky, telling me also that he intended I should retain in my command the Pea Ridge Brigade and Hescock's battery. This latter assurance relieved me greatly, for I feared the loss of these troops in the general redistribution which I knew must soon take place; and being familiar with their valuable service in Missouri, and having brought them up from Mississippi, I hoped they would continue with me. He directed me to take position just below the city with the Pea Ridge Brigade, Hescock's battery, and the Second Michigan Cavalry, informing me, at the same time, that some of the new regiments, then arriving under a recent call of the President for volunteers, would also be assigned

43

to my command. Shortly after the interview eight new regiments and an additional battery joined me, thus making good his promise of more troops.

A few days later came Nelson's tragic end, shocking the whole country. Those of us in camp outside of the city were startled on the morning of September 29 by the news that General Jefferson C. Davis, of the Union Army, had shot General Nelson at the Galt House, and the wildest rumors in regard to the occurrence came thick and fast; one to the effect that Nelson was dead, another having it that he was living and had killed Davis, and still others reflecting on the loyalty of both, it being supposed by the general public at first that the difficulty between the two men had grown out of some political rather than official or personal differences. When the news came, I rode into the city to the Galt House to learn the particulars, reaching there about 10 o'clock in the forenoon. Here I learned that Nelson had been shot by Davis about two hours before, at the foot of the main stairway leading from the corridor just beyond the office to the second floor, and that Nelson was already dead. It was almost as difficult to get reliable particulars of the matter at the hotel as it had been in my camp, but I gathered that the two men had met first at an early hour near the counter of the hotel office, and that an altercation which had begun several days before in relation to something official was renewed by Davis, who, attempting to speak to Nelson in regard to the subject-matter of their previous dispute, was met by an insulting refusal to listen. It now appears that when Nelson made this offensive remark, Davis threw a small paper ball that he was nervously rolling between his fingers into Nelson's face, and that this insult was returned by Nelson slapping Davis in the face.* But at the time, exactly what had taken place just before the shooting was shrouded in mystery by a hundred conflicting stories, the principal and most credited of which was that Davis had demanded from Nelson

*Killed by a Brother Soldier.—Gen. J. B. Fry.

an apology for language used in the original altercation, and that Nelson's refusal was accompanied by a slap in the face, at the same moment denouncing Davis as a coward. However this may be, Nelson, after slapping Davis, moved toward the corridor, from which a stairway led to the second floor, and just as he was about to ascend, Davis fired with a pistol that he had obtained from some one near by after the blow had been struck. The ball entered Nelson's breast just above the heart, but his great strength enabled him to ascend the stairway notwithstanding the mortal character of the wound, and he did not fall till he reached the corridor on the second floor. He died about half an hour later. The tragedy cast a deep gloom over all who knew the men, for they both had many warm personal friends; and affairs at Louisville had hardly recovered as yet from the confused and discouraging condition which preceded the arrival of General Buell's army. General Buell reported the killing of Nelson to the authorities at Washington, and recommended the trial of Davis by court-martial, but no proceedings were ever instituted against him in either a civil or military court, so to this day it has not been determined judicially who was the aggressor. Some months later Davis was assigned to the command of a division in Buell's army after that officer had been relieved from its command.

Two Confederate armies, under General Kirby Smith and General Braxton Bragg, had penetrated into Kentucky, the one under Smith by the way of Cumberland Gap, the other and main army under Bragg by way of the Sequatche Valley, Glasgow, and Mumfordsville. Glasgow was captured by the enemy on the 17th of September, and as the expectation was that Buell would reach the place in time to save the town, its loss created considerable alarm in the North, for fears were now entertained that Bragg would strike Louisville and capture the city before Buell could arrive on the ground. It became necessary therefore to put Louisville in a state of defense, and after the cordon of principal works had been indicated, my troops threw up in one night a heavy line of rifle-pits south of the city, from the Bardstown pike to the river. The apprehended attack by Bragg never came, however, for in the race that was then going on between him and Buell on parallel roads, the Army of the Ohio outmarched the Confederates, its advance arriving at Louisville September 25.

General Buell immediately set about reorganizing the whole force, and on September 29 issued an order designating the troops under my command as the Eleventh Division, Army of the Ohio, and assigning Brigadier-General J. T. Boyle to command the division, and me to command one of its brigades. To this I could not object, of course, for I was a brigadier-general of very recent date, and could hardly expect more than a brigade. I had learned, however, that at least one officer to whom a high command had been given—a corps—had not yet been appointed a general officer by the President, and I considered it somewhat unfair that I should be relegated to a brigade, while men who held no commissions at all were being made chiefs of corps and divisions; so I sought an interview with General Buell's chief-of-staff, Colonel Fry, and, while not questioning Buell's good intentions nor his pure motives, insisted that my rights in the matter should be recognized. That same evening I was assigned to the command of the Eleventh Division, and began preparing it at once for a forward movement, which I knew must soon take place in the resumption of offensive operations by the Army of the Ohio.

During the interval from September 25 till October 1 there was among the officers much criticism of General Buell's management of the recent campaign, which had resulted in his retirement to Louisville; and he was particularly censured by many for not offering battle to General Bragg while the two armies were marching parallel to each other, and so near that an engagement could have been brought on at any one of several points—notably so at Glasgow, Kentucky, if there had been a desire to join issue. It was asserted, and by many conceded, that General

Buell had a sufficient force to risk a fight. He was much blamed for the loss of Mumfordsville also. The capture of this point, with its garrison, gave Bragg an advantage in the race toward the Ohio River, which odds would most likely have ensured the fall of Louisville had they been used with the same energy and skill that the Confederate commander displayed from Chattanooga to Glasgow; but something always diverted General Bragg at the supreme moment, and he failed to utilize the chances falling to him at this time, for, deflecting his march to the north toward Bardstown, he left open to Buell the direct road to Louisville by way of Elizabethtown.

At Bardstown Bragg's army was halted while he endeavored to establish a Confederate government in Kentucky by arranging for the installation of a provisional governor at Lexington. Bragg had been assured that the presence of a Confederate army in Kentucky would so encourage the secession element that the whole State could be forced into the rebellion and his army thereby largely increased; but he had been considerably misled, for he now found that though much latent sympathy existed for his cause, yet as far as giving active aid was concerned, the enthusiasm exhibited by the secessionists of Kentucky in the first year of the war was now replaced by apathy, or at best by lukewarmness. So the time thus spent in political machinations was wholly lost to Bragg; and so little reinforcement was added to his army that it may be said that the recruits gained were not enough to supply the deficiencies resulting from the recent toilsome marches of the campaign.

In the meanwhile Buell had arrived at Louisville, system had been substituted for the chaos which had previously obtained there, and orders were issued for an advance upon the enemy with the purpose of attacking and the hope of destroying him within the limits of the "blue grass" region, and, failing in that, to drive him from Kentucky. The army moved October 1, 1862, and my division, now a part of the Third Corps, commanded by General C. C. Gilbert, marched directly on Bardstown, where it was thought the enemy would make a stand, but Bragg's troops retreated toward Perryville, only resisting sufficiently to enable the forces of General Kirby Smith to be drawn in closer—they having begun a concentration at Frankfort—so they could be used in a combined attack on Louisville as soon as the Confederate commander's political projects were perfected.

Much time was consumed by Buell's army in its march on Perryville, but we finally neared it on the evening of October 7. During the day, Brigadier-General Robert B. Mitchell's division of Gilbert's corps was in the advance on the Springfield pike, but as the enemy developed that he was in strong force on the opposite side of a small stream called Doctor's Creek, a tributary of Chaplin River, my division was brought up and passed to the front. It was very difficult to obtain water in this section of Kentucky, as a drought had prevailed for many weeks, and the troops were suffering so for water that it became absolutely necessary that we should gain possession of Doctor's Creek in order to relieve their distress. Consequently General Gilbert, during the night, directed me to push beyond Doctor's Creek early the next morning. At daylight on the 8th I moved out Colonel Dan McCook's brigade and Barnett's battery for the purpose, but after we had crossed the creek with some slight skirmishing, I found that we could not hold the ground unless we carried and occupied a range of hills, called Chaplin Heights, in front of Chaplin River. As this would project my command in the direction of Perryville considerably beyond the troops that were on either flank, I brought up Laiboldt's brigade and Hescock's battery to strengthen Colonel McCook. Putting both brigades into line we quickly carried the Heights, much to the surprise of the enemy, I think, for he did not hold on to the valuable ground as strongly as he should have done. This success not only ensured us a good supply of water, but also, later in the day, had an important bearing in the battle of Perryville. After taking the Heights, I brought up the rest of my division and intrenched, without much difficulty, by throw-up a strong line of rifle-pits, although the enemy's sharpshooters annoyed us enough to make me order Laiboldt's brigade to drive them in on the main body. This was successfully done in a few minutes, but in pushing them back to Chaplin River, we discovered the Confederates forming a line of battle on the opposite bank, with the apparent purpose of an attack in force, so I withdrew the brigade to our intrenchments on the crest and there awaited the assault.

While this skirmishing was going on, General Gilbert—the corps commander—whose headquarters were located on a hill about a mile distant to the rear, kept sending me messages by signal not to bring on an engagement. I replied to each message that I was not bringing on an engagement, but that the enemy evidently intended to do so, and that I believed I should shortly be attacked. Soon after returning to the crest and getting snugly fixed in the rifle-pits, my attention was called to our left, the high ground we occupied affording me in that direction an unobstructed view. I then saw General A. McD. McCook's corps—the First—advancing toward Chaplin River by the Mackville road, apparently unconscious that the Confederates were present in force behind the stream. I tried by the use of signal flags to get information of the situation to these troops, but my efforts failed, and the leading regiments seemed to approach the river indifferently prepared to meet the sudden attack that speedily followed, delivered as it was from the chosen position of the enemy. The fury of the Confederate assault soon halted this advance force, and in a short time threw it into confusion, pushed it back a considerable distance, and ultimately inflicted upon it such loss of men and guns as to seriously cripple McCook's corps, and prevent for the whole day further offensive movement on his part, though he stoutly resisted the enemy's assaults until 4 o'clock in the afternoon.

Seeing McCook so fiercely attacked, in order to aid him

I advanced Hescock's battery, supported by six regiments, to a very good position in front of a belt of timber on my extreme left, where an enfilading fire could be opened on that portion of the enemy attacking the right of the First Corps, and also on his batteries across Chaplin River. But at this juncture he placed two batteries on my right and began to mass troops behind them, and General Gilbert, fearing that my intrenched position on the heights might be carried, directed me to withdraw Hescock and his supports and return them to the pits. My recall was opportune, for I had no sooner got back to my original line than the Confederates attacked me furiously, advancing almost to my intrenchments, notwithstanding that a large part of the ground over which they had to move was swept by a heavy fire of canister from both my batteries. Before they had quite reached us, however, our telling fire made them recoil, and as they fell back, I directed an advance of my whole division, bringing up my reserve regiments to occupy the crest of the hills; Colonel William P. Carlin's brigade of Mitchell's division meanwhile moving forward on my right to cover that flank. This advance pressed the enemy to Perryville, but he retired in such good order that we gained nothing but some favorable ground that enabled me to establish my batteries in positions where they could again turn their attention to the Confederates in front of McCook, whose critical condition was shortly after relieved, however, by a united pressure of Gilbert's corps against the flank of McCook's assailants, compelling them to retire behind Chaplin River.

The battle virtually ended about 4 o'clock in the afternoon, though more or less desultory firing continued until dark. Considering the severity of the engagement on McCook's front, and the reverses that had befallen him, I question if, from that part of the line, much could have been done toward retrieving the blunders of the day, but it did seem to me that, had the commander of the army been able to be present on the field, he could have taken advantage of Bragg's final repulse, and there would have remained in our hands more than the barren field. But no attempt was made to do anything more till next morning, and then we secured little except the enemy's killed and most severely wounded.

The operations of my division during the engagement pleased General Gilbert very much, and he informed me that he would relax a rigidly enforced order which General Buell had issued some days before, sufficiently to permit my trains to come to the front and supply my almost starving troops with rations. The order in question was one of those issued, doubtless with a good intent, to secure generally the safety of our trains, but General Gilbert was not elastic, and on the march he had construed the order so illiberally that it was next to impossible to supply the men with food, and they were particularly short in this respect on the eve of the battle. I had then endeavored to persuade him to modify his iron-clad interpretation of the order, but without effect, and the only wagons we could bring up from the general parks in rear were ambulances and those containing ammunition. So to gain access to our trains was a great boon, and at that moment a more welcome result than would have been a complete victory minus this concession.

When the battle ceased General Gilbert asked me to join him at Buell's headquarters, which were a considerable distance to the rear, so after making some dispositions for the evening I proceeded there as requested. I arrived just as Buell was about to sit down to his supper, and noticing that he was lame, then learned that he had been severely injured by a recent fall from his horse. He kindly invited me to join him at the table, an invitation which I accepted with alacrity, enjoying the meal with a relish known only to a very hungry man, for I had eaten nothing since morning. Of course the events of the day were the chief topic of discussion—as they were during my stay at headquarters—but the conversation indicated that what had occurred was not fully realized, and I returned to my troops impressed with the belief that General Buell and his staff-officers were unconscious of the magnitude of the battle that had just been fought.

It had been expected by Buell that he would fight the enemy on the 9th of October, but the Confederates disposed of that proposition by attacking us on the 8th, thus disarranging a tactical conception which, with our superior numbers, would doubtless have proved successful had it not been anticipated by an enterprising foe. During the battle on the 8th the Second Corps, under General Thomas L. Crittenden, accompanied by General George H. Thomas, lay idle the whole day for want of orders, although it was near enough to the field to take an active part in the fight; and, moreover, a large part of Gilbert's corps was unengaged during the pressure on McCook. Had these troops been put in on the enemy's left at any time after he assaulted McCook, success would have been beyond question; but there was no one on the ground authorized to take advantage of the situation, and the battle of Perryville remains in history an example of lost opportunities. This was due in some measure probably to General Buell's accident, but is mainly attributable to the fact that he did not clearly apprehend Bragg's aim, which was to gain time to withdraw behind Dick's River all the troops he had in Kentucky, for the Confederate general had no idea of risking the fate of his army on one general battle at a place or on a day to be chosen by the Union commander.

Considering the number of troops actually engaged, the losses to Buell were severe, amounting to something over five thousand in killed, wounded, and missing. Among the killed were two brigade commanders of much promise— General James S. Jackson and General William R. Terrill. McCook's corps lost twelve guns, some of which were recovered next day. The enemy's loss in killed and wounded we never learned, but it must have equalled ours; and about four thousand prisoners, consisting principally of sick and wounded, fell into our hands. In the first report of the battle sent North to the newspapers I was reported among the killed; but I was pleased to notice, when the papers reached us a few days later, that the error had been corrected before my obituary could be written.

The enemy retired from our front the night of the 8th, falling back on Harrodsburg to form a junction with Kirby Smith, and by taking this line of retreat opened to us the road to Danville and the chance for a direct march against his dépôt of supplies at Bryantsville. We did not take advantage of this opening, however, and late in the day— on the 9th—my division marched in pursuit, in the direction of Harrodsburg, which was the apex of a triangle having for its base a line from Perryville to Danville. The pursuit was slow, very slow, consuming the evening of the 9th and all of the 10th and 11th. By cutting across the triangle spoken of above, just south of the apex, I struck the Harrodsburg-Danville road, near Cave Springs, joining there Gilbert's left division, which had preceded me and marched through Harrodsburg. Here we again rested until the intention of the enemy could be divined, and we could learn on which side of Dick's River he would give us battle. A reconnoissance sent toward the Dickville crossing developed to a certainty that we should not have another engagement, however; for it disclosed the fact that Bragg's army had disappeared toward Camp Dick Robinson, leaving only a small rear-guard at Danville, which in turn quickly fled in the direction of Lancaster, after exchanging a few shots with Hescock's battery.

While this parting salute of deadly projectiles was going on, a little daughter of Colonel William J. Landram, whose home was in Danville, came running out from his house and planted a small national flag on one of Hescock's guns. The patriotic act was so brave and touching that it thrilled all who witnessed the scene; and until the close of the war, when peace separated the surviving officers and men of the battery, that little flag was protected and cherished as a memento of the Perryville campaign.

Pursuit of the enemy was not continued in force beyond Crab Orchard, but some portions of the army kept at Bragg's heels until he crossed the Cumberland River, a part of his troops retiring to Tennessee by way of Cumberland Gap, but the major portion through Somerset. As the retreat of Bragg transferred the theatre of operations back to Tennessee, orders were now issued for a concentration of Buell's army at Bowling Green, with a view to marching it to Nashville, and my division moved to that point without noteworthy incident. I reached Bowling Green with a force much reduced by the losses sustained in the battle of Perryville and by sickness. I had started from Louisville on October 1 with twelve regiments of infantry—four old and eight new ones—and two batteries, but many poor fellows, overcome by fatigue, and diseases induced by the heat, dust, and drought of the season, had to be left at roadside hospitals. This was particularly the case with the new regiments, the men of which, much depressed by homesickness, and not yet inured to campaigning, fell easy victims to the hardships of war.

At Bowling Green General Buell was relieved, General W. S. Rosecrans succeeding him. The army as a whole did not manifest much regret at the change of commanders, for the campaign from Louisville on was looked upon generally as a lamentable failure, yet there were many who still had the utmost confidence in General Buell, and they repelled with some asperity the reflections cast upon him by his critics. These admirers held him blameless throughout for the blunders of the campaign, but the greater number laid every error at his door, and even went to the absurdity of challenging his loyalty in a mild way, but they particularly charged incompetency at Perryville, where McCook's corps was so badly crippled while nearly 30,000 Union troops were idle on the field or within striking distance. With these it was no use to argue that Buell's accident stood in the way of his activity, nor that he did not know that the action had assumed the proportions of a battle. The physical disability was denied or contested, but even granting this, his detractors claimed that it did not excuse his ignorance of the true condition of the fight, and finally worsted his champions by pointing out that

Bragg's retreat by way of Harrodsburg beyond Dick's River so jeopardized the Confederate army, that had a skillful and energetic advance of the Union troops been made, instead of wasting precious time in slow and unnecessary tactical manœuvres, the enemy could have been destroyed before he could quit the State of Kentucky.

CHAPTER VI

$\mathbf{M}$Y DIVISION HAD MOVED from Crab Orchard to Bowling Green by easy marches, reaching this place November 1. General Rosecrans assumed command of the department October 30, at Louisville, and joined the army November 2. There had been much pressure brought to bear on General Buell to induce him to take measures looking to the occupancy of East Tennessee, and the clamor to this end from Washington still continued; but now that Bragg was south of the Cumberland River, in a position threatening Nashville, which was garrisoned by but a small force, it was apparent to every one at all conversant with the situation that a battle would have to be fought somewhere in Middle Tennessee. So, notwithstanding the pressure from Washington, the army was soon put in motion for Nashville, and when we arrived there my division went into camp north of the river, on a plateau just outside the little town of Edgefield, until the movements of the enemy should be further developed.

While in this camp, on the plantation of Mr. Hobson, there came to my headquarters one morning an East Tennessean named James Card, who offered to the Union cause his services in any capacity in which they might be made useful. This offer, and the relation of his personal history, were given with such sincerity of speech and manner that in a short time I became convinced of his honesty of purpose. He was a small, active, busy man, with a determined way about him, and his countenance indicated great intelligence. He gave minute information that was of inestimable value to me regarding East and Middle Tennessee and northern Georgia, for, with a view to the army's future movements, I was then making a study of the topography of this region, and posting myself as to Middle Tennessee, for all knew this would be the scene of active operations whenever the campaign was resumed. This man, like most of the East Tennesseans whom I had met, was intensely loyal and patriotic, and the interview led in a few days to his employment as a scout and guide, and subsequently to the engaging in the same capacity of two of his brothers, who were good men, but not quite as active nor so intelligent as he was. Card had been a colporter, having peddled books, especially religious tracts, over all Middle and East Tennessee and Georgia, assisted by his brothers at times, and was therefore thoroughly familiar with these regions, their roads and inhabitants. He also preached to country congregations occasionally, when ministers were scarce, and I have no doubt often performed the functions of family physician in the mountain district. Thus his opportunities were great; and the loyal people in every section of the country being well known to him and his brothers, the three began, at this time, a system of scouting and investigation which bore its first-fruits in specifically locating the different divisions of Bragg's army, with statements of their strength and condition, and all with so much accuracy that I thereafter felt reasonably sure that I could at all times procure such knowledge of the enemy's operations as would well equip me for any contingency that might arise.

By the middle of November the enemy, having assembled his forces in Middle Tennessee, showed considerable

Philip Sheridan

boldness, and it became necessary to rearrange the Union lines; so my troops were moved to the south side of the river, out on the Murfreesboro' pike, to Mill Creek, distant from Nashville about seven miles. While we were in camp on Mill Creek the army was reorganized, and General Joshua W. Sill, at his own request, was assigned to my division, and took command of Colonel Nicholas Greusel's brigade. My division became at the same time the Third Division, Right Wing, Fourteenth Army Corps, its three brigades of four regiments each being respectively commanded by General Sill, Colonel Frederick Schaefer and Colonel Dan McCook; but a few days later Colonel George W. Roberts's brigade, from the garrison at Nashville, was substituted for McCook's.

General Sill was a classmate of mine at the Military Academy, having graduated in 1853. On graduating he was appointed to the Ordnance Corps, and served in that department at various arsenals and ordnance dépôts throughout the country till early in 1861, when he resigned to accept a professorship of mathematics and civil engineering at the Brooklyn Collegiate and Polytechnic Institute. At the breaking out of the war he immediately tendered his services to the Government, and soon rose to the colonelcy of the Thirty-Third Ohio Volunteers, and afterward to the rank of brigadier-general. I knew him well, and was glad that he came to my division, though I was very loth to relieve Colonel Greusel, of the Thirty-Sixth Illinois, who had already indicated much military skill and bravery, and at the battle of Perryville had handled his men with the experience of a veteran. Sill's modesty and courage were exceeded only by a capacity that had already been demonstrated in many practical ways, and his untimely death, almost within a month of his joining me, abruptly closed a career which, had it been prolonged a little more, not only would have shed additional lustre on his name, but would have been of marked benefit to his country.

Colonel Schaefer, of the Second Missouri Infantry, had been absent on sick-leave during the Kentucky campaign, but about this date he returned to duty, and by seniority fell in command of the second brigade. He was of German birth, having come from Baden, where, prior to 1848, he had been a non-commissioned officer in the service of his State. He took part as an insurgent in the so-called revolution which occurred at Baden in that year, and, compelled to emigrate on the suppression of the insurrection, made his way to this country and settled in St. Louis. Here the breaking out of the war found him, and through the personal interest which General Sigel took in him he was commissioned a colonel of volunteers. He had had a pretty fair education, a taste for the military profession, and was of tall and slender build, all of which gave him a student-like appearance. He was extremely excitable and nervous when anticipating a crisis, but always calmed down to cool deliberation when the critical moment came. With such a man I could not be less than well satisfied, although the officer whom he replaced—Colonel Laiboldt—had performed efficient service and shown much capacity in the recent campaign.

Colonel G. W. Roberts, of the Forty-Second Illinois Infantry, also came to me in the reorganization. He was an ideal soldier both in mind and body. He was young, tall, handsome, brave, and dashing, and possessed a balance-wheel of such good judgment that in his sphere of action no occasion could arise from which he would not reap the best results. But he too was destined to lay down his life within a few days, and on the same fatal field. His brigade had been performing garrison duty in Nashville during the siege of that city while Buell's army was in Kentucky, but disliking the prospect of inactivity pending the operations opening before us, Roberts had requested and obtained a transfer to the army in the field. His brigade relieved Colonel Dan McCook's, the latter reluctantly joining the garrison at Nashville, every one in it disappointed and disgusted that the circumstances existing at this time should necessitate their relegation to the harassing and tantalizing duty of protecting our dépôts and line of supply.

I was fortunate in having such brigade commanders, and no less favored in the regimental and battery commanders. They all were not only patriots, but soldiers, and knowing that discipline must be one of the most potent factors in bringing to a successful termination the mighty contest in which our nation was struggling for existence, they studied and practiced its methods ceaselessly, inspiring with the same spirit that pervaded themselves the loyal hearts of their subordinate officers and men. All worked unremittingly in the camp at Mill Creek in preparing for the storm, which now plainly indicated its speedy coming. Drills, parades, scouts, foraging expeditions, picket and guard duty, made up the course in this school of instruction, supplemented by frequent changes in the locations of the different brigades, so that the division could have opportunity to learn to break camp quickly and to move out promptly on the march. Foraging expeditions were particularly beneficial in this respect, and when sent out, though absent sometimes for days, the men went without tents or knapsacks, equipped with only one blanket and their arms, ammunition, and rations, to teach them to shift for themselves with slender means in the event of necessity. The number of regimental and headquarters wagons was cut down to the lowest possible figure, and everything made compact by turning into the supply and ammunition trains of the division all surplus transportation, and restricting the personal baggage of officers to the fewest effects possible.

My own staff also was somewhat reorganized and increased at Mill Creek, and though it had been perfectly satisfactory before, yet, on account of the changes of troops that had occurred in the command, I found it necessary to replace valuable officers in some instances, and secure additional ones in others. The gathering of information about the enemy was also industriously pursued, and Card and his brothers were used constantly on expeditions within the Confederate lines, frequently visiting Murfreesboro', Sparta, Tullahoma, Shelbyville, and other points.

What they learned was reported to army headquarters, often orally through me or personally communicated by Card himself, but much was forwarded in official letters, beginning with November 24, when I transmitted accurate information of the concentration of Bragg's main force at Tullahoma. Indeed, Card kept me so well posted as to every movement of the enemy, not only with reference to the troops in my immediate front, but also throughout his whole army, that General Rosecrans placed the most unreserved reliance on all his statements, and many times used them to check and correct the reports brought in by his own scouts.

Slight skirmishes took place frequently during this period, and now and then heavy demonstrations were made in the neighborhood of Nolensville by reconnoitring parties from both armies, but none of these ever grew into a battle. These affairs sprung from the desire of each side to feel his antagonist, and had little result beyond emphasizing the fact that behind each line of pickets lay a massed and powerful army busily preparing for the inevitable conflict and eager for its opening. So it wore on till the evening of December 25, 1862; then came the order to move forward.

General Rosecrans, in the reorganization of the army, had assigned Major-General A. McD. McCook to command the right wing, Major-General George H. Thomas the centre, and Major-General T. J. Crittenden the left wing. McCook's wing was made up of three divisions, commanded in order of rank by Brigadier-General Jeff. C. Davis; Brigadier-General R. W. Johnson, and Brigadier-General P. H. Sheridan. Although the corps nomenclature established by General Buell was dropped, the grand divisions into which he had organized the army at Louisville were maintained, and, in fact, the conditions established then remained practically unaltered, with the exception of the interchange of some brigades, the transfer of a few general officers from one wing or division to another, and the substitution of General Thomas for Gilbert as a corps commander. The army was thus compact and cohesive, undisturbed by discord and unembarrassed by jealousies of any moment; and it may be said that under a commander who, we believed, had the energy and skill necessary to direct us to success, a national confidence in our invincibility made us all keen for a test of strength with the Confederates. We had not long to wait.

Early on the morning of December 26, 1862, in a heavy rain, the army marched, the movement being directed on Murfreesboro', where the enemy had made some preparation to go into winter-quarters, and to hold which town it was hoped he would accept battle. General Thomas moved by the Franklin and Wilson pikes, General Crittenden by the Murfreesboro' pike, through Lavergne, and General McCook by the Nolensville pike—Davis's division in advance. As McCook's command neared Nolensville, I received a message from Davis informing me that the Confederates were in considerable force, posted on a range of hills in his front, and requesting me to support him in an attack he was about to make. When the head of my column arrived at Nolensville I began massing my troops on the right of the road, and by the time this formation was nearly completed Davis advanced, but not meeting with sufficient resistance to demand active assistance from me, he with his own command carried the hills, capturing one piece of artillery. This position of the Confederates was a strong one, defending Knob's Gap, through which the Nolensville and Triune pike passed. On the 27th Johnson's division, followed by mine, advanced to Triune, and engaged in a severe skirmish near that place, but my troops were not called into action, the stand made by the enemy being only for the purpose of gaining time to draw in his outlying troops, which done, he retired toward Murfreesboro'. I remained inactive at Triune during the 28th, but early on the 29th moved out by the Bole Jack road to the support of Davis in his advance to Stewart's Creek, and encamped at Wilkinson's crossroads, from which point to Murfreesboro', distant about six miles, there was a good turnpike.

The enemy had sullenly resisted the progress of Crittenden and McCook throughout the preceding three days, and as it was thought probable that he might offer battle at Stewart's Creek, Thomas, in pursuance of his original instructions looking to just such a contingency, had now fallen into the centre by way of the Nolensville crossroads.

On the morning of the 30th I had the advance of McCook's corps on the Wilkinson pike, Roberts's brigade leading. At first only slight skirmishing took place, but when we came within about three miles of Murfreesboro' the resistance of the enemy's pickets grew serious, and a little further on so strong that I had to put in two regiments to push them back. I succeeded in driving them about half a mile, when I was directed by McCook to form line of battle and place my artillery in position so that I could act in concert with Davis's division, which he wished to post on my right in the general line he desired to take up. In obedience to these directions I deployed on the right of and oblique to the Wilkinson pike, with a front of four regiments, a second line of four regiments within short supporting distance, and a reserve of one brigade in column of regiments to the rear of my centre. All this time the enemy kept up a heavy artillery and musketry fire on my skirmishers, he occupying, with his sharpshooters, beyond some open fields, a heavy belt of timber to my front and right, where it was intended the left of Davis should finally rest. To gain this point Davis was ordered to swing his division into it in conjunction with a wheeling movement of my right brigade, until our continuous line should face nearly due east. This would give us possession of the timber referred to, and not only rid us of the annoying fire from the skirmishers screened by it, but also place us close in to what was now developing as Bragg's line of battle. The movement was begun about half-past 2, and was successfully executed, after a stubborn resistance. In this preliminary affair the enemy had put in one battery of artillery, which was silenced in a little while, however, by Bush's and Hescock's guns. By sundown I had

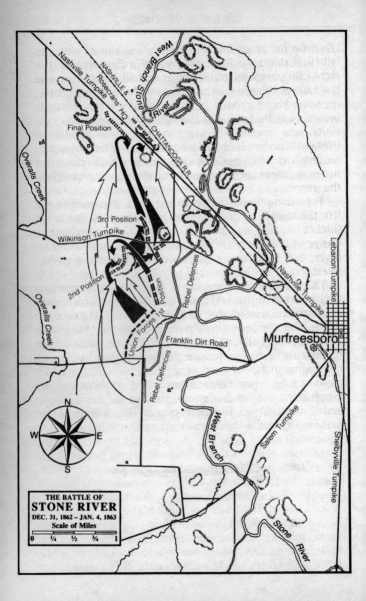

THE BATTLE OF
STONE RIVER
DEC. 31, 1862 – JAN. 4, 1863
Scale of Miles
0   ¼   ½   ¾   1

taken up my prescribed position, facing almost east, my left (Roberts's brigade) resting on the Wilkinson pike, the right (Sill's brigade) in the timber we had just gained, and the reserve brigade (Schaefer's) to the rear of my centre, on some rising ground in the edge of a strip of woods behind Houghtaling's and Hescock's batteries. Davis's division was placed in position on my right, his troops thrown somewhat to the rear, so that his line formed nearly a right angle with mine, while Johnson's division formed in a very exposed position on the right of Davis, prolonging the general line just across the Franklin pike.

The centre, under Thomas, had already formed to my left, the right of Negley's division joining my left in a cedar thicket near the Wilkinson pike, while Crittenden's corps was posted on the left of Thomas, his left resting on Stone River, at a point about two miles and a half from Murfreesboro'.

The precision that had characterized every manœuvre of the past three days, and the exactness with which each corps and division fell into its allotted place on the evening of the 30th, indicated that at the outset of the campaign a well-digested plan of operations had been prepared for us; and although the scheme of the expected battle was not known to subordinates of my grade, yet all the movements up to this time had been so successfully and accurately made as to give much promise for the morrow, and when night fell there was general anticipation of the best results to the Union army.

CHAPTER VII

THE ENEMY UNDER BRAGG lay between us and Stone River in order of battle, his general line conforming to the course of that stream. In my immediate front he appeared to be established in strong force in a dense cedar wood, just beyond an open valley, which varied from two hundred to four hundred yards in width, the cedars extending the entire length of the valley. From the events of the day and evening of the 30th, it was apparent that the two armies were in close proximity, and orders received during the night revealed the fact that Rosecrans intended to attack by throwing his left on the enemy's right, with the expectation of driving it in toward Murfreesboro', so that the right of Crittenden's corps could attack Bragg's centre in reverse, while Thomas supported Crittenden by a simultaneous front assault; and from the movements of the enemy at daylight next morning, it was plainly indicated that Bragg had planned to swing his left on our right by an exactly similar manœuvre, get possession of the railroad and the Nashville pike, and if possible cut us off from our base at Nashville. The conceptions in the minds of the two generals were almost identical; but Bragg took the initiative, beginning his movement about an hour earlier than the time set by Rosecrans, which gained him an immense advantage in execution in the earlier stages of the action.

During the evening of the 30th, feeling keenly all the solicitude which attends one in anticipation of a battle, I examined my position with great care, inspecting its whole length several times to remedy any defects that might exist, and to let the men see that I was alive to their interests and advantages. After dark, I went back to the rear of my reserve brigade, and establishing my headquarters behind the trunk of a large fallen tree, which would shelter me somewhat from the cold December wind, lay down beside a small camp-fire to get some rest.

At 2 o'clock on the morning of the 31st General Sill came back to me to report that on his front a continuous movement of infantry and artillery had been going on all night within the Confederate lines, and that he was convinced that Bragg was massing on our right with the purpose of making an attack from that direction early in the morning. After discussing for a few minutes the probabilities of such a course on the part of the enemy, I thought McCook should be made acquainted with what was going on, so Sill and I went back to see him at his headquarters, not far from the Griscom House, where we found him sleeping on some straw in the angle of a worm-fence. I waked him up and communicated the intelligence, and our consequent impressions. He talked the matter over with us for some little time, but in view of the offensive-defensive part he was to play in the coming battle, did not seem to think that there was a necessity for any further dispositions than had already been taken. He said that he thought Johnson's division would be able to take care of the right, and seemed confident that the early assault which was to be made from Rosecrans's left would anticipate and check the designs which we presaged. We two then returned to my little camp-fire behind the log, and as we continued talking of what might be expected from the indications on the right, and Sill becoming more anxious, I directed two regiments from the reserve to report to him, that they might be placed within very short supporting distance of his line. He then rejoined his brigade, better satisfied, but still adhering to the belief he had expressed when first making his report.

Long before dawn my division breakfasted, and was assembled under arms, the infantry in line, the cannoneers at their pieces, but while we were thus preparing, all the recent signs of activity in the enemy's camp were hushed, a death-like stillness prevailing in the cedars to our front. Shortly after daylight General Hardee opened the engagement, just as Sill had predicted, by a fierce attack on Johnson's division, the extreme right of the Union line. Immediate success attending this assault, Hardee extended the attack gradually along in front of Davis, his movement taking the form of a wheel to the right, the pivot being nearly opposite the left of my division. Johnson's division soon gave way, and two of Davis's brigades were forced to fall back with it, though stubbornly resisting the determined and sweeping onset.

In the meantime the enemy had also attacked me, advancing across an old cotton-field in Sill's front in heavy masses, which were furiously opened upon by Bush's battery from Sill's line, and by Hescock's and Houghtaling's batteries, which had an oblique fire on the field from a commanding position in rear of my centre. The effect of this fire on the advancing column was terrible, but it continued on till it reached the edge of the timber where Sill's right lay, when my infantry opened at a range of not over fifty yards. For a short time the Confederates withstood the fire, but then wavered, broke, and fell back toward their original line. As they retired, Sill's brigade followed in a spirited charge, driving them back across the open ground and behind their intrenchments. In this charge the gallant Sill was killed, a rifle ball passing through his upper lip and penetrating the brain. Although this was a heavy loss, yet the enemy's discomfiture was such as to give us an hour's time, and as Colonel Greusel,

Thirty-sixth Illinois, succeeded to Sill's command, I directed him, as he took charge, to recall the brigade to its original position, for the turning-column on my extreme right was now assuming the most menacing attitude, and it was urgently necessary to prepare for it.

When that portion of the enemy driven back by Sill recovered from its repulse it again advanced to the attack, this time directing its efforts chiefly upon my extreme right, and the front of Woodruff's brigade of Davis's division, which brigade still held on in its first position. In front of my centre the Confederates were again driven back, but as the assault on Woodruff was in conjunction with an advance of the column that had forced Johnson to retire, Woodruff was compelled unfortunately to give way, and two regiments on the right of my line went with him, till they rallied on the two reserve regiments which, in anticipation of the enemy's initiatory attack I had sent to Sill's rear before daylight.

Both Johnson's and Davis's divisions were now practically gone from our line, having retired with a loss of all formation, and they were being closely pursued by the enemy, whose columns were following the arc of a circle that would ultimately carry him in on my rear. In consequence of the fact that this state of things would soon subject me to a fire in reverse, I hastily withdrew Sill's brigade and the reserve regiments supporting it, and ordered Roberts's brigade, which at the close of the enemy's second repulse had changed front toward the south and formed in column of regiments, to cover the withdrawal by a charge on the Confederates as they came into the timber where my right had originally rested. Roberts made the charge at the proper time, and was successful in checking the enemy's advance, thus giving us a breathing-spell, during which I was able to take up a new position with Schaefer's and Sill's brigades on the commanding ground to the rear, where Hescock's and Houghtaling's batteries had been posted all the morning.

The general course of this new position was at right

angles with my original line, and it took the shape of an obtuse angle, with my three batteries at the apex. Davis, and Carlin of his division, endeavored to rally their men here on my right, but their efforts were practically unavailing, though the calm and cool appearance of Carlin, who at the time was smoking a stumpy pipe, had some effect, and was in strong contrast to the excited manner of Davis, who seemed overpowered by the disaster that had befallen his command. But few could be rallied, however, as the men were badly demoralized, and most of them fell back beyond the Wilkinson pike, where they reorganized behind the troops of General Thomas.

At this juncture the enemy's turning-column began advancing again in concert with Cheatham's division, and as the extreme left of the Confederates was directed on Griscom's house, and their right on the Blanton house, my new position was in danger of envelopment. No hope of stemming the tide at this point seemed probable, but to gain time I retained my ground as long as possible, and until, under directions from General McCook, I moved to the front from my left flank and attached myself to the right of Negley's division, which up to this hour had been left almost undisturbed by the enemy in the line it had taken up the night before. Under a heavy fire we succeeded in this manœuvre, Schaefer's brigade marching first, then the batteries, and Roberts's and Sill's brigades following. When my division arrived on this new ground, I posted Roberts on Negley's right, with Hescock's and Bush's guns, the brigade and guns occupying a low rocky ridge of limestone, which faced them toward Murfreesboro', nearly south. The rest of my division was aligned facing west, along the edge of a cedar thicket, the rear rank backed up on the right flank of Roberts, with Houghtaling's battery in the angle. This presented Sill's and Schaefer's brigades in an almost opposite direction to the line we had so confidently taken up the night before, and covered Negley's rear. The enemy, in the meantime, had continued his wheeling movement till he occupied the ground that my batteries and reserve brigade had held in the morning, and I had now so changed my position that the left brigade of my division approached his intrenchments in front of Stone River, while Sill's and Schaeffer's brigades, by facing nearly west, confronted the successful troops that had smashed in our extreme right.

I had hardly got straightened out in this last place when I was attacked by Cheatham's division, which, notwithstanding the staggering blows it had previously received from Sill and Roberts, now again moved forward in conjunction with the wheeling movement under the immediate command of Hardee. One of the most sanguinary contests of the day now took place. In fulfillment of Bragg's original design no doubt, Cheatham's division attacked on my left, while heavy masses under Hardee, covered by batteries posted on the high ground formerly occupied by my guns, assaulted my right, the whole force advancing simultaneously. At the same time the enemy opened an artillery fire from his intrenchments in front of Murfreesboro', and it seemed that he was present on every side. My position was strong, however, located in the edge of a dense cedar thicket and commanding a slight depression of open ground that lay in my front. My men were in good spirits too, notwithstanding they had been a good deal hustled around since daylight, with losses that had told considerably on their numbers. Only a short distance now separated the contending lines, and as the batteries on each side were not much more than two hundred yards apart when the enemy made his assault, the artillery fire was fearful in its effect on the ranks of both contestants, the enemy's heavy masses staggering under the torrent of shell and canister from our batteries, while our lines were thinned by his ricochetting projectiles, that rebounded again and again over the thinly covered limestone formation and sped on to the rear of Negley. But all his efforts to dislodge or destroy us were futile, and for the first time since daylight General Hardee was seriously checked in the turning movement he had begun for the purpose of getting possession of the Nashville pike, and though reinforced until two-fifths of Bragg's army was now at his command, yet he met with repulse after repulse, which created great gaps in his lines and taught him that to overwhelm us was hopeless.

As the enemy was recoiling from his first attack, I received a message from Rosecrans telling me that he was making new dispositions, and directing me to hold on where I was until they were completed. From this I judged that the existing conditions of the battle would probably require a sacrifice of my command, so I informed Roberts and Schaefer that we must be prepared to meet the demand on us by withstanding the assault of the enemy, no matter what the outcome. Every energy was therefore bent to the simple holding of our ground, and as ammunition was getting scarce, instructions were given throughout the command to have it reserve its fire till the most effective moment. In a little while came a second and a third assault, and although they were as daring and furious as the first, yet in each case the Confederates were repulsed, driven back in confusion, but not without deadly loss to us, for the noble Roberts was killed, and Colonel Harrington, of the Twenty-Seventh Illinois, who succeeded to his brigade, was mortally wounded a few minutes later. I had now on the death-roll three brigade commanders, and the loss of subordinate officers and men was appalling, but their sacrifice had accomplished the desired result; they had not fallen in vain. Indeed, the bravery and tenacity of my division gave to Rosecrans the time required to make new dispositions, and exacted from our foes the highest commendations.

A lull followed the third fierce assault, and an investigation showed that, with the exception of a few rounds in my brigade, our ammunition was entirely exhausted; and while it was apparent that the enemy was reluctant to renew the conflict in my front, yet I was satisfied I could not hold on much longer without the danger of ultimate capture, so I prepared to withdraw as soon as the troops of Rousseau's division, which had been ordered to take up a line on my right, came into position. Schaefer's and Sill's brigades being without a cartridge, I directed them to fix bayonets for a charge, and await any attempt of the enemy to embarrass my retreat, while Roberts's brigade, offering such resistance as its small quantity of ammunition would permit, was pulled slowly in toward the Nashville pike. Eighty of the horses of Houghtaling's battery having been killed, an attempt was made to bring his guns back by hand over the rocky ground, but it could not be done, and we had to abandon them. Hescock also had lost most of his horses, but all his guns were saved. Bush's battery lost two pieces, the tangled underbrush in the dense cedars proving an obstacle to getting them away which his almost superhuman exertions could not surmount. Thus far the bloody duel had cost me heavily, one-third of my division being killed or wounded. I had already three brigade commanders killed; a little later I lost my fourth—Colonel Schaefer.

The difficulties of withdrawing were very great, as the ground was exceptionally rocky, and the growth of cedars almost impenetrable for wheeled carriages. Retiring sullenly under a heavy fire, while the general line was reformed to my right and rear, my division was at length drawn through the cedars and debouched into an open space near the Murfreesboro' pike, behind the right of Palmer's division. Two regiments of Sill's brigade, however, on account of the conformation of the ground, were obliged to fall back from the point where Woodruff's brigade of Davis's division had rallied after the disaster of the early morning. The division came out of the cedars with unbroken ranks, thinned by only its killed and wounded—but few missing. When we came into the open ground, McCook directed Roberts's brigade—now commanded by Colonel Luther P. Bradley—to proceed a short distance to the rear on the Nashville pike, to repel the enemy's threatening attempt at our communications. Willingly and cheerfully the brigade again entered the fight under these new conditions, and although it was supplied with but three or four cartridges to the man now, it charged gallantly and recaptured two pieces of artillery which the Union troops had had to abandon at that point.

Shortly after we debouched from the cedars I was directed by Rosecrans to send some aid to the right of General Palmer's division; and two of Schaefer's regiments, having obtained ammunition, were pushed up on Palmer's right, accompanied by four of Hescock's guns; but the advance of the enemy here had already been checked by Palmer, and only a desultory contest ensued. Rosecrans, whom I now met in the open ground west of the railroad, behind Palmer, directed that my command should relieve Wood's division, which was required to fall back and take up the new line that had been marked out while I was holding on in the cedars. His usually florid face had lost its ruddy color, and his anxious eyes told that the disasters of the morning were testing his powers to the very verge of endurance, but he seemed fully to comprehend what had befallen us. His firmly set lips and the calmness with which his instructions were delivered inspired confidence in all around him; and expressing approbation of what my division had done, while deliberately directing it to a new point, he renewed in us all the hope of final victory, though it must be admitted that at this phase of the battle the chances lay largely with the enemy.

Withdrawing the two regiments and Hescock's battery, that I had posted on the right of Palmer, I moved as directed by Rosecrans into the position to the east of the railroad, and formed immediately to the right of Wood, who was now being attacked all along his front, but more particularly where his right rested near the railroad. Under a storm of shot and shell that came in torrents my troops took up the new ground, advancing through a clump of open timber to Wood's assistance. Forming in line in front of the timber we poured a telling fire into the enemy's ranks, which were then attacking across some cleared fields; but when he discovered additional troops confronting him, he gave up the attempt to carry Wood's position. It was here that I lost Schaefer, who was killed instantly, making my fourth brigade commander dead that day. The enemy in front of Wood having been checked, our whole line east of the railroad executed undisturbed its retrograde movement to a position about three hundred yards to its rear. When I fell back to the edge of the clump of timber, where when first coming on the ground I had formed to help Wood, I was ordered by Rosecrans to prepare to make a charge should the enemy again assault us. In anticipation of this work I massed my troops in close column. The expected attack never came, however, but the shot and shell of a furious cannonade told with fatal effect upon men and officers as they lay on their faces hugging the ground. The torments of this trying situation were almost unbearable, but it was obvious to all that it was necessary to have at hand a compact body of troops to repel any assault the enemy might make pending the reconstruction of the extreme right of our line, and a silent determination to stay seemed to take hold of each individual soldier; nor was this grim silence interrupted throughout the cannonade, except in one instance, when one of the regiments broke out in a lusty cheer as a startled rabbit in search of a new hiding-place safely ran the whole length of the line on the backs of the men.

While my troops were still lying here, General Rosecrans, with a part of his staff and a few orderlies, rode out on the re-arranged line to supervise its formation and encourage the men, and in prosecution of these objects moved around the front of my column of attack, within range of the batteries that were shelling us so viciously. As he passed to the open ground on my left, I joined him. The enemy seeing this mounted party, turned his guns upon it, and his accurate aim was soon rewarded, for a solid shot carried away the head of Colonel Gareské, the chief-of-staff, and killed or wounded two or three orderlies. Gareské's appalling death stunned us all, and a momentary expression of horror spread over Rosecrans's face; but at such a time the importance of self-control was vital, and he pursued his course with an appearance of indifference, which, however, those immediately about him saw was assumed, for undoubtedly he felt most deeply the death of his friend and trusted staff-officer.

No other attacks were made on us to the east of the railroad for the rest of the afternoon, and just before dark I was directed to withdraw and take up a position along the west side of the Nashville pike, on the extreme right of our new line, where Roberts's brigade and the Seventy-third and Eighty-eighth Illinois had already been placed by McCook. The day had cost me much anxiety and sadness, and I was sorely disappointed at the general result, though I could not be other than pleased at the part taken by my command. The loss of my brigade commanders—Sill, Roberts, Schaefer, and Harrington—and a large number of regimental and battery officers, with so many of their men, struck deep into my heart. My thinned ranks told the woeful tale of the fierce struggles, indescribable by words, through which my division had passed since 7 o'clock in the morning; and this, added to our hungry and exhausted condition, was naturally disheartening. The men had been made veterans, however, by the fortunes and misfortunes of the day, and as they went into their new places still confident of final success, it was plain to see that they felt a self-confidence inspired by the part they had already played.

My headquarters were now established on the Nashville pike, about three miles and a half from Murfreesboro'; my division being aligned to the west of the pike, bowed out and facing almost west, Cleburn's division of the Confederates confronting it. Davis's division was posted on my right, and Walker's brigade of Thomas's corps, which had reported to me, took up a line that connected my left with Johnson's division.

Late in the evening General Rosecrans, accompanied by General McCook, and several other officers whose names I am now unable to recall, rode by my headquarters on their way to the rear to look for a new line of battle—on Overall's creek it was said—that would preserve our communications with Nashville and offer better facilities for resistance than the one we were now holding. Considerable time had elapsed when they returned from this exploration and proceeded to their respective commands, without intimating to me that anything had been determined upon by the reconnoissance, but a little later it was rumored through the different headquarters that while the party was looking for a new position it discovered the enemy's troops moving toward our right and rear, the head of his columns being conducted in the darkness by the aid of torches, and that no alternative was left us but to hold the lines we then occupied. The torches had been seen unquestionably, and possibly created some alarm at first in the minds of the reconnoitring party, but it was soon ascertained that the lights came from a battalion of the Fourth regular cavalry that was picketing our flank and happened to be starting its bivouac fires at the moment. The fires and the supposed movements had no weight, therefore, in deciding the proposition to take up a line at Overall's creek, but General Rosecrans, fortunately for the army, decided to remain where he was. Doubtless reflections during his ride caused him to realize that the enemy must be quite as much crippled as himself. If it had been decided to fall back to Overall's creek, we could have withdrawn without much difficulty very likely, but such a retrograde movement would have left to the enemy the entire battlefield of Stone River and ultimately compelled our retreat to Nashville.

In the night of December 31 several slight demonstrations were made on my front, but from the darkness neither party felt the effect of the other's fire, and when daylight came again the skirmishers and lines of battle were in about the same position they had taken up the evening before. Soon after daybreak it became evident that the conflict was to be renewed, and a little later the enemy resumed the offensive by an attack along my left front, especially on Walker's brigade. His attempt was ineffectual, however, and so easily repulsed as to demonstrate that the desperate character of his assaults the day before had nearly exhausted his strength. About 3 o'clock in the afternoon he made another feeble charge on my front, but our fire from the barricades and rifle-pits soon demoralized his advancing lines, which fell back in some confusion, thus enabling us to pick up about a hundred prisoners. From this time till the evening of January 3 Bragg's left remained in our front, and continued to show itself at intervals by weak demonstrations, which we afterward ascertained were directly intended to cover the desperate assault he made with Breckenridge on the left of Rosecrans, an assault that really had in view only a defensive purpose, for unless Bragg dislodged the troops which were now massing in front of his right he would be obliged to withdraw General Polk's corps behind Stone River and finally abandon Murfreesboro'. The sequel proved this to be the case; and the ill-judged assault led by Breckenridge ending in entire defeat, Bragg retired from Murfreesboro' the night of January 3.

General Rosecrans occupied Murfreesboro' on the 4th and 5th, having gained a costly victory, which was not decisive enough in its character to greatly affect the general course of the war, though it somewhat strengthened and increased our hold on Middle Tennessee. The enemy in retiring did not fall back very far—only behind Duck River to Shelbyville and Tullahoma—and but little endeavor was made to follow him. Indeed, we were not in condition to pursue, even if it had been the intention at the outset of the campaign.

As soon as possible after the Confederate retreat I went over the battle-field to collect such of my wounded as had not been carried off to the South and to bury my dead. In the cedars and on the ground where I had been so fiercely assaulted when the battle opened on the morning of the 31st, evidences of the bloody struggle appeared on every hand in the form of broken fire-arms, fragments of accoutrements, and splintered trees. The dead had nearly all been left unburied, but as there was likelihood of their mutilation by roving swine, the bodies had mostly been collected in piles at different points and inclosed by rail fences. The sad duties of interment and of caring for the wounded were completed by the 5th, and on the 6th I moved my division three miles south of Murfreesboro' on the Shelbyville pike, going into camp on the banks of Stone River. Here the condition of my command was thoroughly looked into, and an endeavor made to correct such defects as had been disclosed by the recent battle.

During the engagement there had been little straggling, and my list of missing was small and legitimate; still, it was known that a very few had shirked their duty, and an example was necessary. Among this small number were four officers who, it was charged, had abandoned their colors and regiments. When the guilt was clearly established, and as soon as an opportunity occurred, I caused the whole division to be formed in a hollow square, closed in mass, and had the four officers marched to the centre, where, telling them that I would not humiliate any officer or soldier by requiring him to touch their disgraced swords, I compelled them to deliver theirs up to my colored servant, who also cut from their coats every insignia of rank. Then, after there had been read to the command an order from army headquarters dismissing the four from the service, the scene was brought to a close by drumming the cowards out of camp. It was a mortifying spectacle, but from that day no officer in that division ever abandoned his colors.

My effective force in the battle of Stone River was 4,154 officers and men. Of this number I lost 1,633 killed, wounded, and missing, or nearly 40 per cent. In the remaining years of the war, though often engaged in most severe contests, I never experienced in any of my commands so high a rate of casualties. The ratio of loss in the whole of Rosecrans's army was also high, and Bragg's losses were almost equally great. Rosecrans carried into the action about 42,000 officers and men. He lost 13,230, or 31½ per cent. Bragg's effective force was 37,800 officers and men; he lost 10,306, or nearly 28 per cent.

Though our victory was dearly bought, yet the importance of gaining the day at any price was very great, particularly when we consider what might have been the result had not the gallantry of the army and the manœuvring during the early disaster saved us from ultimate defeat. We had started out from Nashville on an offensive campaign, probably with no intention of going beyond Murfreesboro', in midwinter, but still with the expectation of delivering a crushing blow should the enemy accept our challenge to battle. He met us with a plan of attack almost the counterpart of our own. In the execution of his plan he had many advantages, not the least of which was his intimate knowledge of the ground, and he came near destroying us. Had he done so, Nashville would probably have fallen; at all events, Kentucky would have been opened again to his incursions, and the theatre of war very likely transferred once more to the Ohio River. As the case now stood, however, Nashville was firmly established as a base for future operations, Kentucky was safe from the possibility of being again overrun, and Bragg, thrown on the defensive, was compelled to give his thoughts to the protection of the interior of the Confederacy and the security of Chattanooga, rather than indulge in schemes of conquest north of the Cumberland River. While he still held on in Middle Tennessee his grasp was so much loosened that only slight effort would be necessary to push him back into Georgia, and thus give to the mountain region of East Tennessee an opportunity to prove its loyalty to the Union.

The victory quieted the fears of the West and Northwest, destroyed the hopes of the secession element in Kentucky, renewed the drooping spirits of the East Tennesseans, and demoralized the disunionists in Middle Tennessee; yet it was a negative victory so far as concerned the result on the battle-field. Rosecrans seems to have planned the battle with the idea that the enemy would continue passive, remain entirely on the defensive, and that it was necessary only to push forward our left in order to force the evacuation of Murfreesboro'; and notwithstanding the fact that on the afternoon of December 30 McCook received information that the right of Johnson's division, resting near the Franklin pike, extended only to about the centre of the Confederate army, it does not appear that attack from that quarter was at all apprehended by the Union commanders.

The natural line of retreat of the Confederates was not threatened by the design of Rosecrans; and Bragg, without risk to his communications, anticipated it by a counterattack of like character from his own left, and demolished his adversary's plan the moment we were thrown on the defensive. Had Bragg followed up with the spirit which characterized its beginning the successful attack by Hardee on our right wing—and there seems no reason why he should not have done so—the army of Rosecrans still might have got back to Nashville, but it would have been depleted and demoralized to such a degree as to unfit it for offensive operations for a long time afterward. Bragg's intrenchments in front of Stone River were very strong, and there seems no reason why he should not have used his plain advantage as explained, but instead he allowed us to gain time, intrench, and recover a confidence that at first was badly shaken. Finally, to cap the climax of his errors, he directed Breckenridge to make the assault from his right flank on January 2, with small chance for anything but disaster, when the real purpose in view could have been accomplished without the necessity of any offensive manœuvre whatever.

CHAPTER VIII

O N THE 6TH OF JANUARY, 1863, my division settled quietly down in its camp south of Murfreesboro'. Its exhausted condition after the terrible experiences of the preceding week required attention. It needed recuperation, reinforcement, and reorganization, and I set about these matters without delay, in anticipation of active operations early in the spring. No forward movement was made for nearly six months, however, and throughout this period drills, parades, reconnoissances, and foraging expeditions filled in the time profitably. In addition to these exercises the construction of permanent fortifications for the security of Murfreesboro' was undertaken by General Rosecrans, and large details from my troops were furnished daily for the work. Much attention was also given to creating a more perfect system of guard and picket duty—a matter that had hitherto been somewhat neglected in the army, as its constant activity had permitted scant opportunity for the development of such a system. It was at this time that I received my appointment as a major-general of Volunteers. My promotion had been recommended by General Rosecrans immediately after the battle of Stone River, but for some reason it was delayed until April, and though a long time elapsed between the promise and the performance, my gratification was extreme.

My scout, Card, was exceedingly useful while encamped near Murfreesboro', making several trips to East Tennessee within the enemy's lines to collect information as to the condition of the loyal people there, and to encourage them with the hope of early liberation. He also brought back from each trip very accurate statements as to the strength and doings of the Confederate army, fixing almost with certainty its numbers and the locations of its different divisions, and enabling my engineer-officer—Major Morhardt—to construct good maps of the country in our front. On these dangerous excursions Card was always accompanied by one of his brothers, the other remaining with me to be ready for duty if any accident occurred to those who had gone out, or in case I wanted to communicate with them. In this way we kept well posted, although the intelligence these men brought was almost always secured at the risk of their lives.

Early in the spring, before the Tullahoma campaign began, I thought it would be practicable, by sending out a small secret expedition of but three or four men, to break the Nashville and Chattanooga railroad between Chattanooga and the enemy's position at Tullahoma by burning the bridges in Crow Creek valley from its head to Stevenson, Alabama, and then the great bridge across the Tennessee River at Bridgeport. Feeling confident that I could persuade Card to undertake the perilous duty, I broached the contemplated project to him, and he at once jumped at the opportunity of thus distinguishing himself, saying that with one of his brothers and three other loyal East Tennesseeans, whose services he knew could be enlisted, he felt sure of carrying out the idea, so I gave him authority to choose his own assistants. In a few days his men appeared at my headquarters, and when supplied with money in notes of the State Bank of Tennessee, current everywhere as gold in those days, the party, composed of Card, the second brother, and the three East Tennesseeans, started on their precarious enterprise, their course being directed first toward the Cumberland Mountains, intending to strike the Nashville and Chattanooga railroad somewhere above Anderson's station. They expected to get back in about fifteen days, but I looked for some knowledge of the progress of their adventure before the expiration of that period, hoping to hear through Confederate sources—prisoners and the like—of the destruction of the bridges. I waited in patience for such news, but none came, and as the time Card had allotted himself passed by, I watched anxiously for his return, for, as there was scarcely a doubt that the expedition had proved a failure, the fate of the party became a matter of deep concern to Card's remaining brother and to me. Finally this brother volunteered to go to his father's house in East Tennessee to get tidings of the party, and I consented, for the probabilities were that some of them had made their way to that point, or at least that some information had reached there about them. As day after day went by, the time fixed for this brother's return came round, yet he also remained out; but some days after the lad was due Card himself turned up accompanied by the brother he had taken with him, soon explained his delay in getting back, and gave me the story of his adventures while absent.

After leaving my camp, his party had followed various by-ways across the Cumberland Mountains to Crow Creek Valley, as instructed; but when nearing the railroad above Anderson's Station, they were captured by some guerrillas prowling about that vicinity, and being suspected of disloyalty to the Confederacy, were carried to Chattanooga and imprisoned as Yankee spies. Their prospects now were decidedly discouraging, for death stared them in the face. Fortunately, however, some delays occurred relative to the disposition that should be made of them, and they, meanwhile, effected their escape from their jailors by way of one of the prison windows, from which they managed to displace a bar, and by a skiff, in the darkness of night, crossed the Tennessee River a little below Chattanooga. From this point the party made their way back to my camp, traveling only at night, hiding in the woods by day, and for food depending on loyal citizens that Card had become acquainted with when preaching and peddling.

Card's first inquiry after relating his story was for the youngest brother, whom he had left with me. I told him what I had done, in my anxiety about himself, and that more than sufficient time had elapsed for his brother's return. His reply was: "They have caught him. The poor fellow is dead." His surmise proved correct; for news soon came that the poor boy had been captured at his father's house, and hanged. The blow to Card was a severe one, and so hardened his heart against the guerrillas in the neighborhood of his father's home—for he knew they were guilty of his brother's murder—that it was with difficulty I could persuade him to continue in the employment of the Government, so determined was he to avenge his brother's death at the first opportunity. Finally, however, I succeeded in quieting the almost uncontrollable rage that seemed to possess him, and he remained with me during the Tullahoma and Chickamauga campaigns; but when we reached Knoxville the next winter, he took his departure, informing me that he was *going for* the bushwhackers who had killed his brother. A short time after he left me, I saw him at the head of about thirty well-armed East Tennesseeans—refugees. They were determined-looking men, seeking revenge for the wrongs and sufferings that had been put upon them in the last two years, and no doubt wreaked their vengeance right and left on all who had been in any way instrumental in persecuting them.

The feeding of our army from the base at Louisville was attended with a great many difficulties, as the enemy's cavalry was constantly breaking the railroad and intercepting our communications on the Cumberland River at different points that were easily accessible to his then superior force of troopers. The accumulation of reserve stores was therefore not an easy task, and to get forage ahead a few days was wellnigh impossible, unless that brought from the North was supplemented by what we could gather from the country. Corn was abundant in the region to the south and southwest of Murfreesboro', so to make good our deficiences in this respect, I employed a brigade about once a week in the duty of collecting and bringing in forage, sending out sometimes as many as a hundred and fifty wagons to haul the grain which my scouts had previously located. In nearly every one of these expeditions the enemy was encountered, and the wagons were usually loaded while the skirmishers kept up a running fire. Often there would occur a respectable brush, with the loss on each side of a number of killed and wounded. The officer in direct command always reported to me personally whatever had happened during the time he was out—the result of his reconnoissance, so to speak, for that was the real nature of these excursions—and on one occasion the colonel in command, Colonel Conrad, of the Fifteenth Missouri, informed me that he got through without much difficulty; in fact, that everything had gone all right and been eminently satisfactory, except that in returning he had been mortified greatly by the conduct of *the two females belonging to the detachment and division train at my headquarters*. These women, he said, had given much annoyance by getting drunk, and to some extent demoralizing his men. To say that I was astonished at his statement would be a mild way of putting it, and had I not known him to be a most upright man and of sound sense, I should have doubted not only his veracity, but his sanity. Inquiring who they were and for further details, I was informed that there certainly were in the command two females, that in some mysterious manner had attached themselves to the service as soldiers; that one, an East Tennessee woman, was a teamster in the division wagon-train and the other a private soldier in a cavalry company temporarily attached to my headquarters for escort duty. While out on the foraging expedition these Amazons had secured a supply of "apple-jack" by some means, got very drunk, and on the return had fallen into Stone River and been nearly drowned. After they had been fished from the water, in the process of resuscitation their sex was disclosed, though up to this time it appeared to be known only to each other. The story was straight and the circumstance clear, so, convinced of Conrad's continued sanity, I directed the provost-marshal to bring in arrest to my headquarters the two disturbers of Conrad's peace of mind. After some little search the East Tennessee woman was found in camp, somewhat the worse for the experiences of the day before, but awaiting her fate contentedly smoking a cob-pipe. She was brought to me, and put in duress under charge of the division surgeon until her companion could be secured. To the doctor she related that the year before she had "refugeed" from East Tennessee, and on arriving in Louisville assumed men's apparel and sought and obtained employment as a teamster in the quartermaster's department. Her features were very large, and so coarse and masculine was her general appearance that she would readily have passed as a man, and in her case the deception was no doubt easily practiced. Next day the "she dragoon" was caught, and proved to be a rather prepossessing young woman, and though necessarily bronzed and hardened by exposure, I doubt if, even with these marks of campaigning, she could have deceived as readily as did her companion. How the two got acquainted I never learned, and though they had joined the army independently of each other, yet an intimacy had sprung up between them long before the mishaps of the foraging expedition. They both were forwarded to army headquarters, and, when provided with clothing suited to their sex, sent back to Nashville, and thence beyond our lines to Louisville.

On January 9, by an order from the War Department, the Army of the Cumberland had been divided into three corps, designated the Fourteenth, Twentieth, and Twenty-first. This order did not alter the composition of the former grand divisions, nor change the commanders, but the new nomenclature was a decided improvement over the clumsy designations Right Wing, Centre, and Left Wing, which were well calculated to lead to confusion sometimes. McCook's wing became the Twentieth Corps, and my division continued of the same organization, and held the same number as formerly—the Third Division, Twentieth Corps. My first brigade was now commanded by Brigadier-General William H. Lytle, the second by Colonel Bernard Laiboldt, and the third by Colonel Luther P. Bradley.

On the 4th of March I was directed to move in light marching order toward Franklin and join General Gordon Granger, to take part in some operations which he was projecting against General Earl Van Dorn, then at Spring Hill. Knowing that my line of march would carry me through a region where forage was plentiful, I took along a large train of empty wagons, which I determined to fill with corn and send back to Murfreesboro', believing that I could successfully cover the train by Minty's brigade of cavalry, which had joined me for the purpose of aiding in a reconnoissance toward Shelbyville. In marching the column I placed a regiment of infantry at its head, then the wagon-train, then a brigade of infantry—masking the cavalry behind this brigade. The enemy, discovering that the train was with us, and thinking he could capture it, came boldly out with his cavalry to attack. The head of his column came up to the crossroads at Versailles, but holding him there, I passed the train and infantry brigade beyond toward Eagleville, and when my cavalry had been thus unmasked, Minty, followed by the balance of my division, which was still behind, charged him with the sabre. Success was immediate and complete, and pursuit of the routed forces continued through Unionville, until we fell upon and drove in the Confederate outposts at Shelbyville. Here the enemy was taken by surprise evidently, which was most fortunate for us, otherwise the consequences might have been disastrous. Minty captured in the charge about fifty prisoners and a few wagons and mules, and thus enabled me to load my train with corn, and send it back to Murfreesboro' unmolested. In this little fight the sabre was freely used by both sides, and I do not believe that during the whole war I again knew of so large a percentage of wounds by that arm in proportion to the numbers engaged.

That night I encamped at Eagleville, and next day reported to Granger at Franklin, arriving in the midst of much excitement prevailing on account of the loss of Coburn's brigade, which had been captured the day before a little distance south of that point, while marching to form a junction with a column that had been directed on Columbia from Murfreesboro'. Shortly after Coburn's capture General Granger had come upon the scene, and the next day he advanced my division and Minty's troops directly on Spring Hill, with a view to making some reprisal; but Van Dorn had no intention of accommodating us, and retired from Spring Hill, offering but little resistance. He continued to fall back, till finally he got behind Duck River, where operations against him ceased; for, in consequence of the incessant rains of the season, the streams had become almost impassable. Later, I returned by way of Franklin to my old camp at Murfreesboro', passing over on this march the ground on which the Confederate General Hood met with such disaster the following year in his attack on Stanley's corps.

My command had all returned from the Franklin expedition to Murfreesboro' and gone into camp on the Salem pike by the latter part of March, from which time till June it took part in only the little affairs of outposts occurring every now and then on my own front. In the meanwhile General Rosecrans had been materially reinforced by the return of sick and wounded men; his army had become well disciplined, and was tolerably supplied; and he was repeatedly pressed by the authorities at Washington to undertake offensive operations.

During the spring and early summer Rosecrans resisted, with a great deal of spirit and on various grounds, these frequent urgings, and out of this grew up an acrimonious correspondence and strained feeling between him and General Halleck. Early in June, however, stores had been accumulated and other preparations made for a move forward, Rosecrans seeming to have decided that he could safely risk an advance, with the prospect of good results. Before finally deciding, he called upon most of his corps and division commanders for their opinions on certain propositions which he presented, and most of them still opposed the projected movement, I among the number, reasoning that while General Grant was operating against Vicksburg, it was better to hold Bragg in Middle Tennessee than to push him so far back into Georgia that interior means of communication would give the Confederate Government the opportunity of quickly joining a part of his force to that of General Johnson in Mississippi.

At this stage, and in fact prior to it, Rosecrans seemed to manifest special confidence in me, often discussing his plans with me independent of the occasions on which he formally referred them for my views. I recollect that on two different occasions about this time he unfolded his designs to me in this informal way, outlining generally how he expected ultimately to force Bragg south of the Tennessee River, and going into the details of the contemplated move on Tullahoma. His schemes, to my mind, were not only comprehensive, but exact, and showed conclusively, what no one doubted then, that they were original with him. I found in them very little to criticise unfavorably, if we were to move at all, and Rosecrans certainly impressed me that he favored an advance at an early day, though many of his generals were against it until the operations on the Mississippi River should culminate in something definite. There was much, fully apparent in the circumstances about his headquarters, leading to the conviction that Rosecrans originated the Tullahoma campaign, and the record of his prior performances collaterally sustains the visible evidence then existing. In my opinion, then, based on a clear recollection of various occurrences growing out of our intimacy, he conceived the plan of the

Tullahoma campaign and the one succeeding it; and is therefore entitled to every credit that attended their execution, no matter what may be claimed for others.

On the 23d of June Bragg was covering his position north of Duck River with a front extending from McMinnville, where his cavalry rested, through Wartrace and Shelbyville to Columbia, his dépôt being at Tullahoma. Rosecrans, thinking that Bragg would offer strong resistance at Shelbyville—which was somewhat protected by a spur of low mountains or hills, offshoots of the Cumberland Mountains—decided to turn from that place; consequently, he directed the mass of the Union army on the enemy's right flank, about Manchester.

On the 26th of June McCook's corps advanced toward Liberty Gap, my division marching on the Shelbyville pike. I had proceeded but a few miles when I encountered the enemy's pickets, who fell back to Christiana, about nine miles from Murfreesboro'. Here I was assailed pretty wickedly by the enemy's sharpshooters and a section of artillery, but as I was instructed to do nothing more than cover the road from Eagleville, over which Brannan's division was to approach Christiana, I made little reply to this severe annoyance, wishing to conceal the strength of my force. As soon as the head of Brannan's column arrived I marched across-country to the left, and encamped that night at the little town of Millersburg, in the vicinity of Liberty Gap. I was directed to move from Millersburg, on Hoover's Gap—a pass in the range of hills already referred to, through which ran the turnpike from Murfreesboro' to Manchester—but heavy rains had made the country roads almost impassable, and the last of my division did not reach Hoover's Gap till the morning of June 27, after its abandonment by the enemy. Continuing on to Fairfield, the head of my column met, south of that place, a small force of Confederate infantry and cavalry, which after a slight skirmish Laiboldt's brigade drove back toward Wartrace. The next morning I arrived at Manchester, where I remained quiet for the day. Early on the 29th I marched by the Lynchburg road for Tullahoma, where the enemy was believed to be in force, and came into position about six miles from the town.

By the 31st the whole army had been concentrated, in spite of many difficulties, and though, on account of the heavy rains that had fallen almost incessantly since we left Murfreesboro', its movements had been slow and somewhat inaccurate, yet the precision with which it took up a line of battle for an attack on Tullahoma showed that forethought and study had been given to every detail. The enemy had determined to fall back from Tullahoma at the beginning of the campaign, however, and as we advanced, his evacuation had so far progressed that when, on July 1, we reached the earthworks thrown up early in the year for the defense of the place, he had almost wholly disappeared, carrying off all his stores and munitions of war except some little subsistence and eleven pieces of artillery. A strong rear-guard remained to cover the retreat, and on my front the usual encounters between advancing and retreating forces took place. Just before reaching the intrenchments on the Lynchburg road, I came upon an open space that was covered by a network of fallen trees and underbrush, which had been slashed all along in front of the enemy's earthworks. This made our progress very difficult, but I shortly became satisfied that there were only a few of the enemy within the works, so moving a battalion of cavalry that had joined me the day before down the road as rapidly as the obstructions would permit, the Confederate pickets quickly departed, and we gained possession of the town. Three siege guns, four caissons, a few stores, and a small number of prisoners fell into my hands.

That same evening orders were issued to the army to push on from Tullahoma in pursuit, for, as it was thought that we might not be able to cross Elk River on account of its swollen condition, we could do the enemy some damage by keeping close as possible at his heels. I marched on the Winchester road at 3 o'clock on the 2d of July and about 8 o'clock reached Elk River ford. The stream was for the time truly an impassable torrent, and all hope of crossing by the Winchester ford had to be abandoned. Deeming that further effort should be made, however, under guidance of Card I turned the head of my column in the direction of Alisona, marching up the river and nearly parallel with it till I came to Rock Creek. With a little delay we got across Rock Creek, which was also much swollen, and finding a short distance above its mouth a ford on Elk River that Card said was practicable, I determined to attempt it. Some of the enemy's cavalry were guarding this ford, but after a sharp little skirmish my battalion of cavalry crossed and took up a strong position on the other bank. The stream was very high and the current very swift, the water tumbling along over its rocky bed in an immense volume, but still it was fordable for infantry if means could be devised by which the men could keep their feet. A cable was stretched across just below the ford as a life-line for the weaker ones, and then the men of the entire division having secured their ammunition by placing the cartridge-boxes on their shoulders, the column pushed cheerfully into the rushing current. The men as they entered the water joined each other in sets of four in a close embrace, which enabled them to retain a foothold and successfully resist the force of the flood. When they were across I turned the column down the left bank of Elk River, and driving the enemy from some slight works near Estelle Springs, regained the Winchester road.

By this time it was clear that Bragg intended to fall back behind the Tennessee River, and our only chance of accomplishing anything of importance was to smash up his rear-guard before it crossed the Cumberland Mountains, and in pursuance of this idea I was directed to attack such of his force as was holding on to Winchester. At 4 o'clock on the morning of July 2 I moved on that town, and when we got close to it directed my mounted troops to charge a small force of Confederate cavalry that was picketing their front. The Confederates resisted but little, and our men went with them in a disorderly chase through the village to Boiling Fork, a small stream about half a mile beyond. Here the fleeing pickets, rallying behind a stronger force, made a stand, and I was directed by McCook to delay till I ascertained if Davis's division, which was to support me, had made the crossing of Elk River, and until I could open up communication with Brannan's division, which was to come in on my left at Decherd. As soon as I learned that Davis was across I pushed on, but the delay had permitted the enemy to pull his rear-guard up on the mountain, and rendered nugatory all further efforts to hurt him materially, our only returns consisting in forcing him to relinquish a small amount of transportation and forage at the mouth of the pass just beyord Cowan, a station on the line of the Nashville and Chattanooga railroad.

At Cowan, Colonel Watkins, of the Sixth Kentucky Cavalry, reported to me with twelve hundred mounted men. Having heard during the night that the enemy had halted on the mountain near the University—an educational establishment on the summit—I directed Watkins to make a reconnoissance and find out the value of the information. He learned that Wharton's brigade of cavalry was halted at the University to cover a moderately large force of the enemy's infantry which had not yet got down the mountain on the other side, so I pushed Watkins out again on the 5th, supporting him by a brigade of infantry, which I accompanied myself. We were too late, however, for when we arrived at the top of the mountain Wharton had disappeared, and though Watkins pursued to Bridgeport, he was able to do nothing more, and on his return reported that the last of the enemy had crossed the Tennessee River and burned the railroad bridge.

Nothing further could now be done, so I instructed Watkins to rejoin the division at Cowan, and being greatly fatigued by the hard campaigning of the previous ten days, I concluded to go back to my camp in a more comfortable way than on the back of my tired horse. In his retreat the enemy had not disturbed the railway track at all, and as we had captured a hand-car at Cowan, I thought I would have it brought up to the station near the University to carry me down the mountain to my camp, and, desiring company, I persuasively invited Colonel Frank T. Sherman to ride with me. I sent for the car by a courier, and for a long time patiently awaited its arrival, in fact, until all the returning troops had passed us, but still it did not come. Thinking it somewhat risky to remain at the station without protection, Sherman and myself started our horses to Cowan by our orderlies, and set out on foot to meet the car, trudging along down the track in momentary expectation of falling in with our private conveyance. We had not gone very far before night overtook us, and we then began to realize the dangers surrounding us, for there we were alone and helpless, tramping on in the darkness over an unknown railroad track in the enemy's country, liable on the one hand to go tumbling through some bridge or trestle, and on the other, to possible capture or death at the hands of the guerrillas then infesting these mountains. Just after dark we came to a little cabin near the track, where we made bold to ask for water, notwithstanding the fact that to disclose ourselves to the inmates might lead to fatal consequences. The water was kindly given, but the owner and his family were very much exercised lest some misfortune might befall us near their house, and be charged to them, so they encouraged us to move on with a frankness inspired by fear of future trouble to themselves.

At every turn we eagerly hoped to meet the hand-car, but it never came, and we jolted on from tie to tie for eleven weary miles, reaching Cowan after midnight, exhausted and sore in every muscle from frequent falls on the rough, un-ballasted road-bed. Inquiry developed that the car had been well manned, and started to us as ordered, and nobody could account for its non-arrival. Further investigation next day showed, however, that when it reached the foot of the mountain, where the railroad formed a junction, the improvised crew, in the belief no doubt that the University was on the main line instead of near the branch to Tracy City, followed the main stem until it car-

CHAPTER IX

THE TULLAHOMA CAMPAIGN was practically closed by the disappearance of the enemy from the country north of the Tennessee River. Middle Tennessee was once more in the possession of the National troops, and Rosecrans, though strongly urged from Washington to continue on, resisted the pressure until he could repair the Nashville and Chattanooga railroad, which was of vital importance in supplying his army from its secondary base at Nashville. As he desired to hold this road to where it crossed the Tennessee, it was necessary to push a force beyond the mountains, and after a few days of rest at Cowan my division was ordered to take station at Stevenson, Alabama, the junction of the Memphis and Charleston road with the Nashville and Chattanooga, with instructions to occupy Bridgeport also.

The enemy had meanwhile concentrated most of his forces at Chattanooga for the twofold purpose of holding this gateway of the Cumberland Mountains, and to assume a defensive attitude which would enable him to take advantage of such circumstances as might arise in the development of the offensive campaign he knew we must make. The peculiar topography of the country was much to his advantage, and while we had a broad river and numerous spurs and ridges of the Cumberland Mountains to cross at a long distance from our base, he was backed up on his dépôts of supply, and connected by interior lines of railway with the different armies of the Confederacy, so that he could be speedily reinforced.

Bridgeport was to be ultimately a sub-dépôt for storing subsistence supplies, and one of the points at which our army would cross the Tennessee, so I occupied it on July 29 with two brigades, retaining one at Stevenson, however, to protect that railway junction from raids by way of Caperton's ferry. By the 29th of August a considerable quantity of supplies had been accumulated, and then began a general movement of our troops for crossing the river. As there were not with the army enough pontoons to complete the two bridges required, I was expected to build one of them of trestles; and a battalion of the First Michigan Engineers under Colonel Innis was sent me to help construct the bridge. Early on the 31st I sent into the neighboring woods about fifteen hundred men with axes and teams, and by nightfall they had delivered on the riverbank fifteen hundred logs suitable for a trestle bridge. Flooring had been shipped to me in advance by rail, but the quantity was insufficient, and the lack had to be supplied by utilizing planking and weather-boarding taken from barns and houses in the surrounding country. The next day Innis's engineers, with the assistance of the detail that had felled the timber, cut and half-notched the logs, and put the bridge across; spanning the main channel, which was swimming deep, with four or five pontoons that had been sent me for this purpose. On the 2d and 3d of September my division crossed on the bridge in safety, though we were delayed somewhat because of its giving way once where the pontoons joined the trestles. We were followed by a few detachments from other commands, and by nearly all the transportation of McCook's corps.

After getting to the south side of the Tennessee River

I was ordered to Valley Head, where McCook's corps was to concentrate. On the 4th of September I ascended Sand Mountain, but had got only half way across the plateau, on top, when night came, the march having been a most toilsome one. The next day we descended to the base, and encamped near Trenton. On the 10th I arrived at Valley Head, and climbing Lookout Mountain, encamped on the plateau at Indian Falls. The following day I went down into Broomtown Valley to Alpine.

The march of McCook's corps from Valley Head to Alpine was in pursuance of orders directing it to advance on Summerville, the possession of which place would further threaten the enemy's communications, it being assumed that Bragg was in full retreat south, as he had abandoned Chattanooga on the 8th. This assumption soon proved erroneous, however, and as we, while in Broomtown Valley, could not communicate directly with Thomas's corps, the scattered condition of the army began to alarm us all, and McCook abandoned the advance to Summerville, ordering back to the summit of Lookout Mountain such of the corps trains as had got down into Broomtown Valley.

But before this I had grown uneasy in regard to the disjointed situation of our army, and, to inform myself of what was going on, determined to send a spy into the enemy's lines. In passing Valley Head on the 10th my scout Card, who had been on the lookout for some one capable to undertake the task, brought me a Union man with whom he was acquainted, who lived on Sand Mountain, and had been much persecuted by guerrillas on account of his loyal sentiments. He knew the country well, and as his loyalty was vouched for I asked him to go into the enemy's camp, which I believed to be near Lafayette, and bring me such information as he could gather. He said such a journey would be at the risk of his life, and that at best he could not expect to remain in that section of country if he undertook it, but that he would run all the chances if I would enable him to emigrate to the West at the end of the "job," which I could do by purchasing the small "bunch" of stock he owned on the mountain. To this I readily assented, and he started on the delicate undertaking. He penetrated the enemy's lines with little difficulty, but while prosecuting his search for information was suspected, and at once arrested and placed under guard. From this critical situation he escaped, however, making his way through the enemy's picket-line in the darkness by crawling on his belly and deceiving the sentinels by imitating the grunts of the half-wild, sand-colored hogs with which the country abounded. He succeeded in reaching Rosecrans's headquarters finally, and there gave the definite information that Bragg intended to fight, and that he expected to be reinforced by Longstreet.

By this time it was clear that Bragg had abandoned Chattanooga with the sole design of striking us in detail as we followed in pursuit; and to prevent his achieving this purpose orders came at 12 o'clock, midnight, for McCook to draw in toward Chattanooga. This could be done only by recrossing Lookout Mountain, the enemy's army at Lafayette now interposing between us and Thomas's corps. The retrograde march began at once. I moved back over the mountain on the 13th and 14th to Stevens's Mills, and on the 15th and 16th recrossed through Stevens's Gap, in the Lookout range, and encamped at its base in McLamore's cove. The march was made with all possible celerity, for the situation was critical and demanded every exertion. The ascent and descent of the mountains was extremely exhausting, the steep grades often rendering it necessary to drag up and let down by hand both the transportation and artillery. But at last we were in conjunction with the main army, and my division breathed easier.

On the 17th I remained in line of battle all day and night in front of McLamore's cove, the enemy making slight demonstrations against me from the direction of Lafayette. The main body of the army having bodily moved to the left meanwhile, I followed it on the 18th, encamping at Pond Spring. On the 19th I resumed the march to the left and went into line of battle at Crawfish Springs to cover our right and rear. Immediately after forming this line, I again became isolated by the general movement to the left, and in consequence was directed to advance and hold the ford of Chickamauga Creek at Lee and Gordon's Mills, thus coming into close communication with the balance of our forces. I moved into this position rapidly, being compelled, though, first to drive back the enemy's cavalry skirmishers, who, having crossed to the west side of the creek, annoyed the right flank of my column a good deal while *en route*.

Upon arrival at Lee and Gordon's Mills I found the ford over Chickamauga Creek temporarily uncovered, through the hurried movement of Wood to the assistance of Davis's division. The enemy was already present in small force, with the evident intention of taking permanent possession, but my troops at once actively engaged him and recovered the ford with some slight losses. Scarcely had this been done when I was directed to assist Crittenden. Leaving Lytle's brigade at the ford, I proceeded with Bradley's and Laiboldt's to help Crittenden, whose main line was formed to the east of the Chattanooga and Lafayette road, its right trending toward a point on Chickamauga Creek about a mile and a half north of Lee and Gordon's Mills. By the time I had joined Crittenden with my two brigades, Davis had been worsted in an attack Rosecrans had ordered him to make on the left of that portion of the enemy's line which was located along the west bank of the Chicka-mauga, the repulse being so severe that one of Davis's batteries had to be abandoned. Bradley's brigade arrived on the ground first and was hastily formed and thrown into the fight, which up to this moment had been very doubtful, fortune inclining first to one side, then to the other. Bradley's brigade went in with steadiness, and charging across an open corn-field that lay in front of the Lafayette road, recovered Davis's guns and forced the enemy to retire. Meanwhile Laiboldt's brigade had come on the scene, and forming it on Bradley's right, I found myself at the end of the contest holding the ground which was

Davis's original position. It was an ugly fight and my loss was heavy, including Bradley wounded. The temporary success was cheering, and when Lytle's brigade joined me a little later I suggested to Crittenden that we attack, but investigation showed that his troops, having been engaged all day, were not in condition, so the suggestion could not be carried out.

The events of the day had indicated that Bragg's main object was to turn Rosecrans's left; it was therefore still deemed necessary that the army should continue its flank movement to the left, so orders came to draw my troops in toward the widow Glenn's house. By strengthening the skirmish line and shifting my brigades in succession from right to left until the point designated was reached, I was able to effect the withdrawal without much difficulty, calling in my skirmish-line after the main force had retired.

My command having settled down for the night in this new line I rode to army headquarters, to learn if possible the expectations for the morrow and hear the result of the battle in General Thomas's front. Nearly all the superior officers of the army were at headquarters, and it struck me that much depression prevailed, notwithstanding the fact that the enemy's attempts during the day to turn our left flank and also envelop our right had been unsuccessful. It was now positively known, through prisoners and otherwise, that Bragg had been reinforced to such an extent as to make him materially outnumber us, consequently there was much apprehension for the future.

The necessity of protecting our left was most apparent, and the next day the drifting in that direction was to be continued. This movement in the presence of the enemy, who at all points was actively seeking an opportunity to penetrate our line and interpose a column between its right and left, was most dangerous. But the necessity for shifting the army to the left was obvious, hence only the method by which it was undertaken is open to question. The move was made by the flank in the face of an exultant foe superior in numbers, and was a violation of a simple and fundamental military principle. Under such circumstances columns naturally stretch out into attenuated lines, organizations become separated, and intervals occur, all of which we experienced; and had the orders for the movement been construed properly I doubt if it could have been executed without serious danger. Necessity knows no law, however, and when all the circumstances of this battle are fully considered it is possible that justification may be found for the manœuvres by which the army was thus drifted to the left. We were in a bad strait unquestionably, and under such conditions possibly the exception had to be applied rather than the rule.

At daylight on the morning of the 20th a dense fog obscured everything; consequently both armies were passive so far as fighting was concerned. Rosecrans took advantage of the inaction to rearrange his right, and I was pulled back closer to the widow Glenn's house to a strong position, where I threw together some rails and logs as barricades, but I was disconnected from the troops on my left by a considerable interval. Here I awaited the approach of the enemy, but he did not disturb me, although about 9 o'clock in the forenoon he had opened on our extreme left with musketry fire and a heavy cannonade. Two hours later it was discovered by McCook that the interval between the main army and me was widening, and he ordered me to send Laiboldt's brigade to occupy a portion of the front that had been covered by Negley's division. Before getting this brigade into place, however, two small brigades of Davis's division occupied the ground, and I directed Laiboldt to form in column of regiments on the crest of a low ridge in rear of Carlin's brigade, so as to prevent Davis's right flank from being turned. The enemy was now feeling Davis strongly, and I was about sending for Lytle's and Bradley's brigades when I received an order to move these rapidly to the extreme left of the army to the assistance of General Thomas. I rode hastily back toward their position, but in the meanwhile, they had been notified by direct orders from McCook, and were moving out at a

double-quick toward the Lafayette road. By this time the
enemy had assaulted Davis furiously in front and flank,
and driven him from his line, and as the confused mass
came back, McCook ordered Laiboldt to charge by deploying to the front. This he did through Davis's broken
ranks, but failed to check the enemy's heavy lines, and
finally Laiboldt's brigade broke also and fell to the rear.
My remaining troops, headed by Lytle, were now passing
along the rear of the ground where this disaster took
place—*en route* to Thomas, and
as the hundreds of fugitives rushed back, McCook directed
me to throw in Lytle's and Bradley's brigades. This was
hastily done, they being formed to the front under a terrible fire. Scarcely were they aligned when the same horde
of Confederates that had overwhelmed Davis and Laiboldt
poured in upon them a deadly fire and shivered the two
brigades to pieces. We succeeded in rallying them, however, and by a counter attack regained the ridge that Laiboldt had been driven from, where we captured the colors
of the Twenty-fourth Alabama. We could not hold the ridge,
though, and my troops were driven back with heavy loss,
including General Lytle killed, past the widow Glenn's
house, and till I managed to establish them in line of battle
on a range of low hills behind the Dry Valley road.

During these occurrences General Rosecrans passed
down the road behind my line, and sent word that he
wished to see me, but affairs were too critical to admit of
my going to him at once, and he rode on to Chattanooga.
It is to be regretted that he did not wait till I could join
him, for the delay would have permitted him to see that
matters were not in quite such bad shape as he supposed;
still, there is no disguising the fact that at this juncture
his army was badly crippled.

Shortly after my division had rallied on the low hills
already described, I discovered that the enemy, instead of
attacking me in front, was wedging in between my division
and the balance of the army; in short, endeavoring to cut
me off from Chattanooga. This necessitated another ret-

rograde movement, which brought me back to the southern face of Missionary Ridge, where I was joined by Carlin's brigade of Davis's division. Still thinking I could join General Thomas, I rode some distance to the left of my line to look for a way out, but found that the enemy had intervened so far as to isolate me effectually. I then determined to march directly to Rossville, and from there effect a junction with Thomas by the Lafayette road. I reached Rossville about 5 o'clock in the afternoon, bringing with me eight guns, forty-six caissons, and a long ammunition train, the latter having been found in a state of confusion behind the widow Glenn's when I was being driven back behind the Dry Valley road.

The head of my column passed through Rossville, appearing upon Thomas's left about 6 o'clock in the evening, penetrated without any opposition the right of the enemy's line, and captured several of his field-hospitals. As soon as I got on the field I informed Thomas of the presence of my command, and asked for orders. He replied that his lines were disorganized, and that it would be futile to attack; that all I could do was to hold on, and aid in covering his withdrawal to Rossville.

I accompanied him back to Rossville, and when we reached the skirt of the little hamlet General Thomas halted and we dismounted. Going into one of the angles of a worm fence nearby I took a rail from the top and put it through the lower rails at a proper height from the ground to make a seat, and General Thomas and I sat down while my troops were moving by. The General appeared very much exhausted, seemed to forget what he had stopped for, and said little or nothing of the incidents of the day. This was the second occasion on which I had met him in the midst of misfortune, for during the fight in the cedars at Stone River, when our prospects were most disheartening, we held a brief conversation respecting the line he was then taking up for the purpose of helping me. At other times, in periods of inactivity, I saw but little of him. He impressed me now as he did in the cedars, his quiet, unobtrusive demeanor communicating a gloomy rather than a hopeful view of the situation. This apparent depression was due no doubt to the severe trial through which he had gone in the last forty-eight hours, which strain had exhausted him very much both physically and mentally. His success in maintaining his ground was undoubtedly largely influenced by the fact that two-thirds of the National forces had been sent to his succor, but his firm purpose to save the army was the mainstay on which all relied after Rosecrans left the field. As the command was getting pretty well past, I rose to go in order to put my troops into camp. This aroused the General, when, remarking that he had a little flask of brandy in his saddle-holster, he added that he had just stopped for the purpose of offering me a drink, as he knew I must be very tired. He requested one of his staff-officers to get the flask, and after taking a sip himself, passed it to me. Refreshed by the brandy, I mounted and rode off to supervise the encamping of my division, by no means an easy task considering the darkness, and the confusion that existed among the troops that had preceded us into Rossville.

This done, I lay down at the foot of a tree, with my saddle for a pillow, and saddle-blanket for a cover. Some soldiers near me having built a fire, were making coffee, and I guess I must have been looking on wistfully, for in a little while they brought me a tin-cupful of the coffee and a small piece of hard bread, which I relished keenly, it being the first food that had passed my lips since the night before. I was very tired, very hungry, and much discouraged by what had taken place since morning. I had been obliged to fight my command under the most disadvantageous circumstances, disconnected, without supports, without even opportunity to form in line of battle, and at one time contending against four divisions of the enemy. In this battle of Chickamauga, out of an effective strength of 4,000 bayonets, I had lost 1,517 officers and men, including two brigade commanders. This was not satisfactory—indeed, it was most depressing—and then there was much confusion prevailing around Rossville; and, this condition of things doubtless increasing my gloomy reflections, it did not seem to me that the outlook for the next day was at all auspicious, unless the enemy was slow to improve his present advantage. Exhaustion soon quieted all forebodings, though, and I fell into a sound sleep, from which I was not aroused till daylight.

On the morning of the 21st the enemy failed to advance, and his inaction gave us the opportunity for getting the broken and disorganized army into shape. It took a large part of the day to accomplish this, and the chances of complete victory would have been greatly in Bragg's favor if he could have attacked us vigorously at this time. But he had been badly hurt in the two days' conflict, and his inactivity on the 21st showed that he too had to go through the process of reorganization. Indeed, his crippled condition began to show itself the preceding evening, and I have always thought that, had General Thomas held on and attacked the Confederate right and rear from where I made the junction with him on the Lafayette road, the field of Chickamauga would have been relinquished to us; but it was fated to be otherwise.

Rosecrans, McCook, and Crittenden passed out of the battle when they went back to Chattanooga, and their absence was discouraging to all aware of it. Doubtless this had much to do with Thomas's final withdrawal, thus leaving the field to the enemy, though at an immense cost in killed and wounded. The night of the 21st the army moved back from Rossville, and my division, as the rear-guard of the Twentieth Corps, got within our lines at Chattanooga about 8 o'clock the morning of the 22d. Our unmolested retirement from Rossville lent additional force to the belief that the enemy had been badly injured, and further impressed me with the conviction that we might have held on. Indeed, the battle of Chickamauga was somewhat like that of Stone River, victory resting with the side that had the grit to defer longest its relinquishment of the field.

The manoeuvres by which Rosecrans had carried his army over the Cumberland Mountains, crossed the Tennessee River, and possessed himself of Chattanooga, merit the highest commendation up to the abandonment of this town by Bragg on the 8th of September; but I have always fancied that that evacuation made Rosecrans over confident, and led him to think that he could force Bragg south as far as Rome. After the Union army passed the river and Chattanooga fell into our hands, we still kept pressing the enemy's communications, and the configuration of the country necessitated more or less isolation of the different corps. McCook's corps of three divisions had crossed two difficult ridges—Sand and Lookout mountains—to Alpine in Broomtown Valley with intentions against Summerville. Thomas's corps had marched by the way of Stevens's Gap toward Lafayette, which he expected to occupy. Crittenden had passed through Chattanooga, at first directing his march on Ringgold. Thus the corps of the army were not in conjunction, and between McCook and Thomas there intervened a positive and aggressive obstacle in the shape of Bragg's army concentrating and awaiting reinforcement at Lafayette. Under these circumstances Bragg could have taken the different corps in detail, and it is strange that he did not, even before receiving his reinforcements, turn on McCook in Broomtown Valley and destroy him.

Intelligence that Bragg would give battle began to come to us from various sources as early as the 10th of September, and on the 11th McCook found that he could not communicate with Thomas by the direct road through Broomtown Valley; but we did not begin closing in toward Chattanooga till the 13th, and even then the Twentieth Corps had before it the certainty of many delays that must necessarily result from the circuitous and difficult mountain roads which we would be obliged to follow. Had the different corps, beginning with McCook's, been drawn in toward Chattanooga between the 8th and 12th of September, the objective point of the campaign would have remained in our hands without the battle of Chickamauga, but, as has been seen, this was not done. McCook was almost constantly on the march day and night between the 13th and the 19th, ascending and descending mountains, his men worried and wearied, so that when they appeared on the battle-field, their fatigued condition operated greatly against their efficiency. This delay in concentration was also the original cause of the continuous shifting toward our left to the support of Thomas, by which manoeuvre Rosecrans endeavored to protect his communications with Chattanooga, and out of which grew the intervals that offered such tempting opportunities to Bragg. In addition to all this, much transpired on the field of battle tending to bring about disaster. There did not seem to be any well-defined plan of action in the fighting, and this led to much independence of judgment in construing orders among some of the subordinate generals. It also gave rise to much license in issuing orders: too many people were giving important directions, affecting the whole army, without authority from its head. In view, therefore, of all the errors that were committed from the time Chattanooga fell into our hands after our first crossing the Tennessee, it was fortunate that the Union defeat was not more complete, that it left in the enemy's possession not much more than the barren results arising from the simple holding of the ground on which the engagement was fought.

CHAPTER X

B<small>Y 9 O'CLOCK ON THE MORNING OF</small> September 22 my command took up a position within the heavy line of intrenchments at Chattanooga, the greater part of which defenses had been thrown up since the army commenced arriving there the day before. The enemy, having now somewhat recovered from the shock of the recent battle, followed carefully, and soon invested us close into our lines with a parallel system of rifle-pits. He also began at once to erect permanent lines of earthworks on Missionary Ridge and to establish himself strongly on Lookout Mountain. He then sent Wheeler's cavalry north of the Tennessee, and, aided greatly by the configuration of the ground, held us in a state of partial siege, which serious rains might convert into a complete investment. The occupation of Lookout Mountain broke our direct communication with Bridgeport—our sub-dépôt—and forced us to bring supplies by way of the Sequatchie Valley and Waldron's Ridge of the Cumberland Mountains, over a road most difficult even in the summer season, but now liable to be rendered impassable by autumn rains. The distance to Bridgeport by this circuitous route was sixty miles, and the numerous

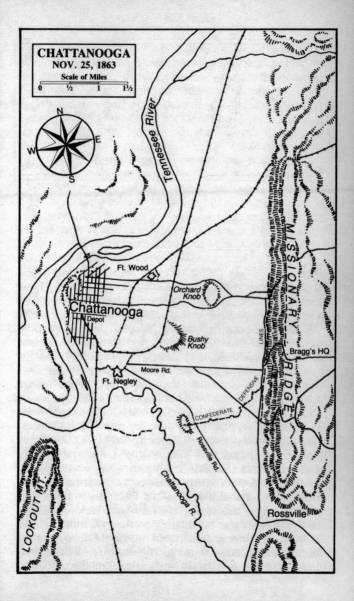

CHATTANOOGA

NOV. 25, 1863

Scale of Miles

0   ½   1   1½

N
W   E
S

Tennessee River

Ft. Wood

Orchard Knob

Chattanooga

Depot

Bushy Knob

MISSIONARY RIDGE

Bragg's HQ

Moore Rd.

Ft. Negley

LINES

DEFENSIVE

CONFEDERATE

Rossville Rd.

Chattanooga R.

LOOKOUT MT.

Rossville

passes, coves, and small valleys through which the road ran offered tempting opportunities for the destruction of trains, and the enemy was not slow to take advantage of them. Indeed, the situation was not promising, and General Rosecrans himself, in communicating with the President the day succeeding the battle of Chickamauga, expressed doubts of his ability to hold the gateway of the Cumberland Mountains.

The position taken up by my troops inside the lines of Chattanooga was near the old iron-works, under the shadow of Lookout Mountain. Here we were exposed to a continual fire from the enemy's batteries for many days, but as the men were well covered by secure though simple intrenchments, but little damage was done. My own headquarters were established on the grounds of Mr. William Crutchfield, a resident of the place, whose devotion to the Union cause knew no bounds, and who rendered me—and, in fact, at one time or another, nearly every general officer in the Army of the Cumberland—invaluable service in the way of information about the Confederate army. My headquarters camp frequently received shots from the point of Lookout Mountain also, but fortunately no casualties resulted from this plunging fire, though, I am free to confess, at first our nerves were often upset by the whirring of twenty-pounder shells dropped inconsiderately into our camp at untimely hours of the night.

In a few days rain began to fall, and the mountain roads by which our supplies came were fast growing impracticable. Each succeeding train of wagons took longer to make the trip from Bridgeport, and the draft mules were dying by the hundreds. The artillery horses would soon go too, and there was every prospect that later the troops would starve unless something could be done. Luckily for my division, a company of the Second Kentucky Cavalry had attached itself to my headquarters, and, though there without authority, had been left undisturbed in view of a coming reorganization of the army incidental to the removal of McCook and Crittenden from the command of their respective corps, a measure that had been determined upon immediately after the battle of Chickamauga. Desiring to remain with me, Captain Lowell H. Thickstun, command-ing this company, was ready for any duty I might find for him, so I ordered him into the Sequatchie Valley for the purpose of collecting supplies for my troops, and sent my scout Card along to guide him to the best locations. The company hid itself away in a deep cove in the upper end of the valley, and by keeping very quiet and paying for everything it took from the people, in a few days was enabled to send me large quantities of corn for my animals and food for the officers and men, which greatly supple-mented the scanty supplies we were getting from the sub-dépôt at Bridgeport. In this way I carried men and animals through our beleaguerment in pretty fair condition, and of the turkeys, chickens, ducks, and eggs sent in for the messes of my officers we often had enough to divide lib-erally among those at different headquarters. Wheeler's cavalry never discovered my detached company, yet the chances of its capture were not small, sometimes giving much uneasiness; still, I concluded it was better to run all risks than to let the horses die of starvation in Chat-tanooga. Later, after the battle of Missionary Ridge, when I started to Knoxville, the company joined me in excellent shape, bringing with it an abundance of food, including a small herd of beef cattle.

The whole time my line remained near the iron-mills the shelling from Lookout was kept up, the screeching shots inquisitively asking in their wellknown, way, "Where are you? Where are you?" but it is strange to see how readily soldiers can become accustomed to the sound of dangerous missiles under circumstances of familiarity, and this case was no exception to the rule. Few casualties occurred, and soon contempt took the place of nervous-ness, and as we could not reply in kind on account of the elevation required for our guns, the men responded by jeers and imprecations whenever a shell fell into their camp.

Meantime, orders having been issued for the organization of the army, additional troops were attached to my command, and it became the Second Division of the Fourth Army Corps, to which Major-General Gordon Granger was assigned as commander. This necessitated a change of position of the division, and I moved to ground behind our works, with my right resting on Fort Negley and my left extending well over toward Fort Wood, my front being parallel to Missionary Ridge. My division was now composed of twenty-five regiments, classified into brigades and demi-brigades, the former commanded by Brigadier-General G. D. Wagner, Colonel C. G. Harker, and Colonel F. T. Sherman; the latter, by Colonels Laiboldt, Miller, Wood, Walworth, and Opdyke. The demibrigade was an awkward invention of Granger's; but at this time it was necessitated—perhaps by the depleted condition of our regiments, which compelled the massing of a great number of regimental organizations into a division—to give it weight and force.

On October 16, 1863, General Grant had been assigned to the command of the "Military Division of the Mississippi," a geographical area which embraced the Departments of the Ohio, the Cumberland, and the Tennessee, thus effecting a consolidation of divided commands which might have been introduced most profitably at an earlier date. The same order that assigned General Grant relieved General Rosecrans, and placed General Thomas in command of the Army of the Cumberland. At the time of the reception of the order, Rosecrans was busy with preparations for a movement to open the direct road to Bridgeport—having received in the interval, since we came back to Chattanooga, considerable reinforcement by the arrival in his department of the Eleventh and Twelfth corps, under General Hooker, from the Army of the Potomac. With this force Rosecrans had already strengthened certain important points on the railroad between Nashville and Stevenson, and given orders to Hooker to concentrate at Bridgeport such portions of his command as were available, and to hold them in readiness to advance toward Chattanooga.

On the 19th of October, after turning the command over to Thomas, General Rosecrans quietly slipped away from the army. He submitted uncomplainingly to his removal, and modestly left us without fuss or demonstration; ever maintaining, though, that the battle of Chickamauga was in effect a victory, as it had ensured us, he said, the retention of Chattanooga. When his departure became known deep and almost universal regret was expressed, for he was enthusiastically esteemed and loved by the Army of the Cumberland, from the day he assumed command of it until he left it, notwithstanding the censure poured upon him after the battle of Chickamauga.

The new position to which my division had been moved, in consequence of the reorganization, required little additional labor to strengthen it, and the routine of fatigue duty and drills was continued as before, its monotony occasionally broken by the excitement of an expected attack, or by amusements of various kinds that were calculated to keep the men in good spirits. Toward this result much was contributed by Mr. James E. Murdock, the actor, who came down from the North to recover the body of his son, killed at Chickamauga, and was quartered with me for the greater part of the time he was obliged to await the successful conclusion of his sad mission. He spent days, and even weeks, going about through the division giving recitations before the camp-fires, and in improvised chapels, which the men had constructed from refuse lumber and canvas. Suiting his selections to the occasion, he never failed to excite intense interest in the breasts of all present, and when circumstances finally separated him from us, all felt that a debt of gratitude was due him that could never be paid. The pleasure he gave, and the confident feeling that was now arising from expected reinforcements, was darkened, however, by one sad incident. Three men of my division had deserted their colors at the beginning of the siege and made their way north. They were soon arrested, and were brought back to stand trial for the worst offense that can be committed by a soldier, convicted of the crime, and ordered to be shot. To make the example effective I paraded the whole division for the execution, and on the 13th of November, in the presence of their former comrades, the culprits were sent, in accordance with the terms of their sentence, to render their account to the Almighty. It was the saddest spectacle I ever witnessed, but there could be no evasion, no mitigation of the full letter of the law; its timely enforcement was but justice to the brave spirits who had yet to fight the rebellion to the end.

General Grant arrived at Chattanooga on October 23, and began at once to carry out the plans that had been formed for opening the shorter or river road to Bridgeport. This object was successfully accomplished by the moving of Hooker's command to Rankin's and Brown's ferries in concert with a force from the Army of the Cumberland which was directed on the same points, so by the 27th of October direct communication with our dépôts was established. The four weeks which followed this cheering result were busy with the work of refitting and preparing for offensive operations as soon as General Sherman should reach us with his troops from West Tennessee. During this period of activity the enemy committed the serious fault of detaching Longstreet's corps—sending it to aid in the siege of Knoxville in East Tennessee—an error which has no justification whatever, unless it be based on the presumption that it was absolutely necessary that Longstreet should ultimately rejoin Lee's army in Virginia by way of Knoxville and Lynchburg, with a chance of picking up Burnside *en route*. Thus depleted, Bragg still held Missionary Ridge in strong force, but that part of his line which extended across the intervening valley to the northerly point of Lookout Mountain was much attenuated.

By the 18th of November General Grant had issued instructions covering his intended operations. They contemplated that Sherman's column, which was arriving by the north bank of the Tennessee, should cross the river on a pontoon bridge just below the mouth of Chickamauga Creek and carry the northern extremity of Missionary Ridge as far as the railroad tunnel; that the Army of the Cumberland—the centre—should co-operate with Sherman; and that Hooker with a mixed command should continue to hold Lookout Valley and operate on our extreme right as circumstances might warrant. Sherman crossed on the 24th to perform his alloted part of the programme, but in the meantime Grant becoming impressed with the idea that Bragg was endeavoring to get away, ordered Thomas to make a strong demonstration in his front, to determine the truth or falsity of the information that had been received. This task fell to the Fourth Corps, and at 12 o'clock on the 23d I was notified that Wood's division would make a reconnoissance to an elevated point in its front called Orchard Knob, and that I was to support it with my division and prevent Wood's right flank from being turned by an advance of the enemy on Moore's road or from the direction of Rossville. For this duty I marched my division out of the works about 2 P.M., and took up a position on Bushy Knob. Shortly after we reached this point Wood's division passed my left flank on its reconnoissance, and my command, moving in support of it, drove in the enemy's picket-line. Wood's took possession of Orchard Knob easily, and mine was halted on a low ridge to the right of the Knob, where I was directed by General Thomas to cover my front by a strong line of rifle-pits, and to put in position two batteries of the Fourth regular artillery that had joined me from the Eleventh Corps. After dark Wood began to feel uneasy about his right flank, for a gap existed between it and my left, so I moved in closer to him, taking up a line where I remained inactive till the 25th, but suffering some inconvenience from the enemy's shells.

On the 24th General Sherman made an attack for the purpose of carrying the north end of Missionary Ridge. His success was not complete, although at the time it was reported throughout the army to be so. It had the effect of disconcerting Bragg, however, and caused him to strengthen his right by withdrawing troops from his left, which circumstance led Hooker to advance on the northerly face of Lookout Mountain. At first, with good glasses, we could plainly see Hooker's troops driving the Confederates up the face of the mountain. All were soon lost to view in the dense timber, but emerged again on the open ground, across which the Confederates retreated at a lively pace, followed by the pursuing line, which was led by a color-bearer, who, far in advance, was bravely waving on his comrades. The gallantry of this man elicited much enthusiasm among us all, but as he was a considerable distance ahead of his comrades I expected to see his rashness punished at any moment by death or capture. He finally got quite near the retreating. Confederates, when suddenly they made a dash at him, but he was fully alive to such a move, and ran back, apparently uninjured, to his friends. About this time a small squad of men reached the top of Lookout and planted the Stars and Stripes on its very crest. Just then a cloud settled down on the mountain, and a heavy bank of fog obscured its whole face.

After the view was lost the sharp rattle of musketry continued some time, but practically the fight had been already won by Hooker's men, the enemy only holding on with a rear-guard to assure his retreat across Chattanooga Valley to Missionary Ridge. Later we heard very heavy cannonading, and fearing that Hooker was in trouble I sent a staff-officer to find out whether he needed assistance, which I thought could be given by a demonstration toward Rossville. The officer soon returned with the report that Hooker was all right, that the cannonading was only a part of a little rear-guard fight, two sections of artillery making all the noise, the reverberations from point to point in the adjacent mountains echoing and re-echoing till it seemed that at least fifty guns were engaged.

On the morning of the 25th of November Bragg's entire army was holding only the line of Missionary Ridge, and our troops, being now practically connected from Sherman to Hooker, confronted it with the Army of the Cumberland in the centre bowed out along the front of Wood's division and mine. Early in the day Sherman, with great determination and persistence, made an attempt to carry the high ground near the tunnel, first gaining and then losing advantage, but his attack was not crowned with the success anticipated. Meanwhile Hooker and Palmer were swinging across Chattanooga Valley, using me as a pivot for the purpose of crossing Missionary Ridge in the neighborhood of Rossville. In the early part of the day I had driven in the Confederate pickets in my front, so as to prolong my line of battle on that of Wood, the necessity of continuing to refuse my right having been obviated by the capture of Lookout Mountain and the advance of Palmer.

About 2 o'clock orders came to carry the line at the foot of the ridge, attacking at a signal of six guns. I had few changes or new dispositions to make. Wagner's brigade, which was next to Wood's division, was formed in double lines, and Harker's brigade took the same formation on Wagner's right. Colonel F. T. Sherman's brigade came on Harker's right, formed in a column of attack, with a front of three regiments, he having nine. My whole front was covered with a heavy line of skirmishers. These dispositions made, my right rested a little distance south of Moore's road, my left joined Wood over toward Orchard Knob, while my centre was opposite Thurman's house— the headquarters of General Bragg—on Missionary Ridge. A small stream of water ran parallel to my front, as far as which the ground was covered by a thin patch of timber, and beyond the edge of the timber was an open plain to the foot of Missionary Ridge, varying in width from four to nine hundred yards. At the foot of the ridge was the enemy's first line of rifle-pits; at a point midway up its face, another line, incomplete; and on the crest was a third line, in which Bragg had massed his artillery.

The enemy saw we were making dispositions for an attack, and in plain view of my whole division he prepared himself for resistance, marching regiments from his left flank with flying colors, and filling up the spaces not already occupied in his intrenchments. Seeing the enemy thus strengthening himself, it was plain that we would have to act quickly if we expected to accomplish much, and I already began to doubt the feasibility of our remaining in the first line of rifle-pits when we should have carried them. I discussed the order with Wagner, Harker, and Sherman, and they were similarly impressed, so while anxiously awaiting the signal I sent Captain Ransom of my staff to Granger, who was at Fort Wood, to ascertain if we were to carry the first line or the ridge beyond. Shortly after Ransom started the signal guns were fired, and I told my brigade commanders to go for the ridge.

Placing myself in front of Harker's brigade, between the line of battle and the skirmishers, accompanied by only an orderly so as not to attract the enemy's fire, we moved out. Under a terrible storm of shot and shell the line pressed forward steadily through the timber, and as it emerged on the plain took the double-quick and with fixed bayonets rushed at the enemy's first line. Not a shot was fired from our line of battle, and as it gained on my skirmishers they melted into and became one with it, and all three of my brigades went over the rifle-pits simultaneously. They then lay down on the face of the ridge, for a breathing-spell and for protection from the terrible fire of canister and musketry pouring over us from the guns on the crest. At the rifle-pits there had been little use for the bayonet, for most of the Confederate troops, disconcerted by the sudden rush, lay close in the ditch and surrendered, though some few fled up the slope to the next line. The prisoners were directed to move out to our rear, and as their intrenchments had now come under fire from the crest, they went with alacrity, and without guard or escort, toward Chattanooga.

After a short pause to get breath the ascent of the ridge began, and I rode into the ditch of the intrenchments to drive out a few skulkers who were hiding there. Just at this time I was joined by Captain Ransom, who, having returned from Granger, told me that we were to carry only the line at the base, and that in coming back, when he struck the left of the division, knowing this interpretation of the order, he in his capacity as an aide-de-camp had directed Wagner, who was up on the face of the ridge, to return, and that in consequence Wagner was recalling his men to the base. I could not bear to order the recall of troops now so gallantly climbing the hill step by step, and believing we could take it, I immediately rode to Wagner's brigade and directed it to resume the attack. In the meantime Harker's and F. T. Sherman's troops were approaching the partial line of works midway of the ridge, and as I returned to the centre of their rear, they were being led by many stands of regimental colors. There seemed to be a rivalry as to which color should be farthest to the front; first one would go forward a few feet, then another would come up to it, the color-bearers vying with one another as to who should be foremost, until finally every standard was planted on the intermediate works. The enemy's fire from the crest during the ascent was terrific in the noise made, but as it was plunging, it over-shot and had little effect on those above the second line of pits, but was very uncomfortable for those below, so I deemed it advisable to seek another place, and Wagner's brigade having reassembled and again pressed up the ridge, I rode up the face to join my troops.

As soon as the men saw me, they surged forward and went over the works on the crest. The parapet of the intrenchment was too high for my horse to jump, so, riding a short distance to the left, I entered through a low place in the line. A few Confederates were found inside, but they turned the butts of their muskets toward me in token of surrender, for our men were now passing beyond them on both their flanks.

The right and right centre of my division gained the summit first, they being partially sheltered by a depression in the face of the ridge, the Confederates in their immediate front fleeing down the southern face. When I crossed the rifle-pits on the top the Confederates were still holding fast at Bragg's headquarters, and a battery located there opened fire along the crest, making things most uncomfortably hot. Seeing the danger to which I was exposed, for I was mounted, Colonel Joseph Conrad, of the Fifteenth Missouri, ran up and begged me to dismount. I accepted his excellent advice, and it probably saved my life, but poor Conrad was punished for his solicitude by being seriously wounded in the thigh at the moment he was thus contributing to my safety.

Wildly cheering, the men advanced along the ridge toward Bragg's headquarters, and soon drove the Confederates from this last position, capturing a number of prisoners, among them Breckenridge's and Bates's adjutant-generals, and the battery that had made such stout resistance on the crest—two guns which were named "Lady Breckenridge" and "Lady Buckner"—General Bragg himself having barely time to escape before his headquarters were taken.

My whole division had now reached the summit, and Wagner and Harker—the latter slightly wounded—joined me as I was standing in the battery just secured. The enemy was rapidly retiring, and though many of his troops, with disorganized wagon-trains and several pieces of artillery, could be distinctly seen in much confusion about half a mile distant in the valley below, yet he was covering them with a pretty well organized line that continued to give us a desultory fire. Seeing this, I at once directed Wagner and Harker to take up the pursuit along Moore's road, which led to Chickamauga Station—Bragg's dépôt of supply— and as they progressed, I pushed Sherman's brigade along the road behind them. Wagner and Harker soon overtook the rear-guard, and a slight skirmish caused it to break, permitting nine guns and a large number of wagons which were endeavoring to get away in the stampede to fall into our hands.

About a mile and a half beyond Missionary Ridge, Moore's road passed over a second ridge or high range of hills, and here the enemy had determined to make a stand for that purpose, posting eight pieces of artillery with such supporting force as he could rally. He was immediately attacked by Harker and Wagner, but the position was strong, the ridge being rugged and difficult of ascent, and after the first onset our men recoiled. A staff-officer from Colonel Wood's demi-brigade informing me at this juncture that that command was too weak to carry the position in its front, I ordered the Fifteenth Indiana and the Twenty-Sixth Ohio to advance to Wood's aid, and then hastening to the front I found his men clinging to the face of the ridge, contending stubbornly with the rear-guard of the enemy. Directing Harker to put Opdyke's demi-brigade in on the right, I informed Wagner that it was necessary to flank the enemy by carrying the high bluff on our left where the ridge terminated, that I had designated the Twenty-Sixth Ohio and Fifteenth Indiana for the work, and that I wished him to join them.

It was now dusk, but the two regiments engaged in the flanking movement pushed on to gain the bluff. Just as they reached the crest of the ridge the moon rose from behind, enlarged by the refraction of the atmosphere, and as the attacking column passed along the summit it crossed the moon's disk and disclosed to us below a most interesting panorama, every figure nearly being thrown out in full relief. The enemy, now outflanked on left and right, abandoned his ground, leaving us two pieces of artillery and a number of wagons. After this ridge was captured I found that no other troops than mine were pursuing the enemy, so I called a halt lest I might become too much isolated. Having previously studied the topography of the country thoroughly, I knew that if I pressed on my line of march would carry me back to Chickamauga station, where we would be in rear of the Confederates that had been fighting General Sherman, and that there was a possibility of capturing them by such action; but I did not feel warranted in marching there alone, so I rode back to Missionary Ridge to ask for more troops, and upon arriving there I found Granger in command, General Thomas having gone back to Chattanooga.

Granger was at Bragg's late headquarters in bed. I informed him of my situation and implored him to follow me up with the Army of the Cumberland, but he declined, saying that he thought we had done well enough. I still insisting, he told me finally to push on to the crossing of Chickamauga Creek, and if I encountered the enemy he would order troops to my support. I returned to my division about 12 o'clock at night, got it under way, and reached the crossing, about half a mile from the station, at 2 o'clock on the morning of the 26th, and there found the bridge destroyed, but that the creek was fordable. I did not encounter the enemy in any force, but feared to go farther without assistance. This I thought I might bring up by practicing a little deception, so I caused two regiments to simulate an engagement by opening fire, hoping that this would alarm Granger and oblige him to respond with troops, but my scheme failed. General Granger afterward told me that he had heard the volleys, but suspected their purpose, knowing that they were not occasioned by a fight, since they were too regular in their delivery.

I was much disappointed that my pursuit had not been supported, for I felt that great results were in store for us should the enemy be vigorously followed. Had the troops under Granger's command been pushed out with mine when Missionary Ridge was gained, we could have reached Chickamauga Station by 12 o'clock the night of the 25th; or had they been sent even later, when I called for them, we could have got there by daylight and worked incalculable danger to the Confederates, for the force that had confronted Sherman did not pass Chickamauga Station in their retreat till after daylight on the morning of the 26th.

My course in following so close was dictated by a thorough knowledge of the topography of the country and a familiarity with its roads, bypaths, and farm-houses, gained with the assistance of Mr. Crutchfield; and sure my column was heading in the right direction, though night had fallen I thought that an active pursuit would almost certainly complete the destruction of Bragg's army. When General Grant came by my bivouac at the crossing of Chickamauga Creek on the 26th, he realized what might have been accomplished had the successful assault on Missionary Ridge been supplemented by vigorous efforts on the part of some high officers, who were more interested in gleaning that portion of the battle-field over which my command had passed than in destroying a panic-stricken enemy.

Although it cannot be said that the result of the two days' operations was reached by the methods which General Grant had indicated in his instructions preceding the battle, yet the general outcome was unquestionably due to his genius, for the manoeuvring of Sherman's and Hooker's commands created the opportunity for Thomas's corps of the Army of the Cumberland to carry the ridge at the centre. In directing Sherman to attack the north end of the ridge, Grant disconcerted Bragg—who was thus made to fear the loss of his dépôt of supplies at Chickamauga Station—and compelled him to resist stoutly; and stout resistance to Sherman meant the withdrawal of the Confederates from Lookout Mountain. While this attack was in process of execution advantage was taken of it by Hooker in a well-planned and well-fought battle, but to my mind an unnecessary one, for our possession of Lookout was the inevitable result that must follow from Sherman's threatening attitude. The assault on Missionary Ridge by Granger's and Palmer's corps was not premeditated by Grant, he directing only the line at its base to be carried, but when this fell into our hands the situation demanded our getting the one at the top also.

I took into the action an effective force of 6,000, and lost 123 officers and 1,181 men killed and wounded. These casualties speak louder than words of the character of the fight, and plainly tell where the enemy struggled most stubbornly, for these figures comprise one-third the casualties of the entire body of Union troops—Sherman's and

CHAPTER XI

THE DAY AFTER THE BATTLE OF Missionary Ridge I was ordered in the evening to return to Chattanooga, and from the limited supply of stores to be had there outfit my command to march to the relief of Knoxville, where General Burnside was still holding out against the besieging forces of General Longstreet. When we left Murfreesboro' in the preceding June, the men's knapsacks and extra clothing, as well as all our camp equipage, had been left behind, and these articles had not yet reached us, so we were poorly prepared for a winter campaign in the mountains of East Tennessee. There was but little clothing to be obtained in Chattanooga, and my command received only a few overcoats and a small supply of India-rubber ponchos. We could get no shoes, although we stood in great need of them, for the extra pair with which each man had started out from Murfreesboro' was now much the worse for wear. The necessity for succoring Knoxville was urgent, however, so we speedily refitted as thoroughly as was possible with the limited means at hand. My division teams were in very fair condition in consequence of the forage we had procured in the Sequatchie Valley, so I left the train behind to bring up clothing when any should arrive in Chattanooga.

Under these circumstances, on the 29th of November the Fourth Corps (Granger's) took up the line of march for Knoxville, my men carrying in their haversacks four days' rations, depending for a further supply of food on a small steamboat loaded with subsistence stores, which was to proceed up the Tennessee River and keep abreast of the column.

Not far from Philadelphia, Tennessee, the columns of General Sherman's army, which had kept a greater distance from the river than Granger's corps, so as to be able to subsist on the country, came in toward our right and the whole relieving force was directed on Marysville, about fifteen miles southwest of Knoxville. We got to Marysville December 5, and learned the same day that Longstreet had shortly before attempted to take Knoxville by a desperate assault, but signally failing, had raised the siege and retired toward Bean's Station on the Rutledge, Rogersville, and Bristol road, leading to Virginia. From Marysville General Sherman's troops returned to Chattanooga, while Granger's corps continued on toward Knoxville, to take part in the pursuit of Longstreet.

Burnside's army was deficient in subsistence, though not to the extent that we had supposed before leaving Chattanooga. It had eaten out the country in the immediate vicinity of Knoxville, however; therefore my division did not cross the Holstein River, but was required, in order to maintain itself, to proceed to the region of the French Broad River. To this end I moved to Sevierville, and making this village my headquarters, the division was spread out over the French Broad country, between Big Pigeon and Little Pigeon rivers, where we soon had all the mills in operation, grinding out plenty of flour and meal. The whole region was rich in provender of all kinds, and as the people with rare exceptions were enthusiastically loyal, we in a little while got more than enough food for ourselves, and by means of flatboats began sending the surplus down the river to the troops at Knoxville.

The intense loyalty of this part of Tennessee exceeded that of any other section I was in during the war. The people could not do too much to aid the Union cause, and brought us an abundance of everything needful. The women were especially loyal, and as many of their sons and husbands, who had been compelled to "refugee" on account of their loyal sentiments, returned with us, numbers of the women went into ecstasies of joy when this part of the Union army appeared among them. So long as we remained in the French Broad region, we lived on the fat of the land, but unluckily our stay was to be of short duration, for Longstreet's activity kept the department commander in a state of constant alarm.

Soon after getting the mills well running, and when the shipment of their surplus product down the river by flatboats had begun, I was ordered to move to Knoxville, on account of demonstrations by Longstreet from the direction of Blain's crossroads. On arriving at Knoxville, an inspection of my command, showed that the shoes of many of the men were entirely worn out, the poor fellows having been obliged to protect their feet with a sort of moccasin, made from their blankets or from such other material as they could procure. About six hundred of the command were in this condition, plainly not suitably shod to withstand the frequent storms of sleet and snow. These men I left in Knoxville to await the arrival of my train, which I now learned was *en route* from Chattanooga with shoes, overcoats, and other clothing, and with the rest of the division proceeded to Strawberry Plains, which we reached the latter part of December.

Mid-winter was now upon us, and the weather in this mountain region of East Tennessee was very cold, snow often falling to the depth of several inches. The thin and scanty clothing of the men afforded little protection, and while in bivouac their only shelter was the ponchos with which they had been provided before leaving Chattanooga;

there was not a tent in the command. Hence great suffering resulted, which I anxiously hoped would be relieved shortly by the arrival of my train with supplies. In the course of time the wagons reached Knoxville, but my troops derived little comfort from this fact, for the train was stopped by General Foster, who had succeeded Burnside in command of the department, its contents distributed *pro rata* to the different organizations of the entire army, and I received but a small share. This was very disappointing, not to say exasperating, but I could not complain of unfairness, for every command in the army was suffering to the same extent as mine, and yet it did seem that a little forethought and exertion on the part of some of the other superior officers, whose transportation was in tolerable condition, might have ameliorated the situation considerably. I sent the train back at once for more clothing, and on its return, just before reaching Knoxville, the quartermaster in charge, Captain Philip Smith, filled the open spaces in the wagons between the bows and load with fodder and hay, and by this clever stratagem passed it through the town safe and undisturbed as a forage train. On Smith's arrival we lost no time in issuing the clothing, and when it had passed into the hands of the individual soldiers the danger of its appropriation for general distribution, like the preceding invoice, was very remote.

General Foster had decided by this time to move his troops to Dandridge for the twofold purpose of threatening the enemy's left and of getting into a locality where we could again gather subsistence from the French Broad region. Accordingly we began an advance on the 15th of January, the cavalry having preceded us some time before. The Twenty-third Corps and Wood's division of the Fourth Corps crossed the Holstein River by a bridge that had been constructed at Strawberry Plains. My division being higher up the stream, forded it, the water very deep and bitter cold, being filled with slushy ice. Marching by way of New Market, I reached Dandridge on the 17th, and here on my arrival met General Sturgis, then commanding our cavalry. He was on the eve of setting out to "whip the enemy's cavalry," as he said, and wanted me to go along and see him do it. I declined, however, for being now the senior officer present, Foster, Parke, and Granger having remained at Knoxville and Strawberry Plains, their absence left me in command, and it was necessary that I should make disposition of the infantry when it arrived. As there were indications of a considerable force of the enemy on the Russellville road I decided to place the troops in line of battle, so as to be prepared for any emergency that might arise in the absence of the senior officers, and I deemed it prudent to supervise personally the encamping of the men. This disposition necessarily required that some of the organizations should occupy very disagreeable ground, but I soon got all satisfactorily posted with the exception of General Willich, who expressed some discontent at being placed beyond the shelter of the timber, but accepted the situation cheerfully when its obvious necessity was pointed out to him.

Feeling that all was secure, I returned to my headquarters in the village with the idea that we were safely established in case of attack, and that the men would now have a good rest if left undisturbed, and plenty to eat, but hardly had I reached my own camp when a staff-officer came post-haste from Sturgis with the information that he was being driven back to my lines, despite the confident invitation to me (in the morning) to go out and witness the whipping which was to be given to the enemy's cavalry. Riding to the front, I readily perceived that the information was correct, and I had to send a brigade of infantry out to help Sturgis, thus relieving him from a rather serious predicament. Indeed, the enemy was present in pretty strong force, both cavalry and infantry, and from his vicious attack on Sturgis it looked very much as though he intended to bring on a general engagement.

Under such circumstances I deemed it advisable that the responsible commanders of the army should be present, and so informed them. My communication brought

Parke and Granger to the front without delay, but Foster could not come, since the hardships of the winter had reopened an old wound received during the Mexican War, and brought on much suffering. By the time Parke and Granger arrived, however, the enemy, who it turned out was only making a strong demonstration to learn the object of our movement on Dandridge, seemed satisfied with the results of his reconnoissance, and began falling back toward Bull's Gap. Meanwhile Parke and Granger concluded that Dandridge was an untenable point, and hence decided to withdraw a part of the army to Strawberry Plains; and the question of supplies again coming up, it was determined to send the Fourth Corps to the south side of the French Broad to obtain subsistence, provided we could bridge the river so that men could get across the deep and icy stream without suffering.

I agreed to undertake the construction of a bridge on condition that each division should send to the ford twenty-five wagons with which to make it. This being acceded to, Harker's brigade began the work next morning at a favorable point a few miles down the river. As my quota of wagons arrived, they were drawn into the stream one after another by the wheel team, six men in each wagon, and as they successively reached the other side of the channel the mules were unhitched, the pole of each wagon run under the hind axle of the one just in front, and the tailboards used so as to span the slight space between them. The plan worked well as long as the material lasted, but no other wagons than my twenty-five coming on the ground, the work stopped when the bridge was only half constructed. Informed of the delay and its cause, in sheer desperation I finished the bridge by taking from my own division all the wagons needed to make up the deficiency.

It was late in the afternoon when the work was finished, and I began putting over one of my brigades; but in the midst of its crossing word came that Longstreet's army was moving to attack us, which caused an abandonment of the foraging project, and orders quickly followed to retire to Strawberry Plains, the retrograde movement to begin forthwith. I sent to headquarters information of the plight I was in—baggage and supplies on the bank and wagons in the stream—begged to know what was to become of them if we were to hurry off at a moment's notice, and suggested that the movement be delayed until I could recover my transportation. Receiving in reply no assurances that I should be relieved from my dilemma—and, in fact, nothing satisfactory—I determined to take upon myself the responsibility of remaining on the ground long enough to get my wagons out of the river; so I sent out a heavy force to watch for the enemy, and with the remainder of the command went to work to break up the bridge.

Before daylight next morning I had recovered everything without interference by Longstreet, who, it was afterward ascertained, was preparing to move east toward Lynchburg instead of marching to attack us; the small demonstration against Dandridge, being made simply to deceive us as to his ultimate object. I marched to Strawberry Plains unmolested, and by taking the route over Bay's Mountain, a shorter one than that followed by the main body of our troops, reached the point of rendezvous as soon as the most of the army, for the road it followed was not only longer, but badly cut up by trains that had recently passed over it.

Shortly after getting into camp, the beef contractor came in and reported that a detachment of the enemy's cavalry had captured my herd of beef cattle. This caused me much chagrin at first, but the commissary of my division soon put in an appearance, and assured me that the loss would not be very disastrous to us nor of much benefit to the enemy, since the cattle were so poor and weak that they could not be driven off. A reconnoissance in force verified the Commissary's statement. From its inability to travel, the herd, after all efforts to carry it off had proved ineffectual, had been abandoned by its captors.

After the troops from Chattanooga arrived in the vicinity

of Knoxville and General Sherman had returned to Chattanooga, the operations in East Tennessee constituted a series of blunders, lasting through the entire winter; a state of affairs doubtless due, in the main, to the fact that the command of the troops was so frequently changed. Constant shifting of responsibility from one to another ensued from the date that General Sherman, after assuring himself that Knoxville was safe, devolved the command on Burnside. It had already been intimated to Burnside that he was to be relieved, and in consequence he was inactive and apathetic, confining his operations to an aimless expedition whose advance extended only as far as Blain's crossroads, whence it was soon withdrawn. Meanwhile General Foster had superseded Burnside, but physical disabilities rendered him incapable of remaining in the field, and then the chief authority devolved on Parke. By this time the transmission of power seemed almost a disease; at any rate it was catching, so, while we were *en route* to Dandridge, Parke transferred the command to Granger. The latter next unloaded it on me, and there is no telling what the final outcome would have been had I not entered a protest against a further continuance of the practice, which remonstrance brought Granger to the front at Dandridge.

While the events just narrated were taking place, General Grant had made a visit to Knoxville—about the last of December—and arranged to open the railroad between there and Chattanooga, with a view to supplying the troops in East Tennessee by rail in the future, instead of through Cumberland Gap by a tedious line of wagon-trains. In pursuance of his plan the railroad had already been opened to Loudon, but here much delay occurred on account of the long time it took to rebuild the bridge over the Tennessee. Therefore supplies were still very scarce, and as our animals were now dying in numbers from starvation, and the men were still on short allowance, it became necessary that some of the troops east of Knoxville should get nearer to their dépôt, and also be in a position to take part in the coming Georgia campaign, or render assistance to

General Thomas, should General Johnston (who had succeeded in command of the Confederate Army) make any demonstration against Chattanooga. Hence my division was ordered to take station at Loudon, Tennessee, and I must confess that we took the road for that point with few regrets, for a general disgust prevailed regarding our useless marches during the winter.

At this time my faithful scout Card and his younger brother left me, with the determination, as I have heretofore related, to avenge their brother's death. No persuasion could induce Card to remain longer, for knowing that my division's next operation would be toward Atlanta, and being ignorant of the country below Dalton, he recognized and insisted that his services would then become practically valueless.

At Loudon, where we arrived January 27, supplies were more plentiful, and as our tents and extra clothing reached us there in a few days, everyone grew contented and happy. Here a number of my regiments, whose terms of service were about to expire, went through the process of "veteranizing," and, notwithstanding the trials and hardships of the preceding nine months, they re-enlisted almost to a man.

When everything was set in motion toward recuperating and refitting my troops, I availed myself of the opportunity during a lull that then existed to take a short leave of absence—a privilege I had not indulged in since entering the service in 1853. This leave I spent in the North with much benefit to my physical condition, for I was much run down by fatiguing service, and not a little troubled by intense pain which I at times still suffered from my experience in the unfortunate hand-car incident on the Cumberland Mountains the previous July. I returned from leave the latter part of March, rejoining my division with the expectation that the campaign in that section would begin as early as April.

On the 12th of March, 1864, General Grant was assigned to the command of the armies of the United States, as general-in-chief. He was already in Washington, whither he had gone to receive his commission as lieutenant-general. Shortly after his arrival there, he commenced to rearrange the different commands in the army to suit the plans which he intended to enter upon in the spring, and out of this grew a change in my career. Many jealousies and much ill-feeling, the outgrowth of former campaigns, existed among officers of high grade in the Army of the Potomac in the winter of 1864, and several general officers were to be sent elsewhere in consequence. Among these, General Alfred Pleasonton was to be relieved from the command of the cavalry, General Grant having expressed to the President dissatisfaction that so little had hitherto been accomplished by that arm of the service, and I was selected as chief of the cavalry corps of the Army of the Potomac, receiving on the night of the 23d of March from General Thomas at Chattanooga the following telegram:

"MARCH 23, 1864.
"MAJOR-GENERAL THOMAS, Chattanooga:
    "Lieutenant-General Grant directs that Major-General Sheridan immediately repair to Washington and report to the Adjutant-General of the Army.
                                    "H. W. HALLECK,
                            "Major-General, Chief-of-Staff."

I was not informed of the purpose for which I was to proceed to Washington, but I conjectured that it meant a severing of my relations with the Second Division, Fourth Army Corps. I at once set about obeying the order, and as but little preparation was necessary, I started for Chattanooga the next day, without taking any formal leave of the troops I had so long commanded. I could not do it; the bond existing between them and me had grown to such depth of attachment that I feared to trust my emotions in any formal parting from a body of soldiers who, from our mutual devotion, had long before lost their official designation, and by general consent within and without the command were called "Sheridan's Division." When I took the train at the station the whole command was collected on the hill-sides around to see me off. They had assembled spontaneously, officers and men, and as the cars moved out for Chattanooga they waved me farewell with demonstrations of affection.

A parting from such friends was indeed to be regretted. They had never given me any trouble, nor done anything that could bring aught but honor to themselves. I had confidence in them, and I believe they had in me. They were ever steady, whether in victory or in misfortune, and as I tried always to be with them, to put them into the hottest fire if good could be gained, or save them from unnecessary loss as occasion required, they amply repaid all my care and anxiety, courageously and readily meeting all demands in every emergency that arose.

In Kentucky, nearly two years before, my lot had been cast with about half of the twenty-five regiments of infantry that I was just leaving, the rest joining me after Chickamauga. It was practically a new arm of the service to me, for although I was an infantry officer, yet the only large command which up to that time I had controlled was composed of cavalry, and most of my experience had been gained in this arm of the service. I had to study hard to be able to master all the needs of such a force, to feed and clothe it and guard all its interests. When undertaking these responsibilities I felt that if I met them faithfully, recompense would surely come through the hearty response that soldiers always make to conscientious exertion on the part of their superiors, and not only that more could be gained in that way than from the use of any species of influence, but that the reward would be quicker. Therefore I always tried to look after their comfort personally; selected their camps, and provided abundantly for their subsistence, and the road they opened for me shows that my work was not in vain. I regretted deeply to have to leave such soldiers, and felt that they were sorry I was going, and even now I could not, if I would, retain other than the warmest sentiments of esteem and the tenderest affection for the officers and men of "Sheridan's Division," Army of the Cumberland.

On reaching Chattanooga I learned from General Thomas the purpose for which I had been ordered to Washington. I was to be assigned to the command of the Cavalry Corps of the Army of the Potomac. The information staggered me at first, for I knew well the great responsibilities of such a position; moreover, I was but slightly acquainted with military operations in Virginia, and then, too, the higher officers of the Army of the Potomac were little known to me, so at the moment I felt loth to undergo the trials of the new position. Indeed, I knew not a soul in Washington except General Grant and General Halleck, and them but slightly, and no one in General Meade's army, from the commanding general down, except a few officers in the lower grades, hardly any of whom I had seen since graduating at the Military Academy.

Thus it is not much to be wondered at that General Thomas's communication momentarily upset me. But there was no help for it, so after reflecting on the matter a little I concluded to make the best of the situation. As in Virginia I should be operating in a field with which I was wholly unfamiliar, and among so many who were strangers, it seemed to me that it would be advisable to have, as a chief staff-officer, one who had had service in the East, if an available man could be found. In weighing all these considerations in my mind, I fixed upon Captain James W. Forsyth, of the Eighteenth Infantry, then in the regular brigade at Chattanooga—a dear friend of mine, who had served in the Army of the Potomac, in the Peninsula and Antietam campaigns. He at once expressed a desire to accept a position on my staff, and having obtained by the next day the necessary authority, he and I started for Washington, accompanied by Lieutenant T. W. C. Moore, one of my aides, leaving behind Lieutenant M. V. Sheridan, my other aide, to forward out horses as soon as they should be sent down to Chattanooga from Loudon, after which he was to join me.

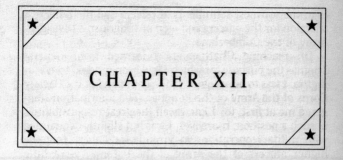

CHAPTER XII

ACCOMPANIED BY Captain Forsyth and Lieutenant Moore, I arrived in Washington on the morning of April 4, 1864, and stopped at Willard's Hotel, where, staying temporarily, were many officers of the Army of the Potomac *en route* to their commands from leave at the North. Among all these, however, I was an entire stranger, and I cannot now recall that I met a single individual whom I had ever before known.

With very little delay after reaching my hotel I made my way to General Halleck's headquarters and reported to that officer, having learned in the meantime that General Grant was absent from the city. General Halleck talked to me for a few minutes, outlining briefly the nature and duties of my new command, and the general military situation in Virginia. When he had finished all he had to say about these matters, he took me to the office of the Secretary of War, to present me to Mr. Stanton. During the ceremony of introduction, I could feel that Mr. Stanton was eying me closely and searchingly, endeavoring to form some estimate of one about whom he knew absolutely nothing, and whose career probably had never been called to his attention until General Grant decided to order me East, after my name had been suggested by General Halleck in an interview the two generals had with Mr. Lincoln. I was rather young in appearance—looking even under than over thirty-three years—but five feet five inches in height, and thin almost to emaciation, weighing only one hundred and fifteen pounds. If I had ever possessed any self-assertion in manner or speech, it certainly vanished in the presence of the imperious Secretary, whose name at the time was the synonym of all that was cold and formal. I never learned what Mr. Stanton's first impressions of me were, and his guarded and rather calculating manner gave at this time no intimation that they were either favorable or unfavorable, but his frequent commendation in after years indicated that I gained his good-will before the close of the war, if not when I first came to his notice; and a more intimate association convinced me that the cold and cruel characteristics popularly ascribed to him were more mythical than real.

When the interview with the Secretary was over, I proceeded with General Halleck to the White House to pay my respects to the President. Mr. Lincoln received me very cordially, offering both his hands, and saying that he hoped I would fulfill the expectations of General Grant in the new command I was about to undertake, adding that thus far the cavalry of the Army of the Potomac had not done all it might have done, and wound up our short conversation by quoting that stale interrogation so prevalent during the early years of the war, "Who ever saw a dead cavalryman?" His manner did not impress me, however, that in asking the question he had meant anything beyond a jest, and I parted from the President convinced that he did not believe all that the query implied.

After taking leave I separated from General Halleck, and on returning to my hotel found there an order from the War Department assigning me to the command of the Cavalry Corps, Army of the Potomac. The next morning, April 5, as I took the cars for the headquarters of the Army of the Potomac, General Grant, who had returned to Washington the previous night from a visit to his family, came aboard the train on his way to Culpeper Court House, and on the journey down I learned among other things that he had wisely determined to continue personally in the field, associating himself with General Meade's army, where he could supervise its movements directly, and at the same time escape the annoyances which, should he remain in Washington, would surely arise from solicitude for the safety of the Capital while the campaign was in progress. When we reached Brandy Station, I left the train and reported to General Meade, who told me that the headquarters of the Cavalry Corps were some distance back from the Station, and indicated the general locations of the different divisions of the corps, also giving me, in the short time I remained with him, much information regarding their composition.

I reached the Cavalry Corps headquarters on the evening of April 5, 1864, and the next morning issued orders assuming command. General Pleasonton had but recently been relieved, and many of his staff-officers were still on duty at the headquarters awaiting the arrival of the permanent commander. I resolved to retain the most of these officers on my staff, and although they were all unknown to me when I decided on this course, yet I never had reason to regret it, nor to question the selections made by my predecessor.

The corps consisted of three cavalry divisions and twelve batteries of horse artillery. Brigadier-General A. T. A. Torbert was in command of the First Division, which was composed of three brigades; Brigadier-General D. McM. Gregg, of the Second, consisting of two brigades; and Brigadier-General J. H. Wilson was afterward assigned to command the Third, also comprising two brigades. Captain Robinson, a veteran soldier of the Mexican war, was chief of artillery, and as such had a general supervision of that arm, though the batteries, either as units or in sections, were assigned to the different divisions in campaign.

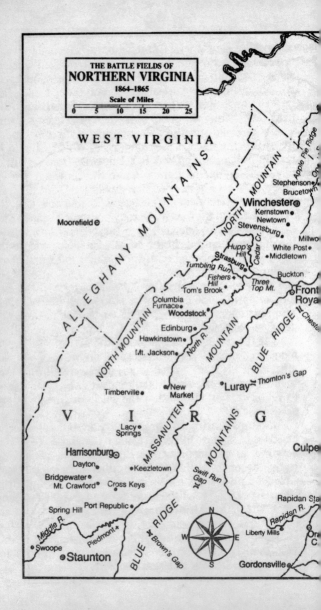

THE BATTLE FIELDS OF
NORTHERN VIRGINIA
1864–1865
Scale of Miles
0   5   10   15   20   25

WEST VIRGINIA

Apple Pie Ridge

NORTH MOUNTAIN

Stephenson
Brucetown

Winchester
Kernstown
Newtown
Stevensburg

Millwo
White Post
Middletown

Moorefield

Hupp's
Hill
Strasburg
Tumbling Run

Cedar Cr.

Buckton

Fishers
Hill
Tom's Brook

Three
Top Mt.

**Front
Roya**

Columbia
Furnace
Woodstock

Chester

Edinburg
Hawkinstown

North R.

BLUE RIDGE MOUNTAIN

Mt. Jackson

Timberville
**New
Market**

Luray Thornton's Gap

A L L E G H A N Y   M O U N T A I N S

NORTH MOUNTAIN

V I R G

Lacy
Springs

Harrisonburg
Dayton
Bridgewater
Mt. Crawford Cross Keys
Keezletown

MASSANUTTEN MOUNTAINS

Swift Run
Gap

Culpe

Spring Hill Port Republic
Middle R. Piedmont
Swoope **Staunton**

BLUE RIDGE
Brown's Gap

Rapidan Sta
Rapidan R.
Liberty Mills

N
W   E
S

Gordonsville

Or
C.

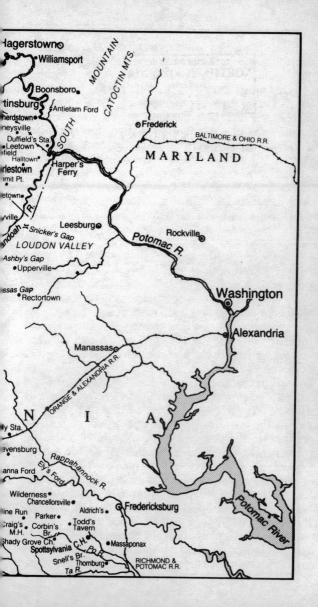

Each one of my division commanders was a soldier by profession. Torbert graduated from the Military Academy in 1855, and was commissioned in the infantry, in which arm he saw much service on the frontier, in Florida, and on the Utah expedition. At the beginning of hostilities in April, 1861, he was made a colonel of New Jersey volunteers, and from that position was promoted in the fall of 1862 to be a brigadier-general, thereafter commanding a brigade of infantry in the Army of the Potomac till, in the redistribution of generals, after Grant came to the East, he was assigned to the First Cavalry Division.

Gregg graduated in 1855 also, and was appointed to the First Dragoons, with which regiment, up to the breaking out of the war, he saw frontier service extending from Fort Union, New Mexico, through to the Pacific coast, and up into Oregon and Washington Territories, where I knew him slightly. In the fall of 1861 he became colonel of the Eighth Pennsylvania Cavalry, and a year later was made a brigadier-general. He then succeeded to the command of a division of cavalry, and continued in that position till the close of his service, at times temporarily commanding the Cavalry Corps. He was the only division commander I had whose experience had been almost exclusively derived from the cavalry arm.

Wilson graduated in 1860 in the Topographical Engineers, and was first assigned to duty in Oregon, where he remained till July, 1861. In the fall of that year his active service in the war began, and he rose from one position to another, in the East and West, till, while on General Grant's staff, he was made a brigadier-general in the fall of 1863 in reward for services performed during the Vicksburg campaign and for engineer duty at Chattanooga preceding the battle of Missionary Ridge. At my request he was selected to command the Third Division. General Grant thought highly of him, and, expecting much from his active mental and physical ability, readily assented to assign him in place of General Kilpatrick. The only other general officers in the corps were Brigadier-General Wesley Merritt, Brigadier-General George A. Custer, and Brigadier-General Henry E. Davies, each commanding a brigade.

In a few days after my arrival at Brandy Station I reviewed my new command, which consisted of about twelve thousand officers and men, with the same number of horses in passable trim. Many of the general officers of the army were present at the review, among them Generals Meade, Hancock, and Sedgwick. Sedgwick being an old dragoon, came to renew his former associations with mounted troops, and to encourage me, as he jestingly said, because of the traditional prejudices the cavalrymen were supposed to hold against being commanded by an infantry officer. The corps presented a fine appearance at the review, and so far as the health and equipment of the men were concerned the showing was good and satisfactory, but the horses were thin and very much worn down by excessive and, it seemed to me, unnecessary picket duty, for the cavalry picket-line almost completely encircled the infantry and artillery camps of the army, covering a distance, on a continuous line, of nearly sixty miles, with hardly a mounted Confederate confronting it at any point. From the very beginning of the war the enemy had shown more wisdom respecting his cavalry than we. Instead of wasting its strength by a policy of disintegration he, at an early day, had organized his mounted force into compact masses, and plainly made it a favorite; and, as usual, he was now husbanding the strength of his horses by keeping them to the rear, so that in the spring he could bring them out in good condition for the impending campaign.

Before and at the review I took in this situation, and determined to remedy it if possible; so in due time I sought an interview with General Meade and informed him that, as the effectiveness of my command rested mainly on the strength of its horses, I thought the duty it was then performing was both burdensome and wasteful. I also gave him my idea as to what the cavalry should do, the main purport of which was that it ought to be kept concentrated to fight the enemy's cavalry. Heretofore, the commander of the Cavalry Corps had been, virtually, but an adjunct at army headquarters—a sort of chief of cavalry—and my proposition seemed to stagger General Meade not a little. I knew that it would be difficult to overcome the recognized custom of using the cavalry for the protection of trains and the establishment of cordons around the infantry corps, and so far subordinating its operations to the movements of the main army that in name only was it a corps at all, but still I thought it my duty to try.

At first General Meade would hardly listen to my proposition, for he was filled with the prejudices that, from the beginning of the war, had pervaded the army regarding the importance and usefulness of cavalry, General Scott then predicting that the contest would be settled by artillery, and thereafter refusing the services of regiment after regiment of mounted troops. General Meade deemed cavalry fit for little more than guard and picket duty, and wanted to know what would protect the transportation trains and artillery reserve, cover the front of moving infantry columns, and secure his flanks from intrusion, if my policy were pursued. I told him that if he would let me use the cavalry as I contemplated, he need have little solicitude in these respects, for, with a mass of ten thousand mounted men, it was my belief that I could make it so lively for the enemy's cavalry that, so far as attacks from it were concerned, the flanks and rear of the Army of the Potomac would require little or no defense, and claimed, further, that moving columns of infantry should take care of their own fronts. I also told him that it was my object to defeat the enemy's cavalry in a general combat, if possible, and by such a result establish a feeling of confidence in my own troops that would enable us after a while to march where we pleased, for the purpose of breaking General Lee's communications and destroying the resources from which his army was supplied.

The idea as here outlined was contrary to Meade's convictions, for though at different times since he commanded the Army of the Potomac considerable bodies of the cavalry had been massed for some special occasion, yet he had never agreed to the plan as a permanency, and could not be bent to it now. He gave little encouragement, therefore, to what I proposed, yet the conversation was immediately beneficial in one way, for when I laid before him the true condition of the cavalry, he promptly relieved it from much of the arduous and harassing picket service it was performing, thus giving me about two weeks in which to nurse the horses before the campaign opened.

The interview also disclosed the fact that the cavalry commander should be, according to General Meade's views, at his headquarters practically as one of his staff, through whom he would give detailed directions as, in his judgment, occasion required. Meade's ideas and mine being so widely divergent, disagreements arose between us later during the battles of the Wilderness, which lack of concord ended in some concessions on his part after the movement toward Spottsylvania Court House began, and although I doubt that his convictions were ever wholly changed, yet from that date on, in the organization of the Army of the Potomac, the cavalry corps became more of a compact body, with the same privileges and responsibilities that attached to the other corps—conditions that never actually existed before.

On the 4th of May the Army of the Potomac moved against Lee, who was occupying a defensive position on the south bank of the Rapidan. After detailing the various detachments which I was obliged to supply for escorts and other mounted duty, I crossed the river with an effective force of about 10,000 troopers. In the interval succeeding my assignment to the command of the cavalry, I had taken the pains to study carefully the topography of the country in eastern Virginia, and felt convinced that, under the policy Meade intended I should follow, there would be little

opportunity for mounted troops to acquit themselves well
in a region so thickly wooded, and traversed by so many
almost parallel streams; but conscious that he would be
compelled sooner or later either to change his mind or
partially give way to the pressure of events, I entered on
the campaign with the loyal determination to aid zealously
in all its plans.

General Lee's army was located in its winter quarters
behind intrenchments that lay along the Rapidan for a
distance of about twenty miles, extending from Barnett's
to Morton's ford. The fords below Morton's were watched
by a few small detachments of Confederate cavalry, the
main body of which, however, was encamped below Hamilton's crossing, where it could draw supplies from the rich
country along the Rappahannock. Only a few brigades of
Lee's infantry guarded the works along the river, the bulk
of it being so situated that it could be thrown to either
flank toward which the Union troops approached.

General Grant adopted the plan of moving by his left
flank, with the purpose of compelling Lee to come out
from behind his intrenchments along Mine Run and fight
on equal terms. Grant knew well the character of country
through which he would have to pass, but he was confident
that the difficulties of operation in the thickly wooded
region of the Wilderness would be counterbalanced by the
facility with which his position would enable him to secure
a new base; and by the fact that as he would thus cover
Washington, there would be little or no necessity for the
authorities there to detach from his force at some inopportune moment for the protection of that city.

In the move forward two divisions of my cavalry took
the advance, Gregg crossing the Rapidan at Ely's ford and
Wilson at Germania ford. Torbert's division remained in
the rear to cover the trains and reserve artillery, holding
from Rapidan Station to Culpeper, and thence through
Stevensburg to the Rappahannock River. Gregg crossed
the Rapidan before daylight, in advance of the Second
Corps, and when the latter reached Ely's ford, he pushed

on to Chancellorsville; Wilson preceded the Fifth Corps to Germania ford, and when it reached the river he made the crossing and moved rapidly by Wilderness Tavern, as far as Parker's Store, from which point he sent a heavy reconnoissance toward Mine Run, the rest of his division bivouacking in a strong position. I myself proceeded to Chancellorsville and fixed my headquarters at that place, where on the 5th I was joined by Torbert's division.

Meanwhile, General Meade had crossed the Rapidan and established his headquarters not far from Germania ford. From that point he was in direct communication with Wilson, whose original instructions from me carried him only as far as Parker's Store, but it being found, during the night of the 4th, that the enemy was apparently unacquainted with the occurrences of the day, Meade directed Wilson to advance in the direction of Craig's Meeting House, leaving one regiment to hold Parker's Store. Wilson with the second brigade encountered Rosser's brigade of cavalry just beyond the Meeting House, and drove it back rapidly a distance of about two miles, holding it there till noon, while his first brigade was halted on the north side of Robinson's Run near the junction of the Catharpen and Parker's Store roads.

Up to this time Wilson had heard nothing of the approach of the Fifth Corps, and the situation becoming threatening, he withdrew the second brigade to the position occupied by the first, but scarcely had he done so when he learned that at an early hour in the forenoon the enemy's infantry had appeared in his rear at Parker's Store and cut off his communication with General Meade. Surprised at this, he determined to withdraw to Todd's Tavern, but before his resolution could be put into execution the Confederates attacked him with a heavy force, and at the same time began pushing troops down the Catharpen road. Wilson was now in a perplexing situation, sandwiched between the Confederates who had cut him off in the rear at Parker's store and those occupying the Catharpen road, but he extricated his command by passing it around the

latter force, and reached Todd's Tavern by crossing the Po
River at Corbin's bridge. General Meade discovering that
the enemy had interposed at Parker's store between Wilson
and the Fifth Corps, sent me word to go to Wilson's relief,
and this was the first intimation I received that Wilson
had been pushed out so far, but surmising that he would
retire in the direction of Todd's Tavern I immediately despatched Gregg's division there to his relief. Just beyond
Todd's Tavern Gregg met Wilson, who was now being followed by the enemy's cavalry. The pursuing force was soon
checked, and then driven back to Shady Grove Church,
while Wilson's troops fell in behind Gregg's line, somewhat
the worse for their morning's adventure.

When the Army of the Potomac commenced crossing
the Rapidan on the 4th, General J. E. B. Stuart, commanding the Confederate cavalry, began concentrating his
command on the right of Lee's infantry, bringing it from
Hamilton's crossing and other points where it had been
wintering. Stuart's force at this date was a little more than
eight thousand men, organized in two divisions, commanded by Generals Wade Hampton and Fitzhugh Lee.
Hampton's division was composed of three brigades, commanded by Generals Gordon, Young, and Rosser; Fitzhugh
Lee's division comprised three brigades also, Generals
W. H. F. Lee, Lomax, and Wickham commanding them.

Information of this concentration, and of the additional
fact that the enemy's cavalry about Hamilton's crossing
was all being drawn in, reached me on the 5th, which
obviated all necessity for my moving on that point as I
intended at the onset of the campaign. The responsibility
for the safety of our trains and of the left flank of the army
still continued, however, so I made such dispositions of
my troops as to secure these objects by holding the line
of the Brock road beyond the Furnaces, and thence around
to Todd's Tavern and Piney Branch Church. On the 6th,
through some false information, General Meade became
alarmed about his left flank, and sent me the following
note:

"Headquarters Army of the Potomac,
             "May 6, 1864—1 o'clock p.m.
"Major-General Sheridan,
     "Commanding Cavalry Corps:
   "Your despatch of 11.45 a.m. received. General Hancock
has been heavily pressed, and his left turned. The major-
general commanding thinks that you had better draw in
your cavalry, so as to secure the protection of the trains.
The order requiring an escort for the wagons to-night has
been rescinded.
                              "A. A. Humphreys,
                      "Major-General, Chief-of-Staff."

On the morning of the 6th Custer's and Devin's brigades
had been severely engaged at the Furnaces before I received
the above note. They had been most successful in repulsing
the enemy's attacks, however, and I felt that the line taken
up could be held; but the despatch from General Humphreys was alarming, so I drew all the cavalry close in
toward Chancellorsville. It was found later that Hancock's
left had not been turned, and the points thus abandoned
had to be regained at a heavy cost in killed and wounded,
to both the cavalry and the infantry.

On the 7th of May, under directions from headquarters,
Army of the Potomac, the trains were put in motion to go
into park at Piney Branch Church, in anticipation of the
movement that was about to be made for the possession
of Spottsylvania Court House. I felt confident that the order
to move the trains there had been given without a full
understanding of the situation, for Piney Branch Church
was now held by the enemy, a condition which had resulted
from the order withdrawing the cavalry on account of the
supposed disaster to Hancock's left the day before; but I
thought the best way to remedy matters was to hold the
trains in the vicinity of Aldrich's till the ground on which
it was intended to park them should be regained.

This led to the battle of Todd's Tavern, a spirited fight
for the possession of the crossroads at that point, partic-

ipated in by the enemy's cavalry and Gregg's division, and two brigades of Torbert's division, the latter commanded by Merritt, as Torbert became very ill on the 6th, and had to be sent to the rear. To gain the objective point—the crossroads—I directed Gregg to assail the enemy on the Catharpen road with Irvin Gregg's brigade and drive him over Corbin's bridge, while Merritt attacked him with the Reserve brigade on the Spottsylvania road in conjunction with Davies's brigade of Gregg's division, which was to be put in on the Piney Branch Church road, and unite with Merritt's left. Davies's and Irvin Gregg's brigades on my right and left flanks met with some resistance, yet not enough to deter them from executing their orders. In front of Merritt the enemy held on more stubbornly, however, and there ensued an exceedingly severe and, at times, fluctuating fight. Finally the Confederates gave way, and we pursued them almost to Spottsylvania Court House; but deeming it prudent to recall the pursuers about dark, I encamped Gregg's and Merritt's divisions in the open fields to the east of Todd's Tavern.

During the preceding three days the infantry corps of the army had been engaged in the various conflicts known as the battles of the Wilderness. The success of the Union troops in those battles had not been all that was desired, and General Grant now felt that it was necessary to throw himself on Lee's communications if possible, while preserving his own intact by prolonging the movement to the left. Therefore, on the evening of the 7th he determined to shift his whole army toward Spottsylvania Court House, and initiated the movement by a night march of the infantry to Todd's Tavern. In view of what was contemplated, I gave orders to Gregg and Merritt to move at daylight on the morning of the 8th, for the purpose of gaining possession of Snell's bridge over the Po River, the former by the crossing at Corbin's bridge and the latter by the Block House. I also directed Wilson, who was at Alsop's house, to take possession of Spottsylvania as early as possible on the morning of the 8th, and then move into position at

Snell's bridge conjointly with the other two divisions. Wilson's orders remained as I had issued them, so he moved accordingly and got possession of Spottsylvania, driving the enemy's cavalry a mile beyond, as will be seen by the following despatch sent me at 9 A.M. of the 8th:

"HEADQUARTERS THIRD DIVISION, CALVARY CORPS,
ARMY OF THE POTOMAC.
"SPOTTSYLVANIA COURT HOUSE, May 8, 1864–9 A.M.
"LIEUTENANT-COLONEL FORSYTH, CHIEF-OF-STAFF, C. C.
"Have run the enemy's cavalry a mile from Spottsylvania Court House; have charged them, and drove them through the village; am fighting now with a considerable force, supposed to be *Lee's* division. Everything all right.
"J. H. WILSON,
"Brigadier-General Commanding."

During the night of the 7th General Meade arrived at Todd's Tavern and modified the orders I had given Gregg and Merritt, directing Gregg simply to hold Corbin's bridge, and Merritt to move out in front of the infantry column marching on the Spottsylvania road. Merritt proceeded to obey, but in advancing, our cavalry and infantry became intermingled in the darkness, and much confusion and delay was the consequence. I had not been duly advised of these changes in Gregg's and Merritt's orders, and for a time I had fears for the safety of Wilson, but while he was preparing to move on to form his junction with Gregg and Merritt at Snell's bridge, the advance of Anderson (who was now commanding Longstreet's corps) appeared on the scene and drove him from Spottsylvania.

Had Gregg and Merritt been permitted to proceed as they were originally instructed, it is doubtful whether the battles fought at Spottsylvania would have occurred, for these two divisions would have encountered the enemy at the Po River, and so delayed his march as to enable our infantry to reach Spottsylvania first, and thus force Lee to take up a line behind the Po. I had directed Wilson to move from the left by "the Gate" through Spottsylvania to Snell's bridge, while Gregg and Merritt were to advance to the same point by Shady Grove and the Block House. There was nothing to prevent at least a partial success of these operations; that is to say, the concentration of the three divisions in front of Snell's bridge, even if we could not actually have gained it. But both that important point and the bridge on the Block House road were utterly ignored, and Lee's approach to Spottsylvania left entirely unobstructed, while three divisions of cavalry remained practically ineffective by reason of disjointed and irregular instructions.

On the morning of the 8th, when I found that such orders had been given, I made some strong remonstrances against the course that had been pursued, but it was then too late to carry out the combinations I had projected the night before, so I proceeded to join Merritt on the Spottsylvania road. On reaching Merritt I found General Warren making complaint that the cavalry were obstructing his infantry column, so I drew Merritt off the road, and the leading division of the Fifth Corps pushed up to the front. It got into line about 11 o'clock, and advanced to take the village, but it did not go very far before it struck Anderson's corps, and was hurled back with heavy loss. This ended all endeavor to take Spottsylvania that day.

A little before noon General Meade sent for me, and when I reached his headquarters I found that his peppery temper had got the better of his good judgment, he showing a disposition to be unjust, laying blame here and there for the blunders that had been committed. He was particularly severe on the cavalry, saying, among other things, that it had impeded the march of the Fifth Corps by occupying the Spottsylvania road. I replied that if this were true, he himself had ordered it there without my knowledge. I also told him that he had broken up my combinations, exposed Wilson's division to disaster, and kept Gregg unnecessarily idle, and further, repelled his insinuations by saying that such disjointed operations as he had been requiring of the cavalry for the last four days would render the corps inefficient and useless before long. Meade was very much irritated, and I was none the less so. One word brought on another, until, finally, I told him that I could whip Stuart if he (Meade) would only let me, but since he insisted on giving the cavalry directions without consulting or even notifying me, he could henceforth command the Cavalry Corps himself—that I would not give it another order.

The acrimonious interview ended with this remark, and after I left him he went to General Grant's headquarters and repeated the conversation to him, mentioning that I had said that I could whip Stuart. At this General Grant remarked: "Did he say so? Then let him go out and do it." This intimation was immediately acted upon by General Meade, and a little later the following order came to me:

> "HEADQUARTERS ARMY OF THE POTOMAC.
> "May 8th, 1864—1 P.M.
>
> "GENERAL SHERIDAN,
>
>   "Commanding Cavalry Corps.
>
>   "The major-general commanding directs you to immediately concentrate your available mounted force, and with your ammunition trains and such supply trains as are filled (exclusive of ambulances) proceed against the enemy's cavalry, and when your supplies are exhausted, proceed *via* New Market and Green Bay to Haxall's Landing on the James River, there communicating with General Butler, procuring supplies and return to this army. Your dismounted men will be left with the train here.
>
> "A. A. HUMPHREYS,
> "Major-General, Chief-of-Staff."

As soon as the above order was received I issued instructions for the concentration of the three divisions of cavalry at Aldrich's to prepare for the contemplated expedition. Three days' rations for the men were distributed, and half rations of grain for one day were doled out for the horses. I sent for Gregg, Merritt, and Wilson and communicated the order to them, saying at the same time, "We are going out to fight Stuart's cavalry in consequence of a suggestion from me; we will give him a fair, square fight; we are strong, and I know we can beat him, and in view of my recent representations to General Meade I shall expect nothing but success." I also indicated to my division commanders the line of march I should take—moving in one column around the right flank of Lee's army to get in its rear—and stated at the same time that it was my intention to fight Stuart wherever he presented himself, and if possible go through to Haxall's Landing; but that if Stuart should successfully interpose between us and that point, we would swing back to the Army of the Potomac by passing around the enemy's left flank by way of Gordonsville. At first the proposition seemed to surprise the division commanders somewhat, for hitherto even the boldest mounted expeditions had been confined to a hurried ride through the enemy's country, without purpose of fighting more than enough to escape in case of molestation, and here and there to destroy a bridge. Our move would be a challenge to Stuart for a cavalry duel behind Lee's lines, in his own country, but the advantages which it was reasonable to anticipate from the plan being quickly perceived, each division commander entered into its support unhesitatingly, and at once set about preparing for the march next day.

CHAPTER XIII

THE EXPEDITION WHICH RESULTED IN the battle of Yellow Tavern and the death of General Stuart started from the vicinity of Aldrich's toward Fredericksburg early on the morning of May 9, 1864, marching on the plank-road, Merritt's division leading. When the column reached Tabernacle Church it headed almost due east to the telegraph road, and thence down that highway to Thornburg, and from that point through Childsburg to Anderson's crossing of the North Anna River, it being my desire to put my command south of that stream if possible, where it could procure forage before it should be compelled to fight. The corps moved at a walk, the three divisions on the same road, making a column nearly thirteen miles in length, and marched around the right flank of the enemy unsuspected until my rear guard had passed Massaponax Church. Although the column was very long, I preferred to move it all on one road rather than to attempt combinations for carrying the divisions to any given point by different routes. Unless the separate commands in an expedition of this nature are very prompt in movement, and each fully equal to overcoming at once any obstacle it may meet,

157

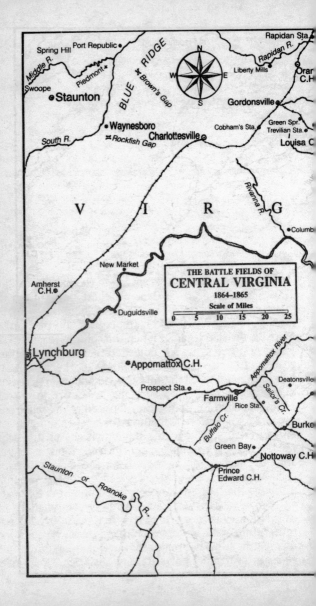

combinations rarely work out as expected; besides, an engagement was at all times imminent, hence it was specially necessary to keep the whole force well together.

As soon as the Ny, Po, and Ta rivers were crossed, each of which streams would have afforded an excellent defensive line to the enemy, all anxiety as to our passing around Lee's army was removed, and our ability to cross the North Anna placed beyond doubt. Meanwhile General Stuart had discovered what we were about, and he set his cavalry in motion, sending General Fitzhugh Lee to follow and attack my rear on the Childsburg road, Stuart himself marching by way of Davenport's bridge, on the North Anna, toward Beaver Dam Station, near which place his whole command was directed to unite the next day.

My column having passed the Ta River, Stuart attacked its rear with considerable vigor, in the hope that he could delay my whole force long enough to permit him to get at least a part of his command in my front; but this scheme was frustrated by Davies's brigade, which I directed to fight as a rear-guard, holding on at one position and then at another along the line of march just enough to deter the enemy from a too rapid advance. Davies performed this responsible and trying duty with tact and good judgment, following the main column steadily as it progressed to the south, and never once permitting Fitzhugh Lee's advance to encroach far enough to compel a halt of my main body. About dark Merritt's division crossed the North Anna at Anderson's ford, while Gregg and Wilson encamped on the north side, having engaged the enemy, who still hung on my rear up to a late hour at night.

After Merritt's division passed the river, Custer's brigade proceeded on to Beaver Dam Station to cut the Virginia Central railroad. Before reaching the station he met a small force of the enemy, but this he speedily drove off, recapturing from it about four hundred Union prisoners, who had been taken recently in the Wilderness and were being conducted to Richmond. Custer also destroyed the station, two locomotives, three trains of cars, ninety wagons, from eight to ten miles of railroad and telegraph lines, some two hundred thousand pounds of bacon and other supplies, amounting in all to about a million and a half of rations, and nearly all the medical stores of General Lee's army, which had been moved from Orange Court House either because Lee wished to have them directly in his rear or because he contemplated falling back to the North Anna.

On the morning of the 10th Gregg and Wilson, while crossing the North Anna, were again attacked, but were covered by the division on the south side of the stream; the passage was effected without much loss, notwithstanding the approach of Stuart on the south bank from the direction of Davenport's bridge. The possession of Beaver Dam gave us an important point, as it opened a way toward Richmond by the Negro-foot road. It also enabled us to obtain forage for our wellnigh famished animals, and to prepare for fighting the enemy, who, I felt sure, would endeavor to interpose between my column and Richmond.

Stuart had hardly united his troops near Beaver Dam when he realized that concentrating there was a mistake, so he began making dispositions for remedying his error, and while we leisurely took the Negro-foot road toward Richmond, he changed his tactics and hauled off from my rear, urging his horses to the death in order to get in between Richmond and my column. This he effected about 10 o'clock on the morning of the 11th, concentrating at Yellow Tavern, six miles from the city, on the Brook turnpike. His change of tactics left my march on the 10th practically unmolested, and we quietly encamped that night on the south bank of the South Anna, near Ground Squirrel Bridge. Here we procured an abundance of forage, and as the distance traveled that day had been only fifteen to eighteen miles, men and horses were able to obtain a good rest during the night.

At 2 o'clock in the morning, May 11, Davies's brigade of Gregg's division marched for Ashland to cut the Fredericksburg railroad. Arriving there before the head of the enemy's column, which had to pass through this same place to reach Yellow Tavern, Davies drove out a small force occupying the town, burnt a train of cars and a locomotive, destroyed the railroad for some distance, and rejoined the main column at Allen's Station on the Fredericksburg and Richmond railroad. From Allen's Station the whole command moved on Yellow Tavern, Merritt in the lead, Wilson following, and Gregg in the rear.

The appearance of Davies's brigade at Ashland in the morning had had the effect of further mystifying the enemy as to my intentions; and while he held it incumbent to place himself between me and Richmond, yet he was still so uncertain of my movements that he committed the same fault that he did the first day, when he divided his force and sent a part to follow me on the Childsburg road. He now divided his command again, sending a portion to hang upon my rear, while he proceeded with the rest to Yellow Tavern. This separation not only materially weakened the force which might have been thrown across my line of march, but it also enabled me to attack with almost my entire corps, while occupying the pursuers with a small rear-guard.

By forced marches General Stuart succeeded in reaching Yellow Tavern ahead of me on May 11; and the presence of his troops on the Ashland and Richmond road becoming known to Merritt as he was approaching the Brook turnpike, this general pressed forward at once to the attack. Pushing his division to the front, he soon got possession of the turnpike and drove the enemy back several hundred yards to the east of it. This success had the effect of throwing the head of my column to the east of the pike, and I quickly brought up Wilson and one of Gregg's brigades to take advantage of the situation by forming a line of battle on that side of the road. Meanwhile the enemy, desperate but still confident, poured in a heavy fire from his line and from a battery which enfiladed the Brook road, and made Yellow Tavern an uncomfortably hot place. Gibbs's and Devin's brigades, however, held fast there, while Custer, supported by Chapman's brigade, attacked the enemy's left and battery in a mounted charge.

Custer's charge, with Chapman on his flank and the rest of Wilson's division sustaining him, was brilliantly executed. Beginning at a walk, he increased his gait to a trot, and then at full speed rushed at the enemy. At the same moment the dismounted troops along my whole front moved forward, and as Custer went through the battery, capturing two of the guns with their cannoneers and breaking up the enemy's left, Gibbs and Devin drove his centre and right from the field. Gregg meanwhile, with equal success, charged the force in his rear—Gordon's brigade—and the engagement ended by giving us complete control of the road to Richmond. We captured a number of prisoners, and the casualties on both sides were quite severe, General Stuart himself falling mortally wounded, and General James B. Gordon, one of his brigade commanders, being killed.

After Custer's charge, the Confederate cavalry was badly broken up, the main portion of it being driven in a rout toward Ashland and a small part in the direction of Richmond, which latter force finally rejoined Fitzhugh Lee near Mechanicsville. A reconnoitring party being now sent up the Brook turnpike toward the city, dashed across the South Fork of the Chickahominy, drove a small force from the enemy's exterior intrenchments and went within them. I followed this party, and after a little exploration found between the two lines of works a country road that led across to the pike which runs from Mechanicsville to Richmond. I thought we could go around within the outer line of works by this country road across to the Mechanicsville pike on the south side of the Chickahominy, and encamp the next night at Fair Oaks; so I determined to make the movement after dark, being influenced in this to some extent by reports received during the afternoon from colored people, to the effect that General B. F. Butler's army had reached a small stream on the south side of the James, about four miles south of Richmond. If I could succeed in getting through by this road, not only would I have a shorter line of march to Haxall's landing, but there was also a possibility that I could help Butler somewhat by joining him so near Richmond. Therefore, after making the wounded as comfortable as possible, we commenced the march about 11 o'clock on the night of the 11th, and massed the command on the plateau south of the Meadow bridge near daylight on the 12th.

The enemy, anticipating that I would march by this route, had planted torpedoes along it, and many of these exploded as the column passed over them, killing several horses and wounding a few men, but beyond this we met with no molestation. The torpedoes were loaded shells planted on each side of the road, and so connected by wires attached to friction-tubes in the shells, that when a horse's hoof struck a wire the shell was exploded by the jerk on the improvised lanyard. After the loss of several horses and the wounding of some of the men by these torpedoes, I gave directions to have them removed, if practicable, so about twenty-five of the prisoners were brought up and made to get down on their knees, feel for the wires in the darkness, follow them up and unearth the shells. The prisoners reported the owner of one of the neighboring houses to be the principal person who had engaged in planting these shells, and I therefore directed that some of them be carried and placed in the cellar of his house, arranged to explode if the enemy's column came that way, while he and his family were brought off as prisoners and held till after daylight.

Meanwhile the most intense excitement prevailed in Richmond. The Confederates, supposing that their capital was my objective point, were straining every effort to put it in a state of defense, and had collected between four and five thousand irregular troops, under General Bragg, besides bringing up three brigades of infantry from the force confronting General Butler south of the James River, the alarm being intensified by the retreat, after the defeat at Yellow Tavern, of Stuart's cavalry, now under General Fitzhugh Lee, by way of Ashland to Mechanicsville, on the north side of the Chickahominy, for falling back in that direction, left me between them and Richmond.

Our march during the night of the 11th was very tedious, on account of the extreme darkness and frequent showers of rain; but at daylight on the 12th the head of my column, under Wilson, reached the Mechanicsville pike. Here Wilson, encountering the enemy's works and batteries manned by General Bragg's troops, endeavored to pass. In this he failed, and as soon as I was notified that it was impracticable to reach Fair Oaks by passing between the works and the Chickahominy, Custer's brigade was directed to make the crossing to the north side of the Chickahominy, at the Meadow bridge. Custer moved rapidly for the bridge, but found it destroyed, and that the enemy's cavalry was posted on the north side, in front of Mechanicsville. When this information came back, I ordered Merritt to take his whole division and repair the bridge, instructing him that the crossing must be made at all hazards; for, in view of an impending attack by the enemy's infantry in Richmond, it was necessary that I should have the bridge as a means of egress in case of serious disaster.

All the time that Merritt was occupied in this important duty, the enemy gave great annoyance to the working party by sweeping the bridge with a section of artillery and a fire from the supporting troops, so a small force was thrown across to drive them away. When Merritt had passed two regiments over, they attacked, but were repulsed. The work on the bridge continued, however, notwithstanding this discomfiture; and when it was finished, Merritt crossed nearly all his division, dismounted, and again attacked the enemy, this time carrying the line of temporary breast-works, built with logs and rails, and pursuing his broken troops toward Gaines's Mills.

While Merritt was engaged in this affair, the Confederates advanced from behind their works at Richmond, and attacked Wilson and Gregg. Wilson's troops were dri-

ven back in some confusion at first; but Gregg, in anticipation of attack, had hidden a heavy line of dismounted
men in a bushy ravine on his front, and when the enemy
marched upon it, with much display and under the eye of
the President of the Confederacy, this concealed line
opened a destructive fire with repeating carbines; and at
the same time the batteries of horse-artillery, under Captain Robinson, joining in the contest, belched forth shot
and shell with fatal effect. The galling fire caused the enemy to falter, and while still wavering Wilson rallied his
men, and turning some of them against the right flank of
the Confederates, broke their line, and compelled them to
withdraw for security behind the heavy works thrown up
for the defense of the city in 1862.

By destroying the Meadow bridge and impeding my
column on the Mechanicsville pike, the enemy thought to
corner us completely, for he still maintained the force in
Gregg's rear that had pressed it the day before; but the
repulse of his infantry ended all his hopes of doing us any
serious damage on the limited ground between the defenses of Richmond and the Chickahominy. He felt certain
that on account of the recent heavy rains we could not
cross the Chickahominy except by the Meadow bridge, and
it also seemed clear to him that we could not pass between
the river and his intrenchments; therefore he hoped to
ruin us, or at least compel us to return by the same route
we had taken in coming, in which case we would run into
Gordon's brigade, but the signal repulse of Bragg's infantry
dispelled these illusions.

Even had it not been our good fortune to defeat him,
we could have crossed the Chickahominy if necessary at
several points that were discovered by scouting parties
which, while the engagement was going on, I had sent out
to look up fords. This means of getting out from the cir-
cumscribed plateau I did not wish to use, however, unless
there was no alternative, for I wished to demonstrate to
the Cavalry Corps the impossibility of the enemy's destroying or capturing so large a body of mounted troops.

The chances of seriously injuring us were more favorable to the enemy this time than ever they were afterward, for with the troops from Richmond, comprising three brigades of veterans and about five thousand irregulars on my front and right flank, with Gordon's cavalry in the rear, and Fitzhugh Lee's cavalry on my left flank, holding the Chickahominy and Meadow bridge, I was apparently hemmed in on every side, but relying on the celerity with which mounted troops could be moved, I felt perfectly confident that the seemingly perilous situation could be relieved under circumstances even worse than those then surrounding us. Therefore, instead of endeavoring to get away without a fight, I concluded that there would be little difficulty in withdrawing, even should I be beaten, and none whatever if I defeated the enemy.

In accordance with this view I accepted battle; and the complete repulse of the enemy's infantry, which assailed us from his intrenchments, and of Gordon's cavalry, which pressed Gregg on the Brook road, ended the contest in our favor. The rest of the day we remained on the battlefield undisturbed, and our time was spent in collecting the wounded, burying the dead, grazing the horses, and reading the Richmond journals, two small newsboys with commendable enterprise having come within our lines from the Confederate capital to sell their papers. They were sharp youngsters, and having come well supplied, they did a thrifty business. When their stock in trade was all disposed of they wished to return, but they were so intelligent and observant that I thought their mission involved other purposes than the mere sale of newspapers, so they were held till we crossed the Chickahominy and then turned loose.

After Merritt had crossed the Chickahominy and reached Mechanicsville, I sent him orders to push on to Gaines's Mills. Near the latter place he fell in with the enemy's cavalry again, and sending me word, about 4 o'clock in the afternoon I crossed the Chickahominy with Wilson and Gregg, but when we overtook Merritt he had already brushed the Confederates away, and my whole command went into camp between Walnut Grove and Gaines's Mills.

The main purposes of the expedition had now been executed. They were "to break up General Lee's railroad communications, destroy such dépôts of supplies as could be found in his rear, and to defeat General Stuart's cavalry." Many miles of the Virginia Central and of the Richmond and Fredericksburg railroads were broken up, and several of the bridges on each burnt. At Beaver Dam, Ashland, and other places, about two millions of rations had been captured and destroyed. The most important of all, however, was the defeat of Stuart. Since the beginning of the war this general had distinguished himself by his management of the Confederate mounted force. Under him the cavalry of Lee's army had been nurtured, and had acquired such prestige that it thought itself wellnigh invincible; indeed, in the early years of the war it had proved to be so. This was now dispelled by the successful march we had made in Lee's rear; and the discomfiture of Stuart at Yellow Tavern had inflicted a blow from which entire recovery was impossible.

In its effect on the Confederate cause the defeat of Stuart was most disheartening, but his death was even a greater calamity, as is evidenced by the words of a Confederate writer (Cooke), who says: "Stuart could be ill spared at this critical moment, and General Lee was plunged into the deepest melancholy at the intelligence of his death. When it reached him he retired from those around him, and remained for some time communing with his own heart and memory. When one of his staff entered and spoke of Stuart, General Lee said: 'I can scarcely think of him without weeping.'"

From the camp near Gaines's Mills I resumed the march to Haxall's Landing, the point on the James River contemplated in my instructions where I was to obtain supplies from General Butler. We got to the James on the 14th with all our wounded and a large number of prisoners, and camped between Haxall's and Shirley. The prisoners, as well as the captured guns, were turned over to General Butler's provost-marshal, and our wounded were quickly and kindly cared for by his surgeons. Ample supplies, also, in the way of forage and rations, were furnished us by General Butler, and the work of refitting for our return to the Army of the Potomac was vigorously pushed. By the 17th all was ready, and having learned by scouting parties sent in the direction of Richmond and as far as Newmarket that the enemy's cavalry was returning to Lee's army I started that evening on my return march, crossing the Chickahominy at Jones's bridge, and bivouacking on the 19th near Baltimore crossroads.

My uncertainty of what had happened to the Army of the Potomac in our absence, and as to where I should find it, made our getting back a problem somewhat difficult of solution, particularly as I knew that reinforcements for Lee had come up from the south to Richmond, and that most likely some of these troops were being held at different points on the route to intercept my column. Therefore I determined to pass the Pamunkey River at the White House, and sent to Fort Monroe for a pontoon-bridge on which to make the crossing. While waiting for the pontoons I ordered Custer to proceed with his brigade to Hanover Station, to destroy the railroad bridge over the South Anna, a little beyond that place; at the same time I sent Gregg and Wilson to Cold Harbor, to demonstrate in the direction of Richmond as far as Mechanicsville, so as to cover Custer's movements. Merritt, with the remaining brigades of his division, holding fast at Baltimore crossroads to await events.

After Gregg and Custer had gone, it was discovered that the railroad bridge over the Pamunkey, near the White House, had been destroyed but partially—the cross-ties and stringers being burned in places only—and that it was practicable to repair it sufficiently to carry us over. In view of this information General Merritt's two brigades were at once put on the duty of reconstructing the bridge. By

sending mounted parties through the surrounding country, each man of which would bring in a board or a plank,
Merritt soon accumulated enough lumber for the flooring,
and in one day the bridge was made practicable. On the
22d Gregg, Wilson, and Custer returned. The latter had
gone on his expedition as far as Hanover Station, destroyed
some commissary stores there, and burned two trestle
bridges over Hanover Creek. This done, he deemed it prudent to retire to Hanovertown. The next morning he again
marched to Hanover Station, and there ascertained that a
strong force of the enemy, consisting of infantry, cavalry,
and artillery, was posted at the South Anna bridges. These
troops had gone there from Richmond *en route* to reinforce
Lee. In the face of this impediment Custer's mission could
not be executed fully, so he returned to Baltimore crossroads.

The whole command was drawn in by noon of the 22d,
and that day it crossed the Pamunkey by Merritt's reconstructed bridge, marching to Ayletts, on the Mattapony
River, the same night. Here I learned from citizens, and
from prisoners taken during the day by scouting parties
sent toward Hanover Court House, that Lee had been
forced from his position near Spottsylvania Court House
and compelled to retire to the line of the North Anna. I
then determined to rejoin the Army of the Potomac at the
earliest moment, which I did by making for Chesterfield
Station, where I reported to General Meade on the 24th
of May.

Our return to Chesterfield ended the first independent
expedition the Cavalry Corps had undertaken since coming
under my command, and our success was commended
highly by Generals Grant and Meade, both realizing that
our operations in the rear of Lee had disconcerted and
alarmed that general so much as to aid materially in forcing his retrograde march, and both acknowledged that, by
drawing off the enemy's cavalry during the past fortnight,
we had enabled them to move the Army of the Potomac
and its enormous trains without molestation in the ma-

nœuvres that had carried it to the North Anna. Then, too, great quantities of provisions and munitions of war had been destroyed—stores that the enemy had accumulated at sub-dépôts from strained resources and by difficult means; the railroads that connected Lee with Richmond broken, the most successful cavalry leader of the South killed, and in addition to all this there had been inflicted on the Confederate mounted troops the most thorough defeat that had yet befallen them in Virginia.

When the expedition set out the Confederate authorities in Richmond were impressed, and indeed convinced, that my designs contemplated the capture of that city, and notwithstanding the loss they sustained in the defeat and death of Stuart, and their repulse the succeeding day, they drew much comfort from the fact that I had not entered their capital. Some Confederate writers have continued to hold this theory and conviction since the war. In this view they were and are in error. When Stuart was defeated the main purpose of my instructions had been carried out, and my thoughts then turned to joining General Butler to get supplies. I believed that I could do this by cutting across to the Mechanicsville pike and Fair Oaks on the south side of the Chickahominy, but the failure of Wilson's column to get possession of the outwork which commanded the pike necessitated my crossing at Meadow bridge, and then moving by Mechanicsville and Gaines's Mills instead of by the shorter route. Moreover, my information regarding General Butler's position was incorrect, so that even had I been successful in getting to Fair Oaks by the direct road I should still have gained nothing thereby, for I should still have been obliged to continue down the James River to Haxall's.

CHAPTER XIV

WHEN I REJOINED THE ARMY of the Potomac, near Chesterfield Station, the heavy battles around Spottsylvania had been fought, and the complicated manoeuvres by which the whole Union force was swung across the North Anna were in process of execution. In conjunction with these manoeuvres Wilson's division was sent to the right flank of the army, where he made a reconnoissance south of the North Anna as far as Little River, crossing the former stream near Jericho Mills. Wilson was to operate from day to day on that flank as it swung to the south, covering to New Castle ferry each advance of the infantry and the fords left behind on the march. From the 26th to the 30th these duties kept Wilson constantly occupied, and also necessitated a considerable dispersion of his force, but by the 31st he was enabled to get all his division together again, and crossing to the south side of the Pamunkey at New Castle ferry, he advanced toward Hanover Court House. Near Dr Price's house he encountered a division of the enemy's cavalry under General W. H. F. Lee, and drove it back across Mechamp's Creek, thus opening communication with the right of our infantry resting near Phillips's

Mills. Just as this had been done, a little before dark, Wilson received an order from General Meade directing him to push on toward Richmond until he encountered the Confederates in such strength that he could no longer successfully contend against them, and in compliance with this order occupied Hanover Court House that same day. Resuming his march at daylight on June 1, he went ahead on the Ashland road while sending Chapman's brigade up the south bank of the South Anna to destroy the bridges on that stream. Chapman having succeeded in this work, Wilson re-united his whole command and endeavored to hold Ashland, but finding the Confederate cavalry and infantry there in strong force, he was obliged to withdraw to Dr. Price's house. Here he learned that the army had gone to the left toward Cold Harbor, so on the 2d of June he moved to Hawe's Shop.

While Wilson was operating thus on the right, I had to cover with Gregg's and Torbert's divisions the crossing of the army over the Pamunkey River at and near Hanovertown. Torbert having recovered from the illness which overtook him in the Wilderness, had now returned to duty. The march to turn the enemy's right began on the 26th, Torbert and Gregg in advance, to secure the crossings of the Pamunkey and demonstrate in such manner as to deceive the enemy as much as possible in the movement, the two cavalry divisions being supported by General D. A. Russell's division of the Sixth Corps.

To attain this end in the presence of an ever-watchful foe who had just recently been reinforced in considerable numbers from Richmond and further south—almost enough to make up the losses he had sustained in the Wilderness and at Spottsylvania—required the most vigorous and zealous work on the part of those to whom had been allotted the task of carrying out the initial manœuvres. Torbert started for Taylor's ford on the Pamunkey with directions to demonstrate heavily at that point till after dark, as if the crossing was to be made there, and having thus impressed the enemy, he was to leave a small guard, withdraw quietly, and march to Hanovertown ford, where the real crossing was to be effected. Meanwhile Gregg marched to Littlepage's crossing of the Pamunkey, with instructions to make feints in the same manner as Torbert until after dark, when he was to retire discreetly, leaving a small force to keep up the demonstration, and then march rapidly to Hanovertown crossing, taking with him the pontoon-bridge.

At the proper hour Russell took up the march and followed the cavalry. The troops were in motion all night, undergoing the usual delays incident to night marches, and early on the morning of the 27th the crossing was made, Custer's brigade of Torbert's division driving from the ford about one hundred of the enemy's cavalry, and capturing between thirty and forty prisoners. The remainder of Torbert's division followed this brigade and advanced to Hanovertown, where General Gordon's brigade of Confederate cavalry was met. Torbert attacked this force with Devin's brigade, while he sent Custer to Hawe's Shop, from which point a road leading to the right was taken that brought him in rear of the enemy's cavalry; when the Confederates discovered this manœuvre, they retired in the direction of Hanover Court House. Pursuit continued as far as a little stream called Crump's Creek, and here Torbert was halted, Gregg moving up on his line meanwhile, and Russell encamping near the crossing of the river. This completed our task of gaining a foothold south of the Pamunkey, and on the 28th the main army crossed unharassed and took up a position behind my line, extending south from the river, with the Sixth Corps on the right across the Hanover Court House road at Crump's Creek, the Second Corps on the left of the Sixth, and the Fifth Corps about two miles in front of Hanovertown, its left extending to the Tolopotomy.

There was now much uncertainty in General Grant's mind as to the enemy's whereabouts, and there were received daily the most conflicting statements as to the nature of Lee's movements. It became necessary, therefore, to find out by an actual demonstration what Lee was doing, and I was required to reconnoitre in the direction of Mechanicsville. For this purpose I moved Gregg's division out toward this town by way of Hawe's Shop, and when it had gone about three-fourths of a mile beyond the Shop the enemy's cavalry was discovered dismounted and disposed behind a temporary breastwork of rails and logs.

This was the first occasion on which, since the battle of Yellow Tavern, the Confederate troopers had confronted us in large numbers, their mounted operations, like ours, having been dependent more or less on the conditions that grew out of the movements in which Lee's infantry had been engaged since the 14th of May. On that date General Lee had foreshadowed his intention of using his cavalry in connection with the manœuvres of his infantry by issuing an order himself, now that Stuart was dead, directing that the "three divisions of cavalry serving with the army [Lee's] will constitute separate commands, and will report directly to and receive orders from the headquarters of the army." The order indicates that since Stuart's death the Confederate cavalry had been re-organized into three divisions, that were commanded respectively by General Wade Hampton, General Fitzhugh Lee, and General W. H. F. Lee, the additional division organization undoubtedly growing out of the fact that General M. C. Butler's brigade of about four thousand men had joined recently from South Carolina.

When this force developed in Gregg's front, he attacked the moment his troops could be dismounted; and the contest became one of exceeding stubbornness, for he found confronting him Hampton's and Fitzhugh Lee's divisions, supported by what we then supposed to be a brigade of infantry, but which, it has since been ascertained, was Butler's brigade of mounted troops, part of them armed with long-range rifles. The contest between the opposing forces was of the severest character and continued till late in the evening. The varying phases of the fight prompted me to reinforce Gregg as much as possible, so I directed

Custer's brigade to report to him, sending, meanwhile, for the other two brigades of Torbert, but these were not available at the time—on account of delays which occurred in relieving them from the line at Crump's Creek—and did not get up till the fight was over. As soon as Custer joined him, Gregg vigorously assaulted the Confederate position along his whole front; and notwithstanding the long-range rifles of the South Carolinians, who were engaging in their first severe combat it appears, and fought most desperately, he penetrated their barricades at several points.

The most determined and obstinate efforts for success were now made on both sides, as the position at Hawe's Shop had become of very great importance on account of the designs of both Lee and Grant. Lee wished to hold this ground while he manœuvred his army to the line of the Tolopotomy, where he could cover the roads to Richmond, while Grant, though first sending me out merely to discover by a strong reconnoissance the movements of the enemy, saw the value of the place to cover his new base at the White House, and also to give us possession of a direct road to Cold Harbor. Hawe's Shop remained in our possession finally, for late in the evening Custer's brigade was dismounted and formed in close column in rear of Gregg, and while it assaulted through an opening near the centre of his line, the other two brigades advanced and carried the temporary works. The enemy's dead and many of his wounded fell into our hands; also a considerable number of prisoners, from whom we learned that Longstreet's and Ewell's corps were but four miles to the rear.

The battle was a decidedly severe one, the loss on each side being heavy in proportion to the number of troops engaged. This fight took place almost immediately in front of our infantry, which, during the latter part of the contest, was busily occupied in throwing up intrenchments. Late in the afternoon I reported to General Meade the presence of the enemy's infantry, and likewise that Hampton's and Fitzhugh Lee's divisions were in my front also, and asked, at the same time, that some of our infantry, which was near at hand, be sent to my assistance. I could not convince Meade that anything but the enemy's horse was fighting us, however, and he declined to push out the foot-troops, who were much wearied by night marches. It has been ascertained since that Meade's conclusions were correct in so far as they related to the enemy's infantry; but the five cavalry brigades far outnumbered my three, and it is to be regretted that so much was risked in holding a point that commanded the roads to Cold Harbor and Meadow bridge, when there was at hand a preponderating number of Union troops which might have been put into action. However, Gregg's division and Custer's brigade were equal to the situation, all unaided as they were till dark, when Torbert and Merritt came on the ground. The contest not only gave us the crossroads, but also removed our uncertainty regarding Lee's movements, clearly demonstrating that his army was retiring by its right flank, so that it might continue to interpose between Grant and the James River, as well as cover the direct route to Richmond.

General Lee reported this battle to his Government as a Confederate victory, but his despatch was sent early in the day, long before the fight ended, and evidently he could not have known the final result when he made the announcement, for the fight lasted until dark. After dark, our own and the Confederate dead having been buried, I withdrew, and moving to the rear of our infantry, marched all night and till I reached the vicinity of Old Church, where I had been instructed to keep a vigilant watch on the enemy with Gregg's and Torbert's divisions. As soon as I had taken position at Old Church my pickets were pushed out in the direction of Cold Harbor, and the fact that the enemy was holding that point in some force was clearly ascertained. But our occupation of Cold Harbor was of the utmost importance; indeed, it was absolutely necessary that we should possess it, to secure our communications with the White House, as well as to cover the extension of our line to the left toward the James River.

Roads from Bethesda Church, Old Church, and the White House centered at Cold Harbor, and from there many roads diverged also toward different crossings of the Chickahominy, which were indispensable to us.

The enemy too realized the importance of the place, for as soon as he found himself compelled to take up the line of the Tolopotomy he threw a body of troops into Cold Harbor by forced marches, and followed it up by pushing a part of this force out on the Old Church road as far as Matadequin Creek, where he established a line of battle, arranging the front of it parallel to the road along the south bank of the Pamunkey; this for the purpose of endangering our trains as they moved back and forth between the army and the White House.

Meanwhile I had occupied Old Church and pushed pickets down toward Cold Harbor. The outposts struck each other just north of Matadequin Creek, and a spirited fight immediately took place. At first our pickets were sorely pressed, but Torbert, who was already preparing to make a reconnoissance, lost no time in reinforcing them on the north side of the creek with Devin's brigade. The fight then became general, both sides, dismounted, stubbornly contesting the ground. Of the Confederates, General Butler's South Carolinians bore the brunt of the fight, and, strongly posted as they were on the south bank of the creek, held their ground with the same obstinacy they had previously shown at Hawe's Shop. Finally, however, Torbert threw Merritt's and Custer's brigades into the action, and the enemy retired, we pursuing to within a mile and a half of Cold Harbor and capturing a number of prisoners. Gregg's division took no part in the actual fighting, but remained near Old Church observing the roads on Torbert's flanks, one leading toward Bethesda Church on his right, the other to his left in the direction of the White House. This latter road Gregg was particularly instructed to keep open, so as to communicate with General W. F. Smith, who was then debarking his corps at the White House, and on the morning of the 31st this general's advance was covered by a brigade which Gregg had sent him for the purpose.

Torbert having pursued toward Cold Harbor the troops he fought at Matadequin Creek, had taken up a position about a mile and a half from that place, on the Old Church road. The morning of the 31st I visited him to arrange for his further advance, intending thus to anticipate an expected attack from Fitzhugh Lee, who was being reinforced by infantry. I met Torbert at Custer's headquarters, and found that the two had already been talking over a scheme to capture Cold Harbor, and when their plan was laid before me it appeared so plainly feasible that I fully endorsed it, at once giving directions for its immediate execution, and ordering Gregg to come forward to Torbert's support with such troops as he could spare from the duty with which he had been charged.

Torbert moved out promptly, Merritt's brigade first, followed by Custer's, on the direct road to Cold Harbor, while Devin's brigade was detached, and marched by a left-hand road that would bring him in on the right and rear of the enemy's line, which was posted in front of the crossroads. Devin was unable to carry his part of the programme farther than to reach the front of the Confederate right, and as Merritt came into position to the right of the Old Church road Torbert was obliged to place a part of Custer's brigade on Merritt's left so as to connect with Devin. The whole division was now in line, confronted by Fitzhugh Lee's cavalry, supported by Clingman's brigade from Hoke's division of infantry; and from the Confederate breastworks, hastily constructed out of logs, rails, and earth, a heavy fire was already being poured upon us that it seemed impossible to withstand. None of Gregg's division had yet arrived, and so stubborn was the enemy's resistance that I began to doubt our ability to carry the place before reinforcements came up, but just then Merritt reported that he could turn the enemy's left, and being directed to execute his proposition, he carried it to a most successful issue with the First and Second regular cavalry. Just as these two regiments passed around the enemy's left and attacked his rear, the remainder of the division assailed him in front. This manœuvre of Merritt's stampeded the Confederates, and the defenses falling into our hands easily, we pushed ahead on the Bottom's bridge road three-fourths of a mile beyond Cold Harbor.

Cold Harbor was now mine, but I was about nine miles away from our nearest infantry, and had been able to bring up only Davies's brigade of cavalry, which arrived after the fight. My isolated position therefore made me a little uneasy. I felt convinced that the enemy would attempt to regain the place, for it was of as much importance to him as to us, and the presence of his infantry disclosed that he fully appreciated this. My uneasiness increased as the day grew late, for I had learned from prisoners that the balance of Hoke's division was *en route* to Cold Harbor, and Kershaw near at hand, interposing between the Union left near Bethesda Church and my position. In view of this state of affairs, I notified General Meade that I had taken Cold Harbor, but could not with safety to my command hold it, and forthwith gave directions to withdraw during the night. The last of my troops had scarcely pulled out, however, when I received a despatch from Meade directing me to hold Cold Harbor at every hazard. General Grant had expected that a severe battle would have to be fought before we could obtain possession of the place; and its capture by our cavalry not being anticipated, no preparation had been made for its permanent occupancy. No time was to be lost, therefore, if the advantages which possession of Cold Harbor gave us were to be improved, so at the same hour that Meade ordered me to hold the place at all hazards the Sixth Corps was started on a forced march, by Grant's directions, to aid in that object, and on arrival to relieve my cavalry.

The moment Meade's order was received, I directed a re-occupation of Cold Harbor, and although a large portion of Torbert's command was already well on its way back to the line we held on the morning of the 31st, this force speedily retraced its steps, and re-entered the place before daylight; both our departure and return having been effected without the enemy being aware of our movements. We now found that the temporary breastworks of rails and logs which the Confederates had built were of incalculable benefit to us in furnishing material with which to establish a line of defense, they being made available by simply reversing them at some points, or at others wholly reconstructing them to suit the circumstances of the ground. The troops, without reserves, were then placed behind our cover dismounted, boxes of ammunition distributed along the line, and the order passed along that the place *must* be held. All this was done in the darkness, and while we were working away at our cover the enemy could be distinctly heard from our skirmish-line giving commands and making preparations to attack.

Just after daylight on the 1st of June the Confederate infantry under General Kershaw endeavored to drive us out, advancing against my right from the Bethesda Church road. In his assault he was permitted to come close up to our works, and when within short range such a fire was opened on him from our horse-artillery and repeating carbines that he recoiled in confusion after the first onset; still, he seemed determined to get the place, and after reorganizing, again attacked; but the lesson of the first repulse was not without effect, and his feeble effort proved wholly fruitless. After his second failure we were left undisturbed, and at 9 A.M. I sent the following despatch to army headquarters:

> "HEADQUARTERS CAVALRY CORPS.
> "ARMY OF THE POTOMAC.
> "Cold Harbor, Va., June 1, 1864—9 A.M.
> "MAJOR-GENERAL HUMPHREYS,
> "Chief-of-Staff.
> "GENERAL: In obedience to your instructions I am holding Cold Harbor. I have captured this morning more prisoners; they belong to three different infantry brigades. The

enemy assaulted the right of my lines this morning, but were handsomely repulsed. I have been very apprehensive, but General Wright is now coming up. I built slight works for my men; the enemy came up to them, and were driven back. General Wright has just arrived.

"P. H. SHERIDAN,
"Major-General Commanding."

About 10 o'clock in the morning the Sixth Corps relieved Torbert and Davies, having marched all night, and these two generals moving out toward the Chickahominy covered the left of the infantry line till Hancock's corps took their place in the afternoon. By this time Gregg had joined me with his two brigades, and both Torbert and Gregg were now marched to Prospect Church, from which point I moved them to a position on the north side of the Chickahominy at Bottom's bridge. Here the enemy's cavalry confronted us, occupying the south bank of the stream, with artillery in position at the fords prepared to dispute our passage; but it was not intended that we should cross; so Gregg and Torbert lay quiet in camp at Bottom's bridge and at Old Church without noteworthy event until the 6th of June.

As before related, Wilson's division struck the enemy's infantry as well as W. H. F. Lee's cavalry near Ashland on the 1st of June, and although Chapman destroyed the bridges over the South Anna, which was his part of the programme, Wilson found it necessary to return to Price's Store. From this point he continued to cover the right of the Army of the Potomac, on the 2d of June driving the rear-guard of the enemy from Hawe's Shop, the scene of the battle of May 28. The same day he crossed Tolopotomy Creek, and passed around the enemy's left flank so far that Lee thought his left was turned by a strong force, and under cover of darkness withdrew from a menacing position which he was holding in front of the Ninth Corps. This successful manœuvre completed, Wilson returned to

Hawe's Shop, and on the 4th went into camp at New Castle ferry, in anticipation of certain operations of the Cavalry Corps, which were to take place while the Army of the Potomac was crossing to the south side of the James.

CHAPTER XV

B Y THE 6TH OF JUNE General Grant again determined to continue the movement of the army by its left flank to the south bank of the James River, his unsuccessful attack on the enemy's works near Cold Harbor having demonstrated that Lee's position north of the Chickahominy could not be carried by assault with results that would compensate for the enormous loss of life which must follow; therefore a further attempt to fight a decisive battle north of Richmond was abandoned. In carrying the army to the James River the hazardous manœuvres would be hampered by many obstacles, such as the thick timber, underbrush, and troublesome swamps to be met in crossing the Chickahominy. Besides, Lee held an interior line, from which all the direct roads to Richmond could be covered with his infantry, leaving his cavalry free to confront our advance on the south bank of the Chickahominy as far down as Jones's bridge, and thence around to Charles City Court House. In view of these difficulties it became necessary to draw off the bulk of the enemy's cavalry while the movement to the James was in process of execution, and General Meade determined to do this by requiring me to proceed with two divisions as far as Charlottesville to destroy the railroad bridge over the Rivanna River near that town, the railroad itself from the Rivanna to Gordonsville, and, if practicable, from Gordonsville back toward Hanover Junction also.

After Meade's instructions reached me they were somewhat modified by General Grant, who on the same evening had received information that General Hunter, commanding the troops in West Virginia, had reached Staunton and engaged with advantage the Confederate commander, General Jones, near that place. General Grant informed me orally that he had directed Hunter to advance as far as Charlottesville, that he expected me to unite with him there, and that the two commands, after destroying the James River canal and the Virginia Central road, were to join the Army of the Potomac in the manner contemplated in my instructions from General Meade; and that in view of what was anticipated, it would be well to break up as much of the railroad as possible on my way westward. A copy of his letter to Hunter comprised my written instructions. A junction with this general was not contemplated when the expedition was first conceived, but became an important though not the paramount object after the reception of the later information. The diversion of the enemy's cavalry from the south side of the Chickahominy was its main purpose, for in the presence of such a force as Lee's contracted lines would now permit him to concentrate behind the Chickahominy, the difficulties of crossing that stream would be largely increased if he also had at hand a strong body of horse, to gain the time necessary for him to oppose the movement at the different crossings with masses of his infantry.

The order calling for two divisions for the expedition, I decided to take Gregg's and Torbert's, leaving Wilson's behind to continue with the infantry in its march to the James and to receive instructions directly from the headquarters of the army. All my dismounted men had been sent to the White House some days before, and they were directed to report to Wilson as they could be provided with mounts.

Owing to the hard service of the preceding month we had lost many horses, so the number of dismounted men was large; and my strength had also been much reduced by killed and wounded during the same period of activity. The effective mounted force of my two divisions was therefore much diminished, they mustering only about six thousand officers and men when concentrated on June 6 at New Castle ferry. Here they were provided with three days' rations, intended to last five days, and with two days' grain for the horses. The rations and forty rounds of ammunition per man were to be carried on the persons of the troopers, the grain on the pommel of the saddle, and the reserve ammunition in wagons. One medical wagon and eight ambulances were also furnished, and one wagon was authorized for each division and brigade headquarters; enough canvas-covered boats for a small pontoon-bridge were also provided.

My instructions permitting latitude in the route I should take, I decided to march along the north bank of the North Anna River, cross that stream at Carpenter's ford, strike the Virginia Central railroad at Trevillian Station, destroy it toward Louisa Court House, march past Gordonsville, strike the railroad again at Cobham's Station, and destroy it thence to Charlottesville as we proceeded west. The success of the last part of this programme would of course depend on the location of General Hunter when I should arrive in the region where it would be practicable for us to communicate with each other.

From my camp at New Castle ferry we crossed the Pamunkey, marched between Aylett's and Dunkirk on the Mattapony River, and on the 8th of June encamped at Polecat Station. The next day we resumed the march along the North Anna—our advance guard skirmishing with a few mounted men of the enemy, who proved to be irregulars—and bivouacked on Northeast Creek, near Young's Mills. This day I learned from some of these irregulars whom we made prisoners that Breckenridge's division of infantry, *en route* to the Shenandoah Valley by way of Gordonsville, was passing slowly up the railroad parallel to me, and that the enemy's cavalry had left its position on the south side of the Chickahominy, and was marching on the old Richmond and Gordonsville road toward Gordonsville, under command of General Wade Hampton, the information being confirmed by a scouting party sent out to cut the telegraph wires along the railroad in the night. Breckenridge had been ordered back to the valley by General Lee as soon as he heard of Hunter's victory near Staunton, but now that my expedition had been discovered, the movement of Breckenridge's troops on the railroad was being timed to correspond with the marches of my command till Hampton could get more nearly parallel with me.

On the 10th we resumed the march, passing by Twyman's store, crossing the North Anna at Carpenter's ford and encamping on the road leading along the south fork of the North Anna to Trevillian Station. During the evening and night of the 10th the boldness of the enemy's scouting parties, with which we had been coming into collision more or less every day, perceptibly increased, thus indicating the presence of a large force, and evidencing that his shorter line of march had enabled him to bring to my front a strong body of cavalry, although it started from Lee's army nearly two days later than I did from Grant's. The arrival of this body also permitted Breckenridge to pass on to Gordonsville, and from there to interpose between General Hunter and me at either Charlottesville or Waynesboro' as circumstances might determine.

On the night of the 10th General Hampton's division camped about three miles northwest of Trevillian, at a place called Green Spring Valley and Fitzhugh Lee's division not far from Louisa Court House, some six miles east of Trevillian. Learning that I was at Carpenter's ford, Hampton marched his division by way of Trevillian Station toward Clayton's store, on the road from Trevillian to Car-

penter's ford, intending to attack me at Clayton's. Fitzhugh
Lee's division was to join Hampton at Clayton's store from
Louisa Court House, but on the morning of the 11th the
two generals were separated by several miles.

At daylight of the 11th my march to Trevillian Station
was resumed on the direct road to that point, and engaging
the enemy's pickets and advanced parties soon after setting
out, we began to drive them in. Torbert had the lead with
Merritt's and Devin's brigades, and as he pressed back the
pickets he came upon the enemy posted behind a line of
barricades in dense timber about three miles from Trevillian. Meanwhile Custer's brigade had been sent from
where we bivouacked, by a wood road found on our left,
to destroy Trevillian Station. In following this road Custer
got to the rear of Hampton's division, having passed between its right flank and Fitzhugh Lee's division, which
was at the time marching on the road leading from Louisa
Court House to Clayton's store to unite with Hampton.

Custer, the moment he found himself in Hampton's
rear, charged the led horses, wagons, and caissons found
there, getting hold of a vast number of each, and also of
the station itself. The stampede and havoc wrought by
Custer in Hampton's rear compelled him to turn Rosser's
brigade in that direction, and while it attacked Custer on
one side, Fitzhugh Lee's division, which had followed Custer toward Trevillian, attacked him on the other. There
then ensued a desperate struggle for the possession of the
captured property, resulting finally in its being retaken by
the enemy. Indeed, the great number of horses and vehicles
could not be kept on the limited space within Custer's line,
which now formed almost a complete circle; and while he
was endeavoring to remove them to a secure place they,
together with Custer's headquarters wagon and four of his
caissons, fell into the hands of their original owners.

As soon as the firing told that Custer had struck the
enemy's rear, I directed Torbert to press the line in front
of Merritt and Devin, aided by one brigade of Gregg's division on their left, Gregg's other brigade in the meantime

attacking Fitzhugh Lee on the Louisa Court House road. The effect of this was to force Hampton back, and his division was so hard pushed that a portion of it was driven pell-mell into Custer's lines, leaving there about five hundred prisoners. The rest of Hampton's men did not rally till they got some distance west of Trevillian, while, in the meantime, Gregg had driven Fitzhugh Lee toward Louisa Court House so far that many miles now intervened between the two Confederate divisions, precluding their union until about noon the next day, when Fitzhugh Lee effected the junction after a circuitous march in the night. The defeat of Hampton at the point where he had determined to resist my further advance, and his retreat westward, gave me undisturbed possession of the station; and after destroying the railroad to some extent toward Gordonsville, I went into camp.

From prisoners taken during the day, I gathered that General Hunter, instead of coming toward Charlottesville, as I had reason to expect, both from the instructions given me and the directions sent him by General Grant, was in the neighborhood of Lexington—apparently moving on Lynchburg—and that Breckenridge was at Gordonsville and Charlottesville. I also heard, from the same source, that Ewell's corps was on its way to Lynchburg, but this intelligence proved afterward to be incorrect, for these troops, commanded by General Early, did not leave Richmond till two days later.

There was no doubt as to the information about Hunter's general location, however. He was marching toward Lynchburg, away from instead of toward me, thus making the junction of our commands beyond all reasonable probability. So in view of this, I made up my mind to abandon that part of the scheme, and to return by leisurely marches, which would keep Hampton's cavalry away from Lee while Grant was crossing the James River. I was still further influenced to this course by the burden which was thrown on me in the large number of wounded—there being about five hundred cases of my own—and the five hundred prisoners that I would probably be forced to abandon, should I proceed farther. Besides, the recent battle had reduced my supply of ammunition to a very small amount—not more than enough for one more respectable engagement; and as the chances were that I would have to fight a great deal before I could reach Hunter, now that the enemy's cavalry and Breckenridge's infantry were between us, the risks of the undertaking seemed too great to warrant it.

The morning of June 12 Gregg's division commenced destroying the railroad to Louisa Court House, and continued the work during the day, breaking it pretty effectually. While Gregg was thus occupied, I directed Torbert to make a reconnoissance up the Gordonsville road, to secure a by-road leading over Mallory's ford, on the North Anna, to the Catharpen road, as I purposed following that route to Spottsylvania Court House on my return, and thence *via* Bowling Green and Dunkirk to the White House. About a mile beyond Trevillian the Gordonsville road forks—the left fork leading to Charlottesville—and about a mile beyond the fork Hampton had taken up and strongly intrenched a line across both roads, being reinforced by Fitzhugh Lee, who, as before related, had joined him about noon by a round-about march. Torbert soon hotly engaged this line, and by the impetuosity of his first attack, gained some advantage; but the appearance of Fitzhugh Lee's troops on the right, and Hampton's strong resistance in front, rendered futile all efforts to carry the position; and, although I brought up one of Gregg's brigades to Torbert's assistance, yet the by-road I coveted was still held by the enemy when night closed in.

This engagement, like that of the day before around Trevillian, was mostly fought dismounted by both sides, as had also been the earlier fights of the cavalry during the summer in the Wilderness, at Todd's Tavern, Hawe's Shop, and Matadequin Creek. Indeed, they could hardly have been fought otherwise than on foot, as there was little chance for mounted fighting in eastern Virginia, the dense woods, the armament of both parties, and the practice of barricading making it impracticable to use the sabre with anything like a large force; and so with the exception of Yellow Tavern the dismounted method prevailed in almost every engagement.

The losses at Mallory's Crossroads were very heavy on both sides. The character of the fighting, together with the day's results, demonstrated that it was impossible to make the passage of the North Anna at Mallory's ford without venturing another battle the next day. This would consume the little ammunition left, and though we might gain the road, yet the possibility of having no ammunition whatever to get back with was too great a hazard, so I gave orders to withdraw during the night of the 12th. We retired along the same road by which we had come, taking with us the prisoners, and all of our wounded who could be moved. Those who could not be transported, some ninety in number, and all the Confederate wounded in my hands, were left at Trevillian in hospitals, under charge of one of our surgeons, with plenty of medical and other stores.

We recrossed the North Anna at Carpenter's ford the following morning, and halting there, unsaddled and turned the horses out to graze, for they were nearly famished, having had neither food nor water during the preceding forty-eight hours. Late in the afternoon we saddled up and proceeded to Twyman's Store, while General Hampton's main body moved down the south bank of the North Anna, with the purpose of intervening between me and the Army of the Potomac, in the hope of preventing my return to it; but his movements took no definite shape beyond watching me, however, till several days later, near St. Mary's Church, when I was crossing the peninsula to the James River.

On the 14th the march was continued, and we reached the Catharpen road, upon which it was originally intended to move if we had been able to cross at Mallory's ford, and this conducted me to Shady Grove Church. The next day we passed over the battle-field of Spottsylvania Court House. The marks of the recent conflicts about there were visible on every hand, and in the neighboring houses were found many Union and Confederate wounded, who had been too severely hurt to be removed from the field-hospitals at the time of the battles. Such of our wounded as were able to travel were brought away.

On the 16th I marched from Edge Hill on the Ta River through Bowling Green to Dr. Butler's, on the north side of the Mattapony. When I arrived here I was unable to ascertain the position of the Army of the Potomac, and was uncertain whether or not the base at the White House had been discontinued. I had heard nothing from the army of nine days except rumors through Southern sources, and under these circumstances did not like to venture between the Mattapony and Pamunkey rivers, embarrassed as I was with some four hundred wounded, five hundred prisoners, and about two thousand negroes that had joined my column in the hope of obtaining their freedom. I therefore determined to push down the north bank of the Mattapony far enough to enable me to send these impediments directly to West Point, where I anticipated finding some of our gunboats and transports, that could carry all to the North. Following this plan, we proceeded through Walkerton to King and Queen Court House, and bivouacked in its vicinity the night of the 18th. Next day I learned that the dépôt at the White House had not yet been broken up entirely, and that supplies were in store for me there; so after sending the wounded, prisoners, and negroes to West Point under an escort of two regiments, I turned back to Dunkirk, on the Mattapony, and crossed to the south side at a place where the stream was narrow enough to bridge with my pontoon-boats.

In returning from Trevillian, as the most of our wounded were hauled in old buggies, carts, and such other vehicles as could be made available in the absence of a sufficient number of ambulances, the suffering was intense, the heat of the season and dusty roads adding much to the discomfort. Each day we halted many times to dress the wounds of the injured and to refresh them as much as possible, but our means for mitigating their distress were limited. The fortitude and cheerfulness of the poor fellows under such conditions were remarkable, for no word of complaint was heard. The Confederate prisoners and colored people being on foot, our marches were necessarily made short, and with frequent halts also, but they too suffered considerably from the heat and dust, though at times the prisoners were relieved by being mounted on the horses of some of our regiments, the owners meantime marching on foot. Where all the colored people came from and what started them was inexplicable, but they began joining us just before we reached Trevillian—men, women, and children—with bundles of all sorts containing their few worldly goods, and the number increased from day to day until they arrived at West Point. Probably not one of the poor things had the remotest idea, when he set out, as to where he would finally land, but to a man they followed the Yankees in full faith that they would lead to freedom, no matter what road they took.

On the morning of the 20th, at an early hour, we resumed our march, and as the column proceeded sounds of artillery were heard in the direction of the White House, which fact caused us to quicken the pace. We had not gone far when despatches from General Abercrombie, commanding some fragmentary organizations at the White House, notified me that the place was about to be attacked. I had previously sent an advance party with orders to move swiftly toward the cannonading and report to me by couriers the actual condition of affairs. From this party I soon learned that there was no occasion to push our jaded animals, since the crisis, if there had been one, was over and the enemy repulsed, so the increased gait was reduced to a leisurely march that took us late in the afternoon to the north bank of the Pamunkey, opposite Abercrombie's camp. When I got to the river the enemy was holding the bluffs surrounding the White House farm, having made no effort to penetrate General Abercrombie's line or do him other hurt than to throw a few shells among the teamsters there congregated.

Next day Gregg's division crossed the Pamunkey dismounted, and Torbert's crossed mounted. As soon as the troops were over, Gregg, supported by Merritt's brigade, moved out on the road to Tunstall's Station to attack Hampton, posted on the west side of Black Creek, Custer's brigade meanwhile moving, mounted, on the road to Cumberland, and Devin's in like manner on the one to Baltimore crossroads. This offer of battle was not accepted, however, and Hampton withdrew from my front, retiring behind the Chickahominy, where his communications with Lee would be more secure.

While at the White House I received orders to break up that dépôt wholly, and also instructions to move the trains which the Army of the Potomac had left there across the peninsula to the pontoon-bridge at Deep Bottom on the James River. These trains amounted to hundreds of wagons and other vehicles, and knowing full well the dangers which would attend the difficult problem of getting them over to Petersburg, I decided to start them with as little delay as circumstances would permit, and the morning of the 22d sent Torbert's division ahead to secure Jones's bridge on the Chickahominy, so that the wagons could be crossed at that point. The trains followed Torbert, while Gregg's division marched by a road parallel to the one on which the wagons were moving, and on their right flank, as they needed to be covered and protected in that direction only.

The enemy made no effort to attack us while we were moving the trains that day, and the wagons were all safely parked for the night on the south side of the Chickahominy, guarded by General Getty, who had relieved Abercrombie from command of the infantry fragments before we started off from the White House.

To secure the crossing at Jones's bridge, Torbert had pushed Devin's brigade out on the Long Bridge road, on the side of the Chickahominy where, on the morning of the 23d, he was attacked by Chambliss's brigade of W. H. F. Lee's division. Devin was driven in some little distance, but being reinforced by Getty with six companies of colored troops, he quickly turned the tables on Chambliss and re-established his picket-posts. From this affair I learned that Chambliss's brigade was the advance of the Confederate cavalry corps, while Hampton discovered from it that we were already in possession of the Jones's bridge crossing of the Chickahominy; and as he was too late to challenge our passage of the stream at this point he contented himself with taking up a position that night so as to cover the roads leading from Long Bridge to Westover, with the purpose of preventing the trains from following the river road to the pontoon-bridge at Deep Bottom.

My instructions required me to cross the trains over the James River on this pontoon-bridge if practicable, and to reach it I should be obliged to march through Charles City Court House, and then by Harrison's Landing and Malvern Hill, the latter point being held by the enemy. In fact, he held all the ground between Long Bridge on the Chickahominy and the pontoon-bridge except the *tête de pont* at the crossing. Notwithstanding this I concluded to make the attempt, for all the delays of ferrying the command and trains would be avoided if we got through to the bridge; and with this object in view I moved Torbert's division out on the Charles City road to conduct the wagons. Just beyond Charles City Court House Torbert encountered Lomax's brigade, which he drove across Herring Creek on the road to Westover Church; and reporting the affair to me, I surmised, from the presence of this force in my front, that Hampton would endeavor to penetrate to the long column of wagons, so I ordered them to go into park near Wilcox's landing, and instructed Gregg, whose division had been marching in the morning along the road leading from Jones's bridge to St. Mary's Church for the purpose of covering the exposed flank of the train, to hold fast near the church without fail till all the transportation had passed Charles City Court House.

Meanwhile, General Hampton, who had conjectured that I would try to get the train across the James by the pontoon-bridge at Deep Bottom, began concentrating all his troops except Lomax's brigade, which was to confront the head of my column on the river road, in the vicinity of Nance's Shop. This was discovered by Gregg at an early hour, and divining this purpose he had prepared to meet it by constructing hasty cover for his men before receiving my instructions. About 4 o'clock in the afternoon Hampton got his force in hand, and with Fitzhugh Lee's division assailed the whole front of Gregg's line, and his left flank with Chambliss's and Geary's brigades. For two hours he continued to attack, but made little impression on Gregg—gain at one point being counterbalanced by failure at another. Because of the evident strength of Hampton, Gregg had placed all his troops in line of battle from the first, and on discovery of the enemy's superior numbers sent message after message to me concerning the situation, but the messengers never arrived, being either killed or captured, and I remained in total ignorance till dark of the strait his division was in.

Toward night it became clear to Gregg that he could maintain the unequal contest no longer, and he then decided to retreat, but not until convinced that the time won had enabled all the trains to pass Charles City Court House in safety. When he had got all his led horses fairly on the way, and such of the wounded as could be transported, he retired by his right flank—in some confusion, it is true, but stubbornly resisting—to Hopewell Church, where Hampton ceased to press him.

Gregg's losses were heavy, and he was forced to abandon his dead and most seriously wounded, but the creditable stand made ensured the safety of the train, the last wagon of which was now parked at Wilcox's Landing. His steady, unflinching determination to gain time for the wagons to get beyond the point of danger was characteristic of the man, and this was the third occasion on which he had exhibited a high order of capacity and sound judgment since coming under my command. The firmness and coolness with which he always met the responsibilities of a dangerous place were particularly strong points in Gregg's make-up, and he possessed so much professional though unpretentious ability, that it is to be regretted he felt obliged a few months later to quit the service before the close of the war.

Gregg's fight fully satisfied me that we could not get the trains up to the pontoon-bridge, for of course Hampton would now throw all his cavalry in my front, on the river road, where it could be backed up by Lee's infantry. Meanwhile, General Meade had become assured of the same thing, and as he was now growing anxious about the fate of Wilson's division—which, during my absence, had been sent out to break the enemy's communications south of Petersburg, by destroying the Southside and Danville railroads—he sent ferryboats to cross me over the James. During the night of the 24th, and next morning, the immense train—which ought never to have been left for the cavalry to escort, after a fatiguing expedition of three weeks—was moved back through Charles City Court House to Douthard's landing, and there ferried over the river, followed by my troops in like manner. When General Hampton discovered this, he moved to Drury's Bluff, and there, on the morning of the 27th, crossed the James by the Confederate pontoon-bridge.

CHAPTER XVI

WHILE I WAS ABSENT on the expedition to Trevillian, the movement of the Army of the Potomac across the James River was effected, and Wilson, whom I had left behind for the purpose, was engaged in the duty of covering its front and rear. Late on the night of June 12 he, with Chapman's brigade, crossed the Chickahominy at Long Bridge, in advance of the Fifth Corps, and by 7 o'clock next morning had driven the enemy's pickets up to White Oak bridge, where he waited for our infantry. When that came up, he pushed on as far as Riddle's Shop, but late that evening the Confederate infantry forced him to withdraw to St. Mary's Church; for early in the morning General Lee had discovered the movement of our army, and promptly threw this column of infantry south of the Chickahominy to White Oak Swamp, with the design of covering Richmond. From St. Mary's Church Wilson guarded all the roads toward White Oak Swamp and Riddle's Shop, McIntosh's brigade joining him on the 14th, by way of Long Bridge, as the rear of the Army of the Potomac passed the Chickahominy. In the performance of this duty Wilson did not have to fight any engagement of magnitude, for the bulk of the enemy's cavalry had followed me to Trevillian. During the 15th and 16th Wilson drew his troops in toward the James River, and next day crossed it on the pontoon-bridge and camped on the Blackwater, near Mt. Sinai Church. Here he remained till the 22d of June—the same day I reached the White House with Gregg and Torbert—when, under orders from General Meade, he set out to cut the enemy's communications to the south and southwest of Petersburg.

His instructions implied that the breaking up of the Petersburg and Lynchburg, and Richmond and Danville railroads at Burkeville was the most important part of his mission, and that when the work of destruction began, it should be continued till he was driven off by the enemy. Wilson's force consisted of about 5,500 men, General A. V. Kautz, with the cavalry of the Army of the James, having joined him for the expedition. In moving out Wilson crossed the Weldon road near Ream's Station, first destroying it effectually at that point. About fourteen miles west of Petersburg he struck the Southside railroad, and broke it up clear to Burkeville, a distance of thirty miles. Having destroyed everything at Burkeville Junction, he moved along the Danville road to Staunton River, completely wrecking about thirty miles of that line also. At Staunton River he found the railroad bridge strongly guarded, and seeing that he could not burn it, he began his return march that night, and reached Nottoway River, some thirty miles south of Petersburg, at noon of the next day—the 28th.

In this expedition Wilson was closely followed from the start by Barringer's brigade of W. H. F. Lee's cavalry, but the operations were not interfered with materially, his success being signal till he reached the vicinity of Stony Creek depot on his return. At this point General Hampton, with his own and Fitzhugh Lee's cavalry, got between Wilson and the Army of the Potomac, there being behind them at Ream's Station, at the same time, two brigades of infantry under General Mahone. A severe battle ensued, resulting in Wilson's defeat, with the loss of twelve guns and all his wagons. In consequence of this discomfiture he was obliged to fall back across the Nottoway River with his own division, and rejoined the army by way of Peter's bridge on that stream, while Kautz's division, unable to unite with Wilson after the two commands had become separated in the fight, made a circuit of the enemy's left, and reached the lines of our army in the night of the 28th.

Neither the presence of Hampton's cavalry at Stony Creek depot, nor the possession of Ream's Station by the Confederate infantry, seems to have been anticipated by Wilson, for in the report of the expedition he states:

"Foreseeing the probability of having to return northward, I wrote to General Meade the evening before starting that I anticipated no serious difficulty in executing his orders; but unless General Sheridan was required to keep Hampton's cavalry engaged, and our infantry to prevent Lee from making detachments, we should probably experience great difficulty in rejoining the army. In reply to this note, General Humphreys, chief-of-staff, informed me it was intended the Army of the Potomac should cover the Weldon road the next day, the Southside road the day after, and that Hampton having followed Sheridan toward Gordonsville, I need not fear any trouble from him."

I doubt that General Meade's letter of instructions and Wilson's note of the same evening, warrant what General Wilson here says. It is true that the Weldon railroad near Ream's Station was not covered by our infantry, as General Humphreys informed him it would be, but Wilson is in error when he intimates that he was assured that I would look after Hampton. I do not think General Meade's instructions are susceptible of this interpretation. I received no orders requiring me to detain Hampton. On the contrary, when I arrived at the White House my instructions required me to break up the dépôt there, and then bring the train across the Peninsula as soon as practicable, nor were these instructions ever modified. I began the duty imposed on me on the morning of the 23d, totally in the dark as to what was expected of Wilson, though it seems, from some correspondence between Generals Grant and Meade, which I never saw till after the war, that Grant thought Wilson could rely on Hampton's absence from his field of operations throughout the expedition.

The moment I received orders from General Meade to go to the relief of Wilson, I hastened with Torbert and Gregg by way of Prince George Court House and Lee's Mills to Ream's Station. Here I found the Sixth Corps, which Meade had pushed out on his left flank immediately on hearing of Wilson's mishap, but I was too late to render any material assistance, Wilson having already disappeared, followed by the enemy. However, I at once sent out parties to gather information, and soon learned that Wilson had got safe across the Nottoway at Peter's bridge and was making for the army by way of Blunt's bridge, on the Blackwater.

The benefits derived from this expedition, in the destruction of the Southside and Danville railroads, were considered by General Grant as equivalent for the losses sustained in Wilson's defeat, for the wrecking of the railroads and cars was most complete, occasioning at this time serious embarrassment to the Confederate Government; but I doubt if all this compensated for the artillery and prisoners that fell into the hands of the enemy in the swamps of Hatcher's Run and Rowanty Creek. Wilson's retreat from the perilous situation at Ream's station was a most creditable performance—in the face of two brigades of infantry and three divisions of cavalry—and in the conduct of the whole expedition the only criticism that can hold against him is that he placed too much reliance on meeting our infantry at Ream's station, seeing that uncontrollable circumstances might, and did, prevent its being there. He ought to have marched on the 28th by Jarrett's Station to Peter's bridge, on the Nottoway, and

Blunt's bridge on the Blackwater, to the rear of the Army of the Potomac.

When the safety of Wilson's command was assured, I was ordered back to Light House Point, where I had gone into camp after crossing the James River to rest and recruit my command, now very much reduced in numbers by reason of casualties to both horses and men. It had been marching and fighting for fifty consecutive days, and the fatiguing service had told so fearfully on my animals that the number of dismounted men in the corps was very large. With the exception of about four hundred horses that I received at the White House, no animals were furnished to supply the deficiencies which had arisen from the wearing marches of the past two months until I got to this camp at Light House Point; here my needs were so obvious that they could no longer be neglected.

I remained at Light House Point from the 2d to the 26th of July, recuperating the cavalry, the intensely warm weather necessitating almost an entire suspension of hostilities on the part of the Army of the Potomac. Meanwhile fifteen hundred horses were sent me here, and these, with the four hundred already mentioned, were all that my troops received while I held the personal command of the Cavalry Corps, from April 6 to August 1, 1864. This was not near enough to mount the whole command, so I disposed the men who could not be supplied in a dismounted camp.

By the 26th of July our strength was pretty well restored, and as General Grant was now contemplating offensive operations for the purpose of keeping Lee's army occupied around Richmond, and also of carrying Petersburg by assault if possible, I was directed to move to the north side of the James River in conjunction with General Hancock's corps, and, if opportunity offered, to make a second expedition against the Virginia Central railroad, and again destroy the bridges on the North Anna, the Little and the South Anna rivers.

I started out on the afternoon of the 26th and crossed

the Appomattox at Broadway landing. At Deep Bottom I was joined by Kautz's small division from the Army of the James, and here massed the whole command, to allow Hancock's corps to take the lead, it crossing to the north bank of the James River by the bridge below the mouth of Bailey's Creek. I moved late in the afternoon, so as not to come within the enemy's view before dark, and after night-fall Hancock's corps passed me and began crossing the pontoon-bridge about 2 o'clock in the morning.

By daylight Hancock was across, the cavalry following. Soon a portion of his corps attacked the enemy's works on the east side of Bailey's Creek, and, aided by the cavalry moving on its right, captured four pieces of artillery. This opened the way for Hancock to push out his whole corps, and as he advanced by a wheel, with his left as a pivot, the cavalry joined in the movement, pressing forward on the New Market and Central or Charles City roads.

We did not go far before we found the enemy's infantry posted across these two roads behind a strong line of in-trenchments on the west bank of Bailey's Creek. His vi-dettes in front of Ruffin's house on the New Market road were soon driven in on their main line, and the high ground before the house was immediately occupied by Torbert and Gregg, supported by Kautz's division. By the time the cavalry line was formed the Confederate General Kershaw, with his own division of infantry and those of Wilcox and Heath, advanced to attack us. Directing the most of his troops against the cavalry, which was still mounted, Kershaw drove it back some distance over the high ground. When it reached the eastern face of the ridge, however, it was quickly dismounted, and the men directed to lie down in line of battle about fifteen yards from the crest, and here the onset of the enemy was awaited. When Kershaw's men reached the crest such a severe fire was opened on them, and at such close quarters, that they could not withstand it, and gave way in disorder. They were followed across the plain by the cavalry, and lost about two hundred and fifty prisoners and two battle-flags. The counter attack against the infantry by Torbert and Gregg re-established our line and gave us the victory of Darbytown, but it also demonstrated the fact that General Lee had anticipated the movement around his left flank by transferring to the north side of the James a large portion of his infantry and W. H. F. Lee's division of cavalry.

This development rendered useless any further effort on Hancock's part or mine to carry out the plan of the expedition, for General Grant did not intend Hancock to assault the enemy's works unless there should be found in them but a very thin line of infantry which could be surprised. In such event, Hancock was to operate so that the cavalry might turn the Confederates on the Central or Charles City road, but the continually increasing force of the enemy showed this to be impracticable. The long front presented by Hancock's corps and the cavalry deceived General Lee, and he undoubtedly thought that nearly all of Grant's army had been moved to the north side of the James River; and to meet the danger he transferred the most of his own strength to the same side to confront his adversary, thinning the lines around Petersburg to reinforce those opposing us on the Central and New Market roads. This was what Grant hoped Lee would do in case the operations of Hancock and myself became impracticable, for Grant had an alternative plan for carrying Petersburg by assault in conjunction with the explosion of a mine that had been driven under the enemy's works from the front of Burnside's corps.

Now that there was no longer a chance for the cavalry to turn the enemy's left, our attention was directed to keeping up the deception of Lee, and on the afternoon of the 28th Hancock's corps withdrew to a line nearer the head of the bridge, the cavalry drawing back to a position on his right. From now on, all sorts of devices and stratagems were practiced—anything that would tend to make the Confederates believe we were being reinforced, while Hancock was preparing for a rapid return to Petersburg at the proper time. In order to delude the enemy still more, after nightfall of the 28th I sent one of my divisions to the south side of the James, first covering the bridgeway with refuse hay to keep the tramp of the horses from being heard. After daylight the next morning, I marched this division back again on foot, in full view of the enemy, to create the impression of a continuous movement of large bodies of infantry to the north side, while at the same time Kautz was made to skirmish with the enemy on our extreme right. These various artifices had the effect intended, for by the evening of the 29th Lee had transferred all his infantry to the north bank of the James, except three divisions, and all his cavalry save one.

The morning of the 30th had been fixed upon to explode the mine and assault the enemy's works, so after dark on the evening of the 29th Hancock hastily but quietly withdrew his corps to the south side to take part in the engagement which was to succeed the explosion, and I was directed to follow Hancock. This left me on the north side of the river confronting two-thirds of Lee's army in a perilous position, where I could easily be driven into Curl's Neck and my whole command annihilated. The situation, therefore, was not a pleasant one to contemplate, but it could not be avoided. Luckily the enemy did not see fit to attack, and my anxiety was greatly relieved by getting the whole command safely across the bridge shortly after daylight, having drawn in the different brigades successively from my right. By 10 o'clock on the morning of the 30th my leading division was well over toward the left of our army in front of Petersburg, marching with the purpose to get around the enemy's right flank during the operations that were to succeed the mine explosion, but when I reached General Meade's headquarters I found that lamentable failure had attended the assault made when the enemy's works were blown up in the morning. Blunder after blunder had rendered the assault abortive, and all the opportunities opened by our expedition to the north side were irretrievably lost, so General Meade at once arrested the movement of the cavalry.

In the expedition to Deep Bottom I was under the command of Major-General Hancock, who, by seniority, was to control my corps as well as his own until the way was opened for me to get out on the Virginia Central railroad. If this opportunity was gained, I was to cut loose and damage Lee's communications with the Shenandoah Valley in such manner as best suited the conditions, but my return was not to be jeopardized nor long delayed. This necessitated that Hancock's line should extend to Bottom's bridge on the Chickahominy. The enemy's early discovery of the movement and his concentration of troops on the north side prevented Hancock from accomplishing the programme laid out for him. Its impracticability was demonstrated early on the 27th, and Hancock's soldierly instincts told him this the moment he unexpectedly discovered Kershaw blocking the New Market and Charles City roads. To Hancock the temptation to assault Kershaw's position was strong indeed, but if he carried it there would still remain the dubious problem of holding the line necessary for my safe return, so with rare judgment he desisted, zealously turning to the alternative proposition— the assault on Petersburg—for more significant results. This was the only occasion during the war in which I was associated with Hancock in campaign. Up till then we had seldom met, and that was the first opportunity I had to observe his quick apprehension, his physical courage, and the soldierly personality which had long before established his high reputation.

On the 1st of August, two days after the mine explosion, I was relieved from the personal command of the Cavalry Corps, and ordered to the Shenandoah Valley, where at a later date Torbert's and Wilson's divisions joined me. Practically, after I went to the valley, my command of the Cavalry Corps became supervisory merely. During the period of my immediate control of the corps, I tried to carry into effect, as far as possible, the views I had advanced before and during the opening of the Wilderness campaign, *i.e.*, "that our cavalry ought to fight the enemy's cavalry, and our infantry the enemy's infantry"; for there was great danger of breaking the spirit of the corps if it was to be pitted against the enemy's compact masses of foot-troops posted behind intrenchments, and unless there was some adequate tactical or strategical advantage to be gained, such a use of it would not be justified. Immediately succeeding the battles of the Wilderness, opportunity offered to put this plan into execution to some extent, and from that time forward—from the battle of Yellow Tavern— our success was almost continuous, resulting finally, before the close of the war, in the nearly total annihilation of the enemy's cavalry.

The constant activity of the corps from May 5 till August 1 gave little opportunity for the various division and brigade commanders to record its work in detail; so there exists but meagre accounts of the numerous skirmishes and graver conflicts in which, in addition to the fights mentioned in this narrative, it engaged. A detailed history of its performances is not within the province of a work of this nature; but in review, it can be said, without trespassing on the reader's time, that the Cavalry Corps led the advance of the Army of the Potomac into the Wilderness in the memorable campaign of 1864; that on the expedition by way of Richmond to Haxall's it marked out the army's line of march to the North Anna; that it again led the advance to the Tolopotomy, and also to Cold Harbor, holding that important strategic point at great hazard; and that by the Trevillian expedition it drew away the enemy's cavalry from the south side of the Chickahominy, and thereby assisted General Grant materially in successfully marching to the James River and Petersburg. Subsequently, Wilson made his march to Staunton bridge, destroying railroads and supplies of inestimable value, and though this was neutralized by his disaster near Ream's Station, the temporary set-back there to one division was soon redeemed by victory over the Confederate infantry at the battle of Darbytown.

In the campaign we were almost always on the march,

CHAPTER XVII

WHEN THE ATTEMPT to take Petersburg in conjunction with the mine explosion resulted in such a dismal failure, all the operations contemplated in connection with that project came to a standstill, and there was every prospect that the intensely hot and sultry weather would prevent further activity in the Army of the Potomac till a more propitious season. Just now, however, the conditions existing in the Shenandoah Valley and along the upper Potomac demanded the special attention of General Grant, for, notwithstanding the successful march that Major-General David Hunter had made toward Lynchburg early in the summer, what he had first gained was subsequently lost by strategical mistakes, that culminated in disaster during the retreat he was obliged to make from the vicinity of Lynchburg to the Kanawha Valley. This route of march uncovered the lower portion of the Valley of the Shenandoah, and with the exception of a small force of Union troops under General Franz Sigel posted at Martinsburg for the purpose of covering the Baltimore and Ohio railroad, there was nothing at hand to defend the lower valley.

The different bodies of Confederates which compelled

Hunter's retreat were under command of General Jubal A. Early, who had been sent to Lynchburg with Ewell's corps after the defeat of the Confederate General W. C. Jones near Staunton on the 5th of June, to take command of the Valley District. When Early had forced Hunter into the Kanawha region far enough to feel assured that Lynchburg could not again be threatened from that direction, he united to his own corps General John C. Breckenridge's infantry division and the cavalry of Generals J. H. Vaughn, John McCausland, B. T. Johnson, and J. D. Imboden, which heretofore had been operating in southwest and western Virginia under General Robert Ransom, Jr., and with the column thus formed, was ready to turn his attention to the lower Shenandoah Valley. At Early's suggestion General Lee authorized him to move north at an opportune moment, cross the upper Potomac into Maryland and threaten Washington. Indeed, General Lee had foreshadowed such a course when Early started toward Lynchburg for the purpose of relieving the pressure in front of Petersburg, but was in some doubt as to the practicability of the movement later, till persuaded to it by the representations of Early after that general had driven Hunter beyond the mountains and found little or nothing opposing except the small force of Sigel, which he thought he could readily overcome by celerity of movement.

By rapid marching Early reached Winchester on the 2d of July, and on the 4th occupied Martinsburg, driving General Sigel out of that place the same day that Hunter's troops, after their fatiguing retreat through the mountains, reached Charlestown, West Virginia. Early was thus enabled to cross the Potomac without difficulty, when, moving around Harper's Ferry, through the gaps of the South Mountain, he found his path unobstructed till he reached the Monocacy, where Ricketts's division of the Sixth Corps, and some raw troops that had been collected by General Lew Wallace, met and held the Confederates till the other reinforcements that had been ordered to the capital from Petersburg could be brought up. Wallace contested the line of the Monocacy with obstinacy, but had to retire finally toward Baltimore. The road was then open to Washington, and Early marched to the outskirts and began against the capital the demonstrations which were designed to divert the Army of the Potomac from its main purpose in front of Petersburg.

Early's audacity in thus threatening Washington had caused some concern to the officials in the city, but as the movement was looked upon by General Grant as a mere foray which could have no decisive issue, the Administration was not much disturbed till the Confederates came in close proximity. Then was repeated the alarm and consternation of two years before, fears for the safety of the capital being magnified by the confusion and discord existing among the different generals in Washington and Baltimore; and the imaginary dangers vanished only with the appearance of General Wright, who, with the Sixth Corps and one division of the Nineteenth Corps, pushed out to attack Early as soon as he could get his arriving troops in hand, but under circumstances that precluded celerity of movement; and as a consequence the Confederates escaped with little injury, retiring across the Potomac to Leesburg, unharassed save by some Union cavalry that had been sent out into Loudoun County by Hunter, who in the meantime had arrived at Harper's Ferry by the Baltimore and Ohio railroad. From Leesburg Early retired through Winchester toward Strasburg, but when the head of his column reached this place he found that he was being followed by General Crook with the combined troops of Hunter and Sigel only, Wright having returned to Washington under orders to rejoin Meade at Petersburg. This reduction of the pursuing force tempting Early to resume the offensive, he attacked Crook at Kernstown, and succeeded in administering such a check as to necessitate this general's retreat to Martinsburg, and finally to Harper's Ferry. Crook's withdrawal restored to Early the line of the upper Potomac, so, recrossing this stream, he advanced again into Maryland, and sending McCausland on to Chambersburg, Pennsylvania, laid that town in ashes, leaving three thousand non-combatants without shelter or food.

When Early fell back from the vicinity of Washington toward Strasburg, General Grant believed that he would rejoin Lee, but later manœuvres of the enemy indicated that Early had given up this idea, if he ever entertained it, and intended to remain in the valley, since it would furnish Lee and himself with subsistence, and also afford renewed opportunities for threatening Washington. Indeed, the possession of the Valley of the Shenandoah at this time was of vast importance to Lee's army, and on every hand there were indications that the Confederate Government wished to hold it at least until after the crops could be gathered in to their dépôts at Lynchburg and Richmond. Its retention, besides being of great advantage in the matter of supplies, would also be a menace to the North difficult for General Grant to explain, and thereby add an element of considerable benefit to the Confederate cause; so when Early's troops again appeared at Martinsburg it was necessary for General Grant to confront them with a force strong enough to put an end to incursions north of the Potomac, which hitherto had always led to National discomfiture at some critical juncture, by turning our army in eastern Virginia from its chief purpose—the destruction of Lee and the capture of the Confederate capital.

This second irruption of Early and his ruthless destruction of Chambersburg led to many recommendations on the part of General Grant looking to a speedy elimination of the confusion then existing among the Union forces along the upper Potomac, but for a time the authorities at Washington would approve none of his propositions. The President and Secretary Stanton seemed unwilling to adopt his suggestions, and one measure which he deemed very important—the consolidation into a single command of the four geographical districts into which, to relieve political pressure no doubt, the territory had been divided—met with serious opposition. Despite Grant's representations, he could not prevail on the Administration to approve this measure, but finally the manœuvres of Early and the raid to Chambersburg compelled a partial compliance, though Grant had somewhat circumvented the difficulty already by deciding to appoint a commander for the forces in the field that were to operate against Early.

On the 31st of July General Grant selected me as this commander, and in obedience to his telegraphic summons I repaired to his headquarters at City Point. In the interview that followed, he detailed to me the situation of affairs on the upper Potomac, telling me that I was to command in the field the troops that were to operate against Early, but that General Hunter, who was at the head of the geographical department, would be continued in his position for the reason that the Administration was reluctant to reconstruct or consolidate the different districts. After informing me that one division of the Cavalry Corps would be sent to my new command, he went on to say that he wanted me to push the enemy as soon as this division arrived, and if Early retired up the Shenandoah Valley I was to pursue, but if he crossed the Potomac I was to put myself south of him and try to compass his destruction. The interview having ended, I returned to Hancock Station to prepare for my departure, and on the evening of August 1 I was relieved from immediate duty with the Army of the Potomac, but not from command of the cavalry as a corps organization.

I arrived at Washington on the 4th of August, and the next day received instructions from General Halleck to report to General Grant at Monocacy Junction, whither he had gone direct from City Point, in consequence of a characteristic despatch from the President indicating his disgust with the confusion, disorder, and helplessness prevailing along the upper Potomac, and intimating that Grant's presence there was necessary.

In company with the Secretary of War I called on the President before leaving Washington, and during a short conversation Mr. Lincoln candidly told me that Mr. Stanton had objected to my assignment to General Hunter's command, because he thought me too young, and that he himself had concurred with the Secretary; but now, since General Grant had "ploughed round" the difficulties of the situation by picking me out to command the "boys in the field," he felt satisfied with what had been done, and "hoped for the best." Mr. Stanton remained silent during these remarks, never once indicating whether he, too, had become reconciled to my selection or not; and although, after we left the White House, he conversed with me freely in regard to the campaign I was expected to make, seeking to impress on me the necessity for success from the political as well as from the military point of view, yet he utterly ignored the fact that he had taken any part in disapproving the recommendation of the general-in-chief.

August 6 I reported to General Grant at the Monocacy, and he there turned over to me the following instructions, which he had previously prepared for General Hunter in the expectation that that general would continue to command the department:

> "HEADQUARTERS IN THE FIELD,
> "Monocacy Bridge, Md., Aug. 5, 1864.
> "GENERAL: Concentrate all your available force without delay in the vicinity of Harper's Ferry, leaving only such railroad guards and garrisons for public property as may be necessary.
> "Use in this concentration the railroad, if by so doing time can be saved. From Harper's Ferry, if it is found that the enemy has moved north of the Potomac in large force, push north, following and attacking him wherever found; following him, if driven south of the Potomac, as long as it is safe to do so. If it is ascertained that the enemy has but a small force north of the Potomac, then push south the main force, detaching, under a competent commander, a sufficient force to look after the raiders and drive them to their homes. In detaching such a force, the brigade of

cavalry now *en route* from Washington *via* Rockville may be taken into account.

"There are now on the way to join you three other brigades of the best of cavalry, numbering at least five thousand men and horses. These will be instructed, in the absence of further orders, to join you by the south side of the Potomac. One brigade will probably start to-morrow.

"In pushing up the Shenandoah Valley, as it is expected you will have to go first or last, it is desirable that nothing should be left to invite the enemy to return. Take all provisions, forage, and stock wanted for the use of your command. Such as cannot be consumed, destroy. It is not desirable that the buildings should be destroyed—they should, rather, be protected; but the people should be informed that so long as an army can subsist among them recurrences of these raids must be expected, and we are determined to stop them at all hazards.

"Bear in mind, the object is to drive the enemy south; and to do this you want to keep him always in sight. Be guided in your course by the course he takes.

"Make your own arrangements for supplies of all kinds, giving regular vouchers for such as may be taken from loyal citizens in the country through which you march.

"Very respectfully,

"U. S. GRANT, Lieut.-General."

"Major-General D. HUNTER,

"Commanding Department of West Virginia."

When I had read the letter addressed to Hunter, General Grant said I would be expected to report directly to him, as Hunter had asked that day to be wholly relieved, not from any chagrin at my assignment to the control of the active forces of his command, but because he thought that his fitness for the position he was filling was distrusted by General Halleck, and he had no wish to cause embarrassment by remaining where he could but remove me one degree from the headquarters of the army. The next day Hunter's unselfish request was complied with, and an order was issued by the President, consolidating the Middle Department, the Department of Washington, the Department of the Susquehanna, and the Department of West Virginia.

Under this order these four geographical districts constituted the Middle Military Division, and I was temporarily assigned to command it. Hunter's men had been bivouacking for some days past in the vicinity of Monocacy Junction and Frederick, but before General Grant's instructions were written out, Hunter had conformed to them by directing the concentration at Halltown, about four miles in front of Harper's Ferry, of all his force available for field service. Therefore the different bodies of troops, with the exception of Averell's cavalry, which had followed McCausland toward Moorefield after the burning of Chambersburg, were all in motion toward Halltown on August 6.

Affairs at Monocacy kept me but an hour or two, and these disposed of, I continued on to Harper's Ferry by the special train which had brought me from Washington, that point being intended as my headquarters while making preparations to advance. The enemy was occupying Martinsburg, Williamsport, and Shepherdstown at the time, sending occasional raiding parties into Maryland as far as Hagerstown. The concentration of my troops at Halltown being an indication to Early that we intended to renew the offensive, however, he immediately began counter preparations by drawing in all his detached columns from the north side of the Potomac, abandoning a contemplated raid into Maryland, which his success against Crook at Kernstown had prompted him to project, and otherwise disposing himself for defense.

At Harper's Ferry I made my headquarters in the second story of a small and very dilapidated hotel, and as soon as settled sent for Lieutenant John R. Meigs, the chief engineer officer of the command, to study with him the maps of my geographical division. It always came rather easy to me to learn the geography of a new section, and its important topographical features as well; therefore I found that, with the aid of Meigs, who was most intelligent in his profession, the region in which I was to operate would soon be well fixed in my mind. Meigs was familiar with every important road and stream, and with all points worthy of note west of the Blue Ridge, and was particularly well equipped with knowledge regarding the Shenandoah Valley, even down to the farm-houses. He imparted with great readiness what he knew of this, clearly pointing out its configuration and indicating the strongest points for Confederate defense, at the same time illustrating scientifically and forcibly the peculiar disadvantages under which the Union army had hitherto labored.

The section that received my closest attention has its northern limit along the Potomac between McCoy's ferry at the eastern base of the North Mountain, and Harper's Ferry at the western base of the Blue Ridge. The southern limit is south of Staunton, on the divide which separates the waters flowing into the Potomac from those that run to the James. The western boundary is the eastern slope of the Alleghany Mountains, the eastern, the Blue Ridge; these two distinct mountain ranges trending about southwest inclose a stretch of quite open, undulating country varying in width from the northern to the southern extremity, and dotted at frequent intervals with patches of heavy woods. At Martinsburg the valley is about sixty miles broad, and on an east and west line drawn through Winchester about forty-five, while at Strasburg it narrows down to about twenty-five. Just southeast of Strasburg, which is nearly midway between the eastern and western walls of the valley, rises an abrupt range of mountains called Massanutten, consisting of several ridges which extend southward between the North and South Forks of the Shenandoah River until, losing their identity, they merge into lower but broken ground between New Market and Harrisonburg. The Massanutten ranges, with their spurs and hills, divide the Shenandoah Valley into two valleys, the one next the Blue Ridge being called the Luray, while that next the North Mountain retains the name of Shenandoah.

A broad macadamized road, leading south from Williamsport, Maryland, to Lexington, Virginia, was built at an early day to connect the interior of the latter State with the Chesapeake and Ohio canal, and along this road are situated the principal towns and villages of the Shenandoah Valley, with lateral lines of communication extending to the mountain ranges on the east and west. The roads running toward the Blue Ridge are nearly all macadamized, and the principal ones lead to the railroad system of eastern Virginia through Snicker's, Ashby's Manassas, Chester, Thornton's Swift Run, Brown's and Rock-fish gaps, tending to an ultimate centre at Richmond. These gaps are low and easy, offering little obstruction to the march of an army coming from eastern Virginia, and thus the Union troops operating west of the Blue Ridge were always subjected to the perils of a flank attack; for the Confederates could readily be brought by rail to Gordonsville and Charlottesville, from which points they could move with such celerity through the Blue Ridge that, on more than one occasion, the Shenandoah Valley had been the theatre of Confederate success, due greatly to the advantage of possessing these interior lines.

Nature had been very kind to the valley, making it rich and productive to an exceptional degree, and though for three years contending armies had been marching up and down it, the fertile soil still yielded ample subsistence for Early's men, with a large surplus for the army of Lee. The ground had long been well cleared of timber, and the rolling surface presented so few obstacles to the movement of armies that they could march over the country in any direction almost as well as on the roads, the creeks and rivers being everywhere fordable, with little or no difficulty beyond that of leveling the approaches.

I had opposing me an army largely composed of troops that had operated in this region hitherto under "Stonewall" Jackson with marked success, inflicting defeat on the Union forces almost every time the two armies had come in contact. These men were now commanded by a veteran officer of the Confederacy—General Jubal A. Early—whose past services had so signalized his ability that General Lee specially selected him to take charge of the Valley District, and, notwithstanding the misfortunes that befell him later, clung to him till the end of the war. The Confederate army at this date was about twenty thousand strong, and consisted of Early's own corps, with Generals Rodes, Ramseur, and Gordon commanding its divisions; the infantry of Breckenridge from southwestern Virginia; three battalions of artillery; and the cavalry brigades of Vaughn, Johnson, McCausland, and Imboden. This cavalry was a short time afterward organized into a division under the command of General Lomax.

After discovering that my troops were massing in front of Harper's Ferry, Early lost not a moment in concentrating his in the vicinity of Martinsburg, in positions from which he could continue to obstruct the Baltimore and Ohio railroad, and yet be enabled to retire up the valley under conditions of safety when I should begin an offensive campaign.

When I took command of the Army of the Shenandoah its infantry force comprised the Sixth Corps, one division of the Nineteenth Corps, and two divisions from West Virginia. The Sixth Corps was commanded by Major-General Horatio G. Wright; its three divisions by Brigadier-Generals David A. Russell, Geo. W. Getty, and James B. Ricketts. The single division of the Nineteenth Corps had for its immediate chief Brigadier-General William Dwight, the corps being commanded by Brigadier-General Wm. H. Emory. The troops from West Virginia were under Brigadier-General George Crook, with Colonels Joseph Thoburn and Isaac H. Duval as division commanders, and though in all not more than one fair-sized division, they had been designated, on account of the department they belonged to, the Army of West Virginia. General Torbert's division, then arriving from the Cavalry Corps of the Army of the Potomac, represented the mounted arm of the service, and in the expectation that Averell would soon join me with his troopers, I assigned General Torbert as chief of cavalry, and General Wesley Merritt succeeded to the command of Torbert's division.

General Wright, the commander of the Sixth Corps, was an officer of high standing in the Corps of Engineers, and had seen much active service during the preceding three years. He commanded the Department of the Ohio throughout the very trying period of the summer and fall of 1862, and while in that position he, with other prominent officers, recommended my appointment as a brigadier-general. In 1863 he rendered valuable service at the battle of Gettysburg, following which he was assigned to the Sixth Corps, and commanded it at the capture of the Confederate works at Rappahannock Station and in the operations at Mine Run. He ranked me as a major-general of volunteers by nearly a year in date of commission, but my assignment by the President to the command of the army in the valley met with Wright's approbation, and, so far as I have ever known, he never questioned the propriety of the President's action. The Sixth Corps division commanders, Getty, Russell, and Ricketts, were all educated soldiers, whose records, beginning with the Mexican War, had already been illustrated in the war of the rebellion by distinguished service in the Army of the Potomac.

General Emory was a veteran, having graduated at the Military Academy in 1831, the year I was born. In early life he had seen much service in the Artillery, the Topographical Engineers, and the Cavalry, and in the war of the rebellion had exhibited the most soldierly characteristics at Port Hudson and on the Red River campaign. At this time he had but one division of the Nineteenth Corps present, which division was well commanded by General Dwight, a volunteer officer who had risen to the grade of brigadier-general through constant hard work. Crook was a classmate of mine—at least, we entered the Military Academy the same year, though he graduated a year ahead of me. We had known each other as boys before we entered the army, and later as men, and I placed implicit faith in his experience and qualifications as a general.

The transfer of Torbert to the position of chief of cavalry left Merritt, as I have already said, in command of the First Cavalry Division. He had been tried in the place before, and from the day he was selected as one of a number of young men to be appointed general officers, with the object of giving life to the Cavalry Corps, he filled the measure of expectation. Custer was one of these young men too, and though as yet commanding a brigade under Merritt, his gallant fight at Trevillian Station, as well as a dozen others during the summer, indicated that he would be equal to the work that was to fall to him when in a few weeks he should succeed Wilson. But to go on down the scale of rank, describing the officers who commanded in the Army of the Shenandoah, would carry me beyond all limit, so I refrain from the digression with regret that I cannot pay to each his well-earned tribute.

The force that I could take with me into the field at this time numbered about 26,000 men. Within the limits of the geographical division there was a much greater number of troops than this. Baltimore, Washington, Harper's Ferry, Hagerstown, Frederick, Cumberland, and a score of other points; besides the strong detachments that it took to keep the Baltimore and Ohio railroad open through the mountains of West Virginia, and escorts for my trains, absorbed so many men that the column which could be made available for field operations was small when compared with the showing on paper. Indeed, it was much less than it ought to have been, but for me, in the face of the opposition made by different interests involved, to detach troops from any of the points to which they had been distributed before I took charge was next to impossible.

In a few days after my arrival preparations were completed, and I was ready to make the first move for the possession of the Shenandoah Valley. For the next five weeks the operations on my part consisted almost wholly of offensive and defensive manœuvring for certain advantages, the enemy confining himself meanwhile to measures intended to counteract my designs. Upon the advent of Torbert, Early immediately grew suspicious, and fell back twelve miles south of Martinsburg, to Bunker Hill and vicinity, where his right flank would be less exposed, but from which position he could continue to maintain the break in the Baltimore and Ohio railroad, and push reconnoitring parties through Smithfield to Charlestown. These reconnoitring parties exhibited considerable boldness at times, but since they had no purpose in view save to discover whether or not we were moving, I did not contest any ground with them except about our outposts. Indeed, I desired that Early might remain at some point well to the north till I was fully prepared to throw my army on his right and rear and force a battle, and hence I abstained from disturbing him by premature activity, for I thought that if I could beat him at Winchester, or north of it, there would be far greater chances of weighty results. I therefore determined to bring my troops, if it were at all possible to do so, into such a position near that town as to oblige Early to fight. The sequel proved, however, that he was accurately informed of all my movements. To anticipate them, therefore, he began his retreat up the valley the day that I moved out from Halltown, and consequently was able to place himself south of Winchester before I could get there.

CHAPTER XVIII

For a clear understanding of the operations which preceded the victories that resulted in almost annihilating General Early's army in the Shenandoah Valley it is necessary to describe in considerable detail the events that took place prior to the 19th of September. My army marched from Harper's Ferry on the 10th of August, 1864, General Torbert with Merritt's division of cavalry moving in advance through Berryville, going into position near White Post. The Sixth Corps, under General Wright, moved by way of Charlestown and Summit Point to Clifton; General Emory, with Dwight's division of the Nineteenth Corps, marched along the Berryville pike through Berryville to the left of the position of the Sixth Corps at Clifton; General Crook's command, moving on the Kabletown road, passed through Kabletown to the vicinity of Berryville, and went into position on the left of Dwight's division, while Colonel Lowell, with a detached force of two small regiments of cavalry, marched to Summit Point; so that on the night of August 10 my infantry occupied a line stretching from Clifton to Berryville, with Merritt's cavalry at White Post and Lowell's at Summit Point. The enemy, as stated before, moved at the same time from Bunker Hill and vicinity, and stretched his line from where the Winchester and Potomac railroad crosses Opequon Creek to the point at which the Berryville and Winchester pike crosses the same stream, thus occupying the west bank to cover Winchester.

On the morning of the 11th the Sixth Corps was ordered to move across the country toward the junction of the Berryville-Winchester pike and the Opequon, and to take the crossing and hold it. Dwight's division being directed to move through Berryville on the White Post road for a mile, then file to the right by heads of regiments at deploying distances, and carry the crossing of Opequon Creek at a ford about three-fourths of a mile from the left of the Sixth Corps, while Crook was instructed to move out on the White Post road, a mile and a half beyond Berryville, then head to the right and secure the ford about a mile to the left of Dwight; Torbert's orders were to push Merritt's division up the Millwood pike toward Winchester, attack any force he might run against, and ascertain the movements of the Confederate army; and lastly, Lowell received instructions to close in from Summit Point on the right of the Sixth Corps.

My object in securing the fords was to further my march on Winchester from the southeast, since, from all the information gathered during the 10th, I still thought Early could be brought to a stand at that point; but in this I was mistaken, as Torbert's reconnoissance proved, for on the morning of the 11th, when Merritt had driven the Confederate cavalry, then covering the Millwood pike west of the Opequon, off toward Kernstown, he found that their infantry and artillery were retreating south, up the Valley pike.

As soon as this information was obtained Torbert moved quickly through the toll-gate on the Front Royal and Winchester road to Newtown, to strike the enemy's flank and harass him in his retreat, Lowell following up through Winchester, on the Valley pike; Crook was turned to the left and ordered to Stony Point, while Emory and Wright, marching to the left also, were directed to take post on the night of the 11th between the Millwood and Front Royal roads, within supporting distance of Crook. Merritt meeting some of the enemy's cavalry at the tollgate, drove it in the direction of Newtown till it got inside the line of Gordon's division of infantry, which had been thrown out and posted behind barricades to cover the flank of the main force in its retreat. A portion of Merritt's cavalry attacked this infantry and drove in its skirmish-line, and though not able to dislodge Gordon, Merritt held the ground gained till night-fall, when the Confederate infantry moved off under cover of darkness to Hupp's Hill, between Strasburg and Cedar Creek.

The next morning Crook marched from Stony Point to Cedar Creek, Emory followed with Dwight, and the cavalry moved to the same point by way of Newtown and the Valley pike, the Sixth Corps following the cavalry. That night Crook was in position at Cedar Creek, on the left of the Valley pike, Emory on the right of the pike, the Sixth Corps on the right of Emory, and the cavalry on the flanks. In the afternoon a heavy skirmish-line had been thrown forward to the heights on the south side of Cedar Creek, and a brisk affair with the enemy's pickets took place, the Confederates occupying with their main force the heights north of Strasburg. On the morning of the 13th my cavalry went out to reconnoitre toward Strasburg, on the middle road, about two and a half miles west of the Valley pike, and discovered that Early's infantry was at Fisher's Hill, where he had thrown up behind Tumbling Run earthworks extending clear across the narrow valley between the Massanutten and North mountains. On the left of these works he had Vaughan's, McCausland's, and Johnson's brigades of cavalry under General Lomax, who at this time relieved General Ramseur from the command of the Confederate mounted forces.

Within the past day or two I had received information that a column of the enemy was moving up from Culpeper

Court House and approaching Front Royal through Chester Gap, and although the intelligence was unconfirmed, it caused me much solicitude; for there was strong probability that such a movement would be made, and any considerable force advancing through Front Royal toward Winchester could fall upon my rear and destroy my communication with Harper's Ferry, or, moving along the base of Massanutten Mountain, could attack my flank in conjunction with the force at Fisher's Hill without a possibility of my preventing it.

Neither Wilson's cavalry nor Grover's infantry had yet joined me, and the necessities, already explained, which obliged me to hold with strong garrisons Winchester and other points heretofore mentioned, had so depleted my line of battle strength that I knew the enemy would outnumber me when Anderson's corps should arrive in the valley. I deemed it advisable, therefore, to act with extreme caution, so, with the exception of a cavalry reconnoissance on the 13th, I remained on the defensive, quietly awaiting developments. In the evening of that day the enemy's skirmishers withdrew to Tumbling Run, his main force remaining inactive behind the intrenchments at Fisher's Hill waiting for the arrival of Anderson.

The rumors in regard to the force advancing from Culpeper kept increasing every hour, so on the morning of the 14th I concluded to send a brigade of cavalry to Front Royal to ascertain definitely what was up. At the same time I crossed the Sixth Corps to the south side of Cedar Creek, and occupied the heights near Strasburg. That day I received from the hands of Colonel Chipman, of the Adjutant-General's Department, the following despatch, to deliver which he had ridden in great haste from Washington through Snicker's Gap, escorted by a regiment of cavalry:

"CITY POINT, August 12, 1864–9 A.M.
"MAJOR-GENERAL HALLECK:
"Inform General Sheridan that it is now certain two (2) divisions of infantry have gone to Early, and some cavalry

and twenty (20) pieces of artillery. This movement commenced last Saturday night. He must be cautious, and act now on the defensive until movements here force them to detach to send this way. Early's force, with this increase, cannot exceed forty thousand men, but this is too much for General Sheridan to attack. Send General Sheridan the remaining brigade of the Nineteenth Corps.

"I have ordered to Washington all the one-hundred-day men. Their time will soon be out, but for the present they will do to serve in the defenses.

"U. S. GRANT, Lieutenant-General."

The despatch explained the movement from Culpeper, and on the morning of the 15th Merritt's two remaining brigades were sent to Front Royal to oppose Anderson, and the Sixth Corps withdrawn to the north side of Cedar Creek, where it would be in a position enabling me either to confront Anderson or to act defensively, as desired by General Grant.

To meet the requirements of his instructions I examined the map of the valley for a defensive line—a position where a smaller number of troops could hold a larger number—for this information led me to suppose that Early's force would greatly exceed mine when Anderson's two divisions of infantry and Fitzhugh Lee's cavalry had joined him. I could see but one such position, and that was at Halltown, in front of Harper's Ferry. Subsequent experience convinced me that there was no other really defensive line in the Shenandoah Valley, for at almost any other point the open country and its peculiar topography invites rather than forbids flanking operations.

This retrograde movement would also enable me to strengthen my command by Grover's division of the Nineteenth Corps and Wilson's cavalry, both of which divisions were marching from Washington by way of Snicker's Gap.

After fully considering the matter, I determined to move back to Halltown, carrying out, as I retired, my instructions to destroy all the forage and subsistence the country afforded. So Emory was ordered to retire to Winchester on the night of the 15th, and Wright and Crook to follow through Winchester to Clifton the next night.

For the cavalry, in this move to the rear, I gave the following instructions:

> "HEADQUARTERS MIDDLE MILITARY DIVISION,
> "Cedar Creek, Va., August 16, 1864.
>
> "GENERAL: In compliance with instructions of the Lieutenant-General commanding, you will make the necessary arrangements and give the necessary orders for the destruction of the wheat and hay south of a line from Millwood to Winchester and Petticoat Gap. You will seize all mules, horses, and cattle that may be useful to our army. Loyal citizens can bring in their claims against the Government for this necessary destruction. No houses will be burned, and officers in charge of this delicate but necessary duty must inform the people that the object is to make this valley untenable for the raiding parties of the rebel army.
>
> "Very respectfully,
>
> "P. H. SHERIDAN,
> "Major-General Commanding.
>
> "BRIGADIER-GENERAL A. T. A. TORBERT,
> "Chief of Cavalry, Middle Military Division."

During his visit to General Hunter at the Monocacy, General Grant had not only decided to retain in the Shenandoah Valley a large force sufficient to defeat Early's army or drive it back to Lee, but he had furthermore determined to make that section, by the destruction of its supplies, untenable for continued occupancy by the Confederates. This would cut off one of Lee's main-stays in the way of subsistence, and at the same time diminish the number of recruits and conscripts he received; the valley district while under his control not only supplying Lee with an abundance of food, but also furnishing him many men for his regular and irregular forces. Grant's instructions to destroy the valley began with the letter of August 5 to

Hunter, which was turned over to me, and this was followed at intervals by more specific directions, all showing the earnestness of his purpose. He had rightly concluded that it was time to bring the war home to a people engaged in raising crops from a prolific soil to feed the country's enemies, and devoting to the Confederacy its best youth. I endorsed the programme in all its parts, for the stores of meat and grain that the valley provided, and the men it furnished for Lee's depleted regiments, were the strongest auxiliaries he possessed in the whole insurgent section. In war a territory like this is a factor of great importance, and whichever adversary controls it permanently reaps all the advantages of its prosperity. Hence, as I have said, I endorsed Grant's programme, for I do not hold war to mean simply that lines of men shall engage each other in battle, and material interests be ignored. This is but a duel, in which one combatant seeks the other's life; war means much more, and is far worse than this. Those who rest at home in peace and plenty see but little of the horrors attending such a duel, and even grow indifferent to them as the struggle goes on, contenting themselves with encouraging all who are able-bodied to enlist in the cause, to fill up the shattered ranks as death thins them. It is another matter, however, when deprivation and suffering are brought to their own doors. Then the case appears much graver, for the loss of property weighs heavy with the most of mankind; heavier often, than the sacrifices made on the field of battle. Death is popularly considered the maximum of punishment in war, but it is not; reduction to poverty brings prayers for peace more surely and more quickly than does the destruction of human life, as the selfishness of man has demonstrated in more than one great conflict.

In the afternoon of the 16th I started back to Winchester, whence I could better supervise our regressive march. As I was passing through Newtown, I heard cannonading from the direction of Front Royal, and on reaching Winchester Merritt's couriers brought me word that he had been attacked at the crossing of the Shenandoah by Kershaw's division of Anderson's corps and two brigades of Fitzhugh Lee's cavalry, but that the attack had been handsomely repulsed, with a capture of two battle-flags and three hundred prisoners. This was an absolute confirmation of the despatch from Grant, and I was now more than satisfied with the wisdom of my withdrawal.

At daylight of the 17th Emory moved from Winchester to Berryville, and the same morning Crook and Wright reached Winchester, having started from Cedar Creek the day before. From Winchester, Crook and Wright resumed their march toward Clifton, Wright, who had the rear guard, getting that day as far as the Berryville crossing of the Opequon, where he was ordered to remain, while Crook went ahead till he reached the vicinity of Berryville. On the afternoon of the 17th Lowell with his two regiments of troopers came into Winchester, where he was joined by Wilson's mounted division, which had come by a rapid march from Snicker's ferry. In the mean time Merritt, after his handsome engagement with Kershaw near Front Royal, had been ordered back to the neighborhood of White Post, so that my cavalry outposts now extended from this last point around to the west of Winchester.

During all these operations the enemy had a signal-station on Three Top Mountain, almost overhanging Strasburg, from which every movement made by our troops could be plainly seen; therefore, early on the morning of the 17th he became aware of the fact that we were retiring down the valley, and at once made after us, and about sundown drove Torbert out of Winchester, he having been left there with Wilson and Lowell, and the Jersey brigade of the Sixth Corps, to develop the character of the enemy's pursuit. After a severe skirmish Wilson and Lowell fell back to Summit Point, and the Jersey brigade joined its corps at the crossing of the Opequon. This affair demonstrated that Early's whole army had followed us from Fisher's Hill, in concert with Anderson and Fitzhugh Lee from Front

Royal, and the two columns joined near Winchester the morning of the 18th.

That day I moved the Sixth Corps by way of Clifton to Flowing Spring, two and a half miles west of Charlestown, on the Smithfield pike; and Emory, with Dwight's and Grover's divisions (Grover's having joined that morning from Washington), to a position about the same distance south of Charlestown, on the Berryville pike. Following these movements, Merritt fell back to Berryville, covering the Berryville pike crossing of the Opequon, and Wilson was stationed at Summit Point, whence he held a line along the Opequon as far north as the bridge at Smithfield. Crook continued to hold on near Clifton until the next day, and was then moved into place on the left of Emory.

This line was practically maintained till the 21st, when the enemy, throwing a heavy force across the Opequon by the bridge at Smithfield, drove in my cavalry pickets to Summit Point, and followed up with a rapid advance against the position of the Sixth Corps near Flowing Spring. A sharp and obstinate skirmish with a heavy picket-line of the Sixth Corps grew out of this manœuvre, and resulted very much in our favor, but the quick withdrawal of the Confederates left no opportunity for a general engagement. It seems that General Early thought I had taken position near Summit Point, and that by moving rapidly around through Smithfield he could fall upon my rear in concert with an attack in front by Anderson, but the warm reception given him disclosed his error, for he soon discovered that my line lay in front of Charlestown instead of where he supposed.

In the manœuvre Merritt had been attacked in front of Berryville and Wilson at Summit Point, the former by cavalry and the latter by Anderson's infantry. The exposed positions of Merritt and Wilson necessitated their withdrawal if I was to continue to act on the defensive; so, after the army had moved back to Halltown the preceding night, without loss or inconvenience, I called them in and posted them on the right of the infantry.

My retrograde move from Strasburg to Halltown caused considerable alarm in the North, as the public was ignorant of the reasons for it; and in the excited state of mind then prevailing, it was generally expected that the reinforced Confederate army would again cross the Potomac, ravage Maryland and Pennsylvania, and possibly capture Washington. Mutterings of dissatisfaction reached me from many sources, and loud calls were made for my removal, but I felt confident that my course would be justified when the true situation was understood, for I knew that I was complying with my instructions. Therefore I paid small heed to the adverse criticisms pouring down from the North almost every day, being fully convinced that the best course was to bide my time, and wait till I could get the enemy into a position from which he could not escape without such serious misfortune as to have some bearing on the general result of the war. Indeed, at this time I was hoping that my adversary would renew the boldness he had exhibited the early part of the month, and strike for the north side of the Potomac, and wrote to General Grant on the 20th of August that I had purposely left everything in that direction open to the enemy.

On the 22d the Confederates moved to Charlestown and pushed well up to my position at Halltown. Here for the next three days they skirmished with my videttes and infantry pickets, Emory and Cook receiving the main attention; but finding that they could make no impression, and judging it to be an auspicious time to intensify the scare in the North, on the 25th of August Early despatched Fitzhugh Lee's cavalry to Williamsport, and moved all the rest of his army but Anderson's infantry and McCausland's cavalry to Kerneysville. This same day there was sharp picket firing along the whole front of my infantry line, arising, as afterward ascertained, from a heavy demonstration by Anderson. During this firing I sent Torbert, with Merritt's and Wilson's divisions, to Kerneysville, whence he was to proceed toward Leetown and learn what had become of Fitz. Lee.

About a mile from Leetown Torbert met a small force of Confederate cavalry, and soon after encountering it, stumbled on Breckenridge's corps of infantry on the march, apparently heading for Shepherdstown. The surprise was mutual, for Torbert expected to meet only the enemy's cavalry, while the Confederate infantry column was anticipating an unobstructed march to the Potomac. Torbert attacked with such vigor as at first to double up the head of Breckenridge's corps and throw it into confusion, but when the Confederates realized that they were confronted only by cavalry, Early brought up the whole of the four infantry divisions engaged in his manœuvre, and in a sharp attack pushed Torbert rapidly back.

All the advantages which Torbert had gained by surprising the enemy were nullified by this counter attack, and he was obliged to withdraw Wilson's division toward my right, to the neighborhood of Duffield's Station, Merritt drawing back to the same point by way of the Shepherdstown ford. Custer's brigade becoming isolated after the fight while assisting the rear guard, was also obliged to retire, which it did to Shepherdstown and there halted, picketing the river to Antietam ford.

When Torbert reported to me the nature of his encounter, and that a part of Early's infantry was marching to the north, while Fitzhugh Lee's cavalry had gone toward Martinsburg, I thought that the Confederate general meditated crossing his cavalry into Maryland, so I sent Wilson by way of Harper's Ferry to watch his movements from Boonesboro', and at the same time directed Averell, who had reported from West Virginia some days before, to take post at Williamsport and hold the crossing there until he was driven away. I also thought it possible that Early might cross the Potomac with his whole army, but the doubts of a movement like this outweighed the probabilities favoring it. Nevertheless, to meet such a contingency I arranged to throw my army on his rear should the occasion arise, and deeming my position at Halltown the most advantageous

in which to await developments, my infantry was retained
there.

If General Early had ever intended to cross the Potomac,
Torbert's discovery of his manœuvre put an end to his
scheme of invasion, for he well knew that any success he
might derive from such a course would depend on his
moving with celerity, and keeping me in ignorance of his
march till it should be well under way; so he settled all
the present uncertainties by retiring with all his troops
about Kerneysville to his old position at Bunker Hill behind
the Opequon, and on the night of the 26th silently withdrew Anderson and McCausland from my front at Halltown
to Stephenson's depot.

By the 27th all of Early's infantry was in position at
Brucetown and Bunker Hill, his cavalry holding the outposts of Leetown and Smithfield, and on that day Merritt's
division attacked the enemy's horse at Leetown, and
pressed it back through Smithfield to the west side of the
Opequon. This reconnoissance determined definitely that
Early had abandoned the projected movement into Maryland, if he ever seriously contemplated it; and I marched
my infantry out from Halltown to the front of Charlestown,
with the intention of occupying a line between Clifton and
Berryville the moment matters should so shape themselves
that I could do so with advantage. The night of the 28th
Wilson joined me near Charlestown from his points of
observation in Maryland, and the next day Averell crossed
the Potomac at Williamsport and advanced to Martinsburg.

Merritt's possession of Smithfield bridge made Early
somewhat uneasy, since it afforded opportunity for interposing a column between his right and left flanks, so he
concluded to retake the crossing, and, to this end, on the
29th advanced two divisions of infantry. A severe fight
followed, and Merritt was forced to retire, being driven
through the village toward Charlestown with considerable
loss. As Merritt was nearing my infantry line, I ordered
Ricketts's division of the Sixth Corps to his relief, and this
in a few minutes turned the tide, the Smithfield crossing

of the Opequon being regained, and afterward held by Lowell's brigade, supported by Ricketts. The next morning I moved Torbert, with Wilson and Merritt, to Berryville, and succeeding their occupation of that point there occurred along my whole line a lull, which lasted until the 3d of September, being undisturbed except by a combat near Bunker Hill between Averell's cavalry and a part of McCausland's, supported by Rodes's division of infantry, in which affair the Confederates were defeated with the loss of about fifty prisoners and considerable property in the shape of wagons and beef-cattle.

Meanwhile Torbert's movement to Berryville had alarmed Early, and as a counter move on the 2d of September he marched with the bulk of his army to Summit Point, but while reconnoitring in that region on the 3d he learned of the havoc that Averell was creating in his rear, and this compelled him to recross to the west side of the Opequon and mass his troops in the vicinity of Stephenson's depot, whence he could extend down to Bunker Hill, continue to threaten the Baltimore and Ohio railroad, and at the same time cover Winchester.

The same day I was moving my infantry to take up the Clifton-Berryville line, and that afternoon Wright went into position at Clifton, Crook occupied Berryville, and Emory's corps came in between them, forming almost a continuous line. Torbert had moved to White Post meanwhile, with directions to reconnoitre as far south as the Front Royal Pike.

My infantry had just got fairly into this position about an hour before sunset, when along Crook's front a combat took place that at the time caused me to believe it was Early's purpose to throw a column between Crook and Torbert, with the intention of isolating the latter, but the fight really arose from the attempt of General Anderson to return to Petersburg with Kershaw's division in response to loud calls from General Lee. Anderson started south on the 3d of September, and possibly this explains Early's reconnoissance that day to Summit Point as a covering movement, but his rapid withdrawal left him in ignorance of my advance, and Anderson marched on heedlessly toward Berryville, expecting to cross the Blue Ridge through Ashby's Gap. At Berryville, however, he blundered into Crook's lines about sunset, and a bitter little fight ensued, in which the Confederates got so much the worst of it that they withdrew toward Winchester. When General Early received word of this encounter he hurried to Anderson's assistance with three divisions, but soon perceiving what was hitherto unknown to him, that my whole army was on a new line, he decided, after some slight skirmishing, that Anderson must remain at Winchester until a favorable opportunity offered for him to rejoin Lee by another route.

Succeeding the discomfiture of Anderson, some minor operations took place on the part of Averell on the right and McIntosh's brigade of Wilson's division on the left, but from that time until the 19th of September no engagement of much importance occurred. The line from Clifton to Berryville was occupied by the Sixth Corps and Grover's and Dwight's divisions of the Nineteenth, Crook being transferred to Summit Point, whence I could use him to protect my right flank and my communication with Harper's Ferry, while the cavalry threatened the enemy's right flank and line of retreat up the valley.

The difference of strength between the two armies at this date was considerably in my favor, but the conditions attending my situation in a hostile region necessitated so much detached service to protect trains, and to secure Maryland and Pennsylvania from raids, that my excess in numbers was almost canceled by these incidental demands that could not be avoided, and although I knew that I was strong, yet, in consequence of the injunctions of General Grant, I deemed it necessary to be very cautious; and the fact that the Presidential election was impending made me doubly so, the authorities at Washington having impressed upon me that the defeat of my army might be followed by the overthrow of the party in power, which event, it was believed, would at least retard the progress of the war, if, indeed, it did not lead to the complete abandonment of all coercive measures. Under circumstances such as these I could not afford to risk a disaster, to say nothing of the intense disinclination every soldier has for such results; so, notwithstanding my superior strength, I determined to take all the time necessary to equip myself with the fullest information, and then seize an opportunity under such conditions that I could not well fail of success.

CHAPTER XIX

WHILE OCCUPYING THE GROUND between Clifton and Berryville, referred to in the last chapter, I felt the need of an efficient body of scouts to collect information regarding the enemy, for the defective intelligence-establishment with which I started out from Harper's Ferry early in August had not proved satisfactory. I therefore began to organize my scouts on a system which I hoped would give better results than had the method hitherto pursued in the department, which was to employ on this service doubtful citizens and Confederate deserters. If these should turn out untrustworthy, the mischief they might do us gave me grave apprehension, and I finally concluded that those of our own soldiers who should volunteer for the delicate and hazardous duty would be the most valuable material, and decided that they should have a battalion organization and be commanded by an officer, Major H. K. Young, of the First Rhode Island Infantry. These men were disguised in Confederate uniforms whenever necessary, were paid from the Secret-Service Fund in proportion to the value of the intelligence they furnished, which often stood us in good stead in checking the forays of Gilmore, Mosby, and other irregulars. Beneficial results came from the plan in many other ways too, and particularly so when in a few days two of my scouts put me in the way of getting news conveyed from Winchester. They had learned that just outside of my lines, near Millwood, there was living an old colored man, who had a permit from the Confederate commander to go into Winchester and return three times a week, for the purpose of selling vegetables to the inhabitants. The scouts had sounded this man, and, finding him both loyal and shrewd, suggested that he might be made useful to us within the enemy's lines; and the proposal struck me as feasible, provided there could be found in Winchester some reliable person who would be willing to co-operate and correspond with me. I asked General Crook, who was acquainted with many of the Union people of Winchester, if he knew of such a person, and he recommended a Miss Rebecca Wright, a young lady whom he had met there before the battle of Kernstown, who, he said, was a member of the Society of Friends and the teacher of a small private school. He knew she was faithful and loyal to the Government, and thought she might be willing to render us assistance, but he could not be certain of this, for on account of her well-known loyalty she was under constant surveillance. I hesitated at first, but finally deciding to try it, despatched the two scouts to the old Negro's cabin, and they brought him to my headquarters late that night. I was soon convinced of the Negro's fidelity, and asking him if he was acquainted with Miss Rebecca Wright, of Winchester, he replied that he knew her well. Thereupon I told him what I wished to do, and after a little persuasion he agreed to carry a letter to her on his next marketing trip. My message was prepared by writing it on tissue paper, which was then compressed into a small pellet, and protected by wrapping it in tin-foil so that it could be safely carried in the man's mouth. The probability of his being searched when he came to the Confederate picket-line was not remote, and in such event he was to swallow the pellet. The letter appealed to Miss Wright's loyalty and patriotism, and requested her to furnish me with information regarding the strength and condition of Early's army. The night before the Negro started one of the scouts placed the odd-looking communication in his hands, with renewed injunctions as to secrecy and promptitude. Early the next morning it was delivered to Miss Wright, with an intimation that a letter of importance was enclosed in the tin-foil, the Negro telling her at the same time that she might expect him to call for a message in reply before his return home. At first Miss Wright began to open the pellet nervously, but when told to be careful, and to preserve the foil as a wrapping for her answer, she proceeded slowly and carefully, and when the note appeared intact the messenger retired, remarking again that in the evening he would come for an answer.

On reading my communication Miss Wright was much startled by the perils it involved, and hesitatingly consulted her mother, but her devoted loyalty soon silenced every other consideration, and the brave girl resolved to comply with my request, notwithstanding it might jeopardize her life. The evening before a convalescent Confederate officer had visited her mother's house, and in conversation about the war had disclosed the fact that Kershaw's division of infantry and Cutshaw's battalion of artillery had started to rejoin General Lee. At the time Miss Wright heard this she attached little if any importance to it, but now she perceived the value of the intelligence, and, as her first venture, determined to send it to me at once, which she did with a promise that in the future she would with great pleasure continue to transmit information by the Negro messenger.

Miss Wright's answer proved of more value to me than she anticipated, for it not only quieted the conflicting reports concerning Anderson's corps, but was most important in showing positively that Kershaw was gone, and this circumstance led, three days later, to the battle of the Opequon, or Winchester as it has been unofficially called. Word to the effect that some of Early's troops were under orders to return to Petersburg, and would start back at the first favorable opportunity, had been communicated to me already from many sources, but we had not been able to ascertain the date for their departure. Now that they had actually started, I decided to wait before offering battle until Kershaw had gone so far as to preclude his return, feeling confident that my prudence would be justified by the improved chances of victory; and then, besides, Mr. Stanton kept reminding me that positive success was necessary to counteract the political dissatisfaction existing in some of the Northern States. This course was advised and approved by General Grant, but even with his powerful backing it was difficult to resist the persistent pressure of those whose judgment, warped by their interests in the Baltimore and Ohio railroad, was often confused and misled by stories of scouts (sent out from Washington), averring that Kershaw and Fitzhugh Lee had returned to Petersburg, Breckenridge to southwestern Virginia, and at one time even maintaining that Early's whole army was east of the Blue Ridge, and its commander himself at Gordonsville.

During the inactivity prevailing in my army for the ten days preceding Miss Wright's communication the infantry was quiet, with the exception of Getty's division, which made a reconnoissance to the Opequon, and developed a heavy force of the enemy at Edwards's Corners. The cavalry, however, was employed a good deal in this interval skirmishing—heavily at times—to maintain a space about six miles in width between the hostile lines, for I wished to control this ground so that when I was released from the instructions of August 12 I could move my men into position for attack without the knowledge of Early. The most noteworthy of these mounted encounters was that of McIntosh's brigade, which captured the Eighth South Carolina at Abraham's Creek September 13.

It was the evening of the 16th of September that I received from Miss Wright the positive information that Kershaw was in march toward Front Royal on his way by

Chester Gap to Richmond. Concluding that this was my opportunity, I at once resolved to throw my whole force into Newtown the next day, but a despatch from General Grant directing me to meet him at Charlestown, whither he was coming to consult with me, caused me to defer action until after I should see him. In our resulting interview at Charlestown, I went over the situation very thoroughly, and pointed out with so much confidence the chances of a complete victory should I throw my army across the Valley pike near Newtown that he fell in with the plan at once, authorized me to resume the offensive, and to attack Early as soon as I deemed it most propitious to do so; and although before leaving City Point he had outlined certain operations for my army, yet he neither discussed nor disclosed his plans, my knowledge of the situation striking him as being so much more accurate than his own.

The interview over, I returned to my army to arrange for its movement toward Newtown, but while busy with these preparations, a report came to me from General Averell which showed that Early was moving with two divisions of infantry toward Martinsburg. This considerably altered the state of affairs, and I now decided to change my plan and attack at once the two divisions remaining about Winchester and Stephenson's depot, and later, the two sent to Martinsburg; the disjointed state of the enemy giving me an opportunity to take him in detail, unless the Martinsburg column should be returned by forced marches.

While General Early was in the telegraph office at Martinsburg on the morning of the 18th, he learned of Grant's visit to me; and anticipating activity by reason of this circumstance, he promptly proceeded to withdraw so as to get the two divisions within supporting distance of Ramseur's, which lay across the Berryville pike about two miles east of Winchester, between Abraham's Creek and Red Bud Run, so by the night of the 18th Wharton's division, under Breckenridge, was at Stephenson's depot, Rodes near there, and Gordon's at Bunker Hill. At daylight of the 19th these positions of the Confederate infantry still obtained, with the cavalry of Lomax, Jackson, and Johnson on the right of Ramseur, while to the left and rear of the enemy's general line was Fitzhugh Lee, covering from Stephenson's depot west across the Valley pike to Apple-pie Ridge.

My army moved at 3 o'clock that morning. The plan was for Torbert to advance with Merritt's division of cavalry from Summit Point, carry the crossings of the Opequon at Stevens's and Lock's fords, and form a junction near Stephenson's depot, with Averell, who was to move south from Darksville by the Valley pike. Meanwhile, Wilson was to strike up the Berryville pike, carry the Berryville crossing of the Opequon, charge through the gorge or cañon on the road west of the stream, and occupy the open ground at the head of this defile. Wilson's attack was to be supported by the Sixth and Nineteenth corps, which were ordered to the Berryville crossing, and as the cavalry gained the open ground beyond the gorge, the two infantry corps, under command of General Wright, were expected to press on after and occupy Wilson's ground, who was then to shift to the south bank of Abraham's Creek and cover my left; Crook's two divisions, having to march from Summit Point, were to follow the Sixth and Nineteenth corps to the Opequon, and should they arrive before the action began, they were to be held in reserve till the proper moment came, and then, as a turning-column, be thrown over toward the Valley pike, south of Winchester.

McIntosh's brigade of Wilson's division drove the enemy's pickets away from the Berryville crossing at dawn, and Wilson following rapidly through the gorge with the rest of the division, debouched from its western extremity with such suddenness as to capture a small earthwork in front of General Ramseur's main line; and notwithstanding the Confederate infantry, on recovering from its astonishment, tried hard to dislodge them, Wilson's troopers obstinately held the work till the Sixth Corps came up. I followed Wilson to select the ground on which to form the infantry. The Sixth Corps began to arrive about 8 o'clock, and taking up the line Wilson had been holding, just beyond the head of the narrow ravine, the cavalry was transferred to the south side of Abraham's Creek.

The Confederate line lay along some elevated ground about two miles east of Winchester, and extended from Abraham's Creek north across the Berryville pike, the left being hidden in the heavy timber on Red Bud Run. Between this line and mine, especially on my right, clumps of woods and patches of underbrush occurred here and there, but the undulating ground consisted mainly of open fields, many of which were covered with standing corn that had already ripened.

Much time was lost in getting all of the Sixth and Nineteenth corps through the narrow defile, Grover's division being greatly delayed there by a train of ammunition wagons, and it was not until late in the forenoon that the troops intended for the attack could be got into line ready to advance. General Early was not slow to avail himself of the advantages thus offered him, and my chances of striking him in detail were growing less every moment, for Gordon and Rodes were hurrying their divisions from Stephenson's depot across-country on a line that would place Gordon in the woods south of Red Bud Run, and bring Rodes into the interval between Gordon and Ramseur.

When the two corps had all got through the cañon they were formed with Getty's division of the Sixth to the left of the Berryville pike, Rickett's division to the right of the pike, and Russell's division in reserve in rear of the other two. Grover's division of the Nineteenth Corps came next on the right of Rickett's, with Dwight to its rear in reserve, while Crook was to begin massing near the Opequon crossing about the time Wright and Emory were ready to attack.

Just before noon the line of Getty, Ricketts, and Grover moved forward, and as we advanced, the Confederates, covered by some heavy woods on their right, slight underbrush and corn-fields along their centre, and a large body of timber on their left along the Red Bud, opened fire from their whole front. We gained considerable ground at first, especially on our left, but the desperate resistance which the right met with demonstrated that the time we had unavoidably lost in the morning had been of incalculable value to Early, for it was evident that he had been enabled already to so far concentrate his troops as to have the different divisions of his army in a connected line of battle in good shape to resist.

Getty and Ricketts made some progress toward Winchester in connection with Wilson's cavalry, which was beyond the Senseny road on Getty's left, and as they were pressing back Ramseur's infantry and Lomax's cavalry Grover attacked from the right with decided effect. Grover in a few minutes broke up Evans's brigade of Gordon's division, but his pursuit of Evans destroyed the continuity of my general line, and increased an interval that had already been made by the deflection of Ricketts to the left, in obedience to instructions that had been given him to guide his division on the Berryville pike. As the line pressed forward, Ricketts observed this widening interval and endeavored to fill it with the small brigade of Colonel Keifer, but at this juncture both Gordon and Rodes struck the weak spot where the right of the Sixth Corps and the left of the Nineteenth should have been in conjunction, and succeeded in checking my advance by driving back a part of Ricketts's division, and the most of Grover's. As these troops were retiring I ordered Russell's reserve division to be put into action, and just as the flank of the enemy's troops in pursuit of Grover was presented, Upton's brigade, led in person by both Russell and Upton, struck it in a charge so vigorous as to drive the Confederates back in turn to their original ground.

The success of Russell enabled me to re-establish the right of my line some little distance in advance of the position from which it started in the morning, and behind Russell's division (now commanded by Upton) the broken regiments of Ricketts's division were rallied. Dwight's division was then brought up on the right, and Grover's men formed behind it.

The charge of Russell was most opportune, but it cost many men in killed and wounded. Among the former was the courageous Russell himself, killed by a piece of shell that passed through his heart, although he had previously been struck by a bullet in the left breast, which wound, from its nature, must have proved mortal, yet of which he had not spoken. Russell's death oppressed us all with sadness, and me particularly. In the early days of my army life he was my captain and friend, and I was deeply indebted to him, not only for sound advice and good example, but for the inestimable service he had just performed, and sealed with his life, so it may be inferred how keenly I felt his loss.

As my lines were being rearranged, it was suggested to me to put Crook into the battle, but so strongly had I set my heart on using him to take possession of the Valley pike and cut off the enemy, that I resisted this advice, hoping that the necessity for putting him in would be obviated by the attack near Stephenson's depot that Torbert's cavalry was to make, and from which I was momentarily expecting to hear. No news of Torbert's progress came, however, so, yielding at last, I directed Crook to take post on the right of the Nineteenth Corps and, when the action was renewed, to push his command forward as a turning-column in conjunction with Emory. After some delay in the annoying defile, Crook got his men up, and posting Colonel Thoburn's division on the prolongation of the Nineteenth Corps, he formed Colonel Duval's division to the right of Thoburn. Here I joined Crook, informing him that I had just got word that Torbert was driving the enemy in confusion along the Martinsburg pike toward Winchester; at the same time I directed him to attack the moment all of Duval's men were in line. Wright was instructed to advance in concert with Crook, by swinging Emory and the right of the Sixth Corps to the left together in a half-wheel. Then leaving Crook, I rode along the Sixth and Nineteenth corps, the open ground over which they were passing affording a rare opportunity to witness the precision with which the attack was taken up from right to left. Crook's success began the moment he started to turn the enemy's left; and assured by the fact that Torbert had stampeded the Confederate cavalry and thrown Breckenridge's infantry into such disorder that it could do little to prevent the envelopment of Gordon's left, Crook pressed forward without even a halt.

Both Emory and Wright took up the fight as ordered, and as they did so I sent word to Wilson, in the hope that he could partly perform the work originally laid out for Crook, to push along the Senseny road and, if possible, gain the valley pike south of Winchester. I then returned toward my right flank, and as I reached the Nineteenth Corps the enemy was contesting the ground in its front with great obstinacy; but Emory's dogged persistence was at length rewarded with success, just as Crook's command emerged from the morass of Red Bud Run, and swept around Gordon, toward the right of Breckenridge, who, with two of Wharton's brigades, was holding a line at right angles with the Valley pike for the protection of the Confederate rear. Early had ordered these two brigades back from Stephenson's depot in the morning, purposing to protect with them his right flank and line of retreat, but while they were *en route* to this end, he was obliged to recall them to his left to meet Crook's attack.

To confront Torbert, Patton's brigade of infantry and some of Fitzhugh Lee's cavalry had been left back by Breckenridge, but, with Averell on the west side of the Valley pike and Merritt on the east, Torbert began to drive this opposing force toward Winchester the moment he struck it near Stephenson's depot, keeping it on the go till it reached the position held by Breckenridge, where it endeavored to make a stand.

The ground which Breckenridge was holding was open, and offered an opportunity such as seldom had been presented during the war for a mounted attack, and Torbert was not slow to take advantage of it. The instant Merritt's division could be formed for the charge, it went at Breckenridge's infantry and Fitzhugh Lee's cavalry with such momentum as to break the Confederate left, just as Averell was passing around it. Merritt's brigades, led by Custer, Lowell, and Devin, met from the start with pronounced success, and with sabre or pistol in hand literally rode down a battery of five guns and took about 1,200 prisoners. Almost simultaneously with this cavalry charge, Crook struck Breckenridge's right and Gordon's left, forcing these divisions to give way, and as they retired, Wright, in a vigorous attack, quickly broke Rodes up and pressed Ramseur so hard that the whole Confederate army fell back, contracting its lines within some breastworks which had been thrown up at a former period of the war, immediately in front of Winchester.

Here Early tried hard to stem the tide, but soon Torbert's cavalry began passing around his left flank, and as Crook, Emory, and Wright attacked in front, panic took possession of the enemy, his troops, now fugitives and stragglers, seeking escape into and through Winchester.

When this second break occurred, the Sixth and Nineteenth corps were moved over toward the Millwood pike to help Wilson on the left, but the day was so far spent that they could render him no assistance, and Ramseur's division, which had maintained some organization, was in such tolerable shape as to check him. Meanwhile Torbert passed around to the west of Winchester to join Wilson, but was unable to do so till after dark. Crook's command pursued the enemy through the town to Mill Creek, I going along.

Just after entering the town Crook and I met, in the main street, three young girls, who gave us the most hearty reception. One of these young women was a Miss Griffith, the other two Miss Jennie and Miss Susie Meredith. During the day they had been watching the battle from the roof of the Meredith residence, with tears and lamentations, they said, in the morning when misfortune appeared to have overtaken the Union troops, but with unbounded exultation when, later, the tide set in against the Confederates. Our presence was, to them, an assurance of victory, and their delight being irrepressible, they indulged in the most unguarded manifestations and expressions. When cautioned by Crook, who knew them well, and reminded that the valley had hitherto been a race-course—one day in the possession of friends, and the next of enemies—and warned of the dangers they were incurring by such demonstrations, they assured him that they had no further fears of that kind, now, adding that Early's army was so demoralized by the defeat it had just sustained that it would never be in condition to enter Winchester again. As soon as we had succeeded in calming the excited girls a little I expressed a desire to find some place where I could write a telegram to General Grant informing him of the result of the battle, and General Crook conducted me to the home of Miss Wright, where I met for the first time the woman who had contributed so much to our success, and on a desk in her schoolroom wrote the despatch announcing that we had sent Early's army whirling up the valley.

My losses in the battle of the Opequon were heavy, amounting to about 4,500 killed, wounded, and missing. Among the killed was General Russell, commanding a division, and the wounded included Generals Upton, McIntosh and Chapman, and Colonels Duval and Sharpe. The Confederate loss in killed, wounded, and prisoners about equaled mine, General Rodes being of the killed, while Generals Fitzhugh Lee and York were severely wounded.

We captured five pieces of artillery and nine battle-flags. The restoration of the lower valley—from the Potomac to Strasburg—to the control of the Union forces caused great rejoicing in the North, and relieved the Administration from further solicitude for the safety of the Maryland and Pennsylvania borders. The President's appreciation of the victory was expressed in a despatch so like Mr. Lincoln in the spirit and the style of it. This he supplemented by promoting me to the grade of brigadier-general in the regular army, and assigning me to the permanent command of the Middle Military Department, and following that came warm congratulations from Mr. Stanton and from Generals Grant, Sherman, and Meade.

The battle was not fought out on the plan in accordance with which marching orders were issued to my troops, for I then hoped to take Early in detail, and with Crook's force cut off his retreat. I adhered to this purpose during the early part of the contest, but was obliged to abandon the idea because of unavoidable delays by which I was prevented from getting the Sixth and Nineteenth corps through the narrow defile and into position early enough to destroy Ramseur while still isolated. So much delay had not been anticipated, and this loss of time was taken advantage of by the enemy to recall the troops diverted to Bunker Hill and Martinsburg on the 17th, thus enabling him to bring them all to the support of Ramseur before I could strike with effect. My idea was to attack Ramseur and Wharton, successively, at a very early hour and before they could get succor, but I was not in condition to do it till nearly noon, by which time Gordon and Rodes had been enabled to get upon the ground at a point from which, as I advanced, they enfiladed my right flank, and gave it such a repulse that to re-form this part of my line I was obliged to recall the left from some of the ground it had gained. It was during this reorganization of my lines that I changed my plan as to Crook, and moved him from my left to my right. This I did with great reluctance, for I hoped to destroy Early's army entirely if Crook continued on his original line of march toward the Valley pike, south of Winchester; and although the ultimate results did, in a measure vindicate the change, yet I have always thought that by adhering to the original plan we might have captured the bulk of Early's army.

CHAPTER XX

THE NIGHT OF THE 19TH OF SEPTEMBER I gave orders for following Early up the valley next morning—the pursuit to begin at daybreak—and in obedience to these directions Torbert moved Averell out on the Back road leading to Cedar Creek, and Merritt up the Valley pike toward Strasburg, while Wilson was directed on Front Royal by way of Stevensburg. Merritt's division was followed by the infantry, Emory's and Wright's columns marching abreast in the open country to the right and left of the pike, and Crook's immediately behind them. The enemy having kept up his retreat at night, presented no opposition whatever until the cavalry discovered him posted at Fisher's Hill, on the first defensive line where he could hope to make any serious resistance. No effort was made to dislodge him, and later in the day, after Wright and Emory came up, Torbert shifted Merritt over toward the Back road till he rejoined Averell. As Merritt moved to the right, the Sixth and Nineteenth corps crossed Cedar Creek and took up the ground the cavalry was vacating, Wright posting his own corps to the west of the Valley pike overlooking Strasburg, and Emory's on his left so as to extend almost to the road leading from Strasburg to Front Royal. Crook, as he came up the same evening, went into position in some heavy timber on the north bank of Cedar Creek.

A reconnoissance made pending these movements convinced me that the enemy's position at Fisher's Hill was so strong that a direct assault would entail unnecessary destruction of life, and, besides, be of doubtful result. At the point where Early's troops were in position, between the Massanutten range and Little North Mountain, the valley is only about three and a half miles wide. All along the precipitous bluff which overhangs Tumbling Run on the south side, a heavy line of earthworks had been constructed when Early retreated to this point in August, and these were now being strengthened so as to make them almost impregnable; in fact, so secure did Early consider himself that, for convenience, his ammunition chests were taken from the caissons and placed behind the breastworks. Wharton, now in command of Breckenridge's division—its late commander having gone to southwest Virginia—held the right of this line, with Gordon next him; Pegram, commanding Ramseur's old division, joined Gordon. Ramseur with Rodes's division, was on Pegram's left, while Lomax's cavalry, now serving as foot-troops, extended the line to the Back road. Fitzhugh Lee being wounded, his cavalry, under General Wickham, was sent to Milford to prevent Fisher's Hill from being turned through the Luray Valley.

In consequence of the enemy's being so well protected from a direct assault, I resolved on the night of the 20th to use again a turning-column against his left, as had been done on the 19th at the Opequon. To this end I resolved to move Crook, unperceived if possible, over to the eastern face of Little North Mountain, whence he could strike the left and rear of the Confederate line, and as he broke it up, I could support him by a left half-wheel of my whole line of battle. The execution of this plan would require perfect secrecy, however, for the enemy from his signal-station on Three Top could plainly see every movement of our troops in daylight. Hence, to escape such observation, I marched Crook during the night of the 20th into some heavy timber north of Cedar Creek, where he lay concealed all day the 21st. This same day Wright and Emory were moved up closer to the Confederate works, and the Sixth Corps, after a severe fight, in which Ricketts's and Getty were engaged, took up some high ground on the right of the Manassas Gap railroad in plain view of the Confederate works, and confronting a commanding point where much of Early's artillery was massed. Soon after General Wright had established this line I rode with him along it to the westward, and finding that the enemy was still holding an elevated position further to our right, on the north side of Tumbling Run, I directed this also to be occupied. Wright soon carried the point, which gave us an unobstructed view of the enemy's works and offered good ground for our artillery. It also enabled me to move the whole of the Sixth Corps to the front till its line was within about seven hundred yards of the enemy's works; the Nineteenth Corps, on the morning of the 22d, covering the ground vacated by the Sixth by moving to the front and extending to the right, but still keeping its reserves on the railroad.

In the darkness of the night of the 21st, Crook was brought across Cedar Creek and hidden in a clump of timber behind Hupp's Hill till daylight of the 22d, when, under cover of the intervening woods and ravines, he was marched beyond the right of the Sixth Corps and again concealed not far from the Back road. After Crook had got into this last position, Ricketts's division was pushed out until it confronted the left of the enemy's infantry, the rest of the Sixth Corps extending from Ricketts's left to the Manassas Gap railroad, while the Nineteenth Corps filled in the space between the left of the Sixth and the North Fork of the Shenandoah.

When Ricketts moved out on this new line, in conjunction with Averell's cavalry on his right, the enemy surmising, from information secured from his signal-station, no doubt, that my attack was to be made from Ricketts's front, prepared for it there, but no such intention ever existed. Ricketts was pushed forward only that he might readily join Crook's turning-column as it swung into the enemy's rear. To ensure success, all that I needed now was enough daylight to complete my arrangements, the secrecy of movement imposed by the situation consuming many valuable hours.

While Ricketts was occupying the enemy's attention, Crook, again moving unobserved into the dense timber on the eastern face of Little North Mountain, conducted his command south in two parallel columns until he gained the rear of the enemy's works, when, marching his divisions by the left flank, he led them in an easterly direction down the mountain-side. As he emerged from the timber near the base of the mountain, the Confederates discovered him, of course, and opened with their batteries, but it was too late—they having few troops at hand to confront the turning-column. Loudly cheering, Crook's men quickly crossed the broken stretch in rear of the enemy's left, producing confusion, and consternation at every step.

About a mile from the mountain's base Crook's left was joined by Ricketts, who in proper time had begun to swing his division into the action, and the two commands moved along in rear of the works so rapidly that, with but slight resistance, the Confederates abandoned the guns massed near the centre. The swinging movement of Ricketts was taken up successively from right to left throughout my line, and in a few minutes the enemy was thoroughly routed, the action, though brief, being none the less decisive. Lomax's dismounted cavalry gave way first, but was shortly followed by all the Confederate infantry in an indescribable panic, precipitated doubtless by fears of being caught and captured in the pocket formed by Tumbling Run and the North Fork of the Shenandoah River. The stampede was complete, the enemy leaving the field without semblance of organization, abandoning nearly all his artillery and such other property as was in the works, and the rout extending through the fields and over the roads toward Woodstock, Wright and Emory in hot pursuit.

Midway between Fisher's Hill and Woodstock there is some high ground, where at night-fall a small squad endeavored to stay us with two pieces of artillery, but this attempt at resistance proved fruitless, and, notwithstanding the darkness, the guns were soon captured. The chase was then taken up by Devin's brigade as soon as it could be passed to the front, and continued till after daylight the next morning, but the delays incident to a night pursuit made it impossible for Devin to do more than pick up stragglers.

Our success was very great, yet I had anticipated results still more pregnant. Indeed, I had high hopes of capturing almost the whole of Early's army before it reached New Market, and with this object in view, during the manœuvres of the 21st I had sent Torbert up the Luray Valley with Wilson's division and two of Merritt's brigades, in the expectation that he would drive Wickham out of the Luray Pass by Early's right, and by crossing the Massanutten Mountain near New Market, gain his rear. Torbert started in good season, and after some slight skirmishing at Gooney Run, got as far as Milford, but failed to dislodge Wickham. In fact, he made little or no attempt to force Wickham from his position, and with only a feeble effort withdrew. I heard nothing at all from Torbert during the 22d, and supposing that everything was progressing favorably, I was astonished and chagrined on the morning of the 23d, at Woodstock, to receive the intelligence that he had fallen back to Front Royal and Buckton ford. My disappointment was extreme, but there was now no help for the situation save to renew and emphasize Torbert's orders, and this was done at once, notwithstanding that I thought the delay had so much diminished the chances of his getting in the rear of Early as to make such a result a very remote possibility, unless, indeed, far greater zeal was displayed than had been in the first attempt to penetrate the Luray Valley.

The battle of Fisher's Hill was, in a measure, a part of

the battle of the Opequon; that is to say, it was an incident of the pursuit resulting from that action. In many ways, however, it was much more satisfactory, and particularly so because the plan arranged on the evening of the 20th was carried out to the very letter by Generals Wright, Crook, and Emory, not only in all their preliminary manœuvres, but also during the fight itself. The only drawback was with the cavalry, and to this day I have been unable to account satisfactory for Torbert's failure. No doubt, Wickham's position near Milford was a strong one, but Torbert ought to have made a fight. Had he been defeated in this, his withdrawal then to await the result at Fisher's Hill would have been justified, but it does not appear that he made any serious effort at all to dislodge the Confederate cavalry: his impotent attempt not only chagrined me very much, but occasioned much unfavorable comment throughout the army.

We reached Woodstock early on the morning of the 23d, and halted there some little time to let the troops recover their organization, which had been broken in the night march they had just made. When the commands had closed up we pushed on toward Edinburg, in the hope of making more captures at Narrow Passage Creek; but the Confederates, to fleet for us, got away; so General Wright halted the infantry not far from Edinburg, till rations could be brought the men. Meanwhile I, having remained at Woodstock, sent Devin's brigade to press the enemy under every favorable opportunity, and if possible prevent him from halting long enough to reorganize. Notwithstanding Devin's efforts the Confederates managed to assemble a considerable force to resist him, and being too weak for the rear-guard, he awaited the arrival of Averell, who, I had informed him, would be hurried to the front with all possible despatch, for I thought that Averell must be close at hand. It turned out, however, that he was not near by at all, and, moreover, that without good reason he had refrained from taking any part whatever in pursuing the enemy in the flight from Fisher's Hill, and in fact had gone into camp and left to the infantry the work of pursuit.

It was nearly noon when Averell came up, and a great deal of precious time had been lost. We had some hot words, but hoping that he would retrieve the mistake of the night before, I directed him to proceed to the front at once, and in conjunction with Devin close with the enemy. He reached Devin's command about 3 o'clock in the afternoon, just as this officer was pushing the Confederates so energetically that they were abandoning Mount Jackson, yet Averell utterly failed to accomplish anything. Indeed, his indifferent attack was not at all worthy the excellent soldiers he commanded, and when I learned that it was his intention to withdraw from the enemy's front, and this, too, on the indefinite report of a signal-officer that a "brigade or division" of Confederates was turning his right flank, and that he had not seriously attempted to verify the information, I sent him this order:

"Headquarters Middle Military Division,
"Woodstock, Va., Sept. 23, 1864.
"Brevet Major-General Averell:

"Your report and report of signal-officer received. I do not want you to let the enemy bluff you or your command, and I want you to distinctly understand this note. I do not advise rashness, but I do desire resolution and actual fighting, with necessary casualties, before you retire. There must now be no backing or filling by you without a superior force of the enemy actually engaging you.

"P. H. Sheridan,
"Major-General Commanding."

Some little time after this note went to Averell, word was brought me that he had already carried out the programme indicated when forwarding the report of the expected turning of his right, and that he had actually withdrawn and gone into camp near Hawkinsburg. I then decided to relieve him from the command of his division, which I did, ordering him to Wheeling, Colonel William H. Powell being assigned to succeed him.

The removal of Averell was but the culmination of a series of events extending back to the time I assumed command of the Middle Military Division. At the outset, General Grant, fearing discord on account of Averell's ranking Torbert, authorized me to relieve the former officer, but I hoped that if any trouble of this sort arose, it could be allayed, or at least repressed, during the campaign against Early, since the different commands would often have to act separately. After that, the dispersion of my army by the return of the Sixth Corps and Torbert's cavalry to the Army of the Potomac would take place, I thought, and this would restore matters to their normal condition; but Averell's dissatisfaction began to show itself immediately after his arrival at Martinsburg, on the 14th of August, and, except when he was conducting some independent expedition, had been manifested on all occasions since. I therefore thought that the interest of the service would be subserved by removing one whose growing indifference might render the best-laid plans inoperative.

The failure of Averell to press the enemy the evening of the 23d gave Early time to collect his scattered forces and take up a position on the east side of the North Fork of the Shenandoah, his left resting on the west side of that stream at Rude's Hill, a commanding point about two miles south of Mt. Jackson. Along this line he had constructed some slight works during the night, and at daylight on the 24th I moved the Sixth and Nineteenth corps through Mt. Jackson to attack him, sending Powell's division to pass around his left flank, toward Timberville, and Devin's brigade across the North Fork, to move along the base of Peaked Ridge and attack his right. The country was entirely open, and none of these manœuvres could be executed without being observed, so as soon as my advance began, the enemy rapidly retreated in line of battle up the valley through New Market, closely followed by Wright and Emory, their artillery on the pike and their columns on its right and left. Both sides moved with celerity, the Confederates stimulated by the desire to escape, and our men animated by the prospect of wholly destroying Early's army. The stern-chase continued for about thirteen miles, our infantry often coming within range, yet whenever we began to deploy, the Confederates increased the distance between us by resorting to a double quick, evading battle with admirable tact. While all this was going on, the open country permitted us a rare and brilliant sight, the bright sun gleaming from the arms and trappings of the thousands of pursuers and pursued.

Near New Market, as a last effort to hold the enemy, I pushed Devin's cavalry—comprising about five hundred men—with two guns right up on Early's lines, in the hope that the tempting opportunity given him to capture the guns would stay his retreat long enough to let my infantry deploy within range, but he refused the bait, and after momentarily checking Devin he continued on with little loss and in pretty good order.

All hope of Torbert's appearing in rear of the Confederates vanished as they passed beyond New Market. Some six miles south of this place Early left the Valley Pike and took the road to Keezletown, a move due in a measure to Powell's march by way of Timberville toward Lacy's Springs, but mainly caused by the fact that the Keezletown road ran immediately along the base of Peaked Mountain— a rugged ridge affording protection to Early's right flank— and led in a direction facilitating his junction with Kershaw, who had been ordered back to him from Culpeper the day after the battle of the Opequon. The chase was kept up on the Keezeltown road till darkness overtook us, when my weary troops were permitted to go into camp; and as soon as the enemy discovered by our fires that the pursuit had stopped, he also bivouacked some five miles farther south toward Port Republic.

The next morning Early was joined by Lomax's cavalry from Harrisonburg, Wickham's and Payne's brigades of cavalry also uniting with him from the Luray Valley. His whole army then fell back to the mouth of Brown's Gap to await Kershaw's division and Cutshaw's artillery, now on their return.

By the morning of the 25th the main body of the enemy had disappeared entirely from my front, and the capture of some small squads of Confederates in the neighboring hills furnished us the only incidents of the day. Among the prisoners was a tall and fine looking officer, much worn with hunger and fatigue. The moment I saw him I recognized him as a former comrade, George W. Carr, with whom I had served in Washington Territory. He was in those days a lieutenant in the Ninth Infantry, and was one of the officers who superintended the execution of the nine Indians at the Cascades of the Columbia in 1856. Carr was very much emaciated, and greatly discouraged by the turn events had recently taken. For old acquaintance sake I gave him plenty to eat, and kept him in comfort at my headquarters until the next batch of prisoners was sent to the rear, when he went with them. He had resigned from the regular army at the commencement of hostilities, and, full of high anticipation, cast his lot with the Confederacy, but when he fell into our hands, his bright dreams having been dispelled by the harsh realities of war, he appeared to think that for him there was no future.

Picking up prisoners here and there, my troops resumed their march directly south on the Valley pike, and when the Sixth and Nineteenth corps reached Harrisonburg they went into camp, Powell in the meanwhile pushing on to Mt. Crawford, and Crook taking up a position in our rear at the junction of the Keezletown road and the Valley pike. Late in the afternoon Torbert's cavalry came in from New Market arriving at that place many hours later than it had been expected.

The succeeding day I sent Merritt to Port Republic to occupy the enemy's attention, while Torbert, with Wilson's division and the regular brigade, was ordered to Staunton, whence he was to proceed to Waynesboro' and blow up the railroad bridge. Having done this, Torbert, as he returned, was to drive off whatever cattle he could find, destroy all forage and breadstuffs, and burn the mills. He took possession of Waynesboro' in due time, but had succeeded in only partially demolishing the railroad bridge when, attacked by Pegram's division of infantry and Wickham's cavalry, he was compelled to fall back to Staunton. From the latter place he retired to Bridgewater and Spring Hill, on the way, however, fully executing his instructions regarding the destruction of supplies.

While Torbert was on this expedition, Merritt had occupied Port Republic, but he happened to get there the very day that Kershaw's division was marching from Swift Run Gap to join Early. By accident Kershaw ran into Merritt shortly after the latter had gained the village. Kershaw's four infantry brigades attacked at once, and Merritt, forced out of Port Republic, fell back toward Cross Keys; and in anticipation that the Confederates could be coaxed to that point, I ordered the infantry there, but Torbert's attack at Waynesboro' had alarmed Early, and in consequence he drew all his forces in toward Rock-fish Gap. This enabled me to re-establish Merritt at Port Republic, send the Sixth and Nineteenth corps to the neighborhood of Mt. Crawford to await the return of Torbert, and to post Crook at Harrisonburg; these dispositions practically obtained till the 6th of October, I holding a line across the valley from Port Republic along North River by Mt. Crawford to the Back road near the mouth of Briery Branch Gap.

It was during this period, about dusk on the evening of October 3, that between Harrisonburg and Dayton my engineer officer, Lieutenant John R. Meigs, was murdered within my lines. He had gone out with two topographical assistants to plot the country, and late in the evening, while riding along the public road on his return to camp, he overtook three men dressed in our uniform. From their dress, and also because the party was immediately behind our lines and within a mile and a half of my headquarters, Meigs and his assistants naturally thought that they were joining friends, and wholly unsuspicious of anything to the contrary, rode on with the three men some little distance; but their perfidy was abruptly discovered by their suddenly turning upon Meigs with a call for his surrender. It has been claimed that, refusing to submit, he fired on the treacherous party, but the statement is not true, for one of the topographers escaped—the other was captured—and reported a few minutes later at my headquarters that Meigs was killed without resistance of any kind whatever, and without even the chance to give himself up. This man was so cool, and related all the circumstances of the occurrence with such exactness, as to prove the truthfulness of his statement. The fact that the murder had been committed inside our lines was evidence that the perpetrators of the crime, having their homes in the vicinity, had been clandestinely visiting them, and been secretly harbored by some of the neighboring residents. Determining to teach a lesson to these abettors of the foul deed—a lesson they would never forget—I ordered all the houses within an area of five miles to be burned. General Custer, who had succeeded to the command of the Third Cavalry division (General Wilson having been detailed as chief of cavalry to Sherman's army), was charged with this duty, and the next morning proceeded to put the order into execution. The prescribed area included the little village of Dayton, but when a few houses in the immediate neighborhood of the scene of the murder had been burned, Custer was directed to cease his desolating work, but to fetch away all the able-bodied males as prisoners.

CHAPTER XXI

WHILE WE LAY IN CAMP at Harrisonburg it became necessary to decide whether or not I would advance to Brown's Gap, and, after driving the enemy from there, follow him through the Blue Ridge into eastern Virginia. Indeed, this question began to cause me solicitude as soon as I knew Early had escaped me at New Market, for I felt certain that I should be urged to pursue the Confederates toward Charlottesville and Gordonsville, and be expected to operate on that line against Richmond. For many reasons I was much opposed to such a plan, but mainly because its execution would involve the opening of the Orange and Alexandria railroad. To protect this road against the raids of the numerous guerrilla bands that infested the region through which it passed, and to keep it in operation, would require a large force of infantry, and would also greatly reduce my cavalry; besides, I should be obliged to leave a force in the valley strong enough to give security to the line of the upper Potomac and the Baltimore and Ohio railroad, and this alone would probably take the whole of Crook's command, leaving me a wholly inadequate number of fighting men to prosecute a campaign against the city of Richmond.

Then, too, I was in doubt whether the besiegers could hold the entire army at Petersburg; and in case they could not, a number of troops sufficient to crush me might be detached by Lee, moved rapidly by rail, and, after overwhelming me, be quickly returned to confront General Meade. I was satisfied, moreover, that my transportation could not supply me further than Harrisonburg, and if in penetrating the Blue Ridge I met with protracted resistance, a lack of supplies might compel me to abandon the attempt at a most inopportune time.

I therefore advised that the Valley campaign be terminated north of Staunton, and I be permitted to return, carrying out on the way my original instructions for desolating the Shenandoah country so as to make it untenable for permanent occupation by the Confederates. I proposed to detach the bulk of my army when this work of destruction was completed, and send it by way of the Baltimore and Ohio railroad through Washington to the Petersburg line, believing that I could move it more rapidly by that route than by any other. I was confident that if a movement of this character could be made with celerity it would culminate in the capture of Richmond, and possibly of General Lee's army, and I was in hopes that General Grant would take the same view of the matter; but just at this time he was so pressed by the Government and by public opinion at the North, that he advocated the wholly different conception of driving Early into eastern Virginia, and adhered to this plan with some tenacity. Considerable correspondence regarding the subject took place between us, throughout which I stoutly maintained that we should not risk, by what I held to be a false move, all that my army had gained. I being on the ground, General Grant left to me the final decision of the question, and I solved the first step by determining to withdraw down the valley at least as far as Strasburg, which movement was begun on the 6th of October.

The cavalry as it retired was stretched across the country from the Blue Ridge to the eastern slope of the Alleghanies, with orders to drive off all stock and destroy all supplies as it moved northward. The infantry preceded the cavalry, passing down the Valley pike, and as we marched along the many columns of smoke from burning stacks, and mills filled with grain, indicated that the adjacent country was fast losing the features which hitherto had made it a great magazine of stores for the Confederate armies.

During the 6th and 7th of October, the enemy's horse followed us up, though at a respectful distance. This cavalry was now under command of General T. W. Rosser, who on October 5 had joined Early with an additional brigade from Richmond. As we proceeded the Confederates gained confidence, probably on account of the reputation with which its new commander had been heralded, and on the third day's march had the temerity to annoy my rear guard considerably. Tired of these annoyances, I concluded to open the enemy's eyes in earnest, so that night I told Torbert I expected him either to give Rosser a drubbing next morning or get whipped himself, and that the infantry would be halted until the affair was over; I also informed him that I proposed to ride out to Round Top Mountain to see the fight. When I decided to have Rosser chastised, Merritt was encamped at the foot of Round Top, an elevation just north of Tom's Brook, and Custer some six miles farther north and west, near Tumbling Run. In the night Custer was ordered to retrace his steps before daylight by the Back road, which is parallel to and about three miles from the Valley pike, and attack the enemy at Tom's Brook crossing, while Merritt's instructions were to assail him on the Valley pike in concert with Custer. About 7 in the morning, Custer's division encountered Rosser himself with three brigades, and while the stirring sounds of the resulting artillery duel were reverberating through the valley Merritt moved briskly to the front and fell upon Generals Lomax and Johnson on the Valley pike. Merritt, by extending his right, quickly established connection with Custer, and the two divisions moved forward together under Torbert's direction, with a determination to inflict on the enemy the sharp and summary punishment his rashness had invited.

The engagement soon became general across the valley, both sides fighting mainly mounted. For about two hours the contending lines struggled with each other along Tom's Brook, the charges and counter charges at many points being plainly visible from the summit of Round Top, where I had my headquarters for the time.

The open country permitting a sabre fight, both sides seemed bent on using that arm. In the centre the Confederates maintained their position with much stubbornness, and for a time seemed to have recovered their former spirit, but at last they began to give way on both flanks, and as these receded, Merritt and Custer went at the wavering ranks in a charge along the whole front. The result was a general smash-up of the entire Confederate line, the retreat quickly degenerating into a rout the like of which was never before seen. For twenty-six miles this wild stampede kept up, with our troopers close at the enemy's heels; and the ludicrous incidents of the chase never ceased to be amusing topics around the camp-fires of Merritt and Custer. In the fight and pursuit Torbert took eleven pieces of artillery, with their caissons, all the wagons and ambulances the enemy had on the ground, and three hundred prisoners. Some of Rosser's troopers fled to the mountains by way of Columbia Furnace, and some up the Valley pike and into the Massanutten Range, apparently not discovering that the chase had been discontinued till south of Mount Jackson they rallied on Early's infantry.

After this catastrophe, Early reported to General Lee that his cavalry was so badly demoralized that it should be dismounted; and the citizens of the valley, intensely disgusted with the boasting and swaggering that had characterized the arrival of the "Laurel Brigade"* in that sec-

---

*When Rosser arrived from Richmond with his brigade he was proclaimed as the savior of the Valley, and his men came all bedecked with laurel branches.

tion, baptized the action (known to us as Tom's Brook) the "Woodstock Races," and never tired of poking fun at General Rosser about his precipitate and inglorious flight.

On the 10th my army, resuming its retrograde movement, crossed to the north side of Cedar Creek. The work of repairing the Manassas Gap branch of the Orange and Alexandria railroad had been begun some days before, out from Washington, and, anticipating that it would be in readiness to transport troops by the time they could reach Piedmont, I directed the Sixth Corps to continue its march toward Front Royal, expecting to return to the Army of the Potomac by that line. By the 12th, however, my views regarding the reconstruction of this railroad began to prevail, and the work on it was discontinued. The Sixth Corps, therefore, abandoned that route, and moved toward Ashby's Gap with the purpose of marching direct to Washington, but on the 13th I recalled it to Cedar Creek, in consequence of the arrival of the enemy's infantry at Fisher's Hill, and the receipt, the night before, of the following despatch, which again opened the question of an advance on Gordonsville and Charlottesville:

(Cipher.)   "WASHINGTON, October 12, 1864, 12 M.
"MAJOR-GENERAL SHERIDAN:

"Lieutenant-General Grant wishes a position taken far enough south to serve as a base for further operations upon Gordonsville and Charlottesville. It must be strongly fortified and provisioned. Some point in the vicinity of Manassas Gap would seem best suited for all purposes. Colonel Alexander, of the Engineers, will be sent to consult with you as soon as you connect with General Augur.

"H. W. HALLECK, Major-General."

As it was well known in Washington that the views expressed in the above despatch were counter to my convictions, I was the next day required by the following telegram from Secretary Stanton to repair to that city:

"WASHINGTON, October 13, 1864.

"MAJOR-GENERAL SHERIDAN
(through General Augur):

"If you can come here, a consultation on several points is extremely desirable. I propose to visit General Grant, and would like to see you first.

"EDWIN M. STANTON,
"Secretary of War."

I got all ready to comply with the terms of Secretary Stanton's despatch, but in the meantime the enemy appeared in my front in force, with infantry and cavalry, and attacked Colonel Thoburn, who had been pushed out toward Strasburg from Crook's command, and also Custer's division of cavalry on the Back road. As afterward appeared, this attack was made in the belief that all of my troops but Crook's had gone to Petersburg. From this demonstration there ensued near Hupp's Hill a bitter skirmish between Kershaw and Thoburn, and the latter was finally compelled to withdraw to the north bank of Cedar Creek. Custer gained better results, however, on the Back road, with his usual dash driving the enemy's cavalry away from his front, Merritt's division then joining him and remaining on the right.

The day's events pointing to a probability that the enemy intended to resume the offensive, to anticipate such a contingency I ordered the Sixth Corps to return from its march toward Ashby's Gap. It reached me by noon of the 14th, and went into position to the right and rear of the Nineteenth Corps, which held a line along the north bank of Cedar Creek, west of the Valley pike. Crook was posted on the left of the Nineteenth Corps and the east of the Valley pike, with Thoburn's division advanced to a round hill, which commanded the junction of Cedar Creek and the Shenandoah River, while Torbert retained both Merritt and Custer on the right of the Sixth Corps, and at the same time covered with Powell the roads toward Front Royal. My headquarters were at the Belle Grove House, which was to the west of the pike and in rear of the Nineteenth Corps. It was my intention to attack the enemy as soon as the Sixth Corps reached me, but General Early having learned from his demonstration that I had not detached as largely as his previous information had led him to believe, on the night of the 13th withdrew to Fisher's Hill; so, concluding that he could not do us serious hurt form there, I changed my mind as to attacking, deciding to defer such action till I could get to Washington, and come to some definite understanding about my future operations.

To carry out this idea, on the evening of the 15th I ordered all of the cavalry under General Torbert to accompany me to Front Royal, again intending to push it thence through Chester Gap to the Virginia Central railroad at Charlottesville, to destroy the bridge over the Rivanna River, while I passed through Manassas Gap to Rectortown, and thence by rail to Washington. On my arrival with the cavalry near Front Royal on the 16th, I halted at the house of Mrs. Richards, on the north bank of the river, and there received the following despatch and inclosure from General Wright, who had been left in command at Cedar Creek:

> "HEADQUARTERS MIDDLE MILITARY DIVISION,
> "October 16, 1864.
>
> "GENERAL:
>
> "I enclose you despatch which explains itself. If the enemy should be strongly re-enforced in cavalry, he might, by turning our right, give us a great deal of trouble. I shall hold on here until the enemy's movements are developed, and shall only fear an attack on my right, which I shall make every preparation for guarding against and resisting.
>
> "Very respectfully, your obedient servant,
> "H. G. WRIGHT, Major-General Commanding.
>
> "MAJOR-GENERAL P. H. SHERIDAN,
> "Commanding Middle Military Division."

> [INCLOSURE.]
>
> "To LIEUTENANT-GENERAL EARLY:

"Be ready to move as soon as my forces join you, and we will crush Sheridan.

"LONGSTREET, Lieutenant-General."

The message from Longstreet had been taken down as it was being flagged from the Confederate signal-station on Three Top Mountain, and afterward translated by our signal officers, who knew the Confederate signal code. I first thought it a ruse, and hardly worth attention, but on reflection deemed it best to be on the safe side, so I abandoned the cavalry raid toward Charlottesville, in order to give General Wright the entire strength of the army, for it did not seem wise to reduce his numbers while reinforcement for the enemy might be near, and especially when such pregnant messages were reaching Early from one of the ablest of the Confederate generals. Therefore I sent the following note to General Wright:

"HEADQUARTERS MIDDLE MILITARY DIVISION,
"Front Royal, October 16, 1864.

"GENERAL: The cavalry is all ordered back to you; make your position strong. If Longstreet's despatch is true, he is under the impression that we have largely detached. I will go over to Augur, and may get additional news. Close in Colonel Powell, who will be at this point. If the enemy should make an advance, I know you will defeat him. Look well to your ground and be well prepared. Get up everything that can be spared. I will bring up all I can, and will be up on Tuesday, if not sooner.

"P. H. SHERIDAN, Major-General.

"MAJOR-GENERAL H. G. WRIGHT,
"Commanding Sixth Army Corps."

At 5 o'clock on the evening of the 16th I telegraphed General Halleck from Rectortown, giving him the information which had come to me from Wright, asking if anything corroborative of it had been received from General Grant, and also saying that I would like to see Halleck; the telegram ending with the question: "Is it best for me to go to see you?" Next morning I sent back to Wright all the cavalry except one regiment, which escorted me through Manassas Gap to the terminus of the railroad from Washington. I had with me Lieutenant-Colonel James W. Forsyth, chief-of-staff, and three of my aides, Major George A. Forsyth, Captain Joseph O'Keefe, and Captain Michael V. Sheridan. I rode my black horse, Rienzi, and the others their own respective mounts.

Before leaving Cedar Creek I had fixed the route of my return to be by rail from Washington to Martinsburg, and thence by horseback to Winchester and Cedar Creek, and had ordered three hundred cavalry to Martinsburg to escort me from that point to the front. At Rectortown I met General Augur, who had brought a force out from Washington to reconstruct and protect the line of railroad, and through him received the following reply from General Halleck:

"HEADQUARTERS ARMIES OF THE UNITED STATES,
"WASHINGTON, D. C., October 16, 1864.
"To MAJOR-GENERAL SHERIDAN,
"Rectortown, Va.
"General Grant says that Longstreet brought with him no troops from Richmond, but I have very little confidence in the information collected at his headquarters. If you can leave your command with safety, come to Washington, as I wish to give you the views of the authorities here.
"H. W. HALLECK, Major-General, Chief-of-Staff."

In consequence of the Longstreet despatch, I felt a concern about my absence which I could hardly repress, but after duly considering what Halleck said, and believing that Longstreet could not unite with Early before I got back, and that even if he did Wright would be able to cope with them both, I and my staff, with our horses, took the cars for Washington, where we arrived on the morning of the 17th at about 8 o'clock. I proceeded at an early hour to the War Department, and as soon as I met Secretary Stanton, asked him for a special train to be ready at 12 o'clock to take me to Martinsburg, saying that in view of existing conditions I must get back to my army as quickly as possible. He at once gave the order for the train, and then the Secretary, Halleck, and I proceeded to hold a consultation in regard to my operating east of the Blue Ridge. The upshot was that my views against such a plan were practically agreed to, and two engineer officers were designated to return with me for the purpose of reporting on a defensive line in the valley that could be held while the bulk of my troops were being detached to Petersburg. Colonel Alexander and Colonel Thom, both of the Engineer Corps, reported to accompany me, and at 12 o'clock we took the train.

We arrived about dark at Martinsburg, and there found the escort of three hundred men which I had ordered before leaving Cedar Creek. We spent that night at Martinsburg, and early next morning mounted and started up the Valley pike for Winchester, leaving Captain Sheridan behind to conduct to the army the Commissioners whom the State of New York had sent down to receive the vote of her troops in the coming Presidential election. Colonel Alexander was a man of enormous weight, and Colonel Thom correspondingly light, and as both were unaccustomed to riding we had to go slowly, losing so much time, in fact, that we did not reach Winchester till between 3 and 4 o'clock in the afternoon, though the distance is but twenty-eight miles. As soon as we arrived at Colonel Edwards's headquarters in the town, where I intended stopping for the night, I sent a courier to the front to bring me a report of the condition of affairs, and then took Colonel Alexander out on the heights about Winchester, in order that he might overlook the country, and make up his mind as to the utility of fortifying there. By the time we had completed our survey it was dark, and just as we reached Colonel Edwards's house on our return a courier came in from Cedar Creek bringing word that everything was all right, that the enemy was quiet at Fisher's Hill, and that a brigade of Grover's division was to make a reconnoissance in the morning, the 19th, so about 10 o'clock I went to bed greatly relieved, and expecting to rejoin my headquarters at my leisure next day.

Toward 6 o'clock the morning of the 19th, the officer on picket duty at Winchester came to my room, I being yet in bed, and reported artillery firing from the direction of Cedar Creek. I asked him if the firing was continuous or only desultory, to which he replied that it was not a sustained fire, but rather irregular and fitful. I remarked: "It's all right; Grover has gone out this morning to make a reconnoissance, and he is merely feeling the enemy." I tried to go to sleep again, but grew so restless that I could not, and soon got up and dressed myself. A little later the picket officer came back and reported that the firing, which could be distinctly heard from his line on the heights outside of Winchester, was still going on. I asked him if it sounded like a battle, and as he again said that it did not, I still inferred that the cannonading was caused by Grover's division banging away at the enemy simply to find out what he was up to. However, I went down-stairs and requested that breakfast be hurried up, and at the same time ordered the horses to be saddled and in readiness, for I concluded to go to the front before any further examinations were made in regard to the defensive line.

We mounted our horses between half-past 8 and 9, and as we were proceeding up the street which leads directly through Winchester, from the Logan residence, where Edwards was quartered, to the Valley pike, I noticed that there were many women at the windows and doors of the houses, who kept shaking their skirts at us and who were otherwise markedly insolent in their demeanor, but supposing this conduct to be instigated by their well-known and perhaps natural prejudices, I ascribed to it no unusual significance. On reaching the edge of the town I halted a moment, and there heard quite distinctly the sound of artillery firing in an unceasing roar. Concluding from this that a battle was in progress, I now felt confident that the women along the street had received intelligence from the battlefield by the "grape-vine telegraph," and were in raptures over some good news, while I as yet was utterly ignorant of the actual situation. Moving on, I put my head down toward the pommel of my saddle and listened intently, trying to locate and interpret the sound, continuing in this position till we had crossed Mill Creek, about half a mile from Winchester. The result of my efforts in the interval was the conviction that the travel of the sound was increasing too rapidly to be accounted for by my own rate of motion, and that therefore my army must be falling back.

At Mill Creek my escort fell in behind, and we were going ahead at a regular pace, when, just as we made the crest of the rise beyond the stream, there burst upon our view the appalling spectacle of a panic-stricken army— hundreds of slightly wounded men, throngs of others unhurt but utterly demoralized, and baggage-wagons by the score, all pressing to the rear in hopeless confusion, telling only too plainly that a disaster had occurred at the front. On accosting some of the fugitives, they assured me that the army was broken up, in full retreat, and that all was lost; all this with a manner true to that peculiar indifference that takes possession of panic-stricken men. I was greatly disturbed by the sight, but at once sent word to Colonel Edwards, commanding the brigade in Winchester, to stretch his troops across the valley, near Mill Creek, and stop all fugitives, directing also that the transportation be passed through and parked on the north side of the town.

As I continued at a walk a few hundred yards farther, thinking all the time of Longstreet's telegram to Early, "Be ready when I join you, and we will crush Sheridan," I was fixing in my mind what I should do. My first thought was to stop the army in the suburbs of Winchester as it came back, form a new line, and fight there; but as the situation was more maturely considered a better conception prevailed. I was sure the troops had confidence in me, for heretofore we had been successful; and as at other times they had seen me present at the slightest sign of trouble or distress, I felt that I ought to try now to restore their broken ranks, or, failing in that, to share their fate because of what they had done hitherto.

About this time Colonel Wood, my chief commissary, arrived from the front and gave me fuller intelligence, reporting that everything was gone, my headquarters captured, and the troops dispersed. When I heard this I took two of my aides-de-camp, Major George A. Forsyth and Captain Joseph O'Keefe, and with twenty men from the escort started for the front, at the same time directing Colonel James W. Forsyth and Colonels Alexander and Thom to remain behind and do what they could to stop the runaways.

For a short distance I traveled on the road, but soon found it so blocked with wagons and wounded men that my progress was impeded, and I was forced to take to the adjoining fields to make haste. When most of the wagons and wounded were past I returned to the road, which was thickly lined with unhurt men, who, having got far enough to the rear to be out of danger, had halted, without any organization, and begun cooking coffee, but when they saw me they abandoned their coffee, threw up their hats, shouldered their muskets, and as I passed along turned to follow with enthusiasm and cheers. To acknowledge this exhibition of feeling I took off my hat, and with Forsyth and O'Keefe rode some distance in advance of my escort, while every mounted officer who saw me galloped out on either side of the pike to tell the men at a distance that I had come back. In this way the news was spread to the stragglers off the road, when they, too, turned their faces to the front and marched toward the enemy, changing in a moment from the depths of depression to the extreme of enthusiasm. I already knew that even in the ordinary condition of mind enthusiasm is a potent element with soldiers, but what I saw that day convinced me that if it can be excited from a state of despondency its power is almost irresistible. I said nothing except to remark, as I rode among those on the road: "If I had been with you this morning this disaster would not have happened. We must face the other way; we will go back and recover our camp."

My first halt was made just north of Newtown, where I met a chaplain digging his heels into the sides of his jaded horse, and making for the rear with all possible speed. I drew up for an instant, and inquired of him how matters were going at the front. He replied, "Everything is lost; but all will be right when you get there"; yet notwithstanding this expression of confidence in me, the parson at once resumed his breathless pace to the rear. At Newtown I was obliged to make a circuit to the left, to get round the village. I could not pass through it, the streets were so crowded, but meeting on this détour Major McKinley, of Crook's staff, he spread the news of my return through the motley throng there.

When nearing the Valley pike, just south of Newtown I saw about three-fourths of a mile west of the pike a body of troops, which proved to be Ricketts's and Wheaton's divisions of the Sixth Corps, and then learned that the Nineteenth Corps had halted a little to the right and rear of these; but I did not stop, desiring to get to the extreme front. Continuing on parallel with the pike, about midway between Newtown and Middletown I crossed to the west of it, and a little later came up in rear of Getty's division of the Sixth Corps. When I arrived, this division and the cavalry were the only troops in the presence of and resisting the enemy; they were apparently acting as a rear guard at a point about three miles north of the line we held at Cedar Creek when the battle began. General Torbert was the first officer to meet me, saying as he rode up, "My God! I am glad you've come." Getty's division, when I found it, was about a mile north of Middletown, posted on the reverse slope of some slightly rising ground, holding a barricade made with fence-rails, and skirmishing slightly with the enemy's pickets. Jumping my horse over the line of rails, I rode to the crest of the elevation, and there taking off my hat, the men rose up from behind their barricade with cheers of recognition. An officer of the Vermont brigade, Colonel A. S. Tracy, rode out to the front, and joining me, informed me that General Louis A. Grant was in command there, the regular division commander, General Getty, having taken charge of the Sixth Corps in place of Ricketts, wounded early in the action, while temporarily commanding the corps. I then turned back to the rear of Getty's division, and as I came behind it, a line of regimental flags rose up out of the ground, as it seemed, to welcome me. They were mostly the colors of Crook's troops, who had been stampeded and scattered in the surprise of the morning. The color-bearers, having withstood the panic, had formed behind the troops of Getty. The line with the colors was largely composed of officers, among whom I recognized Colonel R. B. Hayes, since president of the United States, one of the brigade commanders. At the close of this incident I crossed the little narrow valley, or depression, in rear of Getty's line, and dismounting on the opposite crest, established that point as my headquarters. In a few minutes some of my staff joined me, and the first directions I gave were to have the Nineteenth Corps and the two divisions of Wright's corps brought to the front, so they could be formed on Getty's division, prolonged to the right; for I had already decided to attack the enemy from that line as soon as I could get matters in shape to take the offensive. Crook met me at this time, and strongly favored my idea of attacking, but said, however, that most of his troops were gone. General Wright came up a little later, when I saw that he was wounded, a ball having grazed the point of his chin so as to draw the blood plentifully.

Wright gave me a hurried account of the day's events, and when told that we would fight the enemy on the line which Getty and the cavalry were holding, and that he must go himself and send all his staff to bring up the troops, he zealously fell in with the scheme; and it was *then* that the Nineteenth Corps and two divisions of the Sixth were ordered to the front from where they had been halted to the right and rear of Getty.

After this conversation I rode to the east of the Valley pike and to the left of Getty's division, to a point from which I could obtain a good view of the front, in the mean time sending Major Forsyth to communicate with Colonel Lowell (who occupied a position close in toward the suburbs of Middletown and directly in front of Getty's left) to learn whether he could hold on there. Lowell replied that he could. I then ordered Custer's division back to the right flank, and returning to the place where my headquarters had been established I met near them Ricketts's division under General Keifer and General Frank Wheaton's division, both marching to the front. When the men of these divisions saw me they began cheering and took up the double quick to the front, while I turned back toward Getty's line to point out where these returning troops should be placed. Having done this, I ordered General Wright to resume command of the Sixth Corps, and Getty, who was temporarily in charge of it, to take command of his own division. A little later the Nineteenth Corps came up and was posted between the right of the Sixth Corps and Middle Marsh Brook.

All this had consumed a great deal of time, and I concluded to visit again the point to the east of the Valley pike, from where I had first observed the enemy, to see what he was doing. Arrived there, I could plainly see him getting ready for attack, and Major Forsyth now suggested that it would be well to ride along the line of battle before the enemy assailed us, for although the troops had learned of my return, but few of them had seen me. Following his suggestion I started in behind the men, but when a few paces had been taken I crossed to the front and, hat in hand, passed along the entire length of the infantry line; and it is from this circumstance that many of the officers and men who then received me with such heartiness have since supposed that that was my first appearance on the field. But at least two hours had elapsed since I reached the ground, for it was after mid-day when this incident of riding down the front took place, and I arrived not later, certainly, than half-past 10 o'clock.

After re-arranging the line and preparing to attack I returned again to observe the Confederates, who shortly began to advance on us. The attacking columns did not cover my entire front, and it appeared that their onset would be mainly directed against the Nineteenth Corps, so, fearing that they might be too strong for Emory on account of his depleted condition (many of his men not having had time to get up from the rear), and Getty's division being free from assault, I transferred a part of it from the extreme left to the support of the Nineteenth Corps. The assault was quickly repulsed by Emory, however, and as the enemy fell back Getty's troops were returned to their original place. This repulse of the Confederates made me feel pretty safe from further offensive operations on their part, and I now decided to suspend the fighting till my thin ranks were further strengthened by the men who were continually coming up from the rear, and particularly till Crook's troops could be assembled on the extreme left.

In consequence of the despatch already mentioned, "Be ready when I join you, and we will crush Sheridan," since learned to have been fictitious, I had been supposing all day that Longstreet's troops were present, but as no definite intelligence on this point had been gathered, I concluded, in the lull that now occurred, to ascertain something positive regarding Longstreet; and Merritt having been transferred to our left in the morning, I directed him to attack an exposed battery then at the edge of Middletown, and capture some prisoners. Merritt soon did this work effectually, concealing his intention till his troops got close in to the enemy, and then by a quick dash gobbling up a number of Confederates. When the prisoners were brought in, I learned from them that the only troops of Longstreet's in the fight were of Kershaw's division,

which had rejoined Early at Brown's Gap in the latter part
of September, and that the rest of Longstreet's corps was
not on the field. The receipt of this information entirely
cleared the way for me to take the offensive, but on the
heels of it came information that Longstreet was marching
by the Front Royal pike to strike my rear at Winchester,
driving Powell's cavalry in as he advanced. This renewed
my uneasiness, and caused me to delay the general attack
till after assurances came from Powell denying utterly the
reports as to Longstreet, and confirming the statements
of the prisoners.

Between half-past 3 and 4 o'clock, I was ready to assail,
and decided to do so by advancing my infantry line in a
swinging movement, so as to gain the Valley pike with my
right between Middletown and the Belle Grove House; and
when the order was passed along, the men pushed steadily
forward with enthusiasm and confidence. General Early's
troops extended some little distance beyond our right, and
when my flank neared the overlapping enemy, he turned
on it, with the effect of causing a momentary confusion,
but General McMillan quickly realizing the danger, broke
the Confederates at the reentering angle by a counter
charge with his brigade, doing his work so well that the
enemy's flanking troops were cut off from their main body
and left to shift for themselves. Custer, who was just then
moving in from the west side of Middle Marsh Brook,
followed McMillan's timely blow with a charge of cavalry,
but before starting out on it, and while his men were
forming, riding at full speed himself, to throw his arms
around my neck. By the time he had disengaged himself
from this embrace, the troops broken by McMillan had
gained some little distance to their rear, but Custer's troopers sweeping across the Middletown meadows and down
toward Cedar Creek, took many of them prisoners before
they could reach the stream—so I forgave his delay.

My whole line as far as the eye could see was now driving
everything before it, from behind trees, stone walls, and
all such sheltering obstacles, so I rode toward the left to

ascertain how matters were getting on there. As I passed along behind the advancing troops, first General Grover, and then Colonel Mackenzie, rode up to welcome me. Both were severely wounded, and I told them to leave the field, but they implored permission to remain till success was certain. When I reached the Valley pike Crook had reorganized his men, and as I desired that they should take part in the fight, for they were the very same troops that had turned Early's flank at the Opequon and at Fisher's Hill, I ordered them to be pushed forward; and the alacrity and celerity with which they moved on Middletown demonstrated that their ill-fortune of the morning had not sprung from lack of valor.

Meanwhile Lowell's brigade of cavalry, which, it will be remembered, had been holding on, dismounted, just north of Middletown ever since the time I arrived from Winchester, fell to the rear for the purpose of getting their led horses. A momentary panic was created in the nearest brigade of infantry by this withdrawal of Lowell, but as soon as his men were mounted they charged the enemy clear up to the stone walls in the edge of Middletown; at sight of this the infantry brigade renewed its attack, and the enemy's right gave way. The accomplished Lowell received his death-wound in this courageous charge.

All our troops were now moving on the retreating Confederates, and as I rode to the front Colonel Gibbs, who succeeded Lowell, made ready for another mounted charge, but I checked him from pressing the enemy's right, in the hope that the swinging attack from my right would throw most of the Confederates to the east of the Valley pike, and hence off their line of retreat through Strasburg to Fisher's Hill. The eagerness of the men soon frustrated this anticipation, however, the left insisting on keeping pace with the centre and right, and all pushing ahead till we regained our old camps at Cedar Creek. Beyond Cedar Creek, at Strasburg, the pike makes a sharp turn to the west toward Fisher's Hill, and here Merritt uniting with Custer, they together fell on the flank of the retreating columns, taking many prisoners, wagons, and guns, among the prisoners being Major-General Ramseur, who, mortally wounded, died the next day.

When the news of the victory was received, General Grant directed a salute of one hundred shotted guns to be fired into Petersburg, and the President at once thanked the army in an autograph letter. A few weeks after, he promoted me, and I received notice of this in a special letter from the Secretary of War, saying, "that for the personal gallantry, military skill, and just confidence in the courage and patriotism of your troops, displayed by you on the 19th day of October at Cedar Run, whereby, under the blessing of Providence, your routed army was reorganized, a great National disaster averted, and a brilliant victory achieved over the rebels for the third time in pitched battle within thirty days, Philip H. Sheridan is appointed a major-general in the United States Army."

The direct result of the battle was the recapture of all the artillery, transportation, and camp equipage we had lost, and in addition twenty-four pieces of the enemy's artillery, twelve hundred prisoners, and a number of battle-flags. But more still flowed from this victory, succeeding as it did the disaster of the morning, for the re-occupation of our old-camps at once re-established a *morale* which for some hours had been greatly endangered by ill-fortune.

It was not till after the battle that I learned fully what had taken place before my arrival, and then found that the enemy, having gathered all the strength he could through the return of convalescents and other absentees, had moved quietly from Fisher's Hill, in the night of the 18th and early on the morning of the 19th, to surprise my army, which, it should be remembered, was posted on the north bank of Cedar Creek, Crook holding on the left of the Valley pike, with Thoburn's division advanced toward the creek, and Duval's (under Colonel Rutherford B. Hayes) and Kitching's provisional divisions to the north and rear of Thoburn. The Nineteenth Corps was on the right of Crook, extending in a semi-circular line from the pike nearly to Meadow Brook, while the Sixth Corps lay to the west of the brook in readiness to be used as a movable column. Merritt's division was to the right and rear of the Sixth Corps, and about a mile and a half west of Merritt was Custer covering the fords of Cedar Creek as far west as the Middle road.

General Early's plan was for one column under General Gordon, consisting of three divisions of infantry (Gordon's, Ramseur's, and Pegram's), and Payne's brigade of cavalry, to cross the Shenandoah River directly east of the Confederate works at Fisher's Hill, march around the northerly face of the Massanutten Mountain, and again cross the Shenandoah at Bowman's and McInturff's fords. Payne's task was to capture me at the Belle Grove House. General Early himself, with Kershaw's and Wharton's divisions, was to move through Strasburg, Kershaw, accompanied by Early, to cross Cedar Creek at Robert's ford and connect with Gordon, while Wharton was to continue on the Valley pike to Hupp's Hill and join the left of Kershaw, when the crossing of the Valley pike over Cedar Creek became free.

Lomax's cavalry, then in the Luray Valley, was ordered to join the right of Gordon on the field of battle, while Rosser was to carry the crossing of Cedar Creek on the Back road and attack Custer. Early's conceptions were carried through in the darkness with little accident or delay, Kershaw opening the fight by a furious attack on Thoburn's division, while at dawn and in a dense fog Gordon struck Crook's extreme left, surprising his pickets, and bursting into his camp with such suddenness as to stampede Crook's men. Gordon directing his march on my headquarters (the Belle Grove House), successfully turned our position as he gained the Valley pike, and General Wright was thus forced to order the withdrawal of the Nineteenth Corps from its post at the Cedar Creek crossing, and this enabled Wharton to get over the stream there unmolested and join Kershaw early in the action.

After Crook's troops had been driven from their camps, General Wright endeavored to form a line with the Sixth

Corps to hold the Valley pike to the left of the Nineteenth, but failing in this he ordered the withdrawal of the latter corps, Ricketts, temporarily commanding the Sixth Corps, checking Gordon till Emory had retired. As already stated, Wharton was thus permitted to cross Cedar Creek on the pike, and now that Early had a continuous line, he pressed his advantage so vigorously that the whole Union army was soon driven from its camps in more or less disorder; and though much disjointed resistance was displayed, it may be said that no systematic stand was made until Getty's division, aided by Torbert's cavalry, which Wright had ordered to the left early in the action, took up the ground where, on arriving from Winchester, I found them.

When I left my command on the 16th, little did I anticipate that anything like this would happen. Indeed, I felt satisfied that Early was, of himself, too weak to take the offensive, and although I doubted the Longstreet despatch, yet I was confident that, even should it prove true, I could get back before the junction could be made, and at the worst I felt certain that my army was equal to confronting the forces of Longstreet and Early combined. Still, the surprise of the morning might have befallen me as well as the general on whom it did descend, and though it is possible that this could have been precluded had Powell's cavalry been closed in, as suggested in my despatch from Front Royal, yet the enemy's desperation might have prompted some other clever and ingenious scheme for relieving his fallen fortunes in the Shenandoah Valley.

CHAPTER XXII

EARLY'S BROKEN ARMY practically made no halt in its retreat after the battle of Cedar Creek until it reached New Market, though at Fisher's Hill was left a small rear-guard of cavalry, which hastily decamped, however, when charged by Gibbs's brigade on the morning of the 20th. Between the date of his signal defeat and the 11th of November, the enemy's scattered forces had sufficiently reorganized to permit his again making a reconnoissance in the valley as far north as Cedar Creek, my army having meanwhile withdrawn to Kernstown, where it had been finally decided that a defensive line should be held to enable me to detach troops to General Grant, and where, by reconstructing the Winchester and Potomac railroad from Stephenson's depot to Harper's Ferry, my command might be more readily supplied. Early's reconnoissance north of Cedar Creek ended in a rapid withdrawal of his infantry after feeling my front, and with the usual ill-fortune to his cavalry; Merritt and Custer driving Rosser and Lomax with ease across Cedar Creek on the Middle and Back roads, while Powell's cavalry struck McCausland near Stony Point, and after capturing two pieces of artillery and about three hundred officers and men, chased him into the Luray Valley.

Early got back to New Market on the 14th of November, and, from lack of subsistence, being unable to continue demonstrations to prevent my reinforcement of General Grant, began himself to detach to General Lee by returning Kershaw's division to Petersburg, as was definitely ascertained by Torbert in a reconnoissance to Mount Jackson. At this time General Grant wished me to send him the Sixth Corps, and it was got ready for the purpose, but when I informed him that Torbert's reconnoissance had developed the fact that Early still retained four divisions of infantry and one of cavalry, it was decided, on my suggestion, to let the Sixth Corps remain till the season should be a little further advanced, when the inclemency of the weather would preclude infantry campaigning. These conditions came about early in December, and by the middle of the month the whole of the Sixth Corps was at Petersburg; simultaneously with its transfer to that line Early sending his Second Corps to Lee.

During the entire campaign I had been annoyed by guerrilla bands under such partisan chiefs as Mosby, White, Gilmore, McNeil, and others, and this had considerably depleted my line-of-battle strength, necessitating as it did large escorts for my supply-trains. The most redoubtable of these leaders was Mosby, whose force was made up from the country around Upperville, east of the Blue Ridge, to which section he always fled for a hiding-place when he scented danger. I had not directed any special operations against these partisans while the campaign was active, but as Mosby's men had lately killed, within my lines, my chief quartermaster, Colonel Tolles, and Medical Inspector Ohlenchlager, I concluded to devote particular attention to these "irregulars" during the lull that now occurred; so on the 28th of November, I directed General Merritt to march to the Loudoun Valley and operate against Mosby, taking care to clear the country of forage and subsistence, so as to prevent the guerrillas from being harbored there in the future, their destruction or capture being wellnigh impossible, on account of their intimate knowledge of the mountain region. Merritt carried out his instructions with his usual sagacity and thoroughness, sweeping widely over each side of his general line of march with flankers, who burned the grain and brought in large herds of cattle, hogs and sheep, which were issued to the troops.

While Merritt was engaged in this service the Baltimore and Ohio railroad once more received the attention of the enemy; Rosser, with two brigades of cavalry, crossing the Great North Mountain, capturing the post of New Creek, with about five hundred prisoners and seven guns, destroying all the supplies of the garrison, and breaking up the railroad track. This slight success of the Confederates in West Virginia, and the intelligence that they were contemplating further raids in that section, led me to send Crook there with one division, his other troops going to City Point; and I hoped that all the threatened places would thus be sufficiently protected, but negligence at Beverly resulted in the capture of that station by Rosser on the 11th of January.

In the meanwhile, Early established himself with Wharton's division at Staunton in winter quarters, posting his cavalry in that neighborhood also, except a detachment at New Market, and another small one at the signal-station on Three Top Mountain. The winter was a most severe one, snow falling frequently to the depth of several inches, and the mercury often sinking below zero. The rigor of the season was very much against the success of any mounted operations, but General Grant being very desirous to have the railroads broken up about Gordonsville and Charlottesville, on the 19th of December I started the cavalry out for that purpose, Torbert, with Merritt and Powell, marching through Chester Gap, while Custer moved toward Staunton to make a demonstration in Torbert's favor, hoping to hold the enemy's troops in the valley. Unfortunately, Custer did not accomplish all that was expected of him, and being surprised by Rosser and

Payne near Lacy's Springs before reveille, had to abandon his bivouac and retreat down the valley, with the loss of a number of prisoners, a few horses, and a good many horse equipments, for, because of the suddenness of Rosser's attack, many of the men had no time to saddle up. As soon as Custer's retreat was assured, Wharton's division of infantry was sent to Charlottesville to check Torbert, but this had already been done by Lomax, with the assistance of infantry sent up from Richmond. Indeed, from the very beginning of the movement the Confederates had been closely observing the columns of Torbert and Custer, and in consequence of the knowledge thus derived, Early had marched Lomax to Gordonsville in anticipation of an attack there, at the same time sending Rosser down the valley to meet Custer. Torbert in the performance of his task captured two pieces of artillery from Johnson's and McCausland's brigades, at Liberty Mills on the Rapidan River, but in the main the purpose of the raid utterly failed, so by the 27th of December he returned, many of his men badly frost-bitten from the extreme cold which had prevailed.

This expedition practically closed all operations for the season, and the cavalry was put into winter cantonment near Winchester. The distribution of my infantry to Petersburg and West Virginia left with me in the beginning of the new year, as already stated, but the one small division of the Nineteenth Corps. On account of this diminution of force, it became necessary for me to keep thoroughly posted in regard to the enemy, and I now realized more than I had done hitherto how efficient my scouts had become since under the control of Colonel Young; for not only did they bring me almost every day intelligence from within Early's lines, but they also operated efficiently against the guerrillas infesting West Virginia.

Harry Gilmore, of Maryland, was the most noted of these since the death of McNeil, and as the scouts had reported him in Harrisonburg the latter part of January, I directed two of the most trustworthy to be sent to watch his movements and ascertain his purposes. In a few days these spies returned with the intelligence that Gilmore was on his way to Moorefield, the centre of a very disloyal section in West Virginia, about ninety miles southwest of Winchester, where, under the guise of a camp-meeting, a gathering was to take place, at which he expected to enlist a number of men, be joined by a party of about twenty recruits coming from Maryland, and then begin depredations along the Baltimore and Ohio railroad. Believing that Gilmore might be captured, I directed Young to undertake the task, and as a preliminary step he sent to Moorefield two of his men who early in the war had "refugeed" from that section and enlisted in one of the Union regiments from West Virginia. In about a week these men came back and reported that Gilmore was living at a house between three and four miles from Moorefield, and gave full particulars as to his coming and going, the number of men he had about there and where they rendezvoused.

With this knowledge at hand I directed Young to take twenty of his best men and leave that night for Moorefield, dressed in Confederate uniforms, telling him that I would have about three hundred cavalry follow in his wake when he had got about fifteen miles start, and instructing him to pass his party off as a body of recruits for Gilmore coming from Maryland and pursued by the Yankee cavalry. I knew this would allay suspicion and provide him help on the road; and, indeed, as Colonel Whittaker, who alone knew the secret, followed after the fleeing "Marylanders," he found that their advent had caused so little remark that the trail would have been lost had he not already known their destination. Young met with a hearty welcome wherever he halted on the way, and as he passed through the town of Moorefield learned with satisfaction that Gilmore still made his headquarters at the house where the report of the two scouts had located him a few days before. Reaching the designated place about 12 o'clock on the night of the 5th of February, Young, under the representation that he had come directly from Maryland and was being pursued

by the Union cavalry, gained immediate access to Gilmore's
room. He found the bold guerrilla snugly tucked in bed,
with two pistols lying on a chair near by. He was sleeping
so soundly that to arouse him Young had to give him a
violent shake. As he awoke and asked who was disturbing
his slumbers, Young, pointing at him a cocked six-shooter,
ordered him to dress without delay, and in answer to his
inquiry, informed him that he was a prisoner to one of
Sheridan's staff. Meanwhile Gilmore's men had learned of
his trouble, but the early appearance of Colonel Whittaker
caused them to disperse; thus the last link between Maryland and the Confederacy was carried a prisoner to Winchester, whence he was sent to Fort Warren.

The capture of Gilmore caused the disbandment of the
party he had organized at the "camp-meeting," most of
the men he had recruited returning to their homes discouraged, though some few joined the bands of Woodson
and young Jesse McNeil, which, led by the latter, dashed
into Cumberland, Maryland, at 3 o'clock on the morning
of the 21st of February and made a reprisal by carrying
off General Crook and General Kelly, and doing their work
so silently and quickly that they escaped without being
noticed, and were some distance on their way before the
colored watchman at the hotel where Crook was quartered
could compose himself enough to give the alarm. A troop
of cavalry gave hot chase from Cumberland, striving to
intercept the party at Moorefield and other points, but all
efforts were fruitless, the prisoners soon being beyond
reach.

Although I had adopted the general rule of employing
only soldiers as scouts, there was an occasional exception
to it. I cannot say that these exceptions proved wholly that
an iron-clad observance of the rule would have been best,
but I am sure of it in one instance. A man named Lomas,
who claimed to be a Marylander, offered me his services
as a spy, and coming highly recommended from Mr. Stanton, who had made use of him in that capacity, I employed
him. He made many pretensions, often appearing over-

anxious to impart information seemingly intended to impress me with his importance, and yet was more than ordinarily intelligent, but in spite of that my confidence in him was by no means unlimited. I often found what he reported to me as taking place within the Confederate lines corroborated by Young's men, but generally there were discrepancies in his tales, which led me to suspect that he was employed by the enemy as well as by me. I felt, however, that with good watching he could do me little harm, and if my suspicions were incorrect he might be very useful, so I held on to him.

Early in February Lomas was very solicitous for me to employ a man who, he said, had been with Mosby, but on account of some quarrel in the irregular camp had abandoned that leader. Thinking that with two of them I might destroy the railroad bridges east of Lynchburg, I concluded, after the Mosby man had been brought to my headquarters by Lomas about 12 o'clock one night, to give him employment, at the same time informing Colonel Young that I suspected their fidelity, however, and that he must test it by shadowing their every movement. When Lomas's companion entered my room he was completely disguised, but on discarding the various contrivances by which his identity was concealed he proved to be a rather slender, dark-complexioned, handsome young man, of easy address and captivating manners. He gave his name as Renfrew, answered all my questions satisfactorily, and went into details about Mosby and his men which showed an intimacy with them at some time. I explained to the two men the work I had laid out for them, and stated the sum of money I would give to have it done, but stipulated that in case of failure there would be no compensation whatever beyond the few dollars necessary for their expenses. They readily assented, and it was arranged that they should start the following night. Meanwhile Young had selected his men to shadow them, and in two days reported my spies as being concealed at Strasburg, where they remained, without making the slightest effort to continue on their mission, and were busy, no doubt, communicating with the enemy, though I was not able to fasten this on them. On the 16th of February they returned to Winchester, and reported their failure, telling so many lies about their hazardous adventure as to remove all remaining doubt as to their double-dealing. Unquestionably they were spies from the enemy, and hence liable to the usual penalties of such service; but it struck me that through them I might deceive Early as to the time of opening the spring campaign, I having already received from General Grant an intimation of what was expected of me. I therefore retained the men without even a suggestion of my knowledge of their true character, Young meanwhile keeping close watch over all their doings.

Toward the last of February General Early had at Staunton two brigades of infantry under Wharton. All the rest of the infantry except Echol's brigade, which was in southwestern Virginia, had been sent to Petersburg during the winter, and Fitz. Lee's two brigades of cavalry also. Rosser's men were mostly at their homes, where, on account of a lack of subsistence and forage in the valley, they had been permitted to go, subject to call. Lomax's cavalry was at Millboro', west of Staunton, where supplies were obtainable. It was my aim to get well on the road before Early could collect these scattered forces, and as many of the officers had been in the habit of amusing themselves fox-hunting during the latter part of the winter, I decided to use the hunt as an expedient for stealing a march on the enemy, and had it given out officially that a grand fox-chase would take place on the 29th of February. Knowing that Lomas and Renfrew would spread the announcement South, they were permitted to see several red foxes that had been secured, as well as a large pack of hounds which Colonel Young had collected for the sport, and were then started on a second expedition to burn the bridges. Of course, they were shadowed as usual, and two days later, after they had communicated with friends from their hiding-place in Newtown, they were arrested. On the way north to Fort Warren they escaped from their guards when passing through Baltimore, and I never heard of them again, though I learned that, after the assassination of Mr. Lincoln, Secretary Stanton strongly suspected his friend Lomas of being associated with the conspirators, and it then occurred to me that the good-looking Renfrew may have been Wilkes Booth, for he certainly bore a strong resemblance to Booth's pictures.

On the 27th of February my cavalry entered upon the campaign which cleared the Shenandoah Valley of every remnant of organized Confederates. General Torbert being absent on leave at this time, I did not recall him, but appointed General Merritt Chief of Cavalry, for Torbert had disappointed me on two important occasions—in the Luray Valley during the battle of Fisher's Hill, and on the recent Gordonsville expedition—and I mistrusted his ability to conduct any operations requiring much self-reliance. The column was composed of Custer's and Devin's divisions of cavalry, and two sections of artillery, comprising in all about 10,000 officers and men. On wheels we had, to accompany this column, eight ambulances, sixteen ammunition wagons, a pontoon train for eight canvas boats, and a small supply-train, with fifteen days' rations of coffee, sugar, and salt, it being intended to depend on the country for the meat and bread ration, the men carrying in their haversacks nearly enough to subsist them till out of the exhausted valley.

Grant's orders were for me to destroy the Virginia Central railroad and the James River canal, capture Lynchburg if practicable, and then join General Sherman in North Carolina wherever he might be found, or return to Winchester, but as to joining Sherman I was to be governed by the state of affairs after the projected capture of Lynchburg. The weather was cold, the valley and surrounding mountains being still covered with snow; but this was fast disappearing, however, under the heavy rain that was coming down as the column moved along up the Valley pike at a steady gait that took us to Woodstock the first day.

The second day we crossed the North Fork of the Shenandoah on our pontoon-bridge, and by night-fall reached Lacy's Springs, having seen nothing of the enemy as yet but a few partisans who hung on our flanks in the afternoon.

March 1 we encountered General Rosser at Mt. Crawford, he having been able to call together only some five or six hundred of his troops, our unsuspected march becoming known to Early only the day before. Rosser attempted to delay us here, trying to burn the bridges over the Middle Fork of the Shenandoah, but two regiments from Colonel Capehart's brigade swam the stream and drove Rosser to Kline's Mills, taking thirty prisoners and twenty ambulances and wagons.

Meanwhile General Early was busy at Staunton, but not knowing my objective point, he had ordered the return of Echol's brigade from southwestern Virginia for the protection of Lynchburg, directed Lomax's cavalry to concentrate at Pond Gap for the purpose of harassing me if I moved toward Lynchburg, and at the same time marched Wharton's two brigades of infantry, Nelson's artillery, and Rosser's cavalry to Waynesboro' whither he went also to remain till the object of my movement was ascertained.

I entered Staunton the morning of March 2, and finding that Early had gone to Waynesboro' with his infantry and Rosser, the question at once arose whether I should continue my march to Lynchburg direct, leaving my adversary in my rear, or turn east and open the way through Rockfish Gap to the Virginia Central railroad and James River canal. I felt confident of the success of the latter plan, for I knew that Early numbered there not more than two thousand men; so, influenced by this, and somewhat also by the fact that Early had left word in Staunton that he would fight at Waynesboro', I directed Merritt to move toward that place with Custer, to be closely followed by Devin, who was to detach one brigade to destroy supplies at Swoope's depot. The by-roads were miry beyond description, rain having fallen almost incessantly since we left Winchester, but notwithstanding the down-pour the column pushed on, men and horses growing almost unrecognizable from the mud covering them from head to foot.

General Early was true to the promise made his friends in Staunton, for when Custer neared Waynesboro' he found, occupying a line of breastworks on a ridge west of the town, two brigades of infantry, with eleven pieces of artillery and Rosser's cavalry. Custer, when developing the position of the Confederates, discovered that their left was somewhat exposed instead of resting on South River; he therefore made his dispositions for attack, sending around that flank the dismounted regiments from Pennington's brigade, while he himself, with two brigades, partly mounted and partly dismounted, assaulted along the whole line of breastworks. Pennington's flanking movement stampeded the enemy in short order, thus enabling Custer to carry the front with little resistance, and as he did so the Eighth New York and First Connecticut, in a charge in column, broke through the opening made by Custer, and continued on through the town of Waynesboro', never stopping till they crossed South River. There, finding themselves immediately in the enemy's rear, they promptly formed as foragers and held the east bank of the stream till all the Confederates surrendered except Rosser, who succeeded in making his way back to the valley, and Generals Early, Wharton, Long, and Lilley, who, with fifteen or twenty men, escaped across the Blue Ridge. I followed up the victory immediately by despatching Capehart through Rock-fish Gap, with orders to encamp on the east side of the Blue Ridge. By reason of this move all the enemy's stores and transportation fell into our hands, while we captured on the field seventeen battle flags, sixteen hundred officers and men, and eleven pieces of artillery. This decisive victory closed hostilities in the Shenandoah Valley. The prisoners and artillery were sent back to Winchester next morning, under a guard of 1,500 men, commanded by Colonel J. H. Thompson, of the First New Hampshire.

The night of March 2 Custer camped at Brookfield, Devin remaining at Waynesboro'. The former started for Charlottesville the next morning early, followed by Devin with but two brigades, Gibbs having been left behind to blow up the iron railroad bridge across South River. Because of the incessant rains and spring thaws the roads were very soft, and the columns cut them up terribly, the mud being thrown by the sets of fours across the road in ridges as much as two feet high, making it most difficult to get our wagons along, and distressingly wearing on the animals toward the middle and rear of the columns. Consequently I concluded to rest at Charlottesville for a couple of days and recuperate a little, intending at the same time to destroy, with small parties, the railroad from that point toward Lynchburg. Custer reached Charlottesville the 3d, in the afternoon, and was met at the outskirts by a deputation of its citizens, headed by the mayor, who surrendered the town with mediæval ceremony, formally handing over the keys of the public buildings and of the University of Virginia. But this little scene did not delay Custer long enough to prevent his capturing, just beyond the village, a small body of cavalry and three pieces of artillery. Gibbs's brigade, which was bringing up my mud-impeded train, did not arrive until the 5th of March. In the mean time Young's scouts had brought word that the garrison of Lynchburg was being increased and the fortifications strengthened, so that its capture would be improbable. I decided, however, to move toward the place as far as Amherst Court House, which is sixteen miles short of the town, so Devin, under Merritt's supervision, marched along the James River, destroying the canal, while Custer pushed ahead on the railroad and broke it up. The two columns were to join at New Market, whence I intended to cross the James River at some point east of Lynchburg, if practicable, so as to make my way to Appomattox Court House, and destroy the Southside railroad as far east as Farmville. Owing to its swollen condition the river was unfordable, but knowing that there was a covered bridge at Duguidsville, I hoped to secure it by a dash, and cross there, but the enemy, anticipating this, had filled the bridge with inflammable material, and just as our troops got within striking distance it burst into flames. The bridge at Hardwicksville also having been burned by the enemy, there was now no means of crossing except by pontoons, but, unfortunately, I had only eight of these, and they could not be made to span the swollen river.

Being thus unable to cross until the river should fall, and knowing that it was impracticable to join General Sherman, and useless to adhere to my alternative instructions to return to Winchester, I now decided to destroy still more thoroughly the James River canal and the Virginia Central railroad and then join General Grant in front of Petersburg. I was master of the whole country north of the James as far down as Goochland; hence the destruction of these arteries of supply could be easily compassed, and feeling that the war was nearing its end, I desired my cavalry to be in at the death.

On March 9 the main column started eastward down the James River, destroying locks, dams, and boats, having been preceded by Colonel Fitzhugh's brigade of Devin's division in a forced march to Goochland and Beaver Dam Creek, with orders to destroy everything below Columbia. I made Columbia on the 10th, and from there sent a communication to General Grant reporting what had occurred, informing him of my condition and intention, asking him to send forage and rations to meet me at the White House, and also a pontoon-bridge to carry me over the Pamunkey, for in view of the fact that hitherto it had been impracticable to hold Lee in the trenches around Petersburg, I regarded as too hazardous a march down the south bank of the Pamunkey, where the enemy, by sending troops out from Richmond, might fall upon my flank and rear. It was of the utmost importance that General Grant should receive these despatches without chance of failure, in order that I might depend absolutely on securing supplies at the White House; therefore I sent the message in duplicate, one copy overland direct to City Point by two scouts, Campbell and Rowan, and the other by Fannin and Moore, who were to go down the James River in a small boat to Richmond, join the troops in the trenches in front of Petersburg, and, deserting to the Union lines, deliver their tidings into General Grant's hands. Each set of messengers got through, but the copy confided to Campbell and Rowan was first at Grant's headquarters.

I halted for one day at Columbia to let my trains catch up, for it was still raining and the mud greatly delayed the teams, fatiguing and wearying the mules so much that I believe we should have been forced to abandon most of the wagons except for the invaluable help given by some two thousand negroes who had attached themselves to the column: they literally lifted the wagons out of the mud. From Columbia Merritt, with Devin's division, marched to Louisa Court House and destroyed the Virginia Central to Frederick's Hall. Meanwhile Custer was performing similar work from Frederick's Hall to Beaver Dam Station, and also pursued for a time General Early, who, it was learned from despatches captured in the telegraph office at Frederick's Hall, was in the neighborhood with a couple of hundred men. Custer captured some of these men and two of Early's staff-officers, but the commander of the Valley District, accompanied by a single orderly, escaped across the South Anna and next day made his way to Richmond, the last man of the Confederate army that had so long contended with us in the Shenandoah Valley.

At Frederick's Hall, Young's scouts brought me word from Richmond that General Longstreet was assembling a force there to prevent my junction with Grant, and that Pickett's division, which had been sent toward Lynchburg to oppose my march, and Fitzhugh Lee's cavalry, were moving east on the Southside railroad, with the object of circumventing me. Reasoning that Longstreet could interpose effectually only by getting to the White House ahead of me, I pushed one column under Custer across the South Anna, by way of Ground Squirrel bridge, to

Ashland, where it united with Merritt, who had meanwhile marched through Hanover Junction. Our appearance at Ashland drew the Confederates out in that direction, as was hoped, so, leaving Colonel Pennington's brigade there to amuse them, the united command retraced its route to Mount Carmel church to cross the North Anna. After dark Pennington came away, and all the troops reached the church by midnight of the 15th.

Resuming the march at an early hour next morning, we took the road by way of King William Court House to the White House, where, arriving on the 18th, we found, greatly to our relief, the supplies which I had requested to be sent there. In the meanwhile the enemy had marched to Hanover Court House, but being unable either to cross the Pamunkey there or forestall me at the White House on the south side of the river, he withdrew to Richmond without further effort to impede my column.

The hardships of this march far exceeded those of any previous campaigns by the cavalry. Almost incessant rains had drenched us for sixteen days and nights, and the swollen streams and wellnigh bottomless roads east of Staunton presented grave difficulties on every hand, but surmounting them all, we destroyed the enemy's means of subsistence, in quantities beyond computation, and permanently crippled the Virginia Central railroad, as well as the James River canal, and as each day brought us nearer the Army of the Potomac, all were filled with the comforting reflection that our work in the Shenandoah Valley had been thoroughly done, and every one was buoyed up by the cheering thought that we should soon take part in the final struggle of the war.

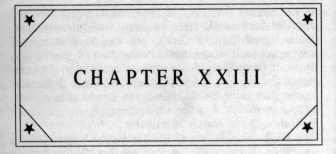

CHAPTER XXIII

THE TRANSFER OF MY COMMAND from the Shenandoah Valley to the field of operations in front of Petersburg was not anticipated by General Grant; indeed, the despatch brought from Columbia by my scouts, asking that supplies be sent me at the White House, was the first word that reached him concerning the move. In view of my message the general-in-chief decided to wait my arrival before beginning spring operations with the investing troops south of the James River, for he felt the importance of having my cavalry at hand in a campaign which he was convinced would wind up the war. We remained a few days at the White House resting and refitting the cavalry, a large amount of shoeing being necessary; but nothing like enough horses were at hand to replace those that had died or been disabled on the mud march from Staunton to the Pamunkey River, so a good many of the men were still without mounts, and all such were sent by boat to the dismounted camp near City Point. When all was ready the column set out for Hancock Station, a point on the military railroad in front of Petersburg, and arriving there on the 27th of March, was in orders reunited with its comrades of the Second Division, who had been serving with the Army of the Potomac since we parted from them the previous August. General Crook, who had been exchanged within a few days, was now in command of this Second Division. The reunited corps was to enter upon the campaign as a separate army, I reporting directly to General Grant; the intention being thus to reward me for foregoing, of my own choice, my position as a department commander by joining the armies at Petersburg.

Taking the road across the Peninsula, I started from the White House with Merritt's column on the 25th of March, and encamped that night at Harrison's Landing. Very early next morning, in conformity with a request from General Grant, I left by boat for City Point, Merritt meanwhile conducting the column across the James River to the point of rendezvous. The trip to City Point did not take long, and on arrival at army headquarters the first person I met was General John A. Rawlins, General Grant's chief-of-staff. Rawlins was a man of strong likes and dislikes, and positive always both in speech and action, exhibiting marked feelings when greeting any one, and on this occasion met me with much warmth. His demonstrations of welcome over, we held a few minutes' conversation about the coming campaign, he taking strong ground against a part of the plan of operations adopted, namely, that which contemplated my joining General Sherman's army. His language was unequivocal and vehement, and when he was through talking, he conducted me to General Grant's quarters, but he himself did not enter.

General Grant was never impulsive, and always met his officers in an unceremonious way, with a quiet "How are you?" soon putting one at his ease, since the pleasant tone in which he spoke gave assurance of welcome, although his manner was otherwise impassive. When the ordinary greeting was over, he usually waited for his visitor to open the conversation, so on this occasion I began by giving him the details of my march from Winchester, my reasons for not joining Sherman, as contemplated in my instruc-

tions, and the motives which had influenced me to march
to the White House. The other provision of my orders on
setting out from Winchester—the alternative return to
that place—was not touched upon, for the wisdom of having ignored that was fully apparent. Commenting on this
recital of my doings, the General referred only to the tor-
tuous course of my march from Waynesboro' down, our
sore trials, and the valuable services of the scouts who had
brought him tidings of me, closing with the remark that
it was rare a department commander voluntarily deprived
himself of independence, and added that I should not suffer
for it. Then turning to the business for which he had called
me to City Point, he outlined what he expected me to do;
saying that I was to cut loose from the Army of the Potomac
by passing its left flank to the southward along the line of
the Danville railroad, and after crossing the Roanoke River,
join General Sherman. While speaking, he handed me a
copy of a general letter of instructions that had been drawn
up for the army on the 24th. The letter contained these
words concerning the movements of my command:

> "The cavalry under General Sheridan, joined by the di-
> vision now under General Davies, will move at the same
> time (29th inst.) by the Weldon road and the Jerusalem
> plank-road, turning west from the latter before crossing
> the Nottoway, and west with the whole column before
> reaching Stony Creek. General Sheridan will then move
> independently under other instructions which will be given
> him. All dismounted cavalry belonging to the Army of the
> Potomac, and the dismounted cavalry from the Middle
> Military Division not required for guarding property be-
> longing to their arm of the service, will report to Brigadier-
> General Benham to be added to the defenses of City Point."

When I had gone over the entire letter I showed plainly
that I was dissatisfied with it, for, coupled with what the
General had outlined orally, which I supposed was the
"other instructions," I believed it foreshadowed my junc-

tion with General Sherman. Rawlins thought so too, as his vigorous language had left no room to doubt, so I immediately began to offer my objections to the programme. These were, that it would be bad policy to send me down to the Carolinas with a part of the Army of the Potomac, to come back to crush Lee after the destruction of General Johnston's army; such a course would give rise to the charge that his own forces around Petersburg were not equal to the task, and would seriously affect public opinion in the North; that in fact my cavalry belonged to the Army of the Potomac, which army was able unaided to destroy Lee, and I could not but oppose any dispersion of its strength.

All this was said in a somewhat emphatic manner, and when I had finished he quietly told me that the portion of my instructions from which I so strongly dissented was intended as a "blind" to cover any check the army in its general move to the left might meet with, and prevent that element in the North which held that the war could be ended only through negotiation, from charging defeat. The fact that my cavalry was not to ultimately join Sherman was a great relief to me, and after expressing the utmost confidence in the plans unfolded for closing the war by directing every effort to the annihilation of Lee's army, I left him to go to General Ingalls's quarters. On the way I again met Rawlins, who, when I told him that General Grant had intimated his intention to modify the written plan of operations so far as regarded the cavalry, manifested the greatest satisfaction, and I judged from this that the new view of the matter had not previously been communicated to the chief-of-staff, though he must have been acquainted of course with the programme made out on the 24th of March.

Toward noon General Grant sent for me to accompany him up the river. When I joined the General he informed me that the President was on board the boat—the steamer *Mary Martin*. For some days Mr. Lincoln had been at City Point, established on the steamer *River Queen*, having come down from Washington to be nearer his generals, no doubt, and also to be conveniently situated for the reception of tidings from the front when operations began, for he could not endure the delays in getting news to Washington. This trip up the James had been projected by General Meade, but on account of demands at the front he could not go, so the President, General Grant, and I composed the party. We steamed up to where my cavalry was crossing on the pontoon-bridge below the mouth of the Dutch Gap canal, and for a little while watched the column as it was passing over the river, the bright sunshine presaging good weather, but only to delude, as was proved by the torrents of rain brought by the succeeding days of March. On the trip the President was not very cheerful. In fact, he was dejected, giving no indication of his usual means of diversion, by which (his quaint stories) I had often heard he could find relief from his cares. He spoke to me of the impending operations and asked many questions, laying stress upon the one, "What would be the result when the army moved out to the left, if the enemy should come down and capture City Point?" the question being prompted, doubtless, by the bold assault on our lines and capture of Fort Steadman two days before by General Gordon. I answered that I did not think it at all probable that General Lee would undertake such a desperate measure to relieve the strait he was in; that General Hartranft's successful check to Gordon had ended, I thought, attacks of such a character; and in any event General Grant would give Lee all he could attend to on the left. Mr. Lincoln said nothing about my proposed route of march, and I doubt if he knew of my instructions, or was in possession at most of more than a very general outline of the plan of campaign. It was late when the *Mary Martin* returned to City Point, and I spent the night there with General Ingalls.

The morning of the 27th I went out to Hancock Station to look after my troops and prepare for moving two days later. In the afternoon I received a telegram from General Grant, saying: "General Sherman will be here this evening to spend a few hours. I should like to have you come down." Sherman's coming was a surprise—at least to me it was—this despatch being my first intimation of his expected arrival. Well knowing the zeal and emphasis with which General Sherman would present his views, there again came into my mind many misgivings with reference to the movement of the cavalry, and I made haste to start for Grant's headquarters. I got off a little after 7 o'clock, taking the rickety military railroad, the rails of which were laid on the natural surface of the ground, with grading only here and there at points of absolute necessity, and had not gone far when the locomotive jumped the track. This delayed my arrival at City Point till near midnight, but on repairing to the little cabin that sheltered the general-in-chief, I found him and Sherman still up talking over the problem whose solution was near at hand. As already stated, thoughts as to the tenor of my instructions became uppermost the moment I received the telegram in the afternoon, and they continued to engross and disturb me all the way down the railroad, for I feared that the telegram foreshadowed, under the propositions Sherman would present, a more specific compliance with the written instructions than General Grant had orally assured me would be exacted.

My entrance into the shanty suspended the conversation for a moment only, and then General Sherman, without prelude, rehearsed his plans for moving his army, pointing out with every detail how he would come up through the Carolinas to join the troops besieging Petersburg and Richmond, and intimating that my cavalry, after striking the Southside and Danville railroads, could join him with ease. I made no comments on the projects for moving his own troops, but as soon as opportunity offered, dissented emphatically from the proposition to have me join the Army of the Tennessee, repeating in substance what I had previously expressed to General Grant. My uneasiness made me somewhat too earnest, I fear, but General Grant soon mollified me, and smoothed matters over by practically repeating what he had told me in regard to this point at the close of our interview the day before, so I pursued the subject no further. In a little while the conference ended, and I again sought lodging at the hospitable quarters of Ingalls.

Very early the next morning, while I was still in bed, General Sherman came to me and renewed the subject of my joining him, but when he saw that I was unalterably opposed to it the conversation turned into other channels, and after we had chatted awhile he withdrew, and later in the day went up the river with the President, General Grant, and Admiral Porter, I returning to my command at Hancock Station, where my presence was needed to put my troops in march next day.

During the entire winter General Grant's lines fronting Petersburg had extended south of the Appomattox River, practically from that stream around to where the Vaughn road crosses Hatcher's Run, and this was nearly the situation when the cavalry concentrated at Hancock Station, General Weitzel holding the line north of the Appomattox, fronting Richmond and Bermuda Hundred.

The instructions of the 24th of March contemplated that the campaign should begin with the movement of Warren's corps (the Fifth) at 3 o'clock on the morning of the 29th, and Humphreys's (the Second) at 6; the rest of the infantry holding on in the trenches. The cavalry was to move in conjunction with Warren and Humphreys, and make its way out beyond our left as these corps opened the road.

The night of the 28th I received the following additional instructions, the general tenor of which again disturbed me, for although I had been assured that I was not to join General Sherman, it will be seen that the supplemental directions distinctly present that alternative, and I therefore feared that during the trip up the James River on the morning of the 28th General Grant had returned to his original views:

"HEADQUARTERS ARMIES OF THE UNITED STATES,
"City Point, Va., March 28, 1865.
"MAJOR-GENERAL P. H. SHERIDAN:

"The Fifth Army Corps will move by the Vaughn road at 3 A.M. to-morrow morning. The Second moves at about 9 A.M., having but about three miles to march to reach the point designated for it to take on the right of the Fifth Corps, after the latter reaches Dinwiddie Court House.

"Move your cavalry at as early an hour as you can, and without being confined to any particular road or roads. You may go out by the nearest roads in rear of the Fifth Corps, pass by its left, and passing near to or through Dinwiddie, reach the right and rear of the enemy as soon as you can. It is not the intention to attack the enemy in his intrenched position, but to force him out if possible. Should he come out and attack us, or get himself where he can be attacked, move in with your entire force in your own way, and with the full reliance that the army will engage or follow the enemy, as circumstances will dictate. I shall be on the field, and will probably be able to communicate with you; should I not do so, and you find that the enemy keeps within his main intrenched line, you may cut loose and push for the Danville road. If you find it practicable I would like you to cross the Southside road, between Petersburg and Burkeville, and destroy it to some extent. I would not advise much detention, however, until you reach the Danville road, which I would like you to strike as near to the Appomattox as possible; make your destruction of that road as complete as possible; you can then pass on to the Southside road, west of Burkeville, and destroy that in like manner.

"After having accomplished the destruction of the two railroads, which are now the only avenues of supply to Lee's army, you may return to this army, selecting your road farther south, or you may go on into North Carolina and join General Sherman. Should you select the latter course, get the information to me as early as possible, so that I may send orders to meet you at Goldsboro'.

U. S. GRANT, Lieut.-General."

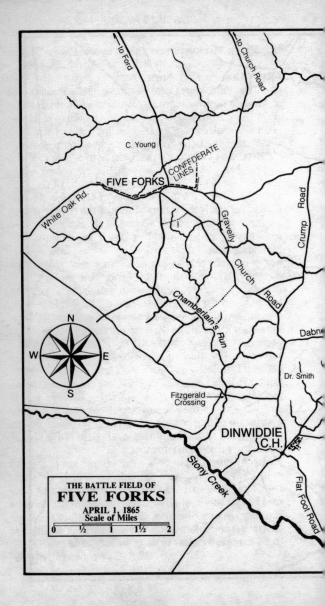

THE BATTLE FIELD OF
FIVE FORKS
APRIL 1, 1865
Scale of Miles
0   ½   1   1½   2

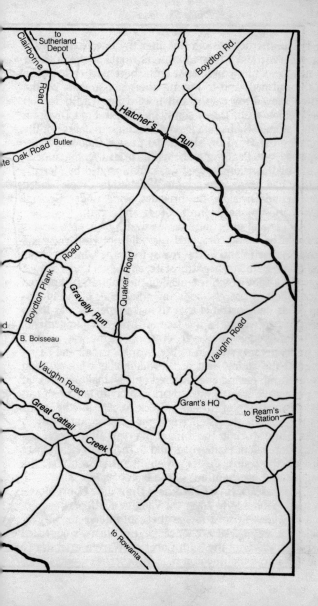

These instructions did not alter my line of march for the morrow, and I trusted matters would so come about as not to require compliance with those portions relative to the railroads and to joining Sherman; so early on the 29th I moved my cavalry out toward Ream's Station on the Weldon road, Devin commanding the First Division, with Colonels Gibbs, Stagg, and Fitzhugh in charge of the brigades; the Third Division under Custer, Colonels Wells, Capehart, and Pennington being the brigade commanders. These two divisions united were commanded by Merritt, as they had been since leaving Winchester. Crook headed the Second Division, his brigades being under General Davies and Colonels John I. Gregg and Smith.

Our general direction was westward, over such routes as could be found, provided they did not embarrass the march of the infantry. The roads, from the winter's frosts and rains, were in a frightful state, and when it was sought to avoid a spot which the head of the column had proved almost bottomless, the bogs and quicksands of the adjoining fields demonstrated that to make a détour was to go from bad to worse. In the face of these discouragements we floundered on, however, crossing on the way a series of small streams swollen to their banks. Crook and Devin reached the county-seat of Dinwiddie about 5 o'clock in the evening, having encountered only a small picket, that at once gave way to our advance. Merritt left Custer at Malon's crossing of Rowanty Creek to care for the trains containing our subsistence and the reserve ammunition, these being stuck in the mire at intervals all the way back to the Jerusalem plank-road; and to make any headway at all with the trains, Custer's men often had to unload the wagons and lift them out of the boggy places.

Crook and Devin camped near Dinwiddie Court House in such manner as to cover the Vaughn, Flatfoot, Boydton, and Five Forks roads; for, as these all intersected at Dinwiddie, they offered a chance for the enemy's approach toward the rear of the Fifth Corps, as Warren extended to the left across the Boydton road. Any of these routes leading to the south or west might also be the one on which, in conformity with one part of my instructions, I was expected to get out toward the Danville and Southside railroads, and the Five Forks road would lead directly to General Lee's right flank, in case opportunity was found to comply with the other part. The place was, therefore, of great strategic value, and getting it without cost repaid us for floundering through the mud.

Dinwiddie Court House, though a most important point in the campaign, was far from attractive in feature, being made up of a half-dozen unsightly houses, a ramshackle tavern propped up on two sides with pine poles, and the weather-beaten building that gave official name to the crossroads. We had no tents—there were none in the command—so I took possession of the tavern for shelter for myself and staff, and just as we had finished looking over its primitive interior a rainstorm set in.

The wagon containing my mess equipment was back somewhere on the road, hopelessly stuck in the mud, and hence we had nothing to eat except some coffee which two young women living at the tavern kindly made for us; a small quantity of the berry being furnished from the haversacks of my escort. By the time we got the coffee, rain was falling in sheets, and the evening bade fair to be a most dismal one; but songs and choruses set up by some of my staff—the two young women playing accompaniments on a battered piano—relieved the situation and enlivened us a little. However, the dreary night brought me one great comfort; for General Grant, who that day had moved out to Gravelly Run, sent me instructions to abandon all idea of the contemplated raid, and directed me to act in concert with the infantry under his immediate command, to turn, if possible, the right flank of Lee's army. The despatch made my mind easy with respect to the objectionable feature of my original instructions, and of course relieved me also from the anxiety growing out of the letter received at Hancock Station the night of the 28th; so, notwithstanding the suspicions excited by some of my staff concerning the Virginia feather-bed that had been assigned me, I turned in at a late hour and slept most soundly.

The night of the 29th the left of General Grant's infantry—Warren's corps—rested on the Boydton road, not far from its intersection with the Quaker road. Humphreys's corps was next to Warren; then came Ord, next Wright, and then Parke, with his right resting on the Appomattox. The moving of Warren and Humphreys to the left during the day was early discovered by General Lee. He met it by extending the right of his infantry on the White Oak road, while drawing in the cavalry of W. H. F. Lee and Rosser along the south bank of Stony Creek to cover a crossroads called Five Forks, to anticipate me there; for assuming that my command was moving in conjunction with the infantry, with the ultimate purpose of striking the Southside railroad, Lee made no effort to hold Dinwiddie, which he might have done with his cavalry, and in this he made a fatal mistake. The cavalry of Fitz. Lee was ordered at this same time from Sunderland depot to Five Forks, and its chief placed in command of all the mounted troops of General Lee's army.

At daylight on the 30th I proceeded to make dispositions under the new conditions imposed by my modified instructions, and directed Merritt to push Devin out as far as the White Oak road to make a reconnoissance to Five Forks, Crook being instructed to send Davies's brigade to support Devin. Crook was to hold, with Gregg's brigade, the Stony Creek crossing of the Boydton plank-road, retaining Smith's near Dinwiddie, for use in any direction required. On the 29th W. H. F. Lee conformed the march of his cavalry with that of ours, but my holding Stony Creek in this way forced him to make a détour west of Chamberlain's Run, in order to get in communication with his friends at Five Forks.

The rain that had been falling all night gave no sign of stopping, but kept pouring down all day long, and the swamps and quicksands mired the horses, whether they marched in the roads or across the adjacent fields. Undismayed, nevertheless, each column set out for its appointed duty, but shortly after the troops began to move I received from General Grant this despatch, which put a new phase on matters:

> "HEADQUARTERS ARMIES OF THE UNITED STATES,
> "GRAVELLY RUN, March 30, 1865.
>
> "MAJOR-GENERAL SHERIDAN:
> "The heavy rain of to-day will make it impossible for us to do much until it dries up a little, or we get roads around our rear repaired. You may, therefore, leave what cavalry you deem necessary to protect the left, and hold such positions as you deem necessary for that purpose, and send the remainder back to Humphrey's Station* where they can get hay and grain. Fifty wagons loaded with forage will be sent to you in the morning. Send an officer back to direct the wagons back to where you want them. Report to me the cavalry you will leave back, and the position you will occupy. Could not your cavalry go back by the way of Stony Creek depot and destroy or capture the store of supplies there?
>
> "U. S. GRANT, Lieut.-General."

When I had read and pondered this, I determined to ride over to General Grant's headquarters on Gravelly Run, and get a clear idea of what it was proposed to do, for it seemed to me that a suspension of operations would be a serious mistake. Mounting a powerful gray pacing horse called Breckenridge (from its capture from one of Breckenridge's staff-officers at Missionary Ridge), and that I knew would carry me through the mud, I set out accompanied by my Assistant Adjutant-General, Colonel Frederick C. Newhall, and an escort of about ten or fifteen men. At first we rode north up the Boydton plank-road, and coming upon our infantry pickets from a direction where the enemy was expected to appear, they began to fire upon

*Humphrey's Station was back on the military railroad.

us, but seeing from our actions that we were friends, they ceased, and permitted us to pass the outposts. We then struggled on in a northeasterly direction across-country, till we struck the Vaughn road. This carried us to army headquarters, which were established south of Gravelly Run in an old corn-field. I rode to within a few yards of the front of General Grant's tent, my horse plunging at every step almost to his knees in the mud, and dismounted near a camp-fire, apparently a general one, for all the staff-officers were standing around it on boards and rails placed here and there to keep them from sinking into the mire.

Going directly to General Grant's tent, I found him and Rawlins talking over the question of suspending operations till the weather should improve. No orders about the matter had been issued yet, except the despatch to me; and Rawlins, being strongly opposed to the proposition, was frankly expostulating with General Grant, who, after greeting me, remarked, in his quiet way: "Well, Rawlins, I think you had better take command." Seeing that there was a difference up between Rawlins and his chief, I made the excuse of being wet and cold, and went outside to the fire. Here General Ingalls met me and took me to his tent, where I was much more comfortable than when standing outside, and where a few minutes later we were joined by General Grant. Ingalls then retired, and General Grant began talking of our fearful plight, resulting from the rains and mud, and saying that because of this it seemed necessary to suspend operations. I at once begged him not to do so, telling him that my cavalry was already on the move in spite of the difficulties, and that although a suspension of operations would not be fatal, yet it would give rise to the very charge of disaster to which he had referred at City Point, and, moreover, that we would surely be ridiculed, just as General Burnside's army was after the mud march of 1863. His better judgment was against suspending operations, but the proposition had been suggested by all sorts of complaints as to the impossibility of moving the trains and the like, so it needed little argument to convince him, and without further discussion he said, in that manner which with him meant a firmness of purpose that could not be changed by further complainings, "We will go on." I then told him that I believed I could break in the enemy's right if he would let me have the Sixth Corps; but saying that the condition of the roads would prevent the movement of infantry, he replied that I would have to seize Five Forks with the cavalry alone.

On my way back to Dinwiddie I stopped at the headquarters of General Warren, but the General being asleep, I went to the tent of one of his staff-officers, Colonel William T. Gentry, an old personal friend with whom I had served in Oregon. In a few minutes Warren came in, and we had a short conversation, he speaking rather despondently of the outlook, being influenced no doubt by the depressing weather.

From Warren's headquarters I returned by the Boydton road to Dinwiddie Court House, fording Gravelly Run with ease. When I got as far as the Dabney road I sent Colonel Newhall out on it toward Five Forks, with orders for Merritt to develop the enemy's position and strength, and then rode on to Dinwiddie to endeavor to get all my other troops up. Merritt was halted at the intersection of the Five Forks and Gravelly Church roads when Newhall delivered the orders, and in compliance moving out Gibbs's brigade promptly, sharp skirmishing was brought on, Gibbs driving the Confederates to Five Forks, where he found them behind a line of breast-works running along the White Oak road. The reconnoissance demonstrating the intention of the enemy to hold this point, Gibbs was withdrawn.

That evening, at 7 o'clock, I reported the position of the Confederate cavalry, and stated that it had been reinforced by Pickett's division of infantry. On receipt of this despatch, General Grant offered me the Fifth Corps, but I declined to take it, and again asked for the Sixth, saying that with it I believed I could turn the enemy's (Pickett's) left, or break through his lines. The morning of the 31st

CHAPTER XXIV

THE NIGHT OF MARCH 30 Merritt, with Devin's division and Davies's brigade, was camped on the Five Forks road about two miles in front of Dinwiddie, near J. Boisseau's. Crook, with Smith and Gregg's brigades, continued to cover Stony Creek, and Custer was still back at Rowanty Creek, trying to get the trains up. This force had been counted while crossing the creek on the 29th, the three divisions numbering 9,000 enlisted men, Crook having 3,300, and Custer and Devin 5,700.

During the 30th, the enemy had been concentrating his cavalry, and by evening General W. H. F Lee and General Rosser had joined Fitzhugh Lee near Five Forks. To this force was added, about dark, five brigades of infantry— three from Pickett's division, and two from Johnson's— all under command of Pickett. The infantry came by the White Oak road from the right of General Lee's intrenchments, and their arrival became positively known to me about dark, the confirmatory intelligence being brought in then by some of Young's scouts who had been inside the Confederate lines.

On the 31st, the rain having ceased, directions were

given at an early hour to both Merritt and Crook to make reconnoissances preparatory to securing Five Forks, and about 9 o'clock Merritt started for the crossroads, Davies's brigade supporting him. His march was necessarily slow because of the mud, and the enemy's pickets resisted with obstinacy also, but the coveted crossroads fell to Merritt without much trouble, as the bulk of the enemy was just then bent on other things. At the same hour that Merritt started, Crook moved Smith's brigade out northwest from Dinwiddie to Fitzgerald's crossing of Chamberlain's Creek, to cover Merritt's left, supporting Smith by placing Gregg to his right and rear. The occupation of this ford was timely, for Pickett, now in command of both the cavalry and infantry, was already marching to get in Merritt's rear by crossing Chamberlain's Creek.

To hold on to Fitzgerald's ford Smith had to make a sharp fight, but Mumford's cavalry attacking Devin, the enemy's infantry succeeded in getting over Chamberlain's Creek at a point higher up than Fitzgerald's ford, and assailing Davies, forced him back in a northeasterly direction toward the Dinwiddie and Five Forks road in company with Devin. The retreat of Davies permitted Pickett to pass between Crook and Merritt, which he promptly did, effectually separating them and cutting off both Davies and Devin from the road to Dinwiddie, so that to get to that point they had to retreat across the country to B. Boisseau's and then down the Boydton road.

Gibbs's brigade had been in reserve near the intersection of the Five Forks and Dabney roads, and directing Merritt to hold on there, I ordered Gregg's brigade to be mounted and brought to Merritt's aid, for if Pickett continued in pursuit north of the Five Forks road he would expose his right and rear, and I determined to attack him, in such case, from Gibbs's position. Gregg arrived in good season, and as soon as his men were dismounted on Gibbs's left, Merritt assailed fiercely, compelling Pickett to halt and face a new foe, thus interrupting an advance that would finally have carried Pickett into the rear of Warren's corps.

It was now about 4 o'clock in the afternoon and we were in a critical situation, but having ordered Merritt to bring Devin and Davies to Dinwiddie by the Boydton road, staff-officers were sent to hurry Custer to the same point, for with its several diverging roads the Court House was of vital importance, and I determined to stay there at all hazards. At the same time orders were sent to Smith's brigade, which, by the advance of Pickett past its right flank and the pressure of W. H. F. Lee on its front, had been compelled to give up Fitzgerald's crossing, to fall back toward Dinwiddie but to contest every inch of ground so as to gain time.

When halted by the attack of Gregg and Gibbs, Pickett, desisting from his pursuit of Devin, as already stated, turned his undivided attention to this unexpected force, and with his preponderating infantry pressed it back on the Five Forks road toward Dinwiddie, though our men, fighting dismounted behind barricades at different points, displayed such obstinacy as to make Pickett's progress slow, and thus give me time to look out a line for defending the Court House. I selected a place about three-fourths of a mile northwest of the crossroads, and Custer coming up quickly with Capehart's brigade, took position on the left of the road to Five Forks in some open ground along the crest of a gentle ridge. Custer got Capehart into place just in time to lend a hand to Smith, who, severely pressed, came back on us here from his retreat along Chamberlain's "bed"—the vernacular for a woody swamp such as that through which Smith retired. A little later the brigades of Gregg and Gibbs, falling to the rear slowly and steadily, took up in the woods a line which covered the Boydton Road some distance to the right of Capehart, the intervening gap to be filled with Pennington's brigade. By this time our horse-artillery, which for two days had been stuck in the mud, was all up, and every gun was posted in this line.

It was now near sunset, and the enemy's cavalry thinking the day was theirs, made a dash at Smith, but just as the assailants appeared in the open fields, Capehart's men opened so suddenly on their left flank as to cause it to recoil in astonishment, which permitted Smith to connect his brigade with Custer unmolested. We were now in good shape behind the familiar barricades, and having a continuous line, excepting only the gap to be filled with Pennington, that covered Dinwiddie and the Boydton Road. My left rested in the woods about half a mile west of the Court House, and the barricades extended from this flank in a semicircle through the open fields in a northeasterly direction, to a piece of thick timber on the right, near the Boydton Road.

A little before the sun went down the Confederate infantry was formed for the attack, and, fortunately for us, Pennington's brigade came up and filled the space to which it was assigned between Capehart and Gibbs, just as Pickett moved out across the cleared fields in front of Custer, in deep lines that plainly told how greatly we were outnumbered.

Accompanied by Generals Merritt and Custer and my staff, I now rode along the barricades to encourage the men. Our enthusiastic reception showed that they were determined to stay. The cavalcade drew the enemy's fire, which emptied several of the saddles—among others Mr. Theodore Wilson, correspondent of the New York *Herald*, being wounded. In reply our horse-artillery opened on the advancing Confederates, but the men behind the barricades lay still till Pickett's troops were within short range. Then they opened, Custer's repeating rifles pouring out such a shower of lead that nothing could stand up against it. The repulse was very quick, and as the gray lines retired to the woods from which but a few minutes before they had so confidently advanced, all danger of their taking Dinwiddie or marching to the left and rear of our infantry line was over, at least for the night. The enemy being thus checked, I sent a staff-officer—Captain Sheridan—to General Grant to report what had taken place during the afternoon, and to say that I proposed to stay at Dinwiddie, but if ultimately compelled to abandon the place, I would do so by retiring on the Vaughn road toward Hatcher's Run, for I then thought the attack might be renewed next morning. Devin and Davies joined me about dark, and my troops being now well in hand, I sent a second staff-officer—Colonel John Kellogg—to explain my situation more fully, and to assure General Grant that I would hold on at Dinwiddie till forced to let go.

By following me to Dinwiddie the enemy's infantry had completely isolated itself, and hence there was now offered the Union troops a rare opportunity. Lee was outside of his works, just as we desired, and the general-in-chief realized this the moment he received the first report of my situation; General Meade appreciated it too from the information he got from Captain Sheridan, *en route* to army headquarters with the first tidings, and sent this telegram to General Grant:

> "HEADQUARTERS OF THE ARMY OF THE POTOMAC,
> "March 31, 1865. 9:45 P.M.
>
> "LIEUTENANT-GENERAL GRANT:
>
> "Would it not be well for Warren to go down with his whole corps and smash up the force in front of Sheridan? Humphreys can hold the line to the Boydton plank-road, and the refusal along with it. Bartlett's brigade is now on the road from G. Boisseau's, running north, where it crosses Gravelly Run, he having gone down the White Oak road. Warren could go at once that way, and take the force threatening Sheridan in rear at Dinwiddie, and move on the enemy's rear with the other two.
>
> "G. G. MEADE, Major-General."

An hour later General Grant replied in these words:

> "HEADQUARTERS ARMIES OF THE UNITED STATES,
> "DABNEY'S MILLS, March 31, 1865. 10:15 P.M.
>
> "MAJOR-GENERAL MEADE,
>
> "Commanding Army of the Potomac.
>
> "Let Warren move in the way you propose, and urge

him not to stop for anything. Let Griffin go on as he was
first directed.*

        "U. S. GRANT, Lieutenant-General."

These two despatches were the initiatory steps in sending the Fifth Corps, under Major-General G. K. Warren,
to report to me, and when I received word of its coming
and also that General Mackenzie's cavalry from the Army
of the James was likewise to be added to my command,
and that discretionary authority was given me to use all
my forces against Pickett, I resolved to destroy him, if it
was within the bounds of possibility, before he could rejoin
Lee.

In a despatch, dated 10:05 P.M., telling me of the coming
of Warren and Mackenzie, General Grant also said that the
Fifth Corps should reach me by 12 o'clock that night, but
at that hour not only had none of the corps arrived, but
no report from it, so believing that if it came all the way
down to Dinwiddie the next morning, our opportunity
would be gone, I concluded that it would be best to order
Warren to move in on the enemy's rear while the cavalry
attacked in front, and, therefore, at 3 o'clock in the morning of April 1 sent this despatch to General Warren:

      "CAVALRY HEADQUARTERS, DINWIDDIE C. H.,
               "April 1, 1865. 3 A.M.

"MAJOR-GENERAL WARREN,
      "Commanding Fifth Army Corps.
  "I am holding in front of Dinwiddie Court House, on
the road leading to Five Forks, for three-quarters of a mile
with General Custer's division. The enemy are in his immediate front, lying so as to cover the road just this side
of A. Adams's house, which leads across Chamberlain's bed,

*Griffin had been ordered by Warren to the Boydton road to protect
his rear.

or run. I understand you have a division at J. Boisseau's;*
if so, you are in rear of the enemy's line and almost on
his flank. I will hold on here. Possibly they may attack
Custer at daylight; if so, attack instantly and in full force.
Attack at daylight anyhow, and I will make an effort to get
the road this side of Adams's house, and if I do, you can
capture the whole of them. Any force moving down the
road I am holding, or on the White Oak road, will be in
the enemy's rear, and in all probability get any force that
may escape you by a flank movement. Do not fear my
leaving here. If the enemy remains, I shall fight at daylight.
                    "P. H. SHERIDAN, Major-General."

With daylight came a slight fog, but it lifted almost
immediately, and Merritt moved Custer and Devin forward.
As these divisions advanced the enemy's infantry fell back
on the Five Forks road, Devin pressing him along the road,
while Custer extended on the left over toward Chamberlain's Run, Crook being held in watch along Stony Creek,
meanwhile, to be utilized as circumstances might require
when Warren attacked.

The order of General Meade to Warren the night of
March 31—a copy being sent me also—was positive in its
directions, but as midnight came without a sign of or word
from the Fifth Corps, notwithstanding that was the hour
fixed for its arrival, I nevertheless assumed that there were
good reasons for its non-appearance, but never once
doubted that measures would be taken to comply with my
despatch of 3 A.M., and therefore hoped that, as Pickett
was falling back slowly toward Five Forks, Griffin's and
Crawford's divisions would come in on the Confederate
left and rear by the Crump road near J. Boisseau's house.

But they did not reach there till after the enemy had
got by. As a matter of fact, when Pickett was passing the
all-important point Warren's men were just breaking from

*This "J." was an error; it should have been "G." J. Boisseau's house
was in possession of the enemy. The division in question was near
G. or Dr. Boisseau's, on the Crump road, north of Gravelly Run.

the bivouac in which their chief had placed them the night before, and the head of Griffin's division did not get to Boisseau's till after my cavalry, which meanwhile had been joined by Ayres's division of the Fifth Corps by way of the Boydton and Dabney roads. By reason of the delay in moving Griffin and Crawford, the enemy having escaped, I massed the Fifth Corps at J. Boisseau's so that the men could be rested, and directed it to remain there; General Warren himself had not then come up. General Mackenzie, who had reported just after daybreak, was ordered at first to stay at Dinwiddie Court House, but later was brought along the Five Forks road to Dr. Smith's, and Crook's division was directed to continue watching the crossings of Stony Creek and Chamberlain's Run.

That we had accomplished nothing but to oblige our foe to retreat was to me bitterly disappointing, but still feeling sure that he would not give up the Five Forks crossroads without a fight, I pressed him back there with Merritt's cavalry, Custer advancing on the Scott road, while Devin drove the rear-guard along that leading from J. Boisseau's to Five Forks.

By 2 o'clock in the afternoon Merritt had forced the enemy inside his intrenchments, which began with a short return about three-quarters of a mile east of the Forks and ran along the south side of the White Oak road to a point about a mile west of the Forks. From the left of the return over toward Hatcher's Run was posted Mumford's cavalry, dismounted. In the return itself was Wallace's brigade, and next on its right came Ransom's, then Stewart's, then Terry's, then Corse's. On the right of Corse was W. H. F. Lee's division of cavalry. Ten pieces of artillery also were in this line, three on the right of the works, three near the centre at the crossroads, and four on the left, in the return. Rosser's cavalry was guarding the Confederate trains north of Hatcher's Run beyond the crossing of the Ford road.

I felt certain the enemy would fight at Five Forks—he had to—so, while we were getting up to his intrenchments,

I decided on my plan of battle. This was to attack his whole front with Merritt's two cavalry divisions, make a feint of turning his right flank, and with the Fifth Corps assail his left. As the Fifth Corps moved into action, its right flank was to be covered by Mackenzie's cavalry, thus entirely cutting off Pickett's troops from communication with Lee's right flank, which rested near the Butler house at the junction of the Claiborne and White Oaks roads. In execution of this plan, Merritt worked his men close in toward the intrenchments, and while he was thus engaged, I ordered Warren to bring up the Fifth Corps, sending the order by my engineer officer, Captain Gillespie, who had reconnoitred the ground in the neighborhood of Gravelly Run Church, where the infantry was to form for attack.

Gillespie delivered the order about 1 o'clock, and when the corps was put in motion, General Warren joined me at the front. Before he came, I had received, through Colonel Babcock, authority from General Grant to relieve him, but I did not wish to do it, particularly on the eve of battle; so, saying nothing at all about the message brought me, I entered at once on the plan for defeating Pickett, telling Warren how the enemy was posted, explaining with considerable detail, and concluding by stating that I wished his troops to be formed on the Gravelly Church road, near its junction with the White Oak road, with two divisions to the front, aligned obliquely to the White Oak road, and one in reserve, opposite the centre of these two.

General Warren seemed to understand me clearly, and then left to join his command, while I turned my attention to the cavalry, instructing Merritt to begin by making demonstrations as though to turn the enemy's right, and to assault the front of the works with his dismounted cavalry as soon as Warren became engaged. Afterward I rode around to Gravelly Run Church, and found the head of Warren's column just appearing, while he was sitting under a tree making a rough sketch of the ground. I was disappointed that more of the corps was not already up, and as the precious minutes went by without any apparent effort to hurry the troops on to the field, this disappointment grew into disgust. At last I expressed to Warren my fears that the cavalry might expend all their ammunition before the attack could be made, that the sun would go down before the battle could be begun, or that troops from Lee's right, which, be it remembered, was less than three miles away from my right, might, by striking my rear, or even by threatening it, prevent the attack on Pickett.

Warren did not seem to me to be at all solicitous; his manner exhibited decided apathy, and he remarked with indifference that "Bobby Lee was always getting people into trouble." With unconcern such as this, it is no wonder that fully three hours' time was consumed in marching his corps from J. Boisseau's to Gravelly Run Church, though the distance was but two miles. However, when my patience was almost worn out, Warren reported his troops ready, Ayres's division being formed on the west side of the Gravelly Church road, Crawford's on the east side, and Griffin in reserve behind the right of Crawford, a little different from my instructions. The corps had no artillery present, its batteries, on account of the mud, being still north of Gravelly Run. Meanwhile Merritt had been busy working his men close up to the intrenchments from the angle of the return west, along the White Oak road.

About 4 o'clock Warren began the attack. He was to assault the left flank of the Confederate infantry at a point where I knew Pickett's intrenchments were refused, almost at right angles with the White Oak road. I did not know exactly how far toward Hatcher's Run this part of the works extended, for here the videttes of Mumford's cavalry were covering, but I did know where the refusal began. This return, then, was the point I wished to assail, believing that if the assault was made with spirit, the line could be turned. I therefore intended that Ayres and Crawford should attack the refused trenches squarely, and when these two divisions and Merritt's cavalry became hotly engaged, Griffin's divisions was to pass around the left of the Confederate line; and I personally instructed Griffin how

I wished him to go in, telling him also that as he advanced, his right flank would be taken care of by Mackenzie, who was to be pushed over toward the Ford road and Hatcher's Run.

The front of the corps was oblique to the White Oak road; and on getting there, it was to swing round to the left till perpendicular to the road, keeping closed to the left. Ayres did his part well, and to the letter, bringing his division square up to the front of the return near the angle; but Crawford did not wheel to the left, as was intended. On the contrary, on receiving fire from Mumford's cavalry, Crawford swerved to the right and moved north from the return, thus isolating his division from Ayres; and Griffin, uncertain of the enemy's position, naturally followed Crawford.

The deflection of this division on a line of march which finally brought it out on the Ford road near C. Young's house, frustrated the purpose I had in mind when ordering the attack, and caused a gap between Ayres and Crawford, of which the enemy quickly took advantage, and succeeded in throwing a part of Ayres's division into confusion. At this juncture I sent word to General Warren to have Crawford recalled; for the direction he was following was not only a mistaken one, but, in case the assault at the return failed, he ran great risk of capture. Warren could not be found, so I then sent for Griffin—first by Colonel Newhall, and then by Colonel Sherman—to come to the aid of Ayres, who was now contending alone with that part of the enemy's infantry at the return. By this time Griffin had observed and appreciated Crawford's mistake, however, and when the staff-officers reached him, was already faced to the left; so, marching across Crawford's rear, he quickly joined Ayres, who meanwhile had rallied his troops and carried the return.

When Ayres's division went over the flank of the enemy's works, Devin's division of cavalry, which had been assaulting the front, went over in company with it; and hardly halting to reform, the intermingling infantry and dismounted cavalry swept down inside the intrenchments, pushing to and beyond Five Forks, capturing thousands of prisoners. The only stand the enemy tried to make was when he attempted to form near the Ford road. Griffin pressed him so hard there, however, that he had to give way in short order, and many of his men, with three pieces of artillery, fell into the hands of Crawford while on his circuitous march.

The right of Custer's division gained a foot-hold on the enemy's works simultaneously with Devin's, but on the extreme left Custer had a very severe combat with W. H. F. Lee's cavalry, as well as with Corse's and Terry's infantry. Attacking Terry and Corse with Pennington's brigade dismounted, he assailed Lee's cavalry with his other two brigades mounted, but Lee held on so obstinately that Custer gained but little ground till our troops, advancing behind the works, drove Corse and Terry out. Then Lee made no further stand except at the west side of the Gillian field, where, assisted by Corse's brigade, he endeavored to cover the retreat, but just before dark Custer, in concert with some Fifth Corps regiments under Colonel Richardson, drove the last of the enemy westward on the White Oak road.

Our success was unqualified; we had overthrown Pickett, taken six guns, thirteen battle-flags, and nearly six thousand prisoners. When the battle was practically over, I turned to consider my position with reference to the main Confederate army. My troops, though victorious, were isolated from the Army of the Potomac, for on the 31st of March the extreme left of that army had been thrown back nearly to the Boydton plank-road, and hence there was nothing to prevent the enemy's issuing from his trenches at the intersection of the White Oak and Claiborne roads and marching directly on my rear. I surmised that he might do this that night or early next morning. It was therefore necessary to protect myself in this critical situation, and General Warren having sorely disappointed me, both in the moving of his corps and in its management during the battle, I felt that he was not the man to rely upon under such circumstances, and deeming that it was to the best interest of the service as well as but just to myself, I relieved him, ordering him to report to General Grant.

I then put Griffin in command of the Fifth Corps, and directed him to withdraw from the pursuit as quickly as he could after following the enemy a short distance, and form in line of battle near Gravelly Run Church, at right angles with the White Oak road, with Ayres and Crawford facing toward the enemy at the junction of the White Oak and Claiborne roads, leaving Bartlett, now commanding Griffin's division, near the Ford road. Mackenzie also was left on the Ford road at the crossing of Hatcher's Run, Merritt going into camp on the widow Gillian's plantation. As I had been obliged to keep Crook's division along Stony Creek throughout the day, it had taken no active part in the battle.

Years after the war, in 1879, a Court of Inquiry was given General Warren in relation to his conduct on the day of the battle. He assumed that the delay in not granting his request for an inquiry, which was first made at the close of the war, was due to opposition on my part. In this he was in error; I never opposed the ordering of the Court, but when it was finally decided to convene it I naturally asked to be represented by counsel, for the authorization of the Inquiry was so peculiarly phrased that it made me practically a respondent.

Briefly stated, in my report of the battle of Five Forks there were four imputations concerning General Warren. The first implied that Warren failed to reach me on the 1st of April, when I had reason to expect him; the second, that the tactical handling of his corps was unskillful; the third, that he did not exert himself to get his corps up to Gravelly Run Church; and the fourth, that when portions of his line gave way he did not exert himself to restore confidence to his troops. The Court found against him on the first and second counts, and for him on the third and fourth. This finding was unsatisfactory to General Warren, for he hoped to obtain such an unequivocal recognition of his services as to cast discredit on my motives for relieving him. These were prompted by the conditions alone—by the conduct of General Warren as described, and my consequent lack of confidence in him.

It will be remembered that in my conversation with General Grant on the 30th, relative to the suspension of operations because of the mud, I asked him to let me have the Sixth Corps to help me in breaking in on the enemy's right, but that it could not be sent me; it will be recalled also that the Fifth Corps was afterward tendered and declined. From these facts it has been alleged that I was prejudiced against General Warren, but this is not true. As we had never been thrown much together I knew but little of him. I had no personal objection to him, and certainly could have none to his corps. I was expected to do an extremely dangerous piece of work, and knowing the Sixth Corps well—my cavalry having campaigned with it so successfully in the Shenandoah Valley—I naturally preferred it, and declined the Fifth for no other reason. But the Sixth could not be given, and the turn of events finally brought me the Fifth after my cavalry, under the most trying difficulties, had drawn the enemy from his works, and into such a position as to permit the realization of General Grant's hope to break up with my force Lee's right flank. Pickett's isolation offered an opportunity which we could not afford to neglect, and the destruction of his command would fill the measure of General Grant's expectations as well as meet my own desires. The occasion was not an ordinary one, and as I thought that Warren had not risen to its demand in the battle, I deemed it injudicious and unsafe under the critical conditions existing to retain him longer. That I was justified in this is plain to all who are disposed to be fair-minded, so with the following extract from General Sherman's review of the proceedings of the Warren Court, and with which I am convinced the judgment of history will accord, I leave the subject:

> "It would be an unsafe and dangerous rule to hold the commander of an army in battle to a technical adherence to any rule of conduct for managing his command. He is responsible for results, and holds the lives and reputations of every officer and soldier under his orders as subordinate to the great end—victory. The most important events are usually compressed into an hour, a minute, and he cannot stop to analyze his reasons. He must act on the impulse, the conviction, of the instant, and should be sustained in his conclusions, if not manifestly unjust. The power to command men, and give vehement impulse to their joint action, is something which cannot be defined by words, but it is plain and manifest in battles, and whoever commands an army in chief must choose his subordinates by reason of qualities which can alone be tested in actual conflict.

> "No one has questioned the patriotism, integrity, and great intelligence of General Warren. These are attested by a long record of most excellent service, but in the clash of arms at and near Five Forks, March 31 and April 1, 1865, his personal activity fell short of the standard fixed by General Sheridan, on whom alone rested the great responsibility for that and succeeding days.

> "My conclusion is that General Sheridan was perfectly justified in his action in this case, and he must be fully and entirely sustained if the United States expects great victories by her arms in the future."

CHAPTER XXV

WHEN THE NEWS OF THE BATTLE at Five Forks reached General Grant, he realized that the decisive character of our victory would necessitate the immediate abandonment of Richmond and Petersburg by the enemy; and fearing that Lee would escape without further injury, he issued orders, the propriety of which must be settled by history, to assault next morning the whole intrenched line. But Lee could not retreat at once. He had not anticipated disaster at Five Forks, and hence was unprepared to withdraw on the moment; and the necessity of getting off his trains and munitions of war, as well as being obliged to cover the flight of the Confederate Government, compelled him to hold on to Richmond and Petersburg till the afternoon of the 2d, though before that Parke, Ord, and Wright had carried his outer intrenchments at several points, thus materially shortening the line of investment.

The night of the 1st of April, General Humphreys's corps—the Second—had extended its left toward the White Oak road, and early next morning, under instructions from General Grant, Miles's division of that corps reported to me, and supporting him with Ayres's and Crawford's divisions of the Fifth Corps, I then directed him to advance toward Petersburg and attack the enemy's works at the intersection of the Claiborne and White Oak roads.

Such of the enemy as were still in the works Miles easily forced across Hatcher's Run, in the direction of Sutherland's depot, but the Confederates promptly took up a position north of the little stream, and Miles being anxious to attack, I gave him leave, but just at this time General Humphreys came up with a request to me from General Meade to return Miles. On this request I relinquished command of the division, when, supported by the Fifth Corps it could have broken in the enemy's right at a vital point; and I have always since regretted that I did so, for the message Humphreys conveyed was without authority from General Grant, by whom Miles had been sent to me, but thinking good feeling a desideratum just then, and wishing to avoid wrangles, I faced the Fifth Corps about and marched it down to Five Forks, and out the Ford road to the crossing of Hatcher's Run. After we had gone, General Grant, intending this quarter of the field to be under my control, ordered Humphreys with his other two divisions to move to the right, in toward Petersburg. This left Miles entirely unsupported, and his gallant attack made soon after was unsuccessful at first, but about 3 o'clock in the afternoon he carried the point which covered the retreat from Petersburg and Richmond.

Merritt had been sent westward, meanwhile, in the direction of Ford's Station, to break the enemy's horse which had been collecting to the north of Hatcher's Run. Meeting with but little opposition, Merritt drove this cavalry force in a northerly direction toward Scott's Corners, while the Fifth Corps was pushed toward Sutherland's depot, in the hope of coming in on the rear of the force that was confronting Miles when I left him. Crawford and Merritt engaged the enemy lightly just before night, but his main column, retreating along the river road south of the Appomattox, had got across Namozine Creek, and the darkness prevented our doing more than to pick up some stragglers. The next morning the pursuit was resumed, the cavalry again in advance, the Fifth Corps keeping up with it all the while, and as we pressed our adversaries hundreds and hundreds of prisoners, armed and unarmed, fell into our hands, together with many wagons and five pieces of artillery. At Deep Creek the rear-guard turned on us, and a severe skirmish took place. Merritt, finding the enemy very strong, was directed to await the arrival of Crook and for the rear division of the Fifth Corps; but by the time they reached the creek, darkness had again come to protect the Confederates, and we had to be content with meagre results at that point.

From the beginning it was apparent that Lee, in his retreat, was making for Amelia Court House, where his columns north and south of the Appomattox River could join, and where, no doubt, he expected to meet supplies, so Crook was ordered to march early on April 4 to strike the Danville railroad, between Jettersville and Burkeville, and then move south along the railroad toward Jettersville, Merritt to move toward Amelia Court House, and the Fifth Corps to Jettersville itself.

The Fifth Corps got to Jettersville about 5 in the afternoon, and I immediately intrenched it across the Burkeville road with the determination to stay there till the main army could come up, for I hoped we could force Lee to surrender at Amelia Court House, since a firm hold on Jettersville would cut him off from his line of retreat toward Burkeville.

Accompanied only by my escort—the First United States Cavalry, about two hundred strong—I reached Jettersville some little time before the Fifth Corps, and having nothing else at hand I at once deployed this handful of men to cover the crossroads till the arrival of the corps. Just as the troopers were deploying, a man on a mule, heading for Burkeville, rode into my pickets. He was arrested, of course, and being searched there was found in his boots this telegram in duplicate, signed by Lee's Commissary General. "The army is at Amelia Court House, short of provisions. Send 300,000 rations quickly to Burke-ville Junction." One copy was addressed to the supply department at Danville, and the other to that at Lynchburg. I surmised that the telegraph lines north of Burkeville had been broken by Crook after the despatches were written, which would account for their being transmitted by messenger. There was thus revealed not only the important fact that Lee was concentrating at Amelia Court House, but also a trustworthy basis for estimating his troops, so I sent word to Crook to strike up the railroad toward me, and to Merritt—who, as I have said, had followed on the heels of the enemy—to leave Mackenzie there and himself close in on Jettersville. Staff-officers were also despatched to hurry up Griffin with the Fifth Corps, and his tired men redoubled their strides.

My troops too were hard up for rations, for in the pursuit we could not wait for our trains, so I concluded to secure if possible these provisions intended for Lee. To this end I directed Young to send four of his best scouts to Burke-ville Junction. There they were to separate, two taking the railroad toward Lynchburg and two toward Danville, and as soon as a telegraph station was reached the telegram was to be transmitted as it had been written and the provisions thus hurried forward.

Although the Fifth Corps arrived at Jettersville the evening of April 4, as did also Crook's and Merritt's cavalry, yet none of the army of the Potomac came up till about 3 o'clock the afternoon of the 5th, the Second Corps, followed by the Sixth, joining us then. General Meade arrived at Jettersville an hour earlier, but being ill, requested me to put his troops in position. The Fifth Corps being already intrenched across the Amelia Court House road facing north, I placed the Sixth on its right and the Second on its left as they reached the ground.

As the enemy had been feeling us ever since morning, to learn what he was up to I directed Crook to send Davies's brigade on a reconnoissance to Paine's crossroads. Davies soon found out that Lee was trying to escape by that flank, for at the crossroads he found the Confederate trains and artillery moving rapidly westward. Having driven away the escort, Davies succeeded in burning nearly two hundred wagons, and brought off five pieces of artillery. Among these wagons were some belonging to General Lee's and to General Fitzhugh Lee's headquarters. This work through, Davies withdrew and rejoined Crook, who, with Smith and Gregg, was established near Flat Creek.

It being plain that Lee would attempt to escape as soon as his trains were out of the way, I was most anxious to attack him when the Second Corps began to arrive, for I felt certain that unless we did so he would succeed in passing by our left flank, and would thus again make our pursuit a stern-chase; but General Meade, whose plan of attack was to advance his right flank on Amelia Court House, objected to assailing before all his troops were up.

I then sent despatches to General Grant, explaining what Davies had done, and telling him that the Second Corps was arriving, and that I wished he himself was present. I assured him of my confidence in our capturing Lee if we properly exerted ourselves, and informed him, finally, that I would put all my cavalry, except Mackenzie, on my left, and that, with such a disposition of my forces, I could see no escape for Lee. I also inclosed him this letter, which had just been captured:

"AMELIA C. H., April 5, 1865.

"DEAR MAMMA:

"Our army is ruined, I fear. We are all safe as yet. Shyron left us sick. John Taylor is well—saw him yesterday. We are in line of battle this morning. General Robert Lee is in the field near us. My trust is still in the justice of our cause, and that of God. General Hill is killed. I saw Murray a few minutes since. Bernard, Terry said, was taken prisoner, but may yet get out. I send this by a negro I see passing up the railroad to Mechlenburg. Love to all.

"Your devoted son,

"WM. B. TAYLOR, Colonel."

General Grant, who on the 5th was accompanying General Ord's column toward Burkeville Junction, did not receive this intelligence till nearly nightfall, when within about ten miles of the Junction. He set out for Jettersville immediately, but did not reach us till near midnight, too late of course to do anything that night. Taking me with him, we went over to see Meade, whom he then directed to advance early in the morning on Amelia Court House. In this interview Grant also stated that the orders Meade had already issued would permit Lee's escape, and therefore must be changed, for it was not the aim only to follow the enemy, but to get ahead of him, remarking during the conversation that "he had no doubt Lee was moving right then." On this same occasion Meade expressed a desire to have in the proposed attack all the troops of the Army of the Potomac under his own command, and asked for the return of the Fifth Corps. I made no objections, and it was ordered to report to him.

When, on the morning of the 6th, Meade advanced toward Amelia Court House, he found, as predicted, that Lee was gone. It turned out that the retreat began the evening of the 5th and continued all night. Satisfied that this would be the case, I did not permit the cavalry to participate in Meade's useless advance, but shifted it out toward the left to the road running from Deatonsville to Rice's station, Crook leading and Merritt close up. Before long the enemy's trains were discovered on this road, but Crook could make but little impression on them, they were so strongly guarded; so, leaving Stagg's brigade and Miller's battery about three miles southwest of Deatonsville— where the road forks, with a branch leading north toward the Appomattox—to harass the retreating column and find a vulnerable point, I again shifted the rest of the cavalry toward the left, across-country, but still keeping parallel to the enemy's line of march.

Just after crossing Sailor's Creek, a favorable opportunity offering, both Merritt and Crook attacked vigorously, gained the Rice's Station road, destroyed several hundred wagons, made many prisoners, and captured sixteen pieces of artillery. This was important, but more valuable still was the fact that we were astride the enemy's line of retreat, and had cut off from joining Longstreet, waiting at Rice's Station, a corps of Confederate infantry under General Ewell, composed of Anderson's, Kershaw's, and Custis Lee's divisions. Stagg's brigade and Miller's battery, which, as I have said, had been left at the forks of the Deatonsville road, had meanwhile broken in between the rear of Ewell's column and the head of Gordon's, forcing Gordon to abandon his march for Rice's Station, and to take the right-hand road at the forks, on which he was pursued by General Humphreys.

The complete isolation of Ewell from Longstreet in his front and Gordon in his rear led to the battle of Sayler's Creek, one of the severest conflicts of the war, for the enemy fought with desperation to escape capture, and we, bent on his destruction, were no less eager and determined. The capture of Ewell, with six of his generals and most of his troops, crowned our success, but the fight was so overshadowed by the stirring events of the surrender three days later, that the battle has never been accorded the prominence it deserves.

The small creek from which the field takes its name flows in a northwesterly direction across the road leading from Deatonsville to Rice's Station. By shifting to the left, Merritt gained the Rice's Station road west of the creek, making havoc of the wagon-trains, while Crook struck them further on and planted himself square across the road. This blocked Ewell, who, advancing Anderson to some high ground west of the creek, posted him behind barricades, with the intention of making a hard fight there, while the main body should escape through the woods in a westerly direction to roads that led to Farmville. This was prevented, however, by Crook forming his division, two brigades dismounted and one mounted, and at once assaulting all along Anderson's front and overlapping his right, while Merritt fiercely attacked to the right of Crook.

The enemy being thus held, enabled the Sixth Corps—which in the meantime I had sent for—to come upon the ground, and Ewell, still contending with the cavalry, found himself suddenly beset by this new danger from his rear. To meet it, he placed Kershaw to the right and Custis Lee to the left of the Rice's Station road, facing them north toward and some little distance from Sayler's Creek, supporting Kershaw with Commander Tucker's Marine brigade. Ewell's skirmishers held the line of Sayler's Creek, which runs through a gentle valley, the north slope of which was cleared ground.

By General Grant's directions the Sixth Corps had been following my route of march since the discovery, about 9 o'clock in the morning, that Lee had decamped from Amelia Court House. Grant had promptly informed me of this in a note, saying, "The Sixth Corps will go in with a vim any place you may dictate," so when I sent word to Wright of the enemy's isolation, and asked him to hurry on with all speed, his gallant corps came as fast as legs could carry them, he sending to me successively Major McClellan and Colonel Franklin, of his staff, to report his approach.

I was well advised as to the position of the enemy through information brought me by an intelligent young soldier, William A. Richardson, Company "A," Second Ohio, who, in one of the cavalry charges on Anderson, had cleared the barricades and made his way back to my front through Ewell's line. Richardson had told me just how the main body of the enemy was posted, so as Seymour's division arrived I directed General Wright to put it on the right of the road, while Wheaton's men, coming up all hot and out of breath, promptly formed on Seymour's left. Both divisions thus aligned faced southwest toward Sayler's Creek, and the artillery of the corps being massed to the left and front of the Hibbon house, without waiting for Getty's division—for I feared that if we delayed longer the enemy might effect his escape toward Farmville—the general attack was begun. Seymour and Wheaton, moving forward together, assailed the enemy's front and left, and

Stagg's brigade, too, which in the mean time had been placed between Wheaton's left and Devin's right, went at him along with them, Merritt and Crook resuming the fight from their positions in front of Anderson. The enemy, seeing little chance of escape, fought like a tiger at bay, but both Seymour and Wheaton pressed him vigorously, gaining ground at all points except just to the right of the road, where Seymour's left was checked. Here the Confederates burst back on us in a counter-charge, surging down almost to the creek, but the artillery, supported by Getty, who in the mean time had come on the ground, opened on them so terribly that this audacious and furious onset was completely broken, though the gallant fellows fell back to their original line doggedly, and not until after they had almost gained the creek. Ewell was now hemmed in on every side, and all those under his immediate command were captured. Merritt and Crook had also broken up Anderson by this time, but he himself, and about two thousand disorganized men escaped by making their way through the woods toward the Appomattox River before they could be entirely enveloped. Night had fallen when the fight was entirely over, but Devin was pushed on in pursuit for about two miles, part of the Sixth Corps following to clinch a victory which not only led to the annihilation of one corps of Lee's retreating army, but obliged Longstreet to move up to Farmville, so as to take a road north of the Appomattox River toward Lynchburg instead of continuing toward Danville.

At the close of the battle I sent one of my staff—Colonel Redwood Price—to General Grant to report what had been done; that we had taken six generals and from nine to ten thousand prisoners. On his way Price stopped at the headquarters of General Meade, where he learned that not the slightest intelligence of the occurrence on my line had been received, for I not being under Meade's command, he had paid no attention to my movements. Price gave the story of the battle, and General Meade, realizing its importance, sent directions immediately to General Wright to make his report of the engagement to the headquarters of the Army of the Potomac, assuming that Wright was operating independently of me in the face of Grant's despatch of 2 o'clock, which said that Wright was following the cavalry and would "go in with a vim" wherever I dictated. Wright could not do else than comply with Meade's orders in the case, and I, being then in ignorance of Meade's reasons for the assumption, could say nothing. But General Grant plainly intending, and even directing, that the corps should be under my command, remedied this phase of the matter, when informed of what had taken place, by requiring Wright to send a report of the battle through me. What he then did, and what his intentions and orders were, are further confirmed by a reference to the episode in his "Memoirs," where he gives his reasons for ordering the Sixth Corps to abandon the move on Amelia Court House and pass to the left of the army. He also says, referring to the 6th of April: "The Sixth Corps now remained with the cavalry under Sheridan's direct command until after the surrender." He unquestionably intended all of this, but his purpose was partly frustrated by General Meade's action next morning in assuming direction of the movements of the corps; and before General Grant became aware of the actual conditions the surrender was at hand.

CHAPTER XXVI

THE FIRST REPORT OF THE BATTLE of Sayler's Creek that General Grant received was, as already stated, an oral message carried by Colonel Price, of my staff. Near midnight I sent a despatch giving the names of the generals captured. These were Ewell, Kershaw, Barton, Corse, Dubose, and Custis Lee. In the same despatch I wrote: "If the thing is pressed, I think that Lee will surrender." When Mr. Lincoln, at City Point, received this word from General Grant, who was transmitting every item of news to the President, he telegraphed Grant the laconic message: "Let the thing be pressed." The morning of the 7th we moved out at a very early hour, Crook's division marching toward Farmville in direct pursuit, while Merritt and Mackenzie were ordered to Prince Edward's Court House to anticipate any effort Lee might make to escape through that place toward Danville, since it had been discovered that Longstreet had slipped away already from the front of General Ord's troops at Rice's Station. Crook overtook the main body of the Confederates at Farmville, and promptly attacked their trains on the north side of the Appomattox with Gregg's brigade, which was fiercely turned upon and forced to recross the river with the loss of a number of prisoners, among them Gregg himself.

When Crook sent word of this fight, it was clear that Lee had abandoned all effort to escape to the southwest by way of Danville. Lynchburg was undoubtedly his objective point now; so, resolving to throw my cavalry again across his path, and hold him till the infantry could overtake him, I directed everything on Appomattox depot, recalling Crook the night of the 7th to Prospect Station, while Merritt camped at Buffalo Creek, and Mackenzie made a reconnoissance along the Lynchburg railroad.

At break of day, April 8, Merritt and Mackenzie united with Crook at Prospect Station, and the cavalry all moved then toward Appomattox depot. Hardly had it started when one of the scouts—Sergeant White—informed me that there were four trains of cars at the depot loaded with supplies for Lee's army; these had been sent from Lynchburg, in compliance with the telegram of Lee's commissary-general, which message, it will be remembered, was captured and transmitted to Lynchburg by two of Young's scouts on the 4th. Sergeant White, who had been on the lookout for the trains ever since sending the despatch, found them several miles west of Appomattox depot, feeling their way along, in ignorance of Lee's exact position. As he had the original despatch with him, and took pains to dwell upon the pitiable condition of Lee's army, he had little difficulty in persuading the men in charge of the trains to bring them east of Appomattox Station, but fearing that the true state of affairs would be learned before long, and the trains be returned to Lynchburg, he was painfully anxious to have them cut off by breaking the track west of the station.

The intelligence as to the trains was immediately despatched to Crook, and I pushed on to join him with Merritt's command. Custer having the advance, moved rapidly, and on nearing the station detailed two regiments to make a détour southward to strike the railroad some distance beyond and break the track. These regiments set off at a gallop, and in short order broke up the railroad enough to prevent the escape of the trains, Custer meanwhile taking possession of the station, but none too soon, for almost at the moment he did so the advance-guard of Lee's army appeared, bent on securing the trains. Without halting to look after the cars further, Custer attacked this advance-guard and had a spirited fight, in which he drove the Confederates away from the station, captured twenty-five pieces of artillery, a hospital train, and a large park of wagons, which, in the hope that they would reach Lynchburg next day, were being pushed ahead of Lee's main body.

Devin coming up a little before dusk, was put in on the right of Custer, and one of Crook's brigades was sent to our left and the other two held in reserve. I then forced the enemy back on the Appomattox road to the vicinity of the Court House, and that the Confederates might have no rest, gave orders to continue the skirmishing throughout the night. Meanwhile the captured trains had been taken charge of by locomotive engineers, soldiers of the command, who were delighted evidently to get back at their old calling. They amused themselves by running the trains to and fro, creating much confusion, and keeping up such an unearthly screeching with the whistles that I was on the point of ordering the cars burned. They finally wearied of their fun, however, and ran the trains off to the east toward General Ord's column.

The night of the 8th I made my headquarters at a little frame house just south of the station. I did not sleep at all, nor did anybody else, the entire command being up all night long; indeed, there had been little rest in the cavalry for the past eight days. The necessity of getting Ord's column up was so obvious now that staff-officer after staff-officer was sent to him and to General Grant requesting that the infantry be pushed on, for if it could get to the front, all knew that the rebellion would be ended on the morrow. Merritt, Crook, Custer, and Devin were present at frequent intervals during the night, and everybody was overjoyed at the prospect that our weary work was about to end so happily. Before sun-up General Ord arrived, and informed me of the approach of his column, it having been marching the whole night. As he ranked me, of course I could give him no orders, so after a hasty consultation as to where his troops should be placed we separated, I riding to the front to overlook my line near Appomattox Court House, while he went back to urge along his weary troops.

The night before General Lee had held a council with his principal generals, when it was arranged that in the morning General Gordon should undertake to break through my cavalry, and when I neared my troops this movement was beginning, a heavy line of infantry bearing down on us from the direction of the village. In front of Crook and Mackenzie firing had already begun, so riding to a slight elevation where a good view of the Confederates could be had, I there came to the conclusion that it would be unwise to offer more resistance than that necessary to give Ord time to form, so I directed Merritt to fall back, and in retiring to shift Devin and Custer to the right so as to make room for Ord, now in the woods to my rear. Crook, who with his own and Mackenzie's divisions was on my extreme left covering some by-roads, was ordered to hold his ground as long as practicable without sacrificing his men, and, if forced to retire, to contest with obstinacy the enemy's advance.

As already stated, I could not direct General Ord's course, he being my senior, but hastily galloping back to where he was, at the edge of the timber, I explained to him what was taking place at the front. Merritt's withdrawal inspired the Confederates, who forthwith began to press Crook, their line of battle advancing with confidence till it reached the crest whence I had reconnoitred them. From this ground they could see Ord's men emerging from the woods, and the hopelessness of a further attack being plain, the gray lines instinctively halted, and then began to retire toward a ridge immediately fronting Appomattox

Court House, while Ord, joined on his right by the Fifth Corps, advanced on them over the ground that Merritt had abandoned.

I now directed my steps toward Merritt, who, having mounted his troopers, had moved them off to the right, and by the time I reached his headquarters flag he was ready for work, so a move on the enemy's left was ordered, and every guidon was bent to the front. As the cavalry marched along parallel with the Confederate line, and in toward its left, a heavy fire of artillery opened on us, but this could not check us at such a time, and we soon reached some high ground about half a mile from the Court House, and from here I could see in the low valley beyond the village the bivouac undoubtedly of Lee's army. The troops did not seem to be disposed in battle order, but on the other side of the bivouac was a line of battle—a heavy rear-guard—confronting, presumably, General Meade.

I decided to attack at once, and formations were ordered at a trot for a charge by Custer's and Devin's divisions down the slope leading to the camps. Custer was soon ready, but Devin's division being in rear its formation took longer, since he had to shift further to the right; Devin's preparations were, therefore, but partially completed when an' aide-de-camp galloped up to me with the word from Custer, "Lee has surrendered; do not charge; the white flag is up." The enemy perceiving that Custer was forming for attack, had sent the flag out to his front and stopped the charge just in time. I at once sent word of the truce to General Ord, and hearing nothing more from Custer himself, I supposed that he had gone down to the Court House to join a mounted group of Confederates that I could see near there, so I, too, went toward them, galloping down a narrow ridge, staff and orderlies following; but we had not got half way to the Court House when, from a skirt of timber to our right, not more than three hundred yards distant, a musketry fire was opened on us. This halted us, when, waving my hat, I called out to the firing party that we were under a truce, and they were violating it. This did not stop them, however, so we hastily took shelter in a ravine so situated as to throw a ridge between us and the danger.

We traveled in safety down this depression to its mouth, and thence by a gentle ascent approached the Court House. I was in advance, followed by a sergeant carrying my battle-flag. When I got within about a hundred and fifty yards of the enemy's line, which was immediately in front of the Court House, some of the Confederates leveled their pieces at us, and I again halted. Their officers kept their men from firing, however, but meanwhile a single-handed contest had begun behind me, for on looking back I heard a Confederate soldier demanding my battle-flag from the color-bearer, thinking, no doubt, that we were coming in as prisoners. The sergeant had drawn his sabre and was about to cut the man down, but at a word from me he desisted and carried the flag back to my staff, his assailant quickly realizing that the boot was on the other leg.

These incidents determined me to remain where I was till the return of a staff-officer whom I had sent over to demand an explanation from the group of Confederates for which I had been heading. He came back in a few minutes with apologies for what had occurred, and informed me that General Gordon and General Wilcox were the superior officers in the group. As they wished me to join them I rode up with my staff, but we had hardly met when in front of Merritt firing began. At the sound I turned to General Gordon, who seemed embarrassed by the occurrence, and remarked: "General, your men fired on me as I was coming over here, and undoubtedly they are treating Merritt and Custer the same way. We might as well let them fight it out." He replied, "There must be some mistake." I then asked, "Why not send a staff-officer and have your people cease firing; they are violating the flag." He answered, "I have no staff-officer to send." Whereupon I said that I would let him have one of mine, and calling for Lieutenant Vanderbilt Allen, I directed him to carry General Gordon's orders to General Geary, commanding a small brigade of South Carolina cavalry, to discontinue firing. Allen dashed off with the message and soon delivered it, but was made a prisoner, Geary saying, "I do not care for white flags: South Carolinians never surrender." By this time Merritt's patience being exhausted, he ordered an attack, and this in short order put an end to General Geary's "last ditch" absurdity, and extricated Allen from his predicament.

When quiet was restored Gordon remarked: "General Lee asks for a suspension of hostilities pending the negotiations which he is having with General Grant." I rejoined: "I have been constantly informed of the progress of the negotiations, and think it singular that while such discussions are going on, General Lee should have continued his march and attempted to break through my lines this morning. I will entertain no terms except that General Lee shall surrender to General Grant on his arrival here. If these terms are not accepted we will renew hostilities." Gordon replied: "General Lee's army is exhausted. There is no doubt of his surrender to General Grant."

It was then that General Ord joined us, and after shaking hands all around, I related the situation to him, and Gordon went away agreeing to meet us again in half an hour. When the time was up he came back accompanied by General Longstreet, who brought with him a despatch, the duplicate of one that had been sent General Grant through General Meade's lines back on the road over which Lee had been retreating.

General Longstreet renewed the assurances that already had been given by Gordon, and I sent Colonel Newhall with the despatch to find General Grant and bring him to the front. When Newhall started, everything on our side of the Appomattox Court House was quiet, for inevitable surrender was at hand, but Longstreet feared that Meade, in ignorance of the new conditions on my front might attack the Confederate rear-guard. To prevent this I offered to send Colonel J. W. Forsyth through the enemy's lines to let Meade know of my agreement, for he too was suspicious that by a renewed correspondence Lee was endeavoring to gain time for escape. My offer being accepted, Forsyth set out accompanied by Colonel Fairfax, of Longstreet's staff, and had no difficulty in accomplishing his mission.

About five or six miles from Appomattox, on the road toward Prospect Station near its intersection with the Walker's Church road, my adjutant-general, Colonel Newhall, met General Grant, he having started from north of the Appomattox River for my front the morning of April 9, in consequence of the following despatches which had been sent him the night before, after we had captured Appomattox Station and established a line intercepting Lee:

"CAVALRY HEADQUARTERS, April 8, 1865—9:20 P.M.
"LIEUTENANT-GENERAL U. S. GRANT,
    "Commanding Armies of the U. S.
"General: I marched early this morning from Buffalo Creek and Prospect Station on Appomattox Station, where my scouts had reported trains of cars with supplies for Lee's army. A short time before dark General Custer, who had the advance, made a dash at the station, capturing four trains of supplies, with locomotives. One of the trains was burned and the others were run back toward Farmville for security. Custer then pushed on toward Appomattox Court House, driving the enemy—who kept up a heavy fire of artillery—charging them repeatedly and capturing, as far as reported, twenty-five pieces of artillery and a number of prisoners and wagons. The First Cavalry Division supported him on the right. A reconnoissance sent across the Appomattox reports the enemy moving on the Cumberland road to Appomattox Station, where they expect to get supplies. Custer is still pushing on. If General Gibbon and the Fifth Corps can get up to-night, we will perhaps finish the job in the morning. I do not think Lee means to surrender until compelled to do so.
            "P. H. SHERIDAN, Major-General."

"HEADQUARTERS CAVALRY, April 8, 1865—9:40 P.M.
"LIEUTENANT-GENERAL U. S. GRANT.

"Commanding Armies U. S.

"GENERAL: Since writing the accompanying despatch, General Custer reports that his command has captured in all thirty-five pieces of artillery, one thousand prisoners—including one general officer—and from one hundred and fifty to two hundred wagons.

"P. H. SHERIDAN, Major-General."

In attempting to conduct the lieutenant-general and staff back by a short route, Newhall lost his bearings for a time, inclining in toward the enemy's lines too far, but regained the proper direction without serious loss of time. General Grant arrived about 1 o'clock in the afternoon, Ord and I, dismounted, meeting him at the edge of the town, or crossroads, for it was little more. He remaining mounted, spoke first to me, saying simply, "How are you, Sheridan?" I assured him with thanks that I was "first-rate," when, pointing toward the village, he asked, "Is General Lee up there?" and I replied, "There is his army down in that valley, and he himself is over in that house (designating McLean's house) waiting to surrender to you." The General then said, "Come, let us go over," this last remark being addressed to both Ord and me. We two then mounted and joined him, while our staff-officers followed, intermingling with those of the general-in-chief as the cavalcade took its way to McLean's house near by, and where General Lee had arrived some time before, in consequence of a message from General Grant consenting to the interview asked for by Lee through Meade's front that morning—the consent having been carried by Colonel Babcock.

When I entered McLean's house General Lee was standing, as was also his military secretary, Colonel Marshall, his only staff-officer present. General Lee was dressed in a new uniform and wore a handsome sword. His tall, commanding form thus set off contrasted strongly with the short figure of General Grant, clothed as he was in a soiled suit, without sword or other insignia of his position except a pair of dingy shoulder-straps. After being presented, Ord and I, and nearly all of General Grant's staff, withdrew to await the agreement as to terms, and in a little while Colonel Babcock came to the door and said, "The surrender had been made; you can come in again."

When we re-entered General Grant was writing; and General Lee, having in his hand two despatches, which I that morning requested might be returned, as I had no copies of them, addressed me with the remark: "I am sorry. It is probable that my cavalry at that point of the line did not fully understand the agreement." These despatches had been sent in the forenoon, after the fighting had been stopped, notifying General Lee that some of his cavalry in front of Crook was violating the suspension of hostilities by withdrawing. About 3 o'clock in the afternoon the terms of surrender were written out and accepted, and General Lee left the house, as he departed cordially shaking hands with General Grant. A moment later he mounted his chunky gray horse, and lifting his hat as he passed out of the yard, rode off toward his army, his arrival there being announced to us by cheering, which, as it progressed, varying in loudness, told he was riding through the bivouac of the Army of Northern Virginia.

The surrender of General Lee practically ended the war of the rebellion. For four years his army had been the mainstay of the Confederacy; and the marked ability with which he directed its operations is evidenced both by his frequent successes and the length of time he kept up the contest. Indeed, it may be said that till General Grant was matched against him, he never met an opponent he did not vanquish, for while it is true that defeat was inflicted on the Confederates at Antietam and Gettysburg, yet the fruits of these victories were not gathered, for after each of these battles Lee was left unmolested till he had a chance to recuperate.

The assignment of General Grant to the command of

the Union armies in the winter of 1863–64 gave presage of success from the start, for his eminent abilities had already been proved, and besides, he was a tower of strength to the Government, because he had the confidence of the people. They knew that henceforth systematic direction would be given to our armies in every section of the vast territory over which active operations were being prosecuted, and further, that this coherence, this harmony of plan, was the one thing needed to end the war, for in the three preceding years there had been illustrated most lamentable effects of the absence of system. From the moment he set our armies in motion simultaneously, in the spring of 1864, it could be seen that we should be victorious ultimately, for though on different lines we were checked now and then, yet we were harassing the Confederacy at so many vital points that plainly it must yield to our blows. Against Lee's army, the forefront of the Confederacy, Grant pitted himself; and it may be said that the Confederate commander was now, for the first time, overmatched, for against all his devices—the products of a mind fertile in defense—General Grant brought to bear not only the wealth of expedient which had hitherto distinguished him, but also an imperturbable tenacity, particularly in the Wilderness and on the march to the James, without which the almost insurmountable obstacles of that campaign could not have been overcome. During it and in the siege of Petersburg he met with many disappointments—on several occasions the shortcomings of generals, when at the point of success, leading to wretched failures. But so far as he was concerned, the only apparent effect of these discomfitures was to make him all the more determined to discharge successfully the stupendous trust committed to his care, and to bring into play the manifold resources of his well-ordered military mind. He guided every subordinate then, and in the last days of the rebellion, with a fund of common sense and superiority of intellect, which have left an impress so distinct as to exhibit his great personality. When his military history is analyzed after the lapse of years, it will show, even more clearly than now, that during these as well as in his previous campaigns he was the steadfast centre about and on which everything else turned.

The surrender at Appomattox put a stop to all military operations on the part of General Grant's forces, and the morning of April 10 my cavalry began its march to Petersburg, the men anticipating that they would soon be mustered out and returned to their homes. At Nottoway Court House I heard of the assassination of the President. The first news came to us the night after the dastardly deed, the telegraph operator having taken it from the wires while in transmission to General Meade. The despatch ran that Mr. Lincoln had been shot at 10 o'clock that morning at Willard's Hotel, but as I could conceive of nothing to take the President there I set the story down as a canard, and went to bed without giving it further thought. Next morning, however, an official telegram confirmed the fact of the assassination, though eliminating the distorted circumstances that had been communicated the night before.

When we reached Petersburg my column was halted, and instructions given me to march the cavalry and the Sixth Corps to Greensboro', North Carolina, for the purpose of aiding General Sherman (the surrender of General Johnston having not yet been effected), so I made the necessary preparations and moved on the 24th of April, arriving at South Boston, on the Dan River, the 28th, the Sixth Corps having reached Danville meanwhile. At South Boston I received a despatch from General Halleck, who immediately after Lee's surrender had been assigned to command at Richmond, informing me that General Johnston had been brought to terms. The necessity for going farther south being thus obviated we retraced our steps to Petersburg, from which place I proceeded by steamer to Washington, leaving the cavalry to be marched thither by easy stages.

The day after my arrival in Washington an important

order was sent me, accompanied by the following letter of instructions, transferring me to a new field of operations:

"HEADQUARTERS ARMIES OF THE UNITED STATES
"Washington, D. C., May 17, 1865.

"GENERAL: Under the orders relieving you from the command of the Middle Military Division and assigning you to command west of the Mississippi, you will proceed without delay to the West to arrange all preliminaries for your new field of duties.

"Your duty is to restore Texas, and that part of Louisiana held by the enemy, to the Union in the shortest practicable time, in a way most effectual for securing permanent peace.

"To do this, you will be given all the troops that can be spared by Major-General Canby, probably twenty-five thousand men of all arms; the troops with Major-General J. J. Reynolds, in Arkansas, say twelve thousand, Reynolds to command; the Fourth Army Corps, now at Nashville, Tennessee, awaiting orders; and the Twenty-Fifth Army Corps, now at City Point, Virginia, ready to embark.

"I do not wish to trammel you with instructions; I will state, however, that if Smith holds out, without even an ostensible government to receive orders from or to report to, he and his men are not entitled to the considerations due to an acknowledged belligerent. Theirs are the conditions of outlaws, making war against the only Government having an existence over the territory where war is now being waged.

"You may notify the rebel commander west of the Mississippi—holding intercourse with him in person, or through such officers of the rank of major-general as you may select—that he will be allowed to surrender all his forces on the same terms as were accorded to Lee and Johnston. If he accedes, proceed to garrison the Red River as high up as Shreveport, the seaboard at Galveston, Malagorda Bay, Corpus Christi, and mouth of the Rio Grande.

"Place a strong force on the Rio Grande, holding it at least to a point opposite Camargo, and above that if supplies can be procured.

"In case of an active campaign (a hostile one) I think a heavy force should be put on the Rio Grande as a first preliminary. Troops for this might be started at once. The Twenty-Fifth Corps is now available, and to it should be added a force of white troops, say those now under Major-General Steele.

"To be clear on this last point, I think the Rio Grande should be strongly held, whether the forces in Texas surrender or not, and that no time should be lost in getting troops there. If war is to be made, they will be in the right place; if Kirby Smith surrenders, they will be on the line which is to be strongly garrisoned.

"Should any force be necessary other than those designated, they can be had by calling for them on Army Headquarters.

"U. S. GRANT,
"Lieutenant-General.

"To MAJOR-GENERAL P. H. SHERIDAN,
      "United States Army."

On receipt of these instructions I called at once on General Grant, to see if they were to be considered so pressing as to preclude my remaining in Washington till after the Grand Review, which was fixed for the 23d and 24th of May, for naturally I had a strong desire to head my command on that great occasion. But the General told me that it was absolutely necessary to go at once to force the surrender of the Confederates under Kirby Smith. He also told me that the States lately in rebellion would be embraced in two or three military departments, the commanders of which would control civil affairs until Congress took action about restoring them to the Union, since that course would not only be economical and simple, but would give the Southern people confidence, and encourage them to go to work, instead of distracting them with politics.

At this same interview he informed me that there was an additional motive in sending me to the new command, a motive not explained by the instructions themselves, and went on to say that, as a matter of fact, he looked upon the invasion of Mexico by Maximilian as a part of the rebellion itself, because of the encouragement that invasion had received from the Confederacy, and that our success in putting down secession would never be complete till the French and Austrian invaders were compelled to quit the territory of our sister republic. With regard to this matter, though, he said it would be necessary for me to act with great circumspection, since the Secretary of State, Mr. Seward, was much opposed to the use of our troops along the border in any active way that would be likely to involve us in a war with European powers.

Under the circumstances, my disappointment at not being permitted to participate in the review had to be submitted to, and I left Washington without an opportunity of seeing again in a body the men who, while under my command, had gone through so many trials and unremittingly pursued and assailed the enemy, from the beginning of the campaign of 1864 till the white flag came into their hands at Appomattox Court House.

A CIVIL WAR CHRONOLOGY

1859

October 16— John Brown, with sixteen whites and five blacks, captures the arsenal at Harpers Ferry in anticipation of fomenting a slave rebellion in Virginia. U. S. troops led by Lt. Col. Robert E. Lee storm the arsenal and capture Brown, on the morning of October 18th.

December 2— John Brown is hanged for treason. Among his final words: "I, John Brown, am now quite certain that the crimes of this guilty land will never be purged away but with blood."

1860

May 3— Democratic party, meeting in Charleston, South Carolina, adjourns unable to agree upon a candidate following the withdrawal of delegates from eight southern states.

May 9— Constitutional Union party, meeting in Baltimore, nominates John Bell of Tennessee for president.

May 16—   Republican party, meeting in Chicago, nominates Abraham Lincoln of Illinois on the third ballot as a compromise candidate. Lincoln promises not to interfere with slavery where it already exists, but opposes its extension.

June 23—   Democratic party, reconvened in Baltimore, nominates Stephen A. Douglas of Illinois on a popular-sovereignty platform regarding slavery (each territory to decide for itself). Outraged southern Democrats walk out and later nominate John C. Breckinridge of Kentucky.

November 6—   Lincoln wins the election. Though he has but 40 percent of the popular vote, his Electoral College count is 180, versus 72 for Breckinridge, 39 for Bell, and 12 for Douglas.

November 9—   The state of South Carolina calls a secession convention.

December 20—   South Carolina secedes from the Union.

December 26—   Major Robert Anderson withdraws federal forces in Charleston to Fort Sumter. He has but eighty men.

1861
January 9—   South Carolina shore batteries open fire on the *Star of the West*, carrying supplies and reinforcements to Fort Sumter. The ship is forced out of Charleston Harbor. On the same day Mississippi secedes from the Union.

January 10—   Florida secedes from the Union.

January 11—   Alabama secedes from the Union.

January 19—   Georgia secedes from the Union.

January 26—   Louisiana secedes from the Union.

February 1—   Texas secedes from the Union. Governor Sam Houston is removed from office for opposing secession.

February 4— A convention meets in Montgomery, Alabama, to create a new government for the seceded states. It passes a constitution on the eighth and elects Jefferson Davis of Mississippi provisional president and Alexander Stephens of Georgia provisional vice-president on the ninth.

February 11— Lincoln departs from Springfield for Washington. "I now leave, not knowing when, or whether ever, I may return, with a task before me greater than that which rested upon Washington," he tells his friends and neighbors.

February 18— Davis is inaugurated at Montgomery, declaring that obstacles "can not long prevent the progress of a movement sanctified by its justice and sustained by a virtuous people."

February 23— Lincoln reaches Washington, entering the city secretly for fear of assassins.

March 4— Lincoln is inaugurated, declaring that "In your hands, my dissatisfied countrymen, and not in mine is the momentous issue of Civil War."

March 6— The Confederate States of America calls for 100,000 volunteers for its army.

April 4— Lincoln orders an expedition to relieve besieged Fort Sumter, and it departs from New York four days later.

April 12— At 4:30 A.M. General P. G. T. Beauregard orders his men to open fire on Fort Sumter. The commander of the fort had been his artillery instructor at West Point.

April 13— Major Anderson surrenders after 34 hours of bombardment.

April 15— Lincoln calls upon the states for 75,000 militia to suppress the insurrection in South Carolina.

April 17—	Virginia secedes from the Union.
April 19—	Lincoln orders a blockade of Confederate ports.
April 20—	Col. Robert E. Lee resigns from the U.S. Army. "Whatever may be the result of the contest," he writes a friend, "I foresee that the country will have to pass through a terrible ordeal, a necessary expiation for our national sins."
May 6—	Arkansas secedes from the Union.
May 6—	Tennessee secedes from the Union.
May 13—	Great Britain declares neutrality, in effect recognizing the Confederacy as a belligerent.
May 20—	North Carolina secedes from the Union.
May 21—	The Confederacy decides to move its capital to Richmond, Virginia.
May 23—	Virginia voters endorse secession.
June 3—	Union troops under Gen. George B. McClellan defeat Confederates at Philippi in western Virginia.
June 10—	France declares neutrality.
June 11—	Pro-Union counties in western Virginia disavow secession and are recognized by Lincoln as the loyal Virginia government. This soon evolves into the new state of West Virginia.
July 16—	Gen. Irvin McDowell, with 30,000 Union troops, advances toward Manassas Junction, Virginia.
July 21—	Battle of Bull Run ends in the defeat of Union forces, although the Rebels are too disorganized to follow up their victory. A strong stand by Thomas J. Jackson's Virginia brigade earns him the nickname "Stonewall." Each side suffers about 625 killed.

July 27— McDowell is replaced by McClellan as commander of the troops around Washington.

August 6— A Confiscation Act is passed which allows the seizure of all property used for insurrectionary purposes. This includes slaves.

August 10— Confederates under Sterling Price and Ben McCulloch defeat a Union force under Gen. Nathaniel Lyon at Wilson's Creek, Missouri. Lyon is killed in action, and each side suffers about 1,300 casualties.

August 30— Gen. John C. Frémont, in command of Union forces in the West, orders the confiscation of all property, including slaves, belonging to Missouri Confederates.

September 10— Gen. Albert Sidney Johnston of Texas assumes command of Confederate forces in the West.

November 1— McClellan replaces Gen. Winfield Scott as Union general in chief.

November 2— Frémont is relieved of his command in the West, and is soon replaced by Gen. Henry W. Halleck.

November 8— Capt. Charles Wilkes of the U.S. Navy stops the British mail steamer *Trent* and arrests Confederate envoys James Mason and John Slidell, setting off an international incident. They will be released on December 27 after British saber rattling.

1862
January 19— Union Gen. George Thomas, a Virginian loyal to the Old Flag, defeats Rebel forces at Mill Springs, Kentucky, securing federal control of the eastern section of that state.

February 6— Gen. Ulysses S. Grant, with 15,000 troops and several naval gunboats under Flag Officer Andrew Foote, attacks Fort Henry on the Tennessee River. The fort quickly falls to Foote's naval forces, but most of its defenders escape to Fort Donelson, a dozen miles away on the Cumberland River.

February 7— Gen. Johnston orders his forces to retreat from southwestern Kentucky.

February 13— Grant, with 40,000 troops, attacks Fort Donelson, defended by 18,000 Confederates.

February 16— Gen. Simon Bolivar Buckner surrenders Fort Donelson. Grant's terms, unconditional surrender, win him a nickname.

February 21— Confederate troops under Gen. Henry H. Sibley defeat Union forces under Gen. Edward Canby and Col. Kit Carson at Valverde, New Mexico. Sibley is then able to occupy Albuquerque and Santa Fe.

February 25— The Confederates are forced to abandon Nashville.

March 3— Andrew Johnson is named military governor of Tennessee by Lincoln.

March 8— Gen. Samuel Curtis defeats Gen. Earl Van Dorn at Pea Ridge and Union control of Missouri is secured.

March 8— The *Virginia*, a Rebel ironclad converted from the captured Union warship the *Merrimac*, destroys the Union wooden warships the *Congress* and the *Cumberland* and drives the *Minnesota* aground at Hampton Roads, Virginia.

March 9— The *Monitor*, a Union iron-plated raft with a revolving gun turret built by John Ericsson, engages the *Virginia* (*Merrimac*) at Hampton Roads. They battle inconclusively all morning, but the *Virginia* withdraws and does not again threaten the Union blockade. A revolution in naval warfare has been wrought. The *Virginia* is burned to prevent its capture a month later. The *Monitor* sinks in a storm off Cape Hatteras on December 31, 1862.

March 11— Lincoln reorganizes the Union high command: Halleck takes charge of all troops west of the Appalachians while McClellan is reduced from general in chief to commander of the Army of the Potomac.

March 17— McClellan begins moving his forces by sea to Fort Monroe in anticipation of the Peninsular Campaign against Richmond.

March 23— Stonewall Jackson is defeated at Kernstown, Virginia, by a much stronger Union force. The battle raises fears in Washington of a Confederate attack, and troops are withheld from McClellan to defend the capital.

March 28— Union forces defeat the Confederate invaders at Glorieta Pass, New Mexico.

April 4— McClellan's forces on the peninsula advance toward Richmond.

April 6— Grant's 37,000 men at Shiloh Church and Pittsburg Landing, Tennessee, are surprised by A. S. Johnston's 42,000 Confederates and almost defeated. Johnston is killed and Beauregard assumes command.

April 7— Grant, reinforced by 25,000 fresh troops under Don Carlos Buell and Lew Wallace, attacks at Shiloh, recapturing all lost ground. Each side suffers 10,000 casualties. Beauregard retreats to Corinth, Mississippi.

April 8— Gen. John Pope captures Island No. 10 in the Mississippi River, taking 5,000 Confederate prisoners.

April 12—   James J. Andrews leads fifteen men on a bold raid to seize a Western and Atlantic Railroad locomotive at Big Shanty, Georgia, and then race north in it burning all bridges on the line between Atlanta and Chattanooga. The raid fails after a wild eight-hour railway chase, and Andrews and seven of his men are eventually hanged.

April 16—   The Confederate Congress passes a conscription bill.

April 16—   Slavery is abolished in the District of Columbia.

April 25—   New Orleans is captured by Union naval forces under Flag Officer David C. Farragut.

May 1—   Union troops under Gen. Benjamin Butler begin the occupation of New Orleans.

May 3—   McClellan's army forces Gen. Joseph E. Johnston to retreat from Yorktown, Virginia.

May 8—   Stonewall Jackson's 10,000 men in the Shenandoah Valley defeat attacking Federals under Gen. Robert Schenk at McDowell, Virginia.

May 9—   Gen. David Hunter at Hilton Head, South Carolina, declares slaves in South Carolina, Georgia, and Florida to be free. His act is later repudiated by Lincoln.

May 9—   Confederate forces retreat from Norfolk.

May 10—   Union forces occupy Pensacola, Florida.

May 12—   Baton Rouge, Louisiana, is occupied by Union forces.

May 25—   Jackson crushes Gen. Nathaniel Banks's 8,000-man force at Winchester, Virginia.

June 1—   Robert E. Lee assumes command of Confederate forces defending Richmond after Joseph E. Johnston is wounded at the Battle of Fair Oaks.

June 8—
At the Battle of Cross Keys, Virginia, Union forces under Gen. John C. Frémont are defeated by Jackson's men.

June 9—
Jackson again defeats Union forces under Frémont and Gen. James Shields at Port Royal.

June 12—
Gen. James E. "Jeb" Stuart leads his Rebel cavalrymen on a bold four-day reconnaissance completely around McClellan's forces on the peninsula.

June 17—
Jackson's victorious army departs the Shenandoah to reinforce Lee.

June 19—
Slavery is abolished in all federal territories.

June 25—
The Seven Days' Battles begin as the forces of McClellan and Lee contend inconclusively.

July 1—
Lee's forces are defeated in their assault on the Army of the Potomac at Malvern Hill. He has lost 20,000 men. Nevertheless, the Seven Days' Battles conclude with the nervous McClellan retreating and Richmond secure.

July 4—
Confederate Col. John Hunt Morgan begins a daring raid into Kentucky.

July 11—
Halleck is named general in chief of Union forces.

July 17—
A second Confiscation Act is passed by Congress, freeing the slaves of those who are in rebellion against the government.

July 29—
The Rebel cruiser *Alabama* departs Liverpool, England, under the command of Captain Raphael Semmes. In the next two years it will capture or destroy sixty-four merchant ships.

August 9—
Jackson defeats Union forces under Banks at Cedar Mountain, Virginia.

August 16— McClellan moves north to unite with the Northern Army of Virginia under Gen. John Pope at Alexandria.

August 26— Jackson captures the railroad line at Manassas Junction.

August 28— Gen. Braxton Bragg leads his Rebel forces from Chattanooga to unite with Gen. Kirby Smith in Kentucky.

August 29— The Second Battle of Bull Run begins as Pope attacks Jackson. The overly confident Pope sends a victory telegram to Washington.

August 30— Confederate reinforcements under Gen. James Longstreet turn the tide at Second Bull Run and Pope's army is routed.

September 2— McClellan is given command of Pope's army and the forces defending Washington.

September 5— Lee leads 55,000 men into Maryland.

September 9— Lee sends Jackson to capture the 12,000 Union troops at Harpers Ferry. Jackson is then to rejoin Lee for a movement against Harrisburg, Pennsylvania.

September 13— Near Frederick, Maryland, two Union soldiers discover a copy of Lee's plans wrapped around three cigars lost by a Confederate officer.

September 14— McClellan, who has 80,000 men and his opponent's plans, still waits eighteen hours before moving. This delay proves crucial in allowing Lee to regroup his army.

September 15— Jackson captures Harpers Ferry.

September 16— Jackson hurriedly rejoins Lee at Sharpsburg, Maryland. McClellan masses his forces a mile east across Antietam Creek.

September 17— The Battle of Antietam becomes the single bloodiest day of the war as the two sides fight to a grisly standstill. 6,000 are killed and 17,000 are wounded.

September 18— Lee escapes into Virginia.

September 22— Lincoln decides to issue the Emancipation Proclamation freeing all slaves in states in rebellion as of January 1.

October 8— Don Carlos Buell's Union forces defeat Gen. Bragg's Confederates at Perryville, Kentucky, repelling the Rebel invasion of Kentucky.

October 30— Gen. William Rosecrans replaces Buell in command of the redesignated Army of the Cumberland.

November 2— Grant moves against Vicksburg, Mississippi.

November 7— McClellan is replaced as commander of the Army of the Potomac by Gen. Ambrose Burnside.

December 13— Burnside is defeated by Lee at Fredericksburg, Virginia.

December 15— The Army of the Potomac retreats.

December 31— Bragg attacks Rosecrans at Stones River near Murfreesboro, Tennessee.

1863
January 1— Lincoln signs the Emancipation Proclamation.

January 2— Rosecrans wins the second day of heavy fighting at Stones River. Bragg retreats on January 3.

January 26— Gen. Joseph Hooker replaces Burnside as commander of the Army of the Potomac.

March 3—   The U.S. Congress passes a conscription act that provides for a draft of all men between twenty and forty-five.

March 9—   Confederate partisan ranger John S. Mosby makes a daring raid behind Union lines and captures Brig. Gen. Edwin H. Stoughton. Lincoln, upon being informed that Mosby has taken Stoughton, thirty-two soldiers, and fifty-eight horses, responds: "Well, I'm sorry for that. I can make new brigadier generals, but I can't make horses."

April 16—   Admiral David Porter's Union gunboats make a daring run past the shore batteries at Vicksburg.

April 17—   Col. Benjamin Grierson leads 1,700 cavalrymen out of La Grange, Tennessee, and heads south. His goal is to disrupt Confederate communications and divert attention from Vicksburg.

April 30—   The Army of the Potomac, 115,000 strong, begins to concentrate at Chancellorsville. Lee faces them with but 60,000 men.

May 1—   Gen. Hooker's 70,000 infantry inconclusively engage Gen. Lee's forces at Chancellorsville. Hooker inexplicably pulls back after fighting in a forest called the Wilderness. That night Lee and Jackson plan a daring flanking attack on Hooker.

May 2—   Lee faces Hooker with but 15,000 men while Jackson leads 30,000 infantry on a flank march across the Union front. Jackson attacks at 5:15 P.M. and rolls up the Union right, but is mistakenly wounded by his own pickets that night while scouting.

May 2—   Grierson's cavalry reach Union lines at Baton Rouge after a daring 600-mile raid.

May 3— Gen. Stuart assumes command of Jackson's corps at Chancellorsville and continues to pound the faltering Federals.

May 4— Gen. John Sedgwick has no success against Lee's rear and retires to Fredericksburg.

May 6— Hooker retreats, and Lee achieves his greatest victory. Confederate forces suffer 13,000 casualties while Union losses are over 17,000.

May 10— Stonewall Jackson dies at Guiney's Station. "Let us cross over the river and rest under the shade of the trees," are his last words.

May 16— Grant, advancing on Vicksburg, defeats Gen. John C. Pemberton's forces at Champion's Hill.

May 18— Pemberton pulls his forces into the Vicksburg defenses.

May 19— Governor John Andrew of Massachusetts presents four flags to Col. Robert Gould Shaw and the 54th Massachusetts Regiment, the first black regiment raised in the Northeast. The regiment is ordered to join Gen. David Hunter at Hilton Head, South Carolina. Already with Hunter is Col. Thomas Wentworth Higginson's First Regiment of South Carolina Volunteers, made up of contrabands (liberated slaves).

May 19— Grant's forces assault Vicksburg but fail to breach the defenses.

May 22— Grant's second assault on Vicksburg is repulsed with heavy losses. He begins a siege.

May 27— Gen. Banks fails in his assaults on Port Hudson, Louisiana, and lays siege.

June 3— Lee departs Fredericksburg for a second invasion of the North. He has three infantry corps and six cavalry brigades—75,000 men.

June 9— Gen. Alfred Pleasonton's 11,000 Union cavalry surprise Stuart's 10,000 horsemen at Brandy Station, and the greatest cavalry engagement of the war follows. Stuart holds his ground but Lee's advance is revealed.

June 15— Gen. Richard S. Ewell captures Winchester in the Shenandoah.

June 20— West Virginia is admitted to the Union.

June 25— Stuart leads three cavalry brigades on a ride around Hooker's army. The raid causes great alarm in Washington, but Stuart's separation from the Army of Northern Virginia will prove costly.

June 28— Gen. Jubal Early captures York, Pennsylvania.

June 28— Gen. George Gordon Meade assumes command of the Army of the Potomac, replacing Hooker.

June 29— Lee orders his forces to reunite near Gettysburg, Pennsylvania.

July 1— Gen. A. P. Hill's infantry, in search of shoes in Gettysburg, clash with two brigades of Union cavalry under Gen. John Buford. Soldiers from both armies rush to the sound of the guns, and the Rebels soon sweep the Yankees in disorder through the town. Union forces dig in on Cemetery Ridge while the Confederates take up positions on Seminary Ridge.

July 2— Lee sends Gen. James Longstreet against the Union left while Gen. Richard Ewell assaults the Union right. Both assaults fail. Stuart finally rejoins the army.

July 3— After a terrific artillery barrage, Lee sends 14,000 men against the Union center in Pickett's Charge. Scarcely half return.

July 4— Gen. Pemberton surrenders his 30,000 men, and Vicksburg, to Grant.

July 8— Gen. John Hunt Morgan leads 2,500 men across the Ohio River into Indiana and toward Ohio.

July 9— Port Hudson surrenders to Gen. Banks. The Mississippi is again a Union river and the Confederacy is split.

July 13— Four days of antidraft rioting begins in New York City. Much of the violence is directed at blacks before troops suppress a mob estimated at 50,000.

July 18— Battery Wagner, defending the entrance to Charleston harbor, is assaulted by Union troops. Spearheading the attack are 600 men of the 54th Massachusetts. The position is impregnable, although the black soldiers of the 54th gain Wagner's parapets and hold them for an hour before falling back. Col. Robert Shaw is killed and the regiment suffers casualties of over 40 percent.

July 19— Over 800 of Morgan's raiders are killed or captured at Buffington, Ohio.

July 26— Gen. Morgan is captured at New Lisbon, Ohio.

August 21— Col. William Clarke Quantrill's Confederate guerrillas sack Lawrence, Kansas.

September 9— Gen. Rosecrans's Federal troops enter Chattanooga as Gen. Bragg's forces retire into northern Georgia.

September 19— Gen. Bragg, reinforced by Longstreet's corps, attacks Gen. George Thomas's corps on the left of Rosecrans's army at Chickamauga Creek, Georgia.

September 20—   Longstreet routs the Union right, and the army is only saved by Thomas's bold stand; Thomas earns the nickname of "Rock of Chickamauga." Rosecrans's army retreats to Chattanooga, where it is besieged. Bragg occupies high ground at Lookout Mountain, south of the city, and along Missionary Ridge to the east. In the fighting each side has suffered 28-percent casualties.

October 15—   The Confederate submarine *Hunley* sinks during a practice run in Charleston harbor, drowning its inventor and seven crewmen.

October 17—   Grant is named commander of all Union forces west of the Appalachians.

October 19—   Thomas replaces Rosecrans as commander of the 35,000-man Army of the Cumberland in Chattanooga.

October 23—   Grant arrives in Chattanooga.

November 4—   Bragg sends Longstreet and 15,000 men to attack Knoxville, thus weakening his forces at Chattanooga.

November 19—   Lincoln, at Gettysburg, gives an immortal speech.

November 20—   Gen. William T. Sherman reaches Chattanooga with 17,000 men from the Army of the Tennessee. Hooker has already arrived on September 24 with 20,000 reinforcements from the Army of the Potomac. Bragg faces them with just over 64,000 troops.

November 24—   Hooker's men take Lookout Mountain at Chattanooga.

November 25—   Sherman's attacks on Bragg's right fail, but Thomas's Army of the Cumberland makes an incredible charge up Missionary Ridge and defeats the Confederates. Bragg, barely escaping capture, retreats into Georgia.

November 27— Gen. Morgan escapes from the Ohio State Penitentiary.

November 29— Longstreet's attack on Knoxville fails, and he soon retreats toward Virginia.

December 16— Gen. Joseph E. Johnston takes command of the Army of Tennessee. Bragg is named an adviser to President Davis.

1864
February 9— Col. Thomas Rose leads 109 Union prisoners in a daring escape from Libby Prison in Richmond. Rose and forty-seven others are recaptured.

February 14— Gen. Sherman occupies Meridian, Mississippi, and his troops begin to dismantle the city.

February 17— The Confederate submarine *Hunley* sinks the *Housatonic* in Charleston harbor, but goes down with the Union sloop.

February 22— Gen. Nathan Bedford Forrest's cavalry defeat Union cavalry under Gen. William Sooy Smith at Okolona, Mississippi.

March 3— Gen. Judson Kilpatrick's cavalry raid on Richmond ends in disaster with Col. Ulrich Dahlgren killed. Papers are found on Dahlgren's body insinuating that his mission was to kill Jefferson Davis.

March 17— Grant is named general in chief and promoted to lieutenant general.

March 18— Sherman is named commander of Union forces in the West.

April 8— Gen. Richard Taylor's Confederates stop Gen. Banks's advance on Shreveport at Sabine Crossroads to end the Union's Red River campaign.

April 12— Gen. Forrest captures Fort Pillow, Tennessee, where surrendering black soldiers are murdered by his troops.

April 17— Grant halts the practice of exchanging prisoners.

May 4— Grant advances across the Rapidan with 122,000 men. Lee faces him with under 70,000. Grant also orders troops under Gen. Benjamin Butler to move up the James River against Richmond. In Chattanooga, Sherman prepares to move south against Atlanta.

May 6— Longstreet reinforces Lee, and Grant is defeated in the Wilderness. Longstreet is seriously wounded.

May 9— Lee's forces entrench at Spottsylvania and repel Union assaults. Union Gen. John Sedgwick is killed.

May 9— Grant sends Gen. Phil Sheridan's 10,000 cavalrymen on a raid against Richmond.

May 11— Sheridan's cavalry defeat Stuart's horsemen at Yellow Tavern. Stuart, mortally wounded, dies the next day.

May 12— Bitter fighting at the "Bloody Angle" at Spotsylvania does not break Lee's lines.

May 15— In the Shenandoah, Gen. John Breckinridge's 5,000-man force, including V.M.I. cadets, defeats Gen. Franz Sigel's 6,500-man Union force at New Market.

May 16— Gen. Butler is defeated at Drewry's Bluff, eight miles south of Richmond, by Gen. Beauregard.

May 20— Grant abandons his Spottsylvania positions in an attempt to flank Lee.

May 24— Lee takes up new positions on the North Anna River.

May 24— Sheridan's victorious cavalrymen rejoin Grant.

May 25— The Battle of New Hope Church, Georgia, begins between the forces of Sherman and Johnston.

May 31— Sheridan's cavalry battles Rebel horsemen under Gen. Fitzhugh Lee and seizes the junction at Cold Harbor.

June 1— Union forces, 109,000 strong, and Confederate forces, numbering 59,000, entrench for seven miles around Cold Harbor. In four weeks of constant fighting, the Federals have suffered 44,000 casualties and the Confederates 25,000.

June 3— Grant launches futile frontal assaults against Lee's lines at Cold Harbor at a cost of 7,000 more casualties.

June 8— Abraham Lincoln and Andrew Johnson are nominated for president and vice-president by the Republican (National Union) Convention in Baltimore.

June 12— Wade Hampton's Rebel cavalry blocks Sheridan's cavalry at Trevilian Station from raiding westward to unite with Gen. David Hunter's forces in the Shenandoah. Both sides suffer 20-percent casualties in the bloodiest cavalry battle of the war.

June 14— Grant begins to move his army across the James River to attack Petersburg.

June 18— Grant's assaults on Petersburg fail and he begins a siege.

June 18— Gen. Jubal Early defeats Gen. Hunter at Lynchburg. Hunter retreats into West Virginia, leaving the Shenandoah to Early.

June 19—	The *Kearsage* sinks the Rebel cruiser *Alabama* in a duel off Cherbourg, France.
June 27—	Johnston repulses Sherman's attacks at Kennesaw Mountain, Georgia.
July 6—	Early invades Maryland.
July 11—	Having swept aside Federal defenders at Monocacy River, Early reaches the defenses of Washington. The Sixth Corps, detached from Grant's forces, arrives on the same day.
July 12—	Early pulls back from Washington, heading for the Shenandoah.
July 17—	Gen. John Bell Hood replaces Johnston as commander of the Army of Tennessee.
July 20—	Hood attacks Thomas's forces at Peachtree Creek, Georgia, and is defeated.
July 22—	Hood attacks Gen. James B. McPherson's Army of the Tennessee and is again defeated. McPherson is killed in action.
July 28—	Hood again attacks the Army of the Tennessee, now commanded by Gen. Oliver Otis Howard, at Ezra Church and is again defeated.
July 30—	A 511-foot tunnel has been dug beneath the Rebel lines at Petersburg and four tons of gunpowder placed at the end. The explosion creates a 170-foot-long, 30-foot-deep crater, but the Federal assault that follows is disorganized and halfhearted. 4,000 casualties and a big hole in the ground is all Grant has by nightfall.
July 31—	Gen. George Stoneman, raiding south from Sherman's army to liberate the prisoners at Andersonville, is captured along with 500 of his men.
August 1—	Sheridan is given command of Union forces in the Shenandoah.

August 5— Admiral Farragut defeats the defending Confederate ships in Mobile Bay. "Damn the torpedoes, full speed ahead," Farragut reportedly exclaims during the action.

August 22— Gen. Judson Kilpatrick's cavalry raid against Hood's Atlanta supply lines fails.

August 23— Fort Morgan, in Mobile Bay, falls to Union forces.

August 29— George B. McClellan is nominated for president by the Democrats.

August 31— Howard defeats Hood at Jonesboro while Gen. John Schofield's forces cut the last railroad line into Atlanta.

September 1— Hood evacuates Atlanta.

September 2— Sherman enters Atlanta.

September 4— John Hunt Morgan is killed at Greeneville, Tennessee.

September 17— John C. Frémont, nominated for president by Radical Republicans unhappy with Lincoln, announces that he will withdraw from the race for fear of splitting the Republican vote.

September 19— Sheridan defeats Early at Winchester.

September 22— Sheridan crushes Early's army at Fisher's Hill.

September 27— Confederate guerrillas under Bloody Bill Anderson loot Centralia, Missouri, and murder twenty-two captured Union soldiers. They then slaughter over 100 pursuing Federals under Maj. A. V. E. Johnston. Young Jesse James kills Maj. Johnston.

September 28— Sherman orders Gen. Thomas to Nashville to defend that city from Hood's army.

September 29— In the fighting around Petersburg, Grant takes Fort Harrison but is repulsed from Fort Gilmore.

October 2— A Federal raid into southwest Virginia is defeated near Saltville, and over 100 Union prisoners, mostly black soldiers, are murdered by their captors.

October 6— Sheridan begins the systematic destruction of the Shenandoah Valley.

October 13— Confederate partisans under Mosby capture a train near Kearneyville and escape with nearly $2 million from Union paymasters on board.

October 16— Sheridan leaves his army for a meeting with Stanton and Halleck on the Valley Campaign.

October 19— Lt. Bennett Young leads Rebel raiders across the Canadian border to St. Albans, Vermont. They rob three banks and escape back over the border.

October 19— Sheridan's army is taken by surprise when Early's army strikes at dawn. The left flank of the Union army, under Gen. George Crook, is routed, but the sudden arrival of Sheridan on the field (he gallops in from Winchester) rallies the men. The Union counterattack destroys the Confederate army. The Battle of Cedar Creek ends the Rebel threat in the Shenandoah. The North is captivated by "Sheridan's Ride," soon immortalized in a popular poem.

October 23— Gen. Curtis defeats Gen. Sterling Price at the Battle of Westport, ending the Confederate threat to Missouri.

October 26— Bloody Bill Anderson is killed in a Union ambush near Richmond, Missouri.

October 27— Lt. William P. Cushing destroys the Confederate ram _Albemarle_ in the Roanoke River, North Carolina.

October 30— Sherman sends Schofield to reinforce Thomas at Nashville.

November 8—   Lincoln is reelected.

November 16—   Sherman's army, 62,000 strong, departs Atlanta to begin the March to the Sea to Savannah. Atlanta burns behind the Federals as they advance.

November 25—   Confederate raiders fail in their attempt to burn New York City.

November 30—   Schofield repulses Hood's assaults at Franklin and retreats under cover of darkness toward Nashville.

December 1—   Schofield unites with Thomas at Nashville.

December 13—   Fort McAllister, guarding Savannah, is captured by Sherman's troops.

December 15—   Thomas attacks Hood before Nashville.

December 16—   Hood's army is routed at Nashville.

December 21—   Sherman's army enters Savannah.

1865
January 7—   Gen. Benjamin Butler is relieved as commander of the Army of the James.

January 15—   Gen. Alfred H. Terry captures Fort Fisher, closing the last major Confederate port at Wilmington, North Carolina.

January 23—   Gen. Richard Taylor is given command of what is left of the Army of Tennessee.

January 31—   The Thirteenth Amendment to the Constitution, abolishing slavery, is passed by the House of Representatives and sent to the states for ratification.

February 6—   Lee is named commander of all Confederate forces.

February 17— Sherman occupies the South Carolina capital, and that night the city burns. Sherman blames fleeing Rebels, but on the eighteenth his troops begin the destruction of what is left of Columbia.

February 17— The Confederates abandon Charleston, and Fort Sumter again comes under Union control.

February 18— Lee speaks out in favor of arming blacks for service in the Confederate army in exchange for their freedom.

February 22— Schofield's Union troops occupy Wilmington.

March 2— Sheridan's cavalry, under Gen. George A. Custer, destroys the last remnant of Early's army at the Battle of Waynesboro.

March 4— Lincoln's second inaugural address calls for reconciliation: "With malice toward none; with charity for all; with firmness in the right as God gives us to see the right, let us strive on to finish the work we are in; to bind up the nation's wounds; to care for him who shall have borne the battle and for his widow, and his orphan—to do all which may achieve and cherish a just and lasting peace among ourselves, and with all nations."

March 13— President Davis signs a bill, narrowly passed by the Confederate Congress after heated debate, that calls for the use of black slaves as soldiers. The question of emancipation in exchange for service is left to the individual states.

March 17— Gen. Edward Canby opens the assault on Mobile, Alabama.

March 22—* Gen. James Wilson begins a cavalry raid through Alabama to capture Selma.

March 26—	Sheridan rejoins Grant before Petersburg.
April 1—	Sheridan defeats Gen. George Pickett at Five Forks, capturing that vital crossroads and large numbers of Rebel prisoners.
April 2—	Grant assaults Lee's weakened lines at Petersburg with great success. Gen A. P. Hill is killed in action. Lee retreats toward Amelia Courthouse.
April 3—	Petersburg is occupied. Richmond surrenders. Jefferson Davis and his cabinet flee to Danville, Virginia.
April 4—	President Lincoln tours Richmond.
April 5—	Sheridan blocks Lee's route southward, forcing the Confederates westward.
April 6—	6,000 Confederates are captured at Sayler's Creek, including Gen. Richard Ewell, as Lee's retreat continues.
April 8—	Custer blocks Lee's retreat route at Appomattox Station.
April 9—	Lee surrenders the Army of Northern Virginia to Grant in the home of Wilmer McLean at Appomattox Courthouse.
April 12—	Wilson captures Montgomery, Alabama. Federal troops occupy Mobile.
April 12—	Grant accords to Gen. Joshua Chamberlain of Maine the honor of accepting the formal surrender of the flags and arms of the Army of Northern Virginia.
April 14—	John Wilkes Booth mortally wounds President Lincoln at Ford's Theater in Washington.
April 15—	President Lincoln dies and Andrew Johnson becomes president.
April 21—	Mosby disbands his rangers.

April 26—	Gen. Johnston surrenders his nearly 30,000 men to Gen. Sherman.
April 26—	Booth is trapped by troops and killed.
May 4—	Gen. Taylor surrenders to Gen. Canby in Alabama.
May 10—	Confederate guerrilla chief William Quantrill is mortally wounded near Taylorsville, Kentucky.
May 10—	Union cavalrymen capture Jefferson Davis and his party in Georgia.
May 22—	Davis is imprisoned at Fort Monroe, Virginia. He will be released in May 1867.
May 23—	Nearly 200,000 Union soldiers begin a two-day grand review up Pennsylvania Avenue in Washington, D.C.—once more the capital of a united nation.